QuickBooks® Online

Online

5th Edition

by Elaine Marmel

A Wiley Brand

QuickBooks® Online For Dummies®, 5th Edition

Published by: **John Wiley & Sons, Inc.,** 111 River Street, Hoboken, NJ 07030-5774, www.wiley.com

Copyright © 2019 by John Wiley & Sons, Inc., Hoboken, New Jersey

Published simultaneously in Canada

For general information on our other products and services, please contact our Customer Care Department within the U.S. at 877-762-2974, outside the U.S. at 317-572-3993, or fax 317-572-4002. For technical support, please visit https://hub.wiley.com/community/support/dummies.

Wiley publishes in a variety of print and electronic formats and by print-on-demand. Some material included with standard print versions of this book may not be included in e-books or in print-on-demand. If this book refers to media such as a CD or DVD that is not included in the version you purchased, you may download this material at http://booksupport.wiley.com. For more information about Wiley products, visit www.wiley.com.

Library of Congress Control Number: 2019939092

ISBN: 978-1-119-59066-8

ISBN: 978-1-119-59067-5 (ePDF)

ISBN: 978-1-119-59074-3 (ePub)

Manufactured in the United States of America

C10010025_050219

Contents at a Glance

Table of Contents

Introduction

Most small business owners do something besides accounting; they sell products or services. Many small business owners address accounting only because they *have* to address it — to meet legal requirements, such as reporting earnings and paying employees.

QuickBooks helps take the pain out of the process; in fact, accounting can become downright tolerable. And QuickBooks Online (QBO) makes accounting almost easy. Because QBO is a web-based product with mobile versions, you can securely do what you need to do from anywhere at any time of day. And, because QBO is web-based, you can easily share your data with your accountant — again, anywhere and at any time.

In most cases, QuickBooks Desktop users who want to stick with something they know but now yearn for the flexibility of a web-based product won't be disappointed. QBO's functionality will feel very familiar to them, and they can migrate their QuickBooks Desktop company to QBO.

Accountants can easily support QuickBooks clients via QuickBooks Online Accountant (QBOA), the sister product of QBO that enables seamless collaboration between accountants and their clients.

Use this book to help you learn how to use QBO and QBOA.

About This Book

Intuit's web-based accounting product is really two products: End users who want to do their accounting on the web or on mobile devices use QBO, whereas accountants use QBOA, which enables the accountant to log in to a client's books and make changes and queries as needed. Although much of QBO and QBOA look and behave alike, QBOA incorporates tools that an accountant needs while working on a client's books. And accountants need to manage multiple client companies, whereas end user clients typically do not.

QBO and QBOA are not for everyone. Before you commit to Intuit's web-based solution, you need to explore the available editions and examine the requirements for the products.

Because these products are both similar and different, I've divided this book into three parts. In the first part of the book, I examine what QBO and QBOA are — and what they aren't — and I describe what you need to be able to use QBO and QBOA. I explain the various editions available and the product costs at the time I wrote this book, and I describe the available features.

The second part of the book focuses on using QBO and is aimed at the end user; but, the accountant who opens a client's company via QBOA will be able to use the same tools that the end user uses to manage lists, enter transactions, and print reports.

The third part of the book is aimed at the accountant and covers using QBOA.

I don't pretend to cover every detail of every feature in QBO or QBOA. Instead, I've focused on covering the tools I think most users will need as they navigate QBO and QBOA.

REMEMBER

As I discuss in Chapter 2, there are different versions of QBO; I used QBO Plus as I rote this book because it contains the most features. Users of other versions might find references in this book to features they don't have because they aren't using the Plus version.

Before diving in, I have to get a few technical convention details out of the way:

>> Text that you're meant to type as it appears in the book is **bold.** The exception is when you're working through a list of steps: Because each step is bold, the text to type is not bold.

>> Web addresses and programming code appear in mono font. If you're reading a digital version of this book on a device connected to the Internet, note that you can tap or click a web address to visit that website, like this: www.dummies.com.

>> You can use QBO and QBOA from their Android and iOS apps, from the Windows desktop app (which works on Windows desktop computers, tablets, and laptops, but not on Windows phones), or from Chrome, Firefox, Safari, or Internet Explorer. At the time I wrote this book, a variety of issues existed if you tried to use QBO and QBOA with Microsoft Edge. In my experience, QBO and QBOA function best in Chrome. For that reason, I used Chrome

throughout this book and I've devoted The Part of Tens chapters in this book to Chrome so that, if you aren't familiar with Chrome, you can get up and running more quickly.

» When I discuss a command to choose, I'll separate the elements of the sequence with a command arrow that looks like this: ⇨ . For example, when you see Chrome Menu ⇨ Settings, that means you should click the Chrome Menu button (on the right side of the Chrome screen — see Chapter 16 for a description of Chrome's screen elements) and, from the drop-down menu that appears, click Settings.

Foolish Assumptions

I had to assume some things about you to write this book. Here are the assumptions I made:

» You know that you need to manage the accounts for your business, and you might even have some sort of setup in place to record this information. I *don't* assume that you know how to do all that on a computer.

» You have some interest in managing the accounts for your business using a web-based product.

» You are probably but not necessarily a QuickBooks Desktop edition user.

» You have a personal computer or Mac (that you know how to turn on). Your PC must be running Microsoft Windows 7, Windows 8.1, or Windows 10; I wrote this book using Windows 10. Your Mac must be running OS X 10.11 or later.

» You might have purchased an edition of QuickBooks Online, but not necessarily.

Icons Used in This Book

TIP

Think of these icons as the fodder of advice columns. They offer (hopefully) wise advice or a bit more information about a topic under discussion.

REMEMBER

This icon points out juicy tidbits that are likely to be repeatedly useful to you — so please don't forget them.

WARNING

Mr. Spock! Scotty! Red Alert! Well, okay, it's really not life-threatening. In this book, you see this icon when I'm trying to help you avoid mistakes that can cost money.

TECHNICAL STUFF

When you see this icon, you've come across material that isn't critical to understand but will satisfy the curious. Think "inquiring minds want to know" when you see this icon.

Beyond the Book

In addition to the content in this book, this product also comes with a free access-anywhere cheat sheet that gives you keyboard shortcuts for QBO and QBOA and some handy tool buttons in QBO. To get this cheat sheet, simply go to www.dummies.com and search for "QuickBooks Online For Dummies Cheat Sheet" in the Search box.

Where to Go from Here

Simply turn the page. Seriously. You can dive in anywhere you want and come back as often as you like. You don't have to read through this book cover to cover because each section stands alone and provides step-by-step instructions for common tasks. You should consider this book a reference that you use when you need it.

That said, if you're just getting started with QBO or QBOA, you might want to turn the page and follow, in order, the chapters in Part 1. Then feel free to explore any topic you want, using the table of contents or the index to help you find a topic.

1

Getting Started with QBO and QBOA

IN THIS PART . . .

Examine what QBO is and what it isn't.

Learn the requirements to use QBO.

Meet the QBO interface.

Chapter **1**

Introducing QBO and QBOA

Q uickBooks Online (QBO) and QuickBooks Online Accountant (QBOA) are web-based products you can use to manage your business's accounting. This chapter introduces these products and discusses whether you should move into the cloud to manage your accounting. It also examines the system requirements for these products.

QBO for the Client and QBOA for the Accountant

QuickBooks Online offers you the ability to manage your business's accounting in the cloud. The software is divided into two products: one for end users and the other for accountants. Interfaces for both products are available on multiple platforms.

QuickBooks Online (QBO) is the cloud-based product for end users who need to perform typical accounting tasks. QBO is based on the same principles as the QuickBooks Desktop product — that is, it uses lists to, for example, manage customers and vendors, and it includes transactions similar to the ones found in the

QuickBooks Desktop product. But, QBO is *not* simply a "rewrite" of the QuickBooks Desktop product for the web. It was designed and developed as a new product, optimized for web-based usage.

QuickBooks Online Accountant (QBOA) is the cloud-based portal that accountants use to access client QBO companies, work in them, and communicate with clients. QBOA also includes a QBO company in its Your Books section that accountants can use to track the accounting of their own businesses.

Comparing interfaces

QBO and QBOA were initially written and optimized to be used in the major web browsers — Chrome, Firefox, Safari, Microsoft Edge, and Internet Explorer. Later, Intuit added QBO apps that you can use to work in QBO on iOS and Android mobile devices. Intuit also offers a desktop version of QBO referred to in this book as, cleverly, QBO Desktop; this version is *not* a mobile app (it won't work on phones and isn't available in the Google Play Store or the Apple App Store) but it will work on any Mac or Windows computer, including "portable" computers like laptops and tablets, making it somewhat mobile. It also is *not* the QuickBooks Desktop product, which is not a cloud-based product.

In this section of the book, you explore what QBO and QBOA look like in a browser; the next section explores what the QBO Desktop edition looks like as well as detailing some of the things you can do in the iOS and Android mobile app versions of QBO.

In a browser, an open company in QBO looks similar to the one shown in Figure 1-1. I cover the interface in more detail in Chapter 3, but for the time being, the most important thing to notice is the Navigation bar that runs down the left side of the screen. If you've been a QuickBooks Desktop user and you've used the Left Icon Bar in that product, you might find the Navigation bar a familiar tool. The Left Icon Bar and the Navigation bar work the same way; you click a link in either of them to navigate to a portion of the program.

Clicking the three-striped button beside the QuickBooks logo above the Navigation bar enables you to collapse the Navigation bar to view just the icons (and clicking it again expands the Navigation bar back to the view in Figure 1-1). When you collapse the Navigation bar (you see an example of it collapsed in Chapter 3), you have more screen real estate to view the right side of the QBO interface.

At the top of the screen, you see tools that help QBO users create transactions, search for existing transactions, and view settings for the QBO company.

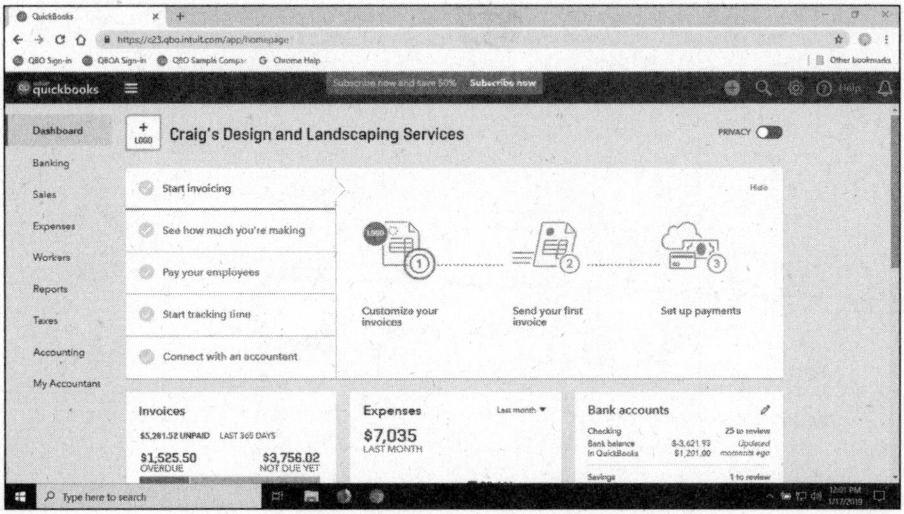

FIGURE 1-1:
An open
company
in QBO.

Figure 1-2 shows what an accountant sees immediately upon logging into QBOA. The Navigation bar changes to support an accountant's needs; you can read more about the QBOA interface in Chapter 11.

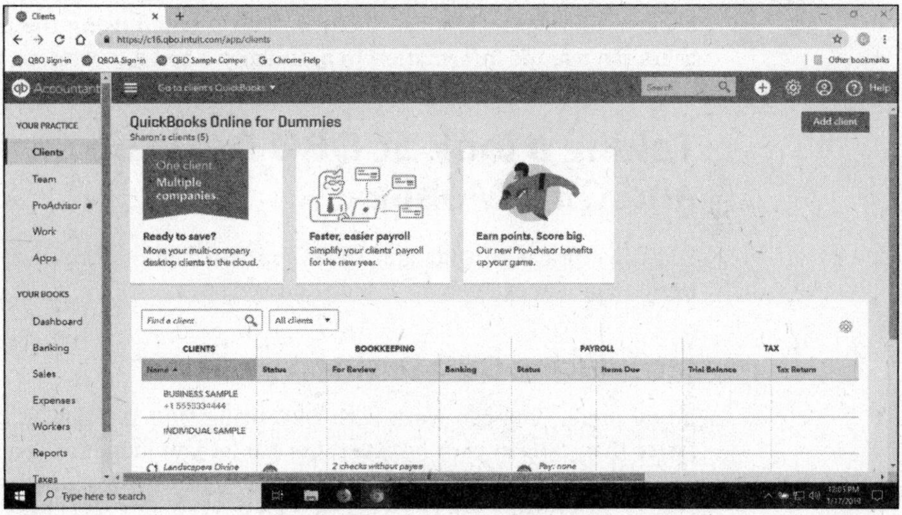

FIGURE 1-2:
The first view
an accountant
has when he
opens QBOA.

When an accountant opens a client's company from within QBOA (see Figure 1-3), the interface resembles what a client sees, with some minor differences. Compare Figure 1-1 with Figure 1-3. First, you know you're using QBOA because the top of the Navigation pane shows QB Accountant. Second, the Accountant Tools menu (the briefcase icon) displays tools not found in QBO that help accountants manage client companies.

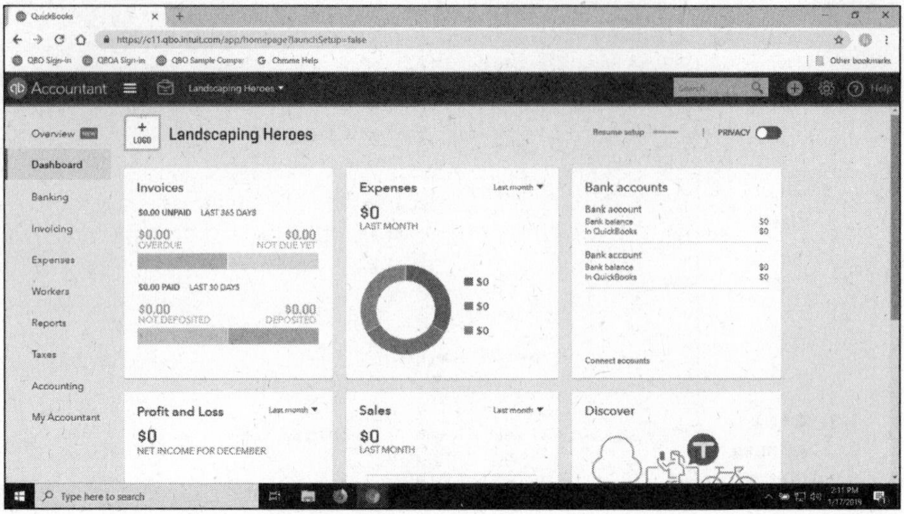

FIGURE 1-3:
An open
company in
QBOA.

Even though an open company looks a bit different depending on whether you open it using QBO or QBOA, the basic functionality doesn't really change, other than accountants have more options than end users have.

REMEMBER

Because QBOA contains functionality that QBO doesn't have, I've organized this book so that QBO users can focus on Part 2 when using the product, and QBOA users can use the information in both Parts 2 and 3 to work in a company online.

Taking a look at QBO Desktop and QBO Mobile

You can work with QBO and QBOA without using a browser; you can use QBO Desktop or you can use the iOS or Android apps.

Introducing QBO Desktop

If you prefer, you can work with QBO using QBO Desktop; it's purported to run faster than QBO in your browser, but I'll let you judge for yourself. To download QBO Desktop, use your browser to navigate to the QBO sign-in page: `quickbooks. intuit.com/apps/`. On the page that appears, you'll see a Free Download button; click it and follow the onscreen instructions to download and install QBO Desktop.

TIP

Both Windows and Mac users can use the same QBO Desktop app; what you download from the QBO sign-in page works on both platforms. Ingenious, don't you think?

WARNING

The word "app" has become a buzzword and is often used when it probably shouldn't be. In this chapter, I'm using the word "app" *only* when I refer to the mobile versions of QBO and QBOA that are available for download from the Google Play Store or the Apple App Store. In many places online, you'll find references to a QBO Windows app — and, at the time I wrote this, there is no Windows app per se. There is QBO Desktop, which allows Windows users (except Windows Phone users) to use QBO while being mobile — on, for example, laptops and tablets — but QBO Desktop *is not* available from any of the "mobile device" stores (Google Play or Apple App) and therefore, I'm not calling it an app.

Figure 1-4 shows QBO Desktop with a QBO company open, and Figure 1-5 shows QBOA just after opening it in QBO Desktop (but before opening any client company).

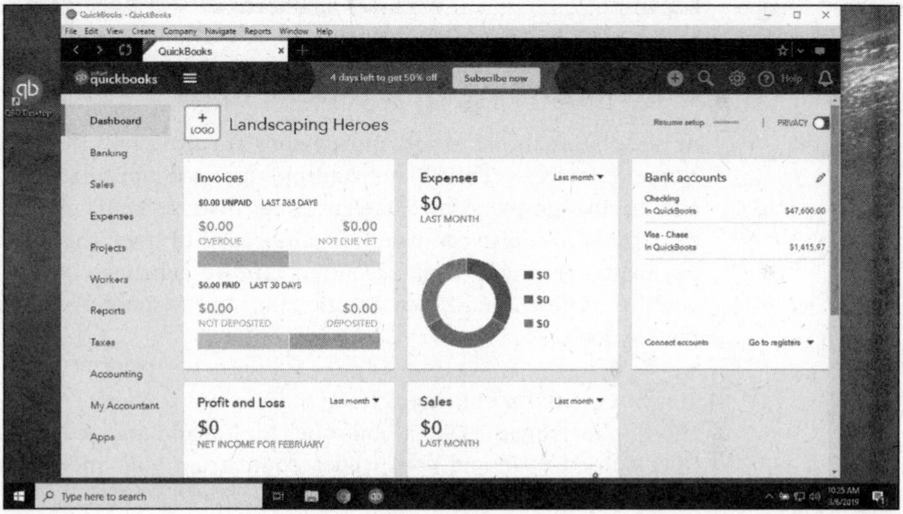

FIGURE 1-4:
QBO while
working in
QBO Desktop.

If you compare Figure 1-5 to Figure 1-1, you'll notice that, once again, QBOA users have the same additional options in QBO Desktop that they have in a browser. The menus at the top of the screen are the biggest visual difference between QBO and QBOA in QBO Desktop and QBO and QBOA in a browser. If you've been a QuickBooks Desktop product user, you know that you can use the menus to navigate. Under the hood, QBO Desktop offers some options that you won't find readily available in a browser, such as the ability to work in multiple windows.

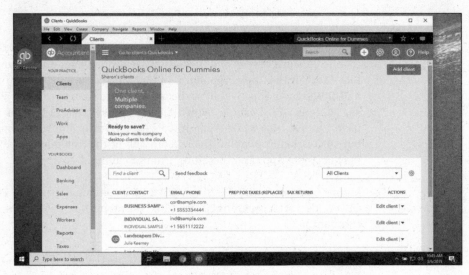

FIGURE 1-5:
QBOA while
working in
QBO Desktop.

Understanding QBO mobile apps

At no additional cost to you, mobile apps are also available for iPhones, iPads, and Android devices. The iOS and Android apps are optimized for touch interaction and on-the-go workflows like customer management, invoicing, estimates, and signatures. You also can use the mobile apps to track the status of invoices, take payments, reconcile bank accounts, capture expenses, and check reports. And, you'll find Pinch and Zoom functionality in the mobile apps and in browsers on mobile devices.

You can get the mobile apps here: `https://quickbooks.intuit.com/mobile`. In addition to using the QBO mobile apps for iOS and Android, you also can access the QBO sign-in page and your QBO account from your mobile device's browser at `https://qbo.intuit.com`.

New features are added often to the mobile apps. For example, you can customize invoice templates from the browser-based QBO and from QBO Desktop. You can customize templates from mobile devices but not using mobile apps; instead, use the browser-based QBO on your mobile device.

REMEMBER

Be aware that the browser-based version of QBO and QBOA has additional functionality and keyboard shortcuts geared towards more in-depth business accounting tasks.

So, take your choice; you're not limited: Work in a browser, work in QBO Desktop, or work in a mobile app, depending on your needs at the moment.

Understanding the Cloud

Just to make sure we're on the same page here, I'm defining the *cloud* as software and data housed securely in remote data centers (not on your office premises) and accessed securely using the Internet. Working in the cloud can increase your efficiency by offering you the opportunity to work anywhere, communicate easily with others, and collaborate in real time.

REMEMBER

Regardless of whether you use QBO or QBOA in a browser, in QBO Desktop, or in an app, both the software and the data are housed on servers controlled by Intuit and accessible via the Internet.

In the traditional model of software use, you buy software and install it on your computer. Or you might buy the software and install it on a vendor's server. QBO and QBOA fall into the category of Software as a Service (SaaS). You typically don't buy SaaS software; instead, you rent it (that is, you purchase a subscription).

Because SaaS software is typically web-based software, you (also typically) access SaaS software over the Internet using a browser. A *browser* is software installed on your local computer or mobile device that you use to, well, browse the Internet, looking up cool stuff like what the stock market is doing today, what kind of weather can you expect on Friday when your vacation starts, how to get to your boss's house for the party he's having, and — oh, yes — to work with web-based software such as QBO and QBOA. In the case of QBO and QBOA, you can work with these web-based SaaS products using a browser, QBO Desktop, or an app you download to your mobile device.

BUSINESS IDENTITY THEFT PROTECTION

If you are concerned about security and business identity theft, you can purchase an add-on service called Detect & Defend, powered by EZShield, a leader in the fraud and identity protection industry. This add-on service costs $9.99/month at the time I wrote this, and the service provides dark-web monitoring, business credit monitoring, and, if your business's identity is stolen, Detect & Defend provides U.S.-based resolution specialists who are trained and certified as Identity Theft Risk Management Specialists by the Institute of Consumer Financial Education and by the Institute of Fraud Risk Management. For more complete details on the features of this service, visit https://intuitmarket.intuit.com/qb-detect-and-defend/features.

Using web-based software can be attractive for a number of reasons. For example, using web-based software, you have access to that software's information anywhere, anytime, from any device — stationary or mobile.

REMEMBER

Some folks see the "anywhere, anytime" feature as a potential disadvantage because it makes information too readily available — and therefore a target for hackers. Intuit stores your data on servers that use bank-level security and encryption, and Intuit automatically backs up your data for you. For added security and protection, see the sidebar, "Business Identity Theft Protection." Other folks see the "anywhere, anytime" feature as a disadvantage for exactly the reason that they have access to the software's information anywhere, anytime, and from any device, offering the opportunity to work more than they'd like. You are in charge of your life, so . . . no comment on this "disadvantage."

In addition, web-based software like QBO and QBOA promotes collaboration and can help you save time. Using QBO and QBOA, accountants, bookkeepers, and clients can communicate about issues that arise, as described in Chapter 14.

Then there's the issue of keeping software up to date. Desktop software such as traditional QuickBooks is updated typically once each year. Unlike their desktop cousin, QBO and QBOA are updated every two to four weeks.

REMEMBER

Because updating occurs so frequently to QBO and QBOA, by the time this book is published, things (and screens) might have changed. Actually, make that "probably have changed."

Should You Move to the Cloud?

Before you make the move to the cloud, you should consider the needs of your business in the following areas:

>> Invoicing, point of sale, electronic payment, and customer relationship management

>> Financial and tax reporting

>> Budgeting

>> Time-tracking and payroll

>> Inventory, job costing, and job scheduling

>> Managing company expenses and vendor bills

Beyond the advantages described in the preceding section, the particular needs of a business might dictate whether you can use QBO. For example, QBO *won't* work for you if your business has industry-specific needs or is mid-sized and needs to use ODBC-compliant applications. In addition, QBO won't work for you if you need to

>> Track your balance sheet by class.

>> Process more than 350,000 transactions annually.

>> Track labor costs.

>> Manage a robust inventory that supports making and selling finished goods.

In any of these cases, you would probably be better off with one of Intuit's "designed for desktop use" products like traditional QuickBooks Pro or Quick-Books Premier.

TIP

When QBO and QBOA were first released, the U.S. version didn't support multiple currencies. That feature has been added to both products. And, you can set a "home currency" without enabling multicurrency support. See Chapter 3 for more information.

System Requirements

Using a web-based software product typically doesn't require a lot of hardware and software; in fact, the demands of QBO and QBOA aren't extensive. In particular, you need a Windows or Intel-based Mac computer using Windows 7, 8.1, or 10, or OS X 10.11 or later. You also need

>> An Internet connection — Intuit recommends a high-speed connection of 3 Mbps or higher

>> One of the five supported Internet browsers:

- Google Chrome

- Mozilla Firefox

- Microsoft Edge

- Microsoft Internet Explorer 11 or higher (32-bit version only)

- Safari 6.1 if your operating system is iOS 7 or higher

Although QBO and QBOA work in all the major browsers, they work best, in my experience, in Chrome, with Firefox coming in a close second. Therefore, I use Chrome throughout this book, and the Part of Tens chapters cover using Chrome so that you can get comfortable with that browser. If you're a Firefox user, give QBO and QBOA a try in Firefox.

The requirements for QBO Desktop and the mobile apps are basically the same as those outlined here, except that you won't really need a browser on your device (although you'll probably have one). You'll still need an Internet connection, and be aware that, although new features are added to the mobile apps all the time, the mobile apps do not support all features of QBO and QBOA.

Whether you work on a desktop computer or on a mobile device, the computer or device needs to meet the basic requirements of the operating system you use on that computer or device — and then some. For example, if you're using a Windows desktop computer, you need the amount of RAM (random access memory) specified by Microsoft to load the version of Windows on the computer before you ever launch your browser. If you don't have sufficient RAM to run the operating system, you certainly won't be happy with the behavior of QBO and QBOA. You won't be happy with the behavior of the computer, either.

Basic requirements (and I stress the word *basic*) for a Windows 7, 8.1, and 10 computer, as specified by Microsoft, are

>> 1-gigahertz (GHz) or faster 32-bit (x86) or 64-bit (x64) processor

>> 1 gigabyte (GB) of RAM (32 bit) or 2GB of RAM (64 bit)

>> 16GB of available hard disk space for the 32-bit version of the operating system or 32GB for the 64-bit versions of the operating system

>> A display that supports at least 800 x 600 dpi

>> DirectX 9 graphics device with WDDM 1.0 or higher driver

>> An Internet connection for both installation and operating system updates

These versions of Windows work with multi-core processors, and all 32-bit versions of Windows can support up to 32 processor cores, whereas 64-bit versions can support up to 256 processor cores.

And a word on the word *basic*. You'll be a whole lot happier if your desktop computer components have higher numbers than the ones I just listed. If you have a computer that's fairly new — say, three to four years old — you might need only to add some RAM or possibly hard disk space. If your computer is older than three or four years, you should consider purchasing new equipment, simply because you'll be unbelievably happier with the computer's performance. Technology continues to improve dramatically in short spurts of time.

If you buy a new computer, you don't need to worry about meeting more than the basic requirements. I'm pretty sure you'd have a hard time finding a new computer containing a 1-gigahertz processor; most computers today come with at least 2.5-gigahertz processors, and they support better graphics than the DirectX 9 graphics listed in the basic requirements. And most monitors available for purchase today don't support low resolutions such as 800 x 600; you most likely own a monitor that supports much higher resolution. In my opinion, 1GB of RAM is insufficient; your desktop computer should have at least 4GB of RAM, and you'll be much happier if it has 8GB of RAM. On the hard drive requirement, if you don't have the 16GB or 20GB of available space specified, you probably should be considering a hard drive replacement for your computer.

QBO and QBOA have their own hardware requirements — that exceed Microsoft's basic requirements. Visit this page to see the system requirements for QBO and QBOA:

`https://community.intuit.com/articles/1145516-system-requirements-for-quickbooks-online`

If you want to use QBO Desktop, visit this page to see system requirements:

`https://community.intuit.com/articles/1458875-quickbooks-windows-app-general-support`

TECHNICAL STUFF

The amount of RAM your computer can successfully use depends on the computer's architecture — in particular, if your computer uses a 32-bit processor, as older computers often did, your computer might not be able to "see" more than 4GB of RAM. So, you could put 16GB of RAM in the computer and only be able to use 4GB. And part of that 4GB goes to other stuff, like your video card; so, with most 32-bit processors (there are a few exceptions), your computer can use only 3GB of RAM. Bottom line here: Newer computers use 64-bit processors and can take advantage of much more RAM, which makes them much faster.

Chapter **2**

Embracing the QBO/QBOA Format

QBO and QBOA are not traditional software that you buy and install on your local computer. This chapter explores the QBO/QBOA software format, and I assume that you've read Chapter 1 and evaluated whether QBO can meet your needs.

It's All about Subscriptions

QBO and QBOA fall into the category of Software as a Service (SaaS). As such, you don't buy the software. Instead, you rent it; that is, you buy a subscription to use the software for a time period specified by the seller.

REMEMBER

Traditionally, you buy a *license* to use software that you install on your computer, and typically, that license permits you to install the software on only one computer.

And, of course, a QBO user can pay varying amounts for a subscription, depending on the subscription level purchased.

QBO is available at five different subscription levels, and each subsequent subscription level costs more and contains more functionality. The QBO subscriptions available at this writing are

>> Self-Employed

>> Simple Start

>> Essentials

>> Plus

>> Advanced

REMEMBER

All versions of QBO share three attributes in common. First, you can use a tablet, Android or iOS smartphone, or desktop computer to access your data. Second, your data is automatically backed up online. And third, all versions of QBO use 128-bit Secure Sockets Layer (SSL), the same security and encryption used by banks to secure data sent over the Internet.

After you assess your needs as described in Chapter 1, use the following information to identify the lowest subscription level that will meet your requirements. At this point in time, you can upgrade to a higher level, but you cannot downgrade to a lower level.

Accounting professionals signing up clients for QBO and creating client companies originally couldn't switch client companies from one version of QBO to another if the accounting professional created the client as part of the Intuit Wholesale Pricing program. However, except for the Self-Employed version, that's no longer true. So, you no longer need to anticipate your client's requirements for more advanced features like the ability to track inventory or prepare 1099s.

The Self-Employed version

This version of QBO is aimed at freelancers and self-employed individuals, basically, those who receive Federal Form 1099 to account for the money they've been paid and pay their taxes using Schedule C of IRS Form 1040. Be aware, though, that the QuickBooks Self-Employed version (QBSE) is not currently part of the QBO product line, and that means that you cannot upgrade from QBSE to any other QBO product directly — an important fact to keep in mind when deciding to start with QBSE. If your business has business bank accounts, you should not use the Self Employed version. QBSE enables you to separate personal and business expenses and mileage, so it's really geared to the "side hustle" gig economy, like Uber and Lyft drivers.

Using the Self-Employed version, you can

>> Download transactions from your bank and credit card accounts.

>> Separate business from personal spending.

>> Create and send invoices at any time, and personalize your invoices using your logo as well as customize the subject line and main message of the invoice email.

>> Send a mobile reminder to customers before payment is due. And, QBSE lets you know when your invoice is viewed and paid.

>> Send receipts for paid invoices.

>> Duplicate prior invoices to send them again, eliminating busy work.

>> Accept mobile payments and take advantage of free bank transfers.

>> Track mileage using your phone's GPS and delete trips, along with mileage, in bulk.

>> Use your phone to take photos of receipts for your expenses; QBSE automatically extracts key data from the receipt and uses the information to match an existing transaction or to create a new expense.

>> Use QBSE's Expense Finder feature to identify more potential deductions by securely connecting your bank accounts to pull in business expenses from the entire past year and sort them into Schedule C categories. When you sign in to QBSE for the first time from March 20 to April 15, select "No, I am still working on 2018 taxes" to access the Expense Finder feature. You can then connect to your bank accounts to securely import all 2018 expenses in just minutes. The Expense Finder feature automatically finds work expenses and organizes them by Schedule C category.

>> Calculate and pay estimated quarterly taxes.

>> Use QBSE Labs to test drive new features.

>> If you need more guidance or have loyalties to a tax preparer, you can invite your tax preparer to work with your QBSE data using QBOA.

Like the other versions of QBO, you can use a tablet, an Android or iOS smartphone, or desktop computer to access your data. In addition, QuickBooks Self-Employed uses the same security and encryption as banks, and your data is automatically backed up online. As you might expect, this version has the fewest reports available, and only one person and an invited accountant can access QBSE.

USAGE LIMITS FOR QBO SIMPLE START, ESSENTIALS, AND PLUS

Because Intuit has introduced the new QBO Advanced subscription (that you can read about in the section "The Advanced version"), Intuit is applying updated usage limits to Simple Start, Essentials, and Plus subscriptions. Customers with these subscriptions who already exceed the usage limits can continue with their current subscription and their existing data, *but* (and this is an important "but") these customers won't be able to manually add to any element that currently exceeds the usage limit for the customer's subscription. After the usage limits go into effect, a customer who wants to add to a QBO element and will exceed the usage limit must upgrade to a higher level subscription that supports their needs.

So, what are the limits? You'll find the limits for all Simple Start, Essentials, and Plus subscriptions in the Usage Limits table.

Usage Limits for Simple Start, Essentials, and Plus Subscriptions

QBO Element	Usage Limit
Chart of Accounts	250
Classes + Locations	40 combined
Billed Users	1 for Simple Start, 3 for Essentials, 5 for Plus
Unbilled Users	2 Accountant users for all plans, for Plus, unlimited users who access for reports only, and, for Essentials and Plus, unlimited users who access for time tracking only.

The Advanced subscription level has only two real limitations: using it, you can have up to 25 billed users and 2 unbilled Accountant users.

So, suppose that your QBO company needs more than 250 accounts or more than a combination of 40 classes and locations. If your company already exceeds these limits, you'll be able to continue in your current subscription, but you won't be able to add accounts or any combination of classes and locations until you delete or deactivate these elements to bring down your total to the limits listed in the table. If you can't reduce your accounts or combination of classes and locations, you'll need to upgrade to an Advanced subscription.

If you opt to include TurboTax in your subscription, you also can pay your estimated quarterly taxes online and export Schedule C information from QBO to TurboTax so that you can prepare your tax return more easily. With TurboTax as part of your subscription, you receive one federal and one state electronic tax return filing at no extra cost.

The Simple Start version

The Simple Start version of QBO is great for a new business with basic bookkeeping needs. With Simple Start, you can

» Track your income and expenses.

» Download transactions from your bank and credit card accounts.

» Create an unlimited number of customers.

» Send unlimited estimates and invoices.

» Print checks and record transactions to track expenses.

» Track, create, and send 1099-Misc forms.

» Import data from Microsoft Excel or QuickBooks Desktop.

» Invite up to two accountants to access your data.

» Integrate with available apps in QBO's App Center.

Although the Simple Start version supports Accounts Receivable functions, you can't set up invoices to bill customers on a recurring basis. You also can't track bills due in the future in the Simple Start version because it doesn't include any Accounts Payable functions. And, one other important consideration: The Simple Start version does include a trial balance and a general ledger.

Although the Simple Start version allows two accountants to work in the client's company, Simple Start is still designed for a single user. Therefore, the accountant cannot create the client's company for the client. At the time the company is created in QBO, whoever creates the company becomes, in QBO parlance, the Master Administrator.

In addition to the single-user restriction, the Simple Start version offers more than 20 reports. And Simple Start users can memorize report settings and produce memorized reports.

REMEMBER

For subscription levels that support multiple users, the accountant can create the company for the client and then assign the master administrator role to the client. And, if the accountant doesn't make the client the master administrator when creating the company, the accountant can, later on, transfer the master administrator role to the client. See Chapter 12 for more information.

The Essentials version

The Essentials version of QBO includes all the features found in Simple Start. In addition, with the Essentials version, you can

>> Set up invoices to automatically bill on a recurring schedule.

>> Prepare and send estimates.

>> Take advantage of Accounts Payable functions, including entering vendor bills and scheduling their payment for later.

>> Compare your sales and profitability with industry trends.

>> Track sales taxes.

>> Create and post recurring transactions.

>> Track time.

>> Control what your users can access.

The Essentials version permits three simultaneous users and two accountant users as well as an unlimited number of users who log in only to use time-tracking tools. In addition, the Essentials version contains the reports found in Simple Start and 20 additional reports.

The Plus version

The Plus version of QBO is the most full-featured version of QBO. It contains all the features found in the Essentials version. In addition, you can

>> Create, send, and track purchase orders.

>> Track inventory using the first in, first out (FIFO) inventory valuation method. QBO supports light inventory needs: If you sell finished goods, QBO should be able to manage your needs. But if you need to assemble finished goods to sell, QBO won't meet your needs on its own. You can look for an add-on app to supplement your inventory needs; I talk about add-on apps at the end of this chapter.

- >> Categorize income and expenses using class tracking.

- >> Track sales and profitability by business location. You can assign only one location to a transaction, but you can assign multiple classes to a transaction.

- >> Give employees and subcontractors limited access to the QBO company to enter time worked.

- >> Track billable hours by customer. QBO supports light job-costing needs, but it does not allow you to automatically cost labor.

- >> Track projects.

- >> Create budgets to estimate future income and expenses, and you can create multiple budgets per year, location, class, or customer.

REMEMBER

I used QBO Plus as I wrote this book because it contains more features needed by most users; therefore, users of other versions might find references in this book to features they don't have. Accounting professionals: The company that comes with QBOA is a Plus company.

The Plus version supports five simultaneous billed users and two accountant users as well as an unlimited number of users who log in only to use reports or time-tracking tools. The Plus version also contains more than 65 reports: all the reports found in both the Simple Start and the Essentials versions, and some additional reports.

The Advanced version

Intuit has recently started offering QBO Advanced, a version aimed at users who have outgrown QBO Plus. In addition to all the features you find in QBO Plus, using QBO Advanced, you can

- >> Have up to 25 simultaneous users with full access.

- >> Connect with a dedicated Customer Success Manager to handle support questions; support calls go to the front of the line instead of waiting in queue. Customer Success Managers also provide information on online training and QuickBooks products; subscribers to QBO Advanced are entitled to five free online training courses annually.

- >> Establish custom permissions for your users.

- >> Efficiently import hundreds of invoice transactions created outside of QuickBooks through a CSV file at one time.

- >> Take advantage of enhanced reporting capabilities called Smart Reporting, powered by Fathom.

Users of QBO Advanced face only two real limitations: They can have up to 25 billed users and 2 unbilled accountant users. For more information on QBO Advanced, see https://quickbooks.intuit.com/accounting/advanced/.

Simple Start, Essentials, Plus, and Advanced with Payroll

If an end user signs up for QBO Simple Start, Essentials, Plus, or Advanced on his own and creates his own company, he can create the company using the Self Service Payroll option or the Full Service Payroll option, or later, he can sign up for payroll from within QBO. An accountant also can create the company that uses Self Service Payroll for a client. For details, see the section "Addressing Payroll Needs" later in this chapter.

What Does It Cost?

The big question: What's it cost? The price is dependent primarily on the QBO version you choose and whether you start with a trial.

If you are an end user who signs up on your own for a QBO subscription, foregoing the trial, the price per month as of the date this book was written appears in Table 2-1.

TABLE 2-1

QBO Subscription Pricing

QBO Version	Regular Price	Sale Price
Self-Employed	$10/month	$5/month
Simple Start	$20/month	$10/month
Essentials	$35/month	$17/month
Plus	$60/month	$30/month
Advanced	$150/month	$75/month

REMEMBER

The prices shown in Table 2-1 are monthly subscription prices, and, at the time I wrote this, the sale price was good for six months. In some cases, when you sign up, you'll be offered the option to pay for an entire year. And, paying for a full year might turn out to be less expensive than paying on a monthly basis.

At the time I wrote this, Intuit offered Simple Start, Essentials, Plus, and Advanced users the ability to add Self Service payroll for $18/month plus $4/employee/month and Full Service payroll for $40/month plus $4/employee/month.

Each month, your credit card is automatically charged for your subscription. You can opt for a free 30-day trial that includes payroll processing along with the rest of the subscription's features. If you opt to continue QBO Payroll after the 30-day trial, your subscription fee increases. You also can use the QBO Payments app for free; it gives you the capability to process online and mobile payments at a rate of, at the time I wrote this book, 2.4 percent for swiped transactions, 2.9 percent for eInvoiced transactions, and 3.4 percent for key-entered transactions. In all cases, there's also a 25 cent per transaction fee, and ACH is free. QuickBooks Self-Employed users can enable mobile payments and enjoy free bank transfers and accept electronic payments.

If you opt for a 30-day free trial, you won't get the sale price for the subscription. But, if you "buy now," Intuit gives you a 60 day, money-back guarantee on your purchase.

If you are an accounting professional, you can sign up for the Wholesale Pricing program and use QBOA for free. If you create a client's company as part of the Wholesale Pricing program and you manage the client's subscription, your credit card is charged automatically for each client subscription. It is your responsibility to bill the client for the QBO subscription. The bill you receive from Intuit is a single consolidated bill for all the QBO subscriptions you manage. For a little more information on the Wholesale Pricing program, see Chapter 11. But, for the complete skinny on the Wholesale Pricing program, contact Intuit. Note that accounting professionals might be able to get QBO for their clients at a reduced price.

If an accounting professional creates a company through QBOA, the company does not come with a 30-day free trial. Instead, at the time the accounting professional creates the company, he must provide a payment method to ensure uninterrupted service.

If your client initially sets up QBO with his or her own subscription, you can move that existing QBO subscription to your consolidated bill at the discounted rate. And, if your arrangement with your client doesn't work out, you can remove the client from your consolidated bill, and the client can begin paying for his own subscription.

Addressing Payroll Needs

QBO can handle payroll regardless of whether an end user or an accountant creates the QBO company.

If an end user signs up for QBO Simple Start, Essentials, Plus or Advanced on his own, he can create his own company using the appropriate "with Payroll" option — Self Service or Full Service Payroll — or, after the fact, he can sign up for QBO Payroll from the Employees screen (see Figure 2-1).

REMEMBER

The distinction between the two options, besides price, is that you choose Self Service Payroll if you want to prepare payroll on your own; for details on preparing payroll in QBO, see Chapter 9. Alternatively, you can subscribe to QBO Full Service Payroll, which integrates with QBO, where Intuit prepares payroll for you. For those with an interest in history, Self Service Payroll is the current name for what used to be called Enhanced Payroll.

REMEMBER

It's easy to get confused here . . . I know I was. Intuit also offers another payroll product, Intuit Full Service Payroll, which is a standalone product that doesn't integrate with QBO.

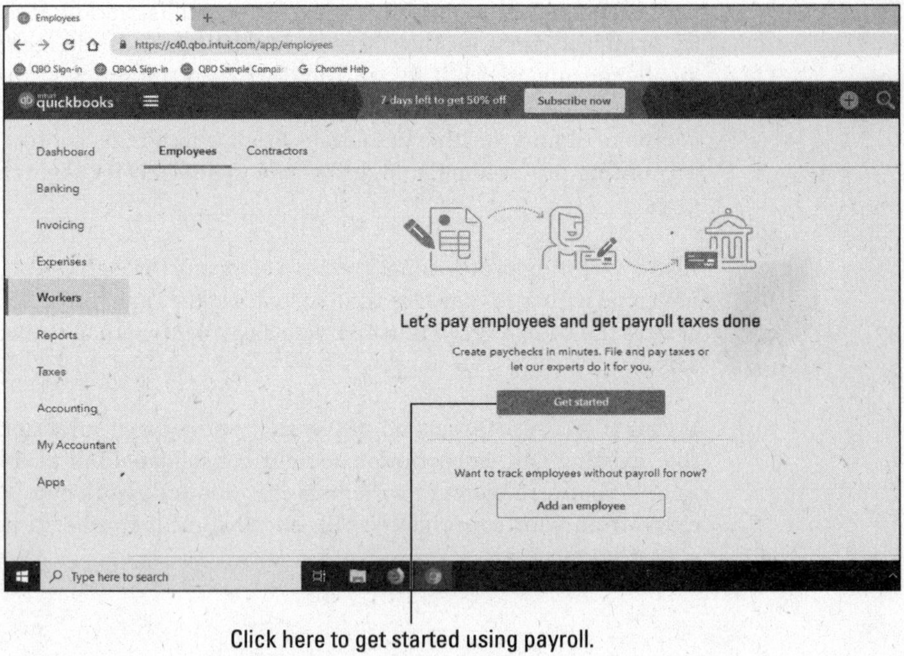

FIGURE 2-1:
If you sign up for QBO on your own, you can turn on payroll from the Employees screen.

Click here to get started using payroll.

Both Self Service and Full Service QBO Payroll sport the following features:

>> Paying employees with printed checks or by directly depositing paychecks

>> Automatically calculating tax payments and paying them electronically

>> Processing federal and state quarterly and annual reports and preparing W-2 forms

>> Processing payroll for employees working in your company's state or another state

>> Keeping payroll tax tables up to date without having to install updates like you do with the QuickBooks Desktop product

>> Using the QBO Payroll mobile app to pay employees, view past paychecks, electronically pay taxes, and electronically file tax forms

If an accountant who is not enrolled in the Intuit Wholesale Pricing program creates a QBO Essentials, Plus, or Advanced company for a client, the client company can turn on QBO payroll (QBOP) from the Employees screen in the client's company (refer to Figure 2-1). Clients can prepare payroll for themselves, or accounting professionals can manage all payroll functions for clients.

If the accountant is enrolled in the Intuit Wholesale Pricing program and creates a QBO Essentials, Plus, or Advanced company for a client as part of the program, the accountant can set up the QBO company to use QBO Payroll (QBOP).

Last, an accountant can add an Intuit Full Service Payroll subscription (where Intuit prepares payroll outside of QBO) to a client company subscription through QBOA, regardless of whether he or she is enrolled in the Wholesale Pricing program.

Switching from QuickBooks Desktop

At this point (or maybe earlier than now), you might have been wondering if you can easily switch to QBO if you have been a QuickBooks Desktop program user. And, the answer is yes. Chapter 12 provides details on importing QuickBooks Desktop data into QBO. And, the import process doesn't affect your original desktop company; it's still available via the desktop product. After you import your data into QBO, you should run the Profit & Loss report and the Balance Sheet using the accrual method for all dates from both QBO and QuickBooks Desktop to ensure both versions show the same information.

And, if you want some reassurance that you'll get the same accurate information from QBO that you got from QuickBooks Desktop, you can "run in parallel" for a time period you specify. For example, you might decide to enter all your transactions in both versions of the software for one month; at the end of that time, you can run reports from both products and make sure you see the same information.

WARNING

Although you can continue to use the QuickBooks Desktop product, once you make the switch to QuickBooks Online, be aware that no synchronization occurs between QuickBooks Desktop and QBO. So, changes you make in one are not reflected in the other. Unless you're temporarily running in parallel, continuing to use both products could really mess up your books because you might accidentally enter transactions into one product and not the other. And it certainly would be time-consuming.

Where Add-On Apps Fit In

QBO doesn't operate as a complete, standalone accounting solution. It has functional limitations. The section "Addressing Payroll Needs" highlights one such limitation — and shows how you can use Intuit add-ons to achieve more functionality in QBO. And, earlier in this chapter, I briefly mention Intuit's Payments app, which supports electronic customer payment processing and integrates with QBO.

But those aren't the only add-on apps available for QBO; third-party developers have been creating apps to enhance the functionality of QBO. And, over time, you can expect more apps to be developed.

REMEMBER

In Chapter 1, I made a distinction about apps: In that chapter, I use the term to describe the versions of QBO available from mobile device stores (Google Play and Apple App) and distinguish them from QBO Desktop, which is not available in mobile device stores but works on both Windows and Mac computers. In this section, when I refer to apps, I refer to products developed to enhance the functionality of QBO; these apps are available through Intuit's app store, called the App Center, and you can find them through QBO.

You can click the Apps link in the Navigation bar that runs down the left side of QBO to visit the App Center and explore available apps (see Figure 2-2).

Click any app to navigate to a web page that describes the app, provides pricing information, and often provides a video about the app (see Figure 2-3).

Although add-on apps can provide additional functionality in QBO, some functionality is still missing; no doubt, that functionality will appear over time. For example, using QBO, you can't

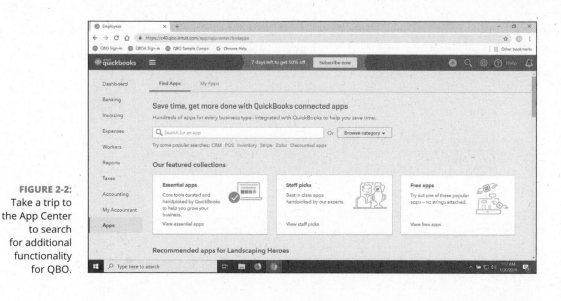

FIGURE 2-2:
Take a trip to
the App Center
to search
for additional
functionality
for QBO.

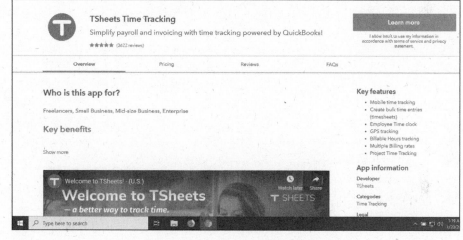

FIGURE 2-3:
When you click
an app in the
App Center,
you see details
for the app.

>> Track your balance sheet by class.

>> Process more than 350,000 transactions annually.

>> Manage a robust inventory.

But apps are making inroads to eliminating these limitations. For example, Lettuce, an app that provided advanced inventory management features for QBO, did such a fine job of handling inventory functions that Intuit acquired Lettuce for the purpose of integrating it into QBO.

2
Managing the Books for the End User

Chapter **3**

Creating a Client Company in QBO

fter you sign up for QBO, you log in. QBO then prompts you to set up your company. With certain limitations, you can import a company if you've been using a QuickBooks Desktop product. Or, you can use the QBO Setup wizard, as shown in this chapter.

For details on importing a company, see Chapter 12 (or ask your accountant to help you with the import). And, don't worry; if you don't import your entire desktop company, you can import just the list information from that company, as described in Chapter 4. And importing lists will still save you a lot of time and setup work.

TIP

Don't have an accountant and need one? You can visit the ProAdvisor marketplace to search for an accountant who is familiar with QBO. Visit www. findaproadvisor.com.

Signing Up for QBO

After you complete the sign-up process for a QBO account, Intuit, by default, logs you in to your account and walks you through the process of setting up your QBO company. The process is short — much shorter than the one you go through when setting up a QuickBooks Desktop product company — and you need the following information:

>> Your company's name and address

>> The industry in which your company operates

>> Your company's legal organization (such as S-Corp or Limited Liability Partnership)

>> Whether you want to import company information from a QuickBooks Desktop product

>> The types of payments you accept from your customers (that is, cash, checks, and credit cards)

>> The way you want to handle payroll

To sign up for a QBO account, follow these steps:

1. **Visit** `quickbooks.intuit.com/pricing`.

You might get redirected; double-check the address in the browser's address bar to make sure you're on the "pricing" page.

2. **Scroll down the page to find five boxes describing each version of QBO — Simple Start, Essentials, Plus, Advanced, and Self-Employed.**

REMEMBER

Intuit has recently started offering QBO Advanced, a version aimed at users who have outgrown QBO Plus. QBO Advanced is *not* available as a free trial. For more information, see Chapter 2 and `https://quickbooks.intuit.com/accounting/advanced`.

3. **To use QBO as a free trial, click the slider button above the versions of QBO to change the slider's position from Buy Now for the current promotional price to Free Trial for 30 Days (see Figure 3-1).**

REMEMBER

Be aware that the price you ultimately pay for QBO depends on whether you choose the Buy Now option or the Free Trial for 30 Days option. If you opt to "buy now," you pay less for your subscription because discounts don't apply to the free trials. And, be aware that promotional pricing usually ends after 6 to 12 months.

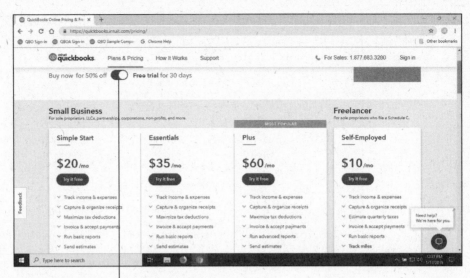

Click here to opt for a free trial or buy QBO.

4. **In the version of QBO that you want to try, click Try It Free.**

   The page in Figure 3-2 appears.

5. **Fill in your email address (and confirm it), a mobile number if you want (it's optional, but Intuit uses it as a way to verify your identity if you need help recovering your account), and a password.**

   Your password must be between 6 and 32 characters and consist of a mix of letters and numbers. The password can also contain some special characters; I included an exclamation point (!) in my password and it was accepted. The user ID and password you supply are the ones you use each time you log in to QBO. If you've previously created an Intuit login, you can use the same one again.

6. **Click the Sign Up with Email button below the boxes you completed in Step 5.**

   At the time that I wrote this, a window appeared that offered the option to skip the free trial and buy the product at a discounted rate. You can buy, but I opted to click the Continue to Trial button.

QBO sets up your free trial, logs you in to QBO, and displays the Set Up wizard . . . read on.

TIP

If, at any time, you find you need help from a real person, you can take advantage of QBO's SmartLook feature to work with Intuit in your QBO company. Phone or chat with QBO technical support and, in your QBO company, click Gear⇨Smart-Look (you'll find it at the bottom of the Tools list on the Gear menu). QBO will display a number that you supply to your technical support representative, giving permission to share your QBO screen (and only your QBO screen). And, just so you know, I first thought the SmartLook feature functioned like a bat signal, and that an agent would just show up. But, my highly qualified and competent technical editor set me straight.

Setting Up a New Company

When you first sign up for a QBO account, Intuit logs you in to your QBO account and, by default, displays the Set Up wizard. The first screen of the wizard, shown in Figure 3-3, asks for basic company information.

TIP

Notice that you can opt to bring in QuickBooks Desktop data. For this exercise, I didn't check that box. Be aware that you can later import QuickBooks Desktop data; the decision you make here isn't your last chance.

Click Next in the lower right corner, and QBO displays the screen shown in Figure 3-4, where you select activities for which you intend to use QBO. Don't worry about making a mistake here; this is just a "get up and running" page. You don't need to select all activities. If you don't select an activity now, you can always add it later. As you select a particular activity, QBO displays a check in the box for that activity. You can choose any or all of the following that apply to you:

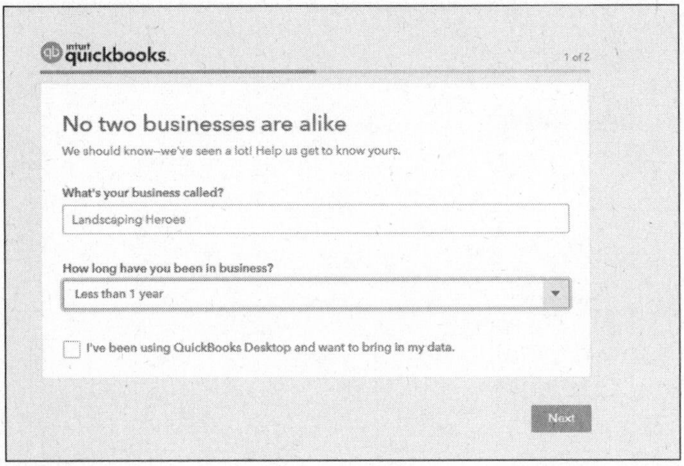

quickbooks.

No two businesses are alike

We should know—we've seen a lot! Help us get to know yours.

What's your business called?

Landscaping Heroes

How long have you been in business?

Less than 1 year

☐ I've been using QuickBooks Desktop and want to bring in my data.

Next

FIGURE 3-3:
Provide basic
company
information.

» Send and track invoices.

» Organize your expenses.

» Manage your inventory.

» Track your retail sales.

» Track your bills.

» Track your sales tax.

» Pay your employees.

» Track billable hours.

When you finish selecting activities, click All Set.

TIP

If you choose the option to pay your employees, QBO assumes you want to use QBOP — and that's fine; you can read more about payroll and using QBOP in Chapter 9. But, if you have any future expectation of importing any QuickBooks Desktop data into your QBO company, don't turn on payroll *or* plan to start another QBO company when you're ready to import. Turning on payroll in a QBO company before you import QuickBooks Desktop data effectively nullifies your ability to successfully import the data. So, turn on payroll with the expectation that you're using this QBO company to play around and see how QBO works, but that you won't be keeping any data you store in it once you get around to importing Quick-Books Desktop data (described in detail in Chapter 12).

QBO displays a short tour and then your company's Dashboard page (formerly called the Home page) as well as links to options you might want to set up to get started (see Figure 3-5).

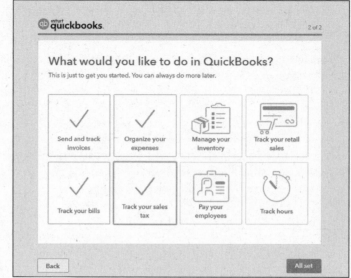

FIGURE 3-4:
Select activities
for which you
expect to
use QBO.

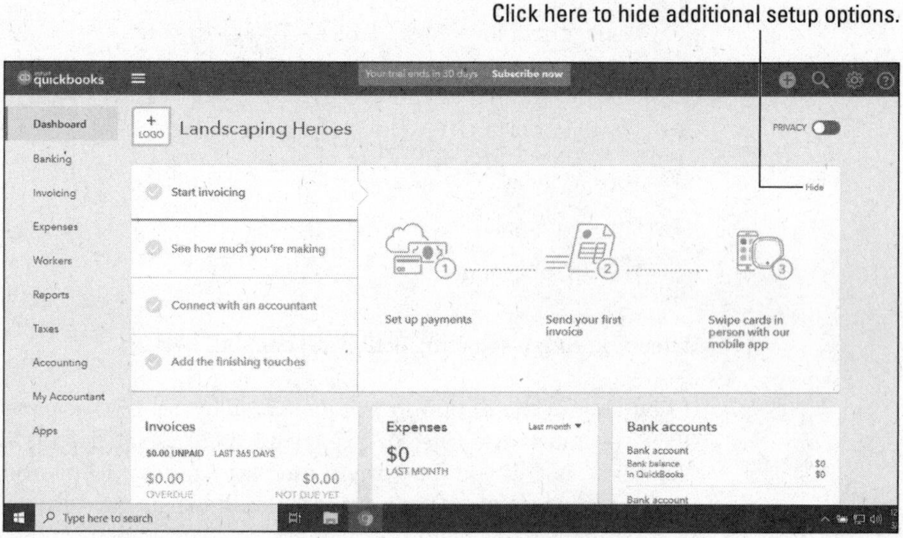

Click here to hide additional setup options.

FIGURE 3-5:
Your QBO
Dashboard page
just after creating
your company.

I examine the Dashboard page in the next section, but essentially you've just completed most of the initial setup work; I cover other program settings later in this chapter.

Understanding the Dashboard Page

When you first see your QBO company, your Dashboard page contains boxes with links to options you can use to set up features in QBO that are important to you (refer to Figure 3-5). You can use those links and set up those options now, or you can wait until later. To hide the options, click Hide in the upper right corner of the box. Don't worry, you can still set up the options associated with any of these boxes; in Figure 3-6, notice the Resume Setup link in the upper right corner of the Dashboard. Click it to redisplay the setup options. And, once you close the boxes, your Dashboard page displays information specific to your company.

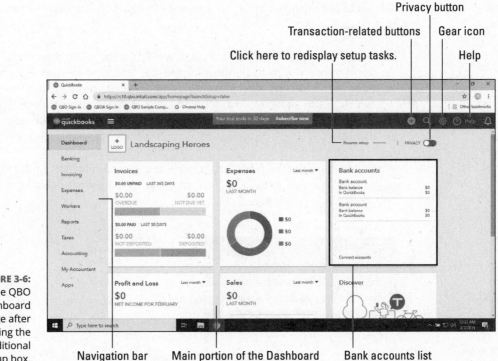

FIGURE 3-6:
The QBO Dashboard page after closing the additional setup box.

In the center of Figure 3-6, using most of the Dashboard page real estate, you find information that changes depending on what you have clicked while using QBO. For example, when you initially open QBO, the information is overview company information. If you click an entry in the Navigation bar (on the left side of the screen), the information in the center of the Dashboard page changes to information related to the entry you clicked. If you select an option on the Gear menu (discussed later in this section), the information you see relates to the option you select.

TIP

You might have noticed the Privacy button in Figure 3-6. You can use this button to temporarily hide financial information on your Dashboard page. For example, you might want to turn Privacy on if you're using QuickBooks in a public place or even in your office when you're not alone. Once you turn Privacy on, it remains on until you turn it off again.

As I just mentioned, the Navigation bar runs down the left side of the screen. You use the Navigation bar the same way you'd use a menu; click an item in the Navigation bar to, well, navigate to that part of QBO. For example, you can click Sales in the Navigation bar to see existing sales transactions in QBO and to create a new Sales transaction.

The highlighted entry in the Navigation bar helps you identify the section of QBO that you are using.

On the right side of the Dashboard page, you find a list of the bank accounts you've set up; if you scroll to the bottom of the list, you find options to connect your accounts to their banks, select an account and open its register, and view all activity, which is the audit log in QBO. The audit log lists every transaction created, changed, or deleted in QBO, as well as every instance of someone logging in to and out of QBO.

When you click the Help button, you see a menu of common topics QBO thinks might be of interest to you, and you can type in the Search box to find help on a particular topic (see Figure 3-7).

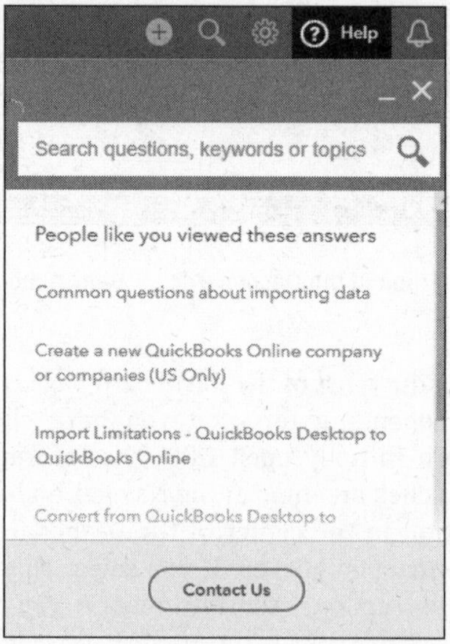

FIGURE 3-7:
The Help menu.

For example, when you click the Create a New QuickBooks Online Company or Companies (US Only) link, QBO displays the How to Create a New QuickBooks Online Company or Companies page, which provides instructions for that topic (see Figure 3-8).

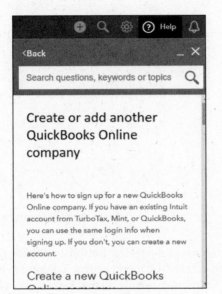

FIGURE 3-8:
A sample Help topic.

At the right edge of the top of the screen, you see two transaction-related buttons that display lists you can use to work with transactions. Figure 3-9 shows the Create menu that appears when you click the Create button, which appears as a plus sign (+) when the menu is closed and an X when the menu is open; compare Figures 3-6 and 3-9.

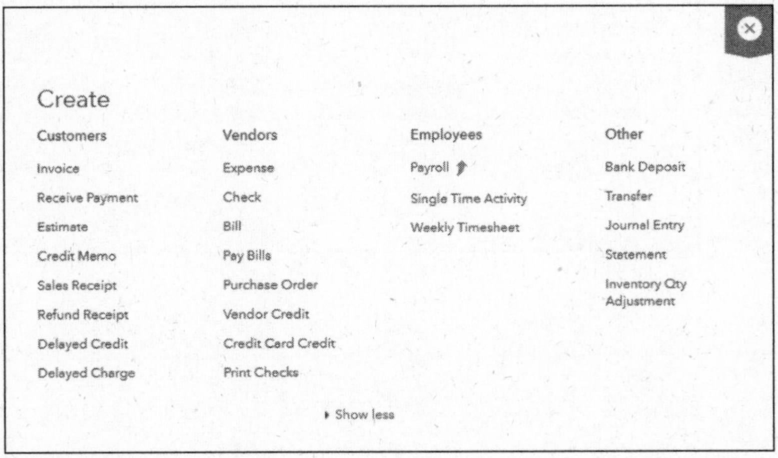

FIGURE 3-9:
Click the Create button to create a new transaction.

Figure 3-10 shows what you see when you click the Search button, which appears as a magnifying glass to the right of the Create menu button. You see a list of recently entered transactions; you can click any transaction in the list to open that transaction. Or, you can use the Search Transactions box to search for a transaction.

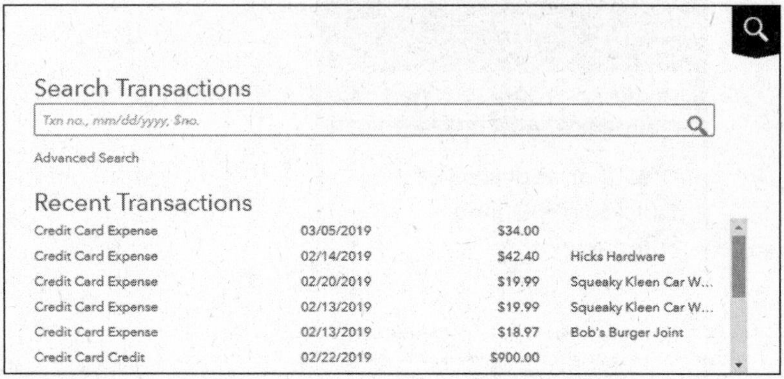

FIGURE 3-10:
Click the Search button to search for previously entered transactions.

To the right of the two transaction-related buttons, you see the Gear button. If you click the Gear button, you see the menu shown in Figure 3-11, which you use to look at and change QBO company settings; view lists; work with tools such as import and export, reconciliation, and budgeting tools; and view information about your QBO account. Note that the Gear menu is divided into four columns that organize related commands.

FIGURE 3-11:
Use the Gear menu to work with settings, lists, tools, and your QBO account.

Establishing Company Settings

After you set up your company, you should review the default settings Intuit established and make changes as appropriate. To examine and make changes to payroll settings, see Chapter 9.

Examining company preferences

Choose Gear ⇨ Account and Settings to display the Company tab of the Account and Settings dialog box (see Figure 3-12).

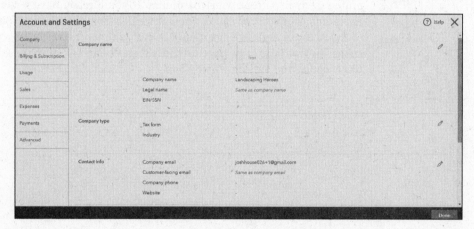

FIGURE 3-12: Review company settings.

On this tab, you can make changes to your company name, address, and contact information and your preferences for communication with Intuit.

To change any setting, click anywhere in the group where the setting appears. When you finish making changes, click the Save button that appears in the group of settings. You can then move on to other settings on the page.

When you finish working with Account and Settings, click Done in the lower right corner of the screen.

Examining billing and subscription settings and usage limits

To review the settings related to your QBO billing and subscription, click the Gear icon and select the appropriate option. QBO users, choose Gear ⇨ Account and

Settings to display the Account and Settings dialog box. Then, click Billing & Subscription in the pane on the left. QBOA users choose Gear⇨Your Account.

REMEMBER

You won't see the Billing & Subscription pane if the QBO company is being managed by an accountant who is part of the Wholesale Billing program.

This page, shown in Figure 3-13, shows you the status of your QBO, Payroll, and Payments subscriptions. From this page, you can convert your trial version of QBO and of the QBO Payroll product to a regular subscription; converting cancels your trial. You also can use this page to order checks and supplies, should you need them.

REMEMBER

The subscription Payments product that Intuit offers enables you to receive online payments from your customers. If you already have a subscription to the Payments product, you can connect it to QBO from the Billing & Subscription page of the Account and Settings dialog box. If you don't have a subscription, you can subscribe from the Apps page on the Navigation bar or from the Payments page of the Account and Settings dialog box.

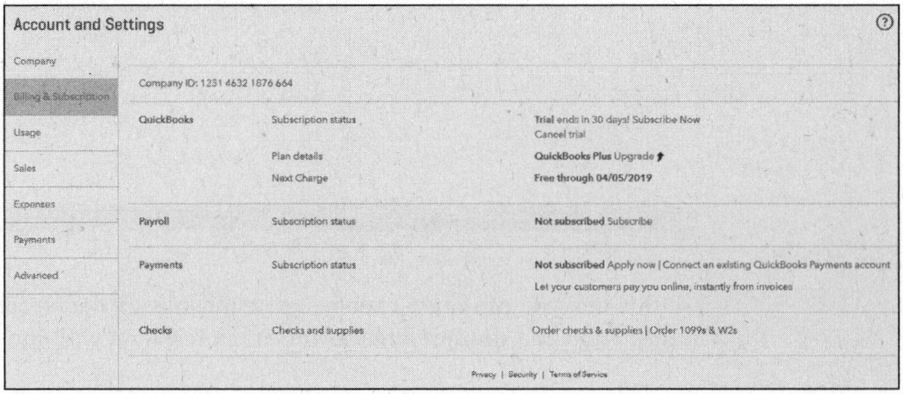

FIGURE 3-13:
Review QBO billing and subscription settings.

When you click the Usage pane on the left side of the Account and Settings dialog box, QBO displays the usage limits applied to your QBO company based on the version of QBO you selected when you created your company (Simple Start, Essential, Plus, or Advanced).

Setting sales preferences

To review the Sales preferences of your QBO company, choose Gear⇨Account and Settings to display the Account and Settings dialog box. Then, click Sales in the pane on the left.

At the top of the page that appears (see Figure 3-14), you can click the Customize Look and Feel button to customize the appearance of the invoice you send to customers. I return to the customization process at the end of this section; first, I examine the settings available to you.

Account and Settings

Company			
Billing & Subscription	Customize	Customize the way forms look to your customers	Customize look and feel
Usage	Sales form content	Preferred invoice terms	Net 30
Sales		Preferred delivery method	None
Expenses		Shipping	Off
Payments		Custom fields	Off
Advanced		Custom transaction numbers	Off
		Service date	Off
		Discount	Off
		Deposit	Off
		Tips (Gratuity)	Off
	Products and services	Show Product/Service column on sales forms	On
		Show SKU column	Off
		Turn on price rules BETA	Off
		Track quantity and price/rate	On
		Track inventory quantity on hand	Off

FIGURE 3-14: The Sales page of the Account and Settings dialog box.

Examining sales settings

You can set a variety of options related to sales:

>> In the Sales Form Content section, you can define the fields that appear on the form you complete to prepare invoices, sales receipts, and other sales forms.

>> In the Products and Services section, you can make changes to the product- and service-related fields that appear on sales forms. If you're using QBO Plus, this is where you turn on inventory tracking and where you can try out using price rules. You can read more about inventory and price rules in Chapter 4.

>> In the Messages section, you can control the default email message sent to customers with sales forms and the default message that appears on those sales forms.

>> In the Reminders section, you set up the standard language to be used in email messages sent with reminders.

>> In the Online Delivery section, you can set email delivery options for sales forms such as attaching the sales form as a PDF, showing a summary or details of the sales form in the email, and email formatting options for invoices.

>> In the Statements section, you can specify whether to show the aging table at the bottom of the statement.

Customizing form appearance

To customize forms that your customers receive, click Customize Look and Feel at the top of the Sales page in the Account and Settings dialog box to display the Custom Form Styles page shown in Figure 3-15.

				New style ▾
Custom form styles				Import style
‹ All lists				Invoice
NAME	FORM TYPE	LAST EDITED		Estimate
Standard	Master	03/06/2019		Sales receipt

Dashboard
Banking
Invoicing
Expenses
Workers
Reports
Taxes
Accounting
My Accountant
Apps

FIGURE 3-15: Use this page to edit an existing form style or set up a new form style.

The Custom Form Styles page lists any form styles you have already created. By default, QBO creates one form style for you when you sign up; that form style is named Standard and is used by default for invoices, estimates, and sales receipts.

If you are satisfied with the appearance of the majority of the form style, you can edit it instead of creating a form style. Alternatively, you can create separate customized forms for invoices, estimates, and sales receipts. To do so, click New Style in the upper right corner of the Custom Form Styles page and choose the type of form you want to create. For this example, I chose Invoice, and QBO displayed the page shown in Figure 3-16, which varies only slightly if you opt to edit a different form. In particular, if you opt to create a form style, the page displays a form name for the form you are creating (see Figure 3-16).

REMEMBER

The option to Import Style appears only if you have enabled importing form styles in QuickBooks Labs, as described in the next section, "Importing form styles."

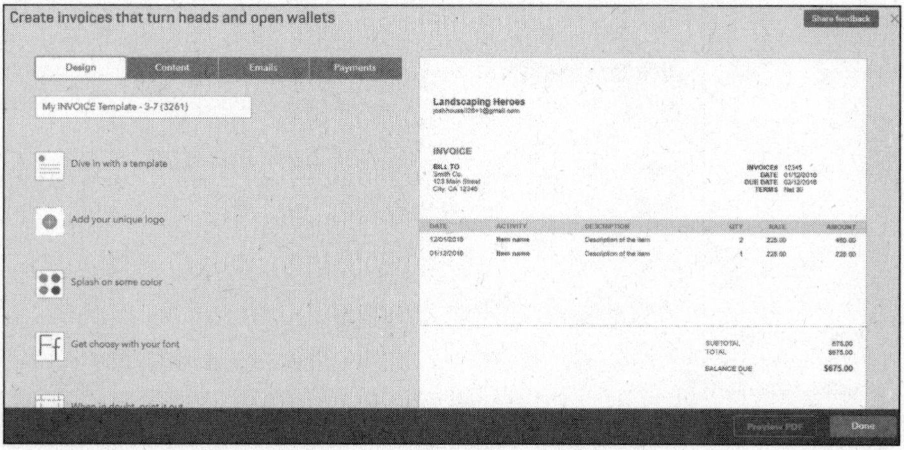

FIGURE 3-16:
The page you
use to customize
sales forms.

You use the tabs that run across the top left side of the page to establish form style settings:

>> From the Design tab, shown in Figure 3-16, you can select a style for the form: Airy, Modern, Fresh, Friendly, or Bold. The preview shown in Figure 3-16 is the Fresh form style. You also can modify the appearance and placement of your logo, set the form's font, and try different colors.

>> From the Content tab, you can edit directly on the form. Just click a pencil in the upper right corner of a form section and make changes using the boxes that appear on the left side of the page.

>> From the Emails tab, shown in Figure 3-17, you can edit the standard and reminder email messages your customer receives with each new or reminder form you send them. You make changes on the left side of the page, and the right side of the page shows a preview of what your customer receives.

>> From the Payments tab, choose whether you want to give your customers the option to pay online and, if so, the methods you want to offer your customers — using bank transfers, by credit card (where fees apply), or both. Note that you need to finish setting up your payments profile before customers can pay you online.

You can click the Preview PDF button at the bottom right side of the screen to preview your invoice in PDF format.

Click the Done button in the lower right corner of the screen to save changes you make to the appearance of your forms.

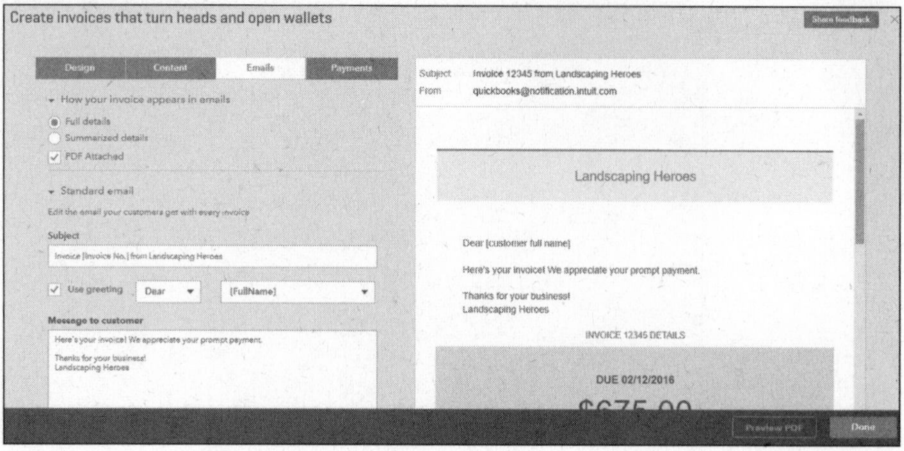

Make changes to the email your customers receive with their forms.

FIGURE 3-17:

Importing form styles

REMEMBER

At the time I wrote this, importing form styles was a feature "under construction" in QBO and therefore not available unless you enable it using QuickBooks Labs. For details on using QuickBooks Labs, see "Taking Advantage of QuickBooks Labs," later in this chapter. For purposes of this discussion, I have enabled the feature.

If the form templates supplied with QBO don't meet your needs, you can use Microsoft Word 2010 or later to create a form style and then upload it into QBO. As part of the import process, you map fields you've identified on your Word document form style to QBO fields.

The tricky part of this process is getting the form correctly designed in Word. But, luckily, Intuit anticipated the challenge and provides sample forms and instructions to simplify the process. To download the samples and instructions, you need to pretend you've already created your form style in Word. If this feels like I'm putting the cart in front of the horse, well . . . I am, sort of.

To get the sample information and instructions, enable the Import Form Styles feature through QuickBooks Labs. Then, choose Gear➪ Custom Form Styles. On the Custom Form Styles page, click the down arrow beside New Style, and choose Import Style. QBO displays the page shown in Figure 3-18.

To download the sample information, click the Download a Sample Invoice link. A Zip file downloads, containing two sample forms — one for Windows users and one for Mac users — that you can use as starting points.

REMEMBER

The Zip file also contains detailed instructions that describe what to do and what not to do when creating a form style. For example, the instructions list the fonts QBO will recognize and also describe the best way to use Word tables. Suffice it to say, use these instructions and save yourself some pain.

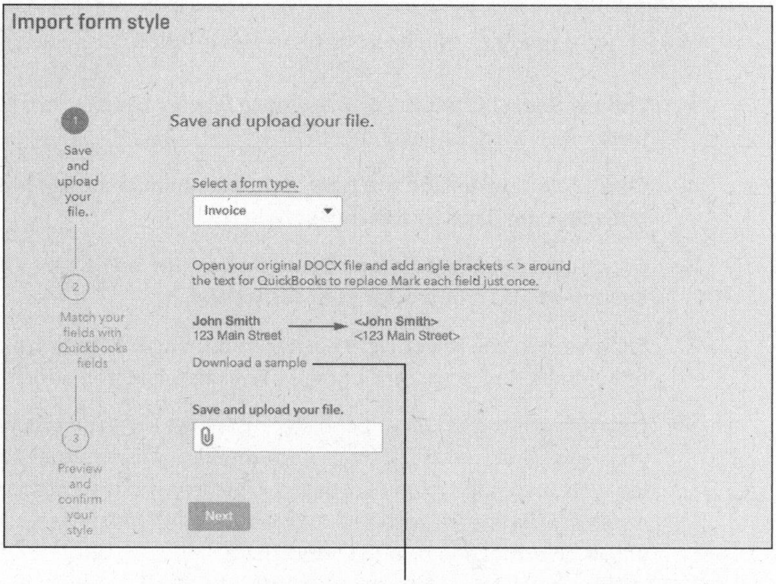

FIGURE 3-18:
Use the Import
Form Style page
to download
sample forms
and instructions
to create your
own form style.

Click here to download sample files and instructions.

Open either of the sample files to see how a customized form style should look in Word (see Figure 3-19). Note, for example, that you simply type information that won't change, but you place less than and greater than brackets (< and >) around fields you want to replace with QBO data, such as your customer's billing and shipping addresses and item information.

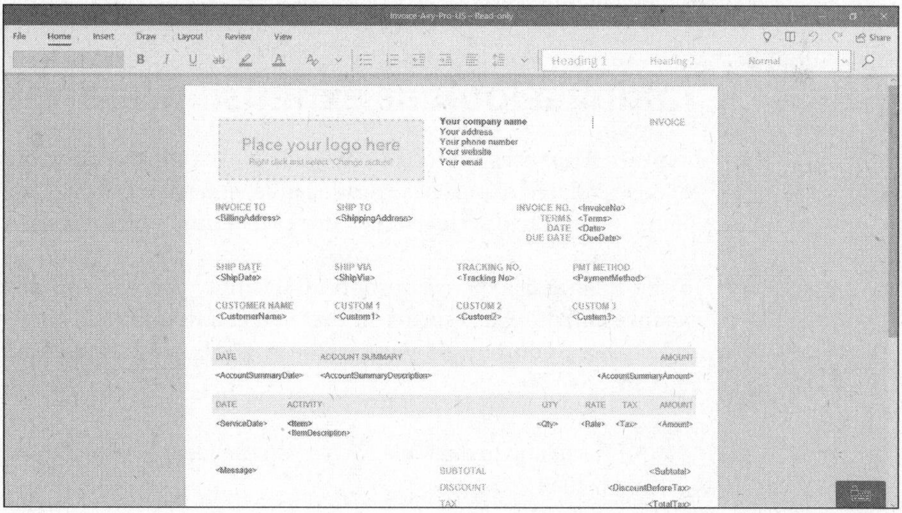

FIGURE 3-19:
In Word, place
information that
QBO should
replace in
brackets.

When you're ready to upload your form style, follow these steps:

1. **Choose Gear ⇨ Custom Form Styles to display the Custom Form Style page.**

2. **Click the arrow beside the New Style button and choose Import Style to redisplay the page shown in Figure 3-18.**

3. **Click in the Save and Upload Your File box and navigate to the Word document you created for your form style.**

4. **Click Next in the lower right corner of the page (appears in gray and unavailable in Figure 3-18 because I haven't selected a form to upload).**

   QBO uploads the document and scans it for fields you placed in brackets. If you successfully upload the Word document, you'll see a message telling you that you succeeded in uploading. If this process is not successful you will see errors; review the instruction document included with the sample file for details on errors and how to correct them.

   Assuming your document uploads successfully, a page appears where you can map the fields on your form style to fields in QBO.

5. **Match the fields on your form style to QBO fields; when you finish, click Next.**

   A preview of the new form style appears on the Confirm Style page.

6. **If you're happy with what you see, click Save and supply a name for your form style.**

   It's now ready to use. If you're not happy, click Back and correct any problems.

Taking a look at expense preferences

From the Expenses tab of the Account and Settings dialog box, you can control expenses related to purchase orders, bills, and payments you make to vendors (see Figure 3-20). Choose Gear ⇨ Account and Settings ⇨ Expenses.

In the Bills and Expenses group of settings, you can opt to display a table on expense and purchase forms so that you can itemize and categorize the products and services you buy. If you purchase goods and services for your customers, you can

» Add a column to the table so that you can identify the customer for whom you made the purchase.

» Add a column where you identify expenses and items for which you want to bill customers.

Account and Settings			
Company	Bills and expenses	Show Items table on expense and purchase forms	On
Billing & Subscription		Track expenses and items by customer	Off
		Make expenses and items billable	Off
Usage		Default bill payment terms	
Sales			
	Purchase orders	Use purchase orders	Off
Expenses			
Payments	Messages	Default email message sent with purchase orders	
Advanced			
		Privacy | Security | Terms of Service	

FIGURE 3-20:
Expense preferences you can control.

You also can set default bill payment terms.

In the Purchase Orders group, you can opt to use purchase orders and you can opt to copy estimates to purchase orders. For more information about converting an estimate to a purchase order, see Chapter 6.

In the Messages group, you can establish the settings for the default email message sent with purchase orders, including the salutation, subject, and message. You also can opt to send yourself a copy of the message that goes out with each purchase order.

Examining options to receive customer payments

The Payments tab of the Account and Settings dialog box offers you a way to connect with Intuit Merchant Services via a QuickBooks Payments account. If you don't have a QuickBooks Payments account with Intuit and you want one, click the Learn More button. If you already have a QuickBooks Payments account, you can click the Connect button to connect your QBO account with your QuickBooks Payments account.

TIP

Bank transfers are free, and there are no monthly fees associated with accepting credit card payments — just a "per transaction" fee, and that fee varies, depending on whether you swipe a card, accept a payment online, or key in a credit card number. QBO users who use QuickBooks Payments now have money from qualifying credit or debit card transactions deposited in the bank the next business day. No extra fees, no extra waiting.

REMEMBER

QuickBooks Payments is the name Intuit uses to describe the service it offers that enables you to accept credit cards or bank transfers from your customers and email invoices that contain a Pay Now button so that your customers can pay you online. You might also know this service as GoPayment or Merchant Services.

Reviewing advanced preferences

The Advanced tab of the Account and Settings dialog box enables you to make changes to a variety of QBO settings (see Figure 3-21). Choose Gear ⇨ Account and Settings ⇨ Advanced to view and update these settings:

» In the Accounting group, you can control fiscal year settings and the accounting method your company uses (cash or accrual).

» Use the Company Type group to select the tax form your company uses, based on its legal organization.

» When you create a new company, QBO automatically sets up the Chart of Accounts it thinks you'll need. Because QBO doesn't use account numbers in the Chart of Accounts, you can turn them on in the Chart of Accounts group — something most accountants prefer you do.

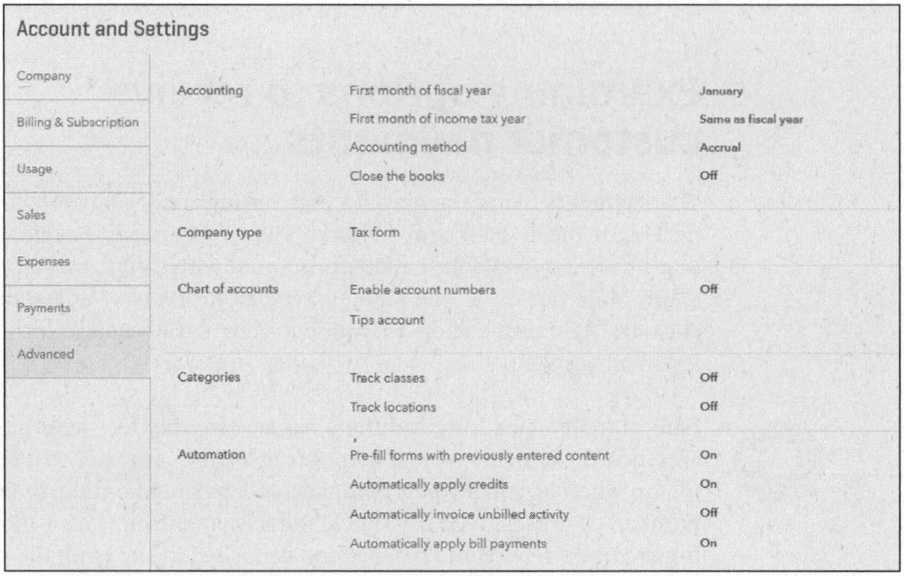

Account and Settings			
Company	Accounting	First month of fiscal year	January
Billing & Subscription		First month of income tax year	Same as fiscal year
		Accounting method	Accrual
Usage		Close the books	Off
Sales			
Expenses	Company type	Tax form	
Payments	Chart of accounts	Enable account numbers	Off
Advanced		Tips account	
	Categories	Track classes	Off
		Track locations	Off
	Automation	Pre-fill forms with previously entered content	On
		Automatically apply credits	On
		Automatically invoice unbilled activity	Off
		Automatically apply bill payments	On

FIGURE 3-21:
The Advanced tab of the Account and Settings dialog box.

CATEGORIES, CLASSES, AND LOCATIONS . . . OH, MY!

Don't confuse the options you see in the Categories section of the Account and Settings dialog box (QBO classes and locations) with QBO categories. The QBO Category feature is entirely separate from the class and location features shown in the Categories section of the Account and Settings dialog box.

If you turn on the Class and Location options shown here in the Account and Settings dialog box, you can then assign classes and locations to transactions to help you further break down financial data beyond the account level. To create classes and locations, first enable them in the Account and Settings dialog box. Then choose Gear ⇨ All Lists, and click Classes to create new classes and click Locations to create new locations.

QBO categories, NOT shown in the Account and Settings dialog box (and no need to turn them on), replace sub-items and are available to users of QBO Plus to help organize item information for reporting purposes; see Chapter 4 for details.

TIP

>> You can replace the Chart of Accounts QBO sets up with a Chart of Accounts that you create outside QBO using an Excel file that you then import into QBO. The process is very similar to the one described earlier in this chapter in the section "Importing form styles." The file you import needs to follow a particular format, and you can download a sample layout file.

>> Depending on the version of QBO you use, you can use the Categories section to opt to track information using classes, locations, or both. You also can opt to have QBO warn you if you don't assign a class to a transaction, and you can opt to assign classes individually to each line of a transaction or assign one class to the entire transaction. For locations, you can choose from seven different labels; one of these choices might better describe your intended use of the Location category.

>> In the Automation group, you can control some of QBO's automated behavior. For example, if you don't want QBO to prefill new forms with information from forms you entered previously, feel free to turn that setting off.

>> In the Projects section, you can opt to use QBO's project tracking features; if you do, QBO organizes all job-related activity in one place. You can read more about projects in Chapter 6.

>> In the Time Tracking section, you can control the appearance of timesheets. For example, you can opt to add a service field to timesheets so that you can select services performed for each time entry. By default, QBO includes a

customer field on timesheets so that you can optionally charge work performed to a customer.

If time tracking is an integral part of your business, you might consider purchasing the add-on app, TSheets Time Tracking. It integrates with QBO and gives you extensive time-tracking capabilities, including, for example, scheduling employees and letting employees track billable and non-billable time using the mobile version of the app. Visit the QBO App Center by clicking Apps in the Navigation bar of QBO for more information.

» Use the Currency section to turn on multicurrency tracking and to set your company's home currency. If you change the home currency symbol, QBO changes the symbol for future transactions; existing transactions will still be calculated at the original currency value. For more information about Multicurrency and Home Currency, see the section "Working with Multiple Currencies" next in this chapter.

Think long and hard before you turn on multicurrency, and turn it on only if you really need it. Why? Because turning on multicurrency eliminates your ability to change your home currency. Further, you can't turn multicurrency off after you turn it on.

» In the Other Preferences group, you can make changes to a variety of settings, such as date and number formats; whether QBO warns you if you reuse a check number or bill number you used previously; and how long QBO should wait before signing you out because you haven't done any work. And, if you prefer to call your customers something other than Customer (such as Client, Patron, or Shopper), you can change the label you use to refer to those who buy stuff from you.

Working with Multiple Currencies

The Plus version of QBO supports using multiple currencies. Typically, you use the Multicurrency feature when you sell products and services to customers or buy products and services from vendors whose base currency is different from your home currency. If you don't need to record transactions in multiple currencies, don't turn on this feature because you can't turn it off again.

Also be aware that the Multicurrency feature in QBO doesn't support customer- or currency-specific pricing. If you need either of those features, you need to use QuickBooks Desktop.

WARNING

DO I NEED THE MULTICURRENCY FEATURE?

You need the Multicurrency feature *only if* you work with customers or vendors whose base currency is different from your own base currency. Suppose that your home country does not work in U.S. dollars but you only buy and sell using your home country's currency. In this case, you work in a single currency and you don't need the Multicurrency feature. Instead, you need to use the International version of QBO and set your home currency to the proper denomination — and you'll find steps to set your home currency in the section "Turning on the Multicurrency feature."

If you turn on the Multicurrency feature, you cannot change your home currency.

Because you can assign only one currency to each account, customer, or vendor, you need to add new asset and liability accounts, customers, and vendors for each different currency that you will use in transactions; as you create these new elements in QBO, you assign to them the currency you want to use. Be aware that, once you've posted a transaction to an account, a vendor, or a customer, you cannot change the currency of the account, vendor, or customer.

REMEMBER

Income and expense accounts continue to use your home currency — the currency of the country where your business is physically located.

So, if you've decided to use the Multicurrency feature, do these things in the order listed:

1. Choose your Home Currency.

2. Turn on the Multicurrency feature.

3. Set up the currencies you intend to use.

4. Add customers, vendors, and necessary asset and liability accounts for each currency you expect to use. Note that QBO automatically creates Accounts Receivable and Accounts Payable accounts in the foreign currency after you create one foreign sales and one foreign purchasing transaction, so you don't need to set up those accounts.

5. Enter transactions.

How the Multicurrency feature changes QBO

After you turn on the Multicurrency feature, you will see new fields in QBO. Specifically, you'll see changes on these screens:

>> When you open the Gear menu, you'll see the Currencies option at the bottom of the Lists column. You use the Currencies list to establish the foreign currency you want to use, along with the exchange rate. I describe using this option after I show you how to turn on the Multicurrency feature.

>> When you view the Chart of Accounts, you'll find a Currency column that shows the currency assigned to each account. You'll also find a new account — an Other Expense account called Exchange Gain or Loss.

>> When you view Bank and Credit Card registers, the currency of each transaction appears in parentheses in the Payment, Deposit (Charge in Credit Card registers), Sales Tax, and Balance Due columns. You'll also see a Foreign Currency Exchange Rate column in these registers.

>> Sales and purchase forms use both your home currency and the foreign currency; QBO does all the conversions for you on the screen.

>> On QuickBooks reports, you find that QBO converts all foreign currency amounts to home currency amounts, automatically reflecting exchange rate changes.

Turning on the Multicurrency feature

You can change your home currency from the same place that you enable the Multicurrency feature. Follow these steps:

WARNING

Once you turn on the Multicurrency feature, you cannot change your home currency. And, you can't turn off the Multicurrency feature because it affects many accounts and balances in QBO.

1. **Choose Gear ⇨ Account and Settings.**

   QBO displays the Account and Settings dialog box.

2. **Click Advanced.**

3. **Scroll down to the Currency section.**

4. **Set your home currency by clicking the Home Currency list box.**

   Choose the currency of your country. If you're not in the United States, don't set the United States as your home currency.

5. **Select Multicurrency (see Figure 3-22).**

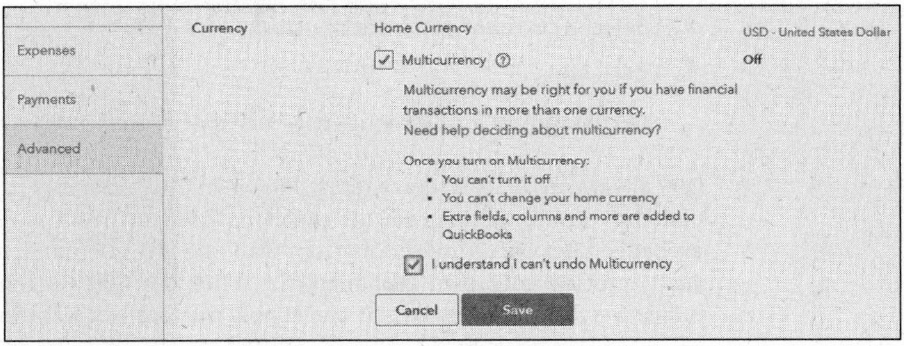

FIGURE 3-22:
Turning on
Multicurrency.

QBO warns you that, once you turn on the Multicurrency feature

a) You can't turn it off, and

b) You can't change your home currency.

6. **Select I Understand I Can't Undo Multicurrency.**

7. **Click Save.**

8. **Click Done.**

Setting up currencies

After enabling the Multicurrency option, you'll find an option to display the Currencies list if you click the Gear button; the Currencies option appears at the bottom of the Lists section on the Gear menu. Follow these steps to set up the currencies you need to use:

1. **Choose Gear ⇨ Currencies.**

   QBO displays the Currencies page (see Figure 3-23).

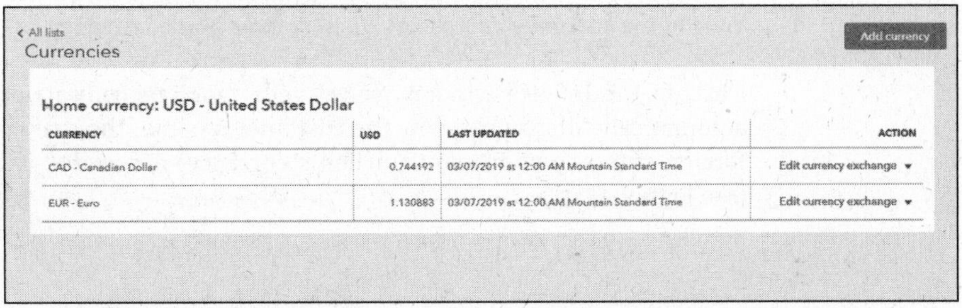

FIGURE 3-23:
The Currencies
page.

2. **In the upper right corner of the page, click Add Currency.**

QBO displays a drop-down list.

3. **Select a currency you want to use.**

4. **Click Add.**

QBO redisplays the Currencies page with the new currency added.

QBO always records exchange rates, shown on the Currencies page, as the number of home currency units needed to equal one foreign currency unit. QBO downloads exchange rates every four hours from Wall Street On Demand, but you can, if you want, provide your own exchange rate. Click the Edit Currency Exchange link beside the rate you want to edit and supply the rate you want to use.

Using multiple currencies

Take a brief look at the effects of creating an invoice that uses multiple currencies; creating a purchase transaction for a foreign vendor works in a similar fashion.

Suppose that you have a customer whose base currency is the Canadian dollar and your home currency is the U.S. dollar. So, in this example, when I refer to the "foreign currency," I mean the Canadian dollar.

REMEMBER

At this time, QBO doesn't support letting either your employees or contractors record time entries (using either the Weekly Timesheet or the Single Time Activity) associated with a foreign currency customer.

First, create the customer: click Sales and, on the Sales page, choose Customers➪New Customer. Fill in the window as you usually would with the following addition: Click the Payment and Billing tab. Then, open the This Customer Pays Me With list and select the customer's currency. In Figure 3-24, my customer, uninspiringly named Foreign Currency, uses the Canadian Dollar. You'll find a similar setting available when you create a new vendor.

Once you save the customer, if you look at the Customer list page, you'll see the customer listed, and, in the Currency column, you'll see the foreign currency. Your home currency customers display your home currency.

Next, in the Invoice window, select your "foreign transaction" customer. QBO automatically displays, below the customer's name, the two currencies (first the foreign currency and then your home currency) associated with the transaction (see Figure 3-25).

Use the Payment and Billing tab to select the customer's currency.

Foreign currency followed by domestic currency

Once you add products or services to the invoice, as shown in Figure 3-26, the amounts for each line appear in the foreign currency, and totals appear in both currencies. The Balance Due on the transaction appears in the foreign (customer's) currency so that your customer knows how much to pay.

REMEMBER

Saving your first sales or purchase document for a customer or vendor using a foreign currency makes QBO automatically establish a foreign currency–related Accounts Receivable and Accounts Payable account.

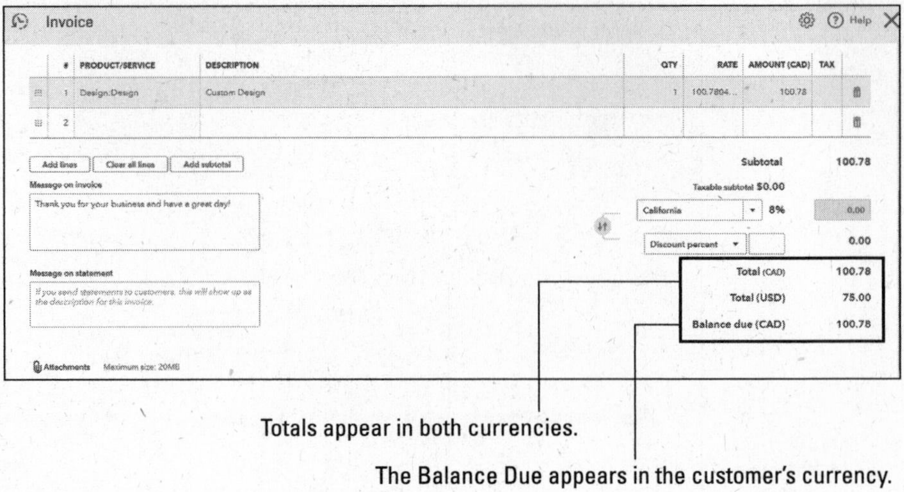

FIGURE 3-26:
An invoice for a foreign-currency customer shows values in both the home and foreign currency.

Totals appear in both currencies.

The Balance Due appears in the customer's currency.

Reports in QBO show values in your home currency. Figure 3-27 shows the A/R Aging Summary; the customer who uses a foreign currency is the third customer on the list.

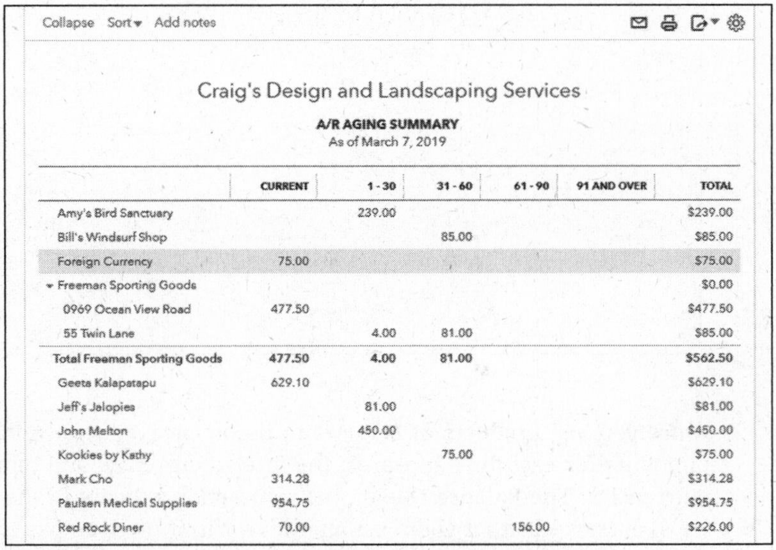

FIGURE 3-27:
Values on reports appear in your home currency.

Figure 3-28, the Balance Sheet, shows the multiple Accounts Receivable accounts QBO uses when you've enabled the Multicurrency feature and created a sales transaction using a foreign currency; the values on the report appear in the home currency.

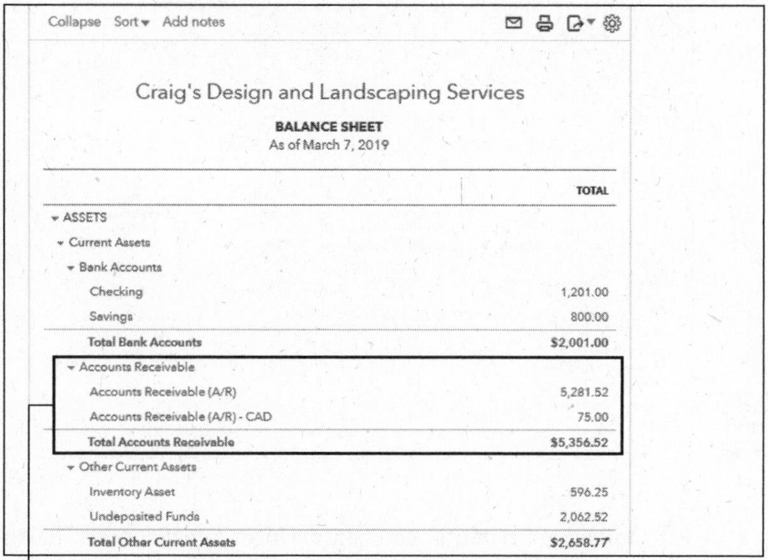

Craig's Design and Landscaping Services

BALANCE SHEET
As of March 7, 2019

	TOTAL
▾ ASSETS	
▾ Current Assets	
▾ Bank Accounts	
Checking	1,201.00
Savings	800.00
Total Bank Accounts	**$2,001.00**
▾ Accounts Receivable	
Accounts Receivable (A/R)	5,281.52
Accounts Receivable (A/R) - CAD	75.00
Total Accounts Receivable	**$5,356.52**
▾ Other Current Assets	
Inventory Asset	596.25
Undeposited Funds	2,062.52
Total Other Current Assets	**$2,658.77**

FIGURE 3-28: QBO establishes separate Accounts Receivable accounts for transactions involving foreign-currency customers.

Multiple Accounts Receivable accounts when you use the Multicurrency feature

Updating the Chart of Accounts

As I mention earlier in this chapter, when discussing advanced options for your company, QBO automatically sets up the Chart of Accounts it thinks you'll need when you create a new company. If you feel that the Chart of Accounts QBO creates doesn't closely match what you'll need, you can replace that Chart of Accounts with one you set up in Excel or as a CSV file using a process very similar to the one described earlier in this chapter in the section "Importing form styles." Because I suspect that most QBO users will feel like importing a Chart of Accounts is an undertaking they prefer to avoid, I don't cover the process here; instead, I leave that to accountants. If you want to import a Chart of Accounts, you'll find details in Chapter 13.

As a QBO user, though, you probably will want to modify the Chart of Accounts QBO sets up for your company. To make changes to those accounts, choose Gear➪Chart of Accounts or Accounting➪Chart of Accounts. On the page that appears, click the See Your Chart of Accounts button, and QBO displays a page similar to the one shown in Figure 3-29; from this page, you can perform a variety of functions. For example, you can print a list of your accounts if you click the Run Report button, which is at the top of the page.

If you've enabled the Multicurrency feature, you'll see a Currency column on the Chart of Accounts page.

REMEMBER

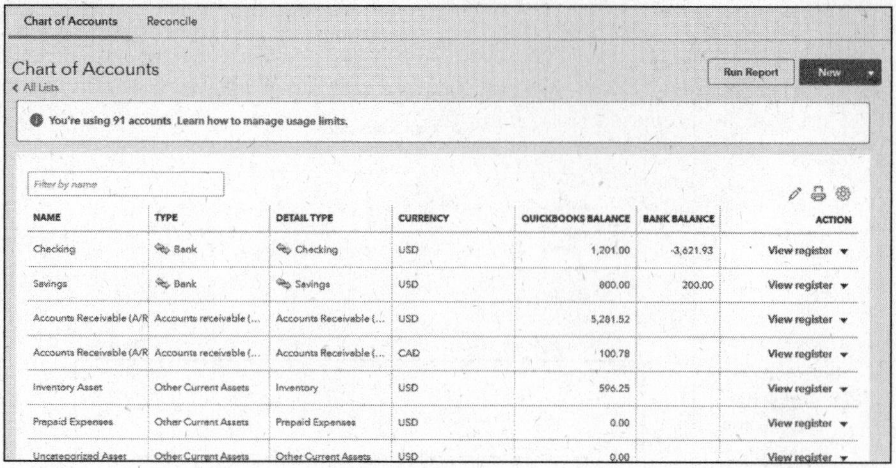

FIGURE 3-29:
The Chart of
Accounts page.

For individual accounts, you can perform a few actions. Balance Sheet accounts have registers; you can view the transactions in the account by clicking View Register in the Action column. You can identify Balance Sheet accounts by looking in the Type column. Balance Sheet accounts display one of the following account types:

>> Bank

>> Accounts Receivable

>> Other Current Assets

>> Fixed Assets

>> Other Assets

>> Credit Card

>> Other Current Liabilities

>> Long Term Liabilities

>> Accounts Payable

>> Equity

For other accounts — the ones without registers — you can run reports for the account by clicking Run Report in the Action column.

You also can edit any account and you can delete an account you have not yet used. Click the down arrow in the Action column (at the right edge of the account's row) to display a short menu of the actions you can take for the account.

WARNING

If you edit an account, don't change its type unless you're sure you know what you're doing. Consider consulting your accountant before you make a change to an account's category or detail type. You also can identify if the account is actually a sub-account of another account.

If you decided to turn on account numbers, you can click the Batch Edit icon (it looks like a pencil and appears just above the Action column). The appearance of the Chart of Accounts page changes to enable you to quickly assign account numbers (see Figure 3-30).

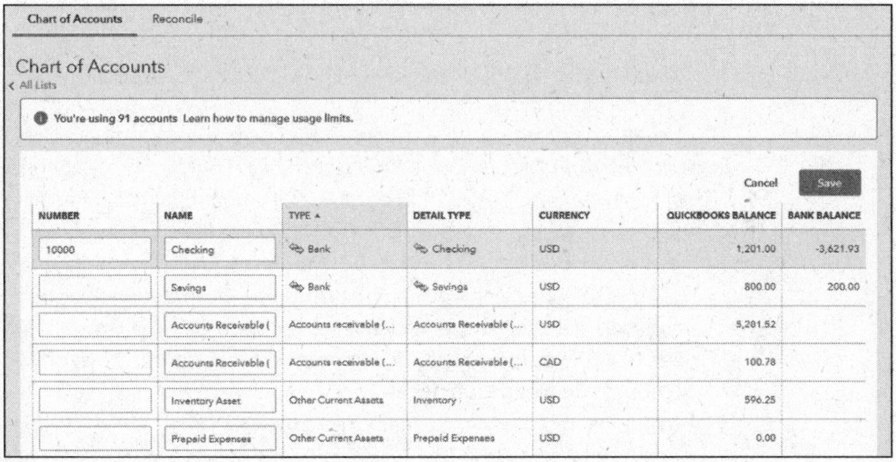

FIGURE 3-30:
The Chart of Accounts page in Batch Edit mode.

REMEMBER

If you've enabled the Multicurrency feature, the Chart of Accounts page in Batch Edit mode also contains a Currency column.

Type a number for each account; when you finish entering all the numbers, click the Save button at the top of the page. QBO displays the account number as part of the account name on the Chart of Accounts screen. You also can establish budgets for accounts; see Appendix A for details.

The screens you use to add or edit an account look almost exactly alike. Because you'll need a Bank account for your company, I examine the screens as you create your Bank account. If you plan to connect your QBO Bank account to its corresponding account at a financial institution, don't follow these steps; instead, see Chapter 8 for details on creating the account. And, if you decide now that you don't want to connect and later you decide that you *do* want to connect, all isn't lost. Once again, see Chapter 8 for details on merging the Bank account you create here with an online version.

A FEW NOTES ON PAYING OWNERS

Many small business owners wonder about the accounts they should use to pay themselves. Owners and partners typically are not considered employees and therefore are not paid through payroll. To pay an owner or partner, use the Chart of Accounts page to set up a Draw account (Owner's Draw, Partner's Draw, whatever is appropriate; if you have multiple partners, set up Draw accounts for each partner) and use it to pay owners. The Draw account is an equity account. Similarly, owners and partners sometimes put their own money into the business; to account for these contributions, set up equity accounts (again, one for each owner or partner) called Owner's Contribution, Partner's Contribution — again, whatever is appropriate.

Note that you use the Draw account not only to pay the owner but also to account for personal items an owner might buy using the business's money. You record the withdrawals using the appropriate bank account and the appropriate Draw account. Note that these transactions don't show up on your Profit and Loss report because they are *not* business expenses. To find out the total amount paid to an owner, run a report for the Draw account.

And, finally, housekeeping about the Draw and Contribution accounts: At the end of your fiscal year, you need to enter a journal entry, dated on the last day of your fiscal year, that moves the dollar amounts from the appropriate Draw or Contribution account to Retained Earnings — another equity account. If I just lost you, talk to your accountant about how to handle closing the year.

To ensure an accurate bank balance in QBO, reconcile your bank account before you set up the account in QBO. Follow these steps to create an account in QBO:

1. **Click the New button on the Chart of Accounts page to open the Account dialog box (see Figure 3-31).**

2. **Open the Category Type list and choose Bank.**

3. **Click the entry in the Detail Type list that most closely matches the type of account you want to add.**

   QBO uses the choice you make in the Detail Type list as the account's name, but you can change the name to something else. For my example, I chose Checking, changed the account name to Checking-Chase Bank, and supplied Chase Checking account as the description.

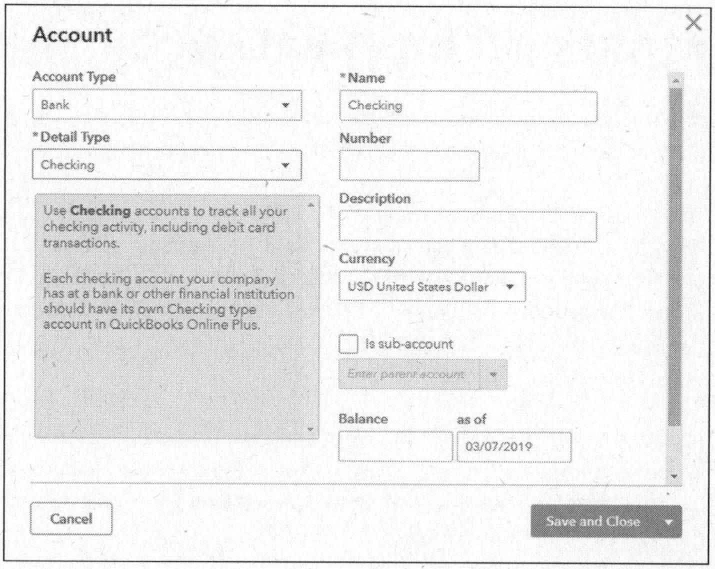

Account

Account Type

Bank

*Detail Type

Checking

Use **Checking** accounts to track all your checking activity, including debit card transactions.

Each checking account your company has at a bank or other financial institution should have its own Checking type account in QuickBooks Online Plus.

*Name

Checking

Number

Description

Currency

USD United States Dollar

☐ Is sub-account

Enter parent account

Balance   as of

03/07/2019

Cancel

Save and Close

FIGURE 3-31:
The dialog box you use to create an account.

4. **If you're using account numbers, supply a number for the new account.**

   You can, optionally, supply a description for the account.

   If you've enabled the Multicurrency feature, the dialog box you use to create a Bank account — or any type of asset or liability account except an Accounts Receivable (A/R) or Accounts Payable (A/P) account — also contains a list box from which you select the currency for the account. QBO automatically creates currency-related A/R and A/P accounts when you create transactions for foreign customers and vendors.

REMEMBER

5. **You can enter your account's balance as it appears on the last statement you received from your bank.**

   My example company is just starting out and has no opening balance yet, so I'm not entering an opening balance. See the sidebar "Proper account balances" for details on what to do here.

6. **Click Save.**

   QBO redisplays the Chart of Accounts page and your new account appears in the list.

PROPER ACCOUNT BALANCES

If you've been in business for a while, transactions have occurred. To ensure accurate account balances, you need to account for these transactions in QBO.

To make sure that you start your work in QBO with correct account balances, begin by deciding on the first date you intend to use QBO. This date determines the "as of" date of historical information you need to collect. Try to start using QBO on the first day of an accounting period — either on the first day of your company's fiscal year or on the first day of a month. If you start using QBO Payroll (QBOP) on January 1, you do not need to enter any historical payroll information.

Although it might seem like more work, I suggest that the easiest way for you to ensure proper account balances is to enter $0 as your Bank account's opening balance in Step 5 in the preceding steps for creating a Bank account. Then, enter all transactions that have occurred so far this year.

If you've been in business since before the beginning of the year, enter $0 for your Bank account's balance and ask your accountant for opening amounts for your Balance Sheet accounts as of December 31 of last year. Enter these amounts by entering a journal entry: Click the plus sign (+) icon at the top of QBO and choose Journal Entry from the Other column in the list. To avoid later confusion, reconcile the account as of December 31 before you do any more work. That way, when you perform your first "real" reconciliation of QBO transactions, QBO transactions will line up more closely with your bank statement.

The transactions you enter for the current year will ultimately affect your bank balance (for example, a customer eventually pays an invoice), and, when you finish entering the transactions, your QBO Bank account balance should agree with the one your financial institution has. So, I suggest that you enter transactions for *all* customer invoices (and corresponding payments customers made) and *all* vendor bills (and corresponding payments you made) during the current year.

If you choose to ignore my suggestion and enter an opening amount for your bank balance in Step 5, you need to then enter all transactions that have affected your bank account *since the last statement*.

QBO posts balances you enter while creating an account to the Opening Balance Equity (Equity) account, an account created by QuickBooks. Most accountants don't like this account and will want to create journal entries to move the balances to proper accounts.

That second approach sounds like a lot less work and, if you don't use payroll, or you make payroll payments from a separate bank account, you can safely ignore my suggestion and enter an opening amount for your bank balance in Step 5 and then enter outstanding customer invoices and unpaid vendor bills.

But, if your company does prepare payroll, has prepared one or more payrolls so far this year, and you use only one bank account, I strongly urge you to take my suggestion because you need accurate *annual* information to successfully manage payroll. The easiest way to ensure that you have accurate annual payroll information is to enter all payrolls you've completed this year so far — and these payrolls will affect your Bank account, so, entering a Bank account balance in Step 5 will lead you into trouble. Yes, you can try to do a mix of both approaches and subtract payroll amounts from the bank balance you previously entered in Step 5, but that approach is seriously error-prone.

If you use one bank account for everything and you feel that entering all transactions that have occurred so far this year is just too much work, I suggest that you enter your Bank account's balance as of your last bank statement, enter outstanding invoices and unpaid vendor bills, and then contact Intuit technical support for help entering historical payroll information.

If you intend to connect your Bank account to your financial institution — and details appear in Chapter 8 — I still recommend that you set the Bank account opening balance to $0. You can connect a Bank account to your financial institution at the time you create it or later — the choice is yours and I suggest you wait and get other things set up, like outstanding customer invoices and vendor bills. When you connect, as described in Chapter 8, you still need to review each transaction the financial institution downloads into QBO to make sure the transactions are properly assigned in QBO. So, while connecting might seem like a timesaver because it enters transactions into QBO, it really isn't because you need to review each transaction.

Taking Advantage of QuickBooks Labs

You might be wondering about the QuickBooks Labs option on the Gear menu (you can see it if you refer to Figure 3-11). Intuit calls QuickBooks Labs its "high-tech playground." If you're adventurous, check out the lab and turn on experimental features to see how they work. In most cases, features you find in QuickBooks Labs eventually become part of QBO.

For example, when I wrote this, the Import Style feature discussed earlier in this chapter was a QuickBooks Labs feature and therefore didn't appear by default. Here's how you turn on a QuickBooks Lab feature:

1. **Log in to your company.**

2. **Choose Gear ⇨ QuickBooks Labs.**

   The QuickBooks Labs window appears (see Figure 3-32).

FIGURE 3-32: Use this page to turn on features not yet available by default in QuickBooks.

TIP

Note that you can provide feedback on QuickBooks Labs features. The more positive feedback a feature receives, the more likely that feature will become a standard part of QBO.

3. **Check out the features available and, for any you want to try, click the Off button.**

   The Off button changes to the On button.

TIP

One of the features available in QuickBooks Labs is the Routines feature. Using it, you can automate repetitive tasks such as notifying your customers when you receive their payments or when their invoices are past due. And you can remind yourself about upcoming bills.

4. **When you finish turning on features, click Done, which appears in the lower right corner of the window.**

   Your QBO company reappears, with the features you selected enabled.

REMEMBER

You might need to refresh the browser page to see the new features you chose to make available. Click your browser's Refresh button or press F5 on your keyboard.

Signing In to and Out of QBO

If you followed the process in this chapter to sign up for QBO, you're currently signed in to QBO. But, obviously, you don't sign up for QBO every time you want to use it. And then, of course, there's the question of how you sign out of QBO each time you finish using it.

To sign out of QBO, click the Gear button and, from the menu shown earlier in Figure 3-11, click Sign Out (at the bottom of the list of commands under Your Company).

To sign in to QBO in the future, visit `qbo.intuit.com` (you get redirected to a long web address you don't need to type) and supply your username and password. I suggest you bookmark this page to make signing in easy.

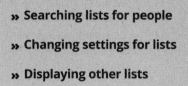
Chapter **4**

Managing List Information

Like its cousin the QuickBooks Desktop product, QBO relies on lists to help you store background information that you'll use again and again. For the most part, you enter information about the people with whom you do business — customers, vendors, and employees — and the stuff you sell or buy. But you also store other background information in lists, such as the accounts your company uses and the payment methods your company accepts. In this chapter, you'll find information that you need to set up customers and vendors, as well as setting up items you sell or buy. Finally, at the end of the chapter, you learn where to find other lists you might need.

Importing People into a List

If you've been running your business for a while, you probably have lists of customers and vendors. If they're stored electronically, you might be able to save yourself some setup time in QBO if you import them. And, because most people tend to worry about accounting "later," after they've been running the business for a bit, I'll start this chapter by assuming you do have lists stored in some electronic form. In the "Adding New People to a List" section of this chapter, I'll show you how to manually set up a customer or vendor. That will be important to those of you who don't have anything already in electronic form, and to all of you as your business grows and you add new customers and vendors.

If you've been using the QuickBooks Desktop product, you can import your list information from it into your free trial of QBO, which can help you become accustomed to QBO using list information you already recognize.

REMEMBER

Importing list information is not the same thing as importing a QuickBooks Desktop company. For details on importing a company, see Chapter 12 in Part 3. Be aware that you can't import your list of Employees, who are "people," because payroll setup cannot be imported. You can import employees if you import a QuickBooks Desktop company containing employees.

Even if you haven't been using QuickBooks Desktop, be aware that you can import list information from an Excel file or a CSV file. CSV stands for *comma-separated values*; most programs, including QuickBooks Desktop, enable you to export information to a CSV format. Coincidentally, Excel can open and save CVS files. So, you can open a CSV file, edit it in Excel as needed, and then resave it as a CSV file. Or, after editing, you can save the file as an Excel 97-2003 workbook.

TIP

You can create a CSV file by saving an Excel file in CSV format. With the Excel file open, choose File ⇨ Save As. In the Save As dialog box, change the Save as Type list below the filename from Excel Workbook to CSV (Comma Delimited).

You use the same process to import both customers and vendors from a Quick-Books Desktop product. QBO offers a tip that encourages you to import customers, as you can see from the bottom of Figure 4-1. You can display Figure 4-1 when you use the Navigation bar to choose Sales ⇨ Customers before you've added any customers. Because the screens for importing customers or vendors are the same *after* the first screen, I'll show you how to import vendors.

REMEMBER

In my screens, most often the Navigation bar refers to Sales, and sometimes it refers to Invoicing. They are the same, so, if necessary, click Invoicing when I say click Sales. The wording of the titles on the Navigation bar are influenced by some of the decisions you make while creating your company, so, if your company's appearance doesn't match mine, don't worry.

To successfully import information into QBO from a CSV file or an Excel work-book, the information must conform to a specific format. And, luckily, QBO gives you the option to download a sample file in Excel format so that you can view the required format for importing list information; you can use this sample as a guideline for setting up the data in your own file.

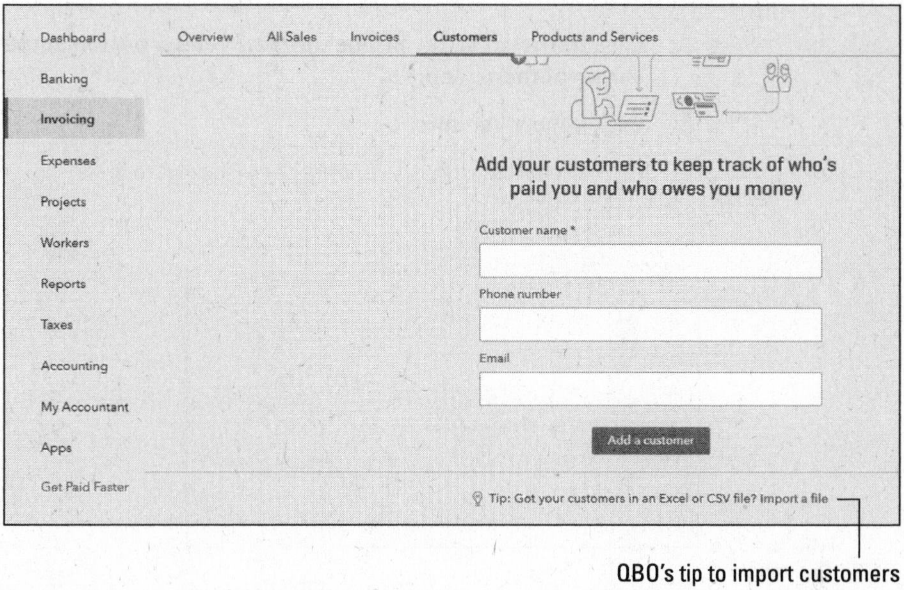

Add your customers to keep track of who's
paid you and who owes you money

Customer name *

Phone number

Email

Add a customer

Tip: Got your customers in an Excel or CSV file? Import a file

QBO's tip to import customers

**TECHNICAL
STUFF**

The steps that follow assume you have installed Excel on your computer. If you don't own a copy of Excel, you can use Excel Mobile, the free app from Microsoft. To make editing changes to your files in Excel Mobile, you need to sign in to Excel Mobile with your Microsoft account email and password.

To download and view the sample file for vendors, follow these steps:

1. **Click Expenses in the Navigation bar and then click Vendors to display the Vendors page (see Figure 4-2).**

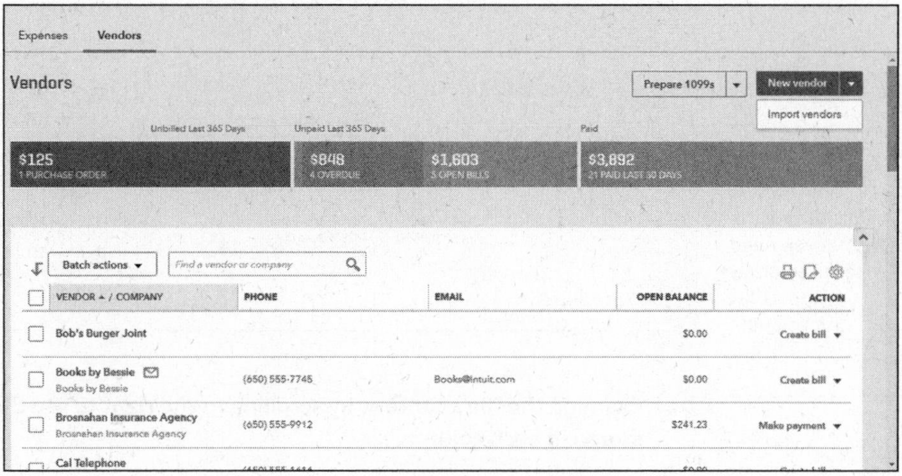

Expenses   Vendors

Vendors   Prepare 1099s ▼   New vendor ▼
                                                              Import vendors

| Unbilled Last 365 Days | Unpaid Last 365 Days | | Paid |
| $125 1 PURCHASE ORDER | $848 4 OVERDUE | $1,603 3 OPEN BILLS | $3,892 21 PAID LAST 30 DAYS |

Batch actions ▼   Find a vendor or company

VENDOR ▲ / COMPANY	PHONE	EMAIL	OPEN BALANCE	ACTION
Bob's Burger Joint			$0.00	Create bill ▼
Books by Bessie ✉ Books by Bessie	(650) 555-7745	Books@Intuit.com	$0.00	Create bill ▼
Brosnahan Insurance Agency Brosnahan Insurance Agency	(650) 555-9912		$241.23	Make payment ▼
Cal Telephone	(650) 555-1111		$0.00	Create bill ▼

FIGURE 4-2:
Start from the
appropriate page
when you want to
create a list entry
for a new person.

2. **Click the down arrow beside the New Vendor button in the upper right corner of the screen.**

3. **Click Import Vendors.**

   QBO displays the Import Vendors page (see Figure 4-3).

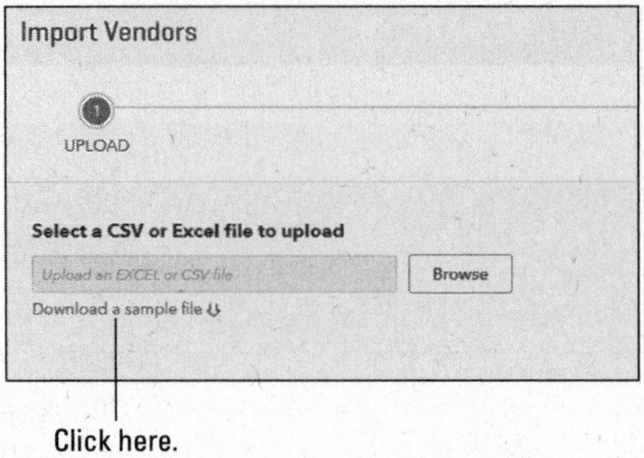

Import Vendors

①
UPLOAD

Select a CSV or Excel file to upload

[Upload an EXCEL or CSV file]   [Browse]

Download a sample file ⬇

FIGURE 4-3:
The Import
Vendors page.

Click here.

4. **Click the Download a Sample File link.**

   Once you click the link, QBO downloads the sample file and displays a button in the Windows taskbar for it, assuming you're using Chrome.

5. **Click the sample file's button in the Windows taskbar.**

   The sample file opens in Excel (see Figure 4-4).

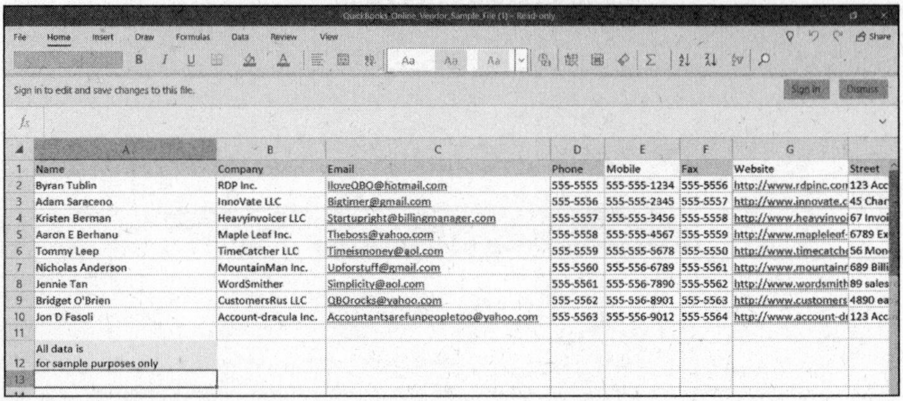

	Name	Company	Email	Phone	Mobile	Fax	Website	Street
2	Byran Tublin	RDP Inc.	IloveQBO@hotmail.com	555-5555	555-555-1234	555-5556	http://www.rdpinc.com	123 Acc
3	Adam Saraceno	InnoVate LLC	Bigtimer@gmail.com	555-5556	555-555-2345	555-5557	http://www.innovate.c	45 Char
4	Kristen Berman	Heavyinvoicer LLC	Startupright@billingmanager.com	555-5557	555-555-3456	555-5558	http://www.heavyinvoi	67 Invoi
5	Aaron E Berhanu	Maple Leaf Inc.	Theboss@yahoo.com	555-5558	555-555-4567	555-5559	http://www.mapleleaf-	6789 Ex
6	Tommy Leep	TimeCatcher LLC	Timeismoney@aol.com	555-5559	555-555-5678	555-5550	http://www.timecatch	56 Mon
7	Nicholas Anderson	MountainMan Inc.	Upforstuff@gmail.com	555-5560	555-556-6789	555-5561	http://www.mountainn	689 Billi
8	Jennie Tan	WordSmither	Simplicity@aol.com	555-5561	555-556-7890	555-5562	http://www.wordsmith	89 sales
9	Bridget O'Brien	CustomersRus LLC	QBOrocks@yahoo.com	555-5562	555-556-8901	555-5563	http://www.customers	4890 ea
10	Jon D Fasoli	Account-dracula Inc.	Accountantsarefunpeopletoo@yahoo.com	555-5563	555-556-9012	555-5564	http://www.account-dr	123 Acc
11								
12	All data is for sample purposes only							

FIGURE 4-4:
A file showing the
format you need
to successfully
import list
information.

6. **Examine the file's content by scrolling to the right to see the information stored in each column.**

THE DATA FILE'S LAYOUT IN EXCEL

Excel stores the information in the sample file (and you'll need to store the information in your data file) in a table format, where each row in the Excel file contains all the information about a single vendor or customer (each row is referred to as a *record*), and each column contains the same piece of information for all customers and vendors (each column is referred to as one *field* in a record). For example, in Figure 4-4, all the information about Adam Saraceno appears in Row 3, and all vendor email addresses appear in Column C. Also note that Row 1 contains a label that identifies the type of information found in each column; don't forget to include identifying labels in your data file.

7. **Create your own file, modeling it on the sample file.**

   If you've been using QuickBooks Desktop, you can export lists to CSV or Excel files; see QuickBooks Desktop Help for details.

REMEMBER

You'll find that importing your data works best if you can match the headings in your data file to the ones found in the sample data file. Also, your data file cannot contain more than 1,000 rows or exceed 2MB in size. Don't forget to save your data file as either an Excel 97-2003 workbook or a CSV (comma-delimited) file.

After you have created an Excel file or a CSV file containing your list information, you can import it. Follow these steps:

1. **Make sure your data file is not open.**

2. **Follow Steps 1 to 3 to display the Import Vendors (or Import Customers) page.**

3. **Click the Browse button.**

4. **Navigate to the folder where you saved the file containing your list information.**

5. **Select the file and choose Open.**

   QBO updates the Import Vendors page with the name of the file you selected.

6. **Click Next.**

   QBO uploads your file and displays the Map Data screen shown in Figure 4-5.

7. **Make sure that the fields in your data file correctly match fields in QBO.**

   As needed, open the list box beside each QBO field name and match it to the labels in your data file.

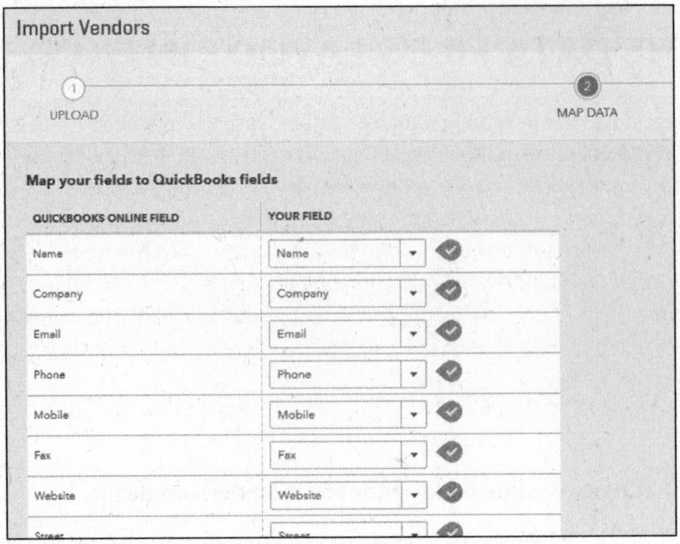

FIGURE 4-5:
Match the fields
in your data file
to QBO fields.

8. **Click Next, which appears in the lower right corner of the screen (and isn't shown in Figure 4-5).**

   QBO displays the records it has identified (see Figure 4-6).

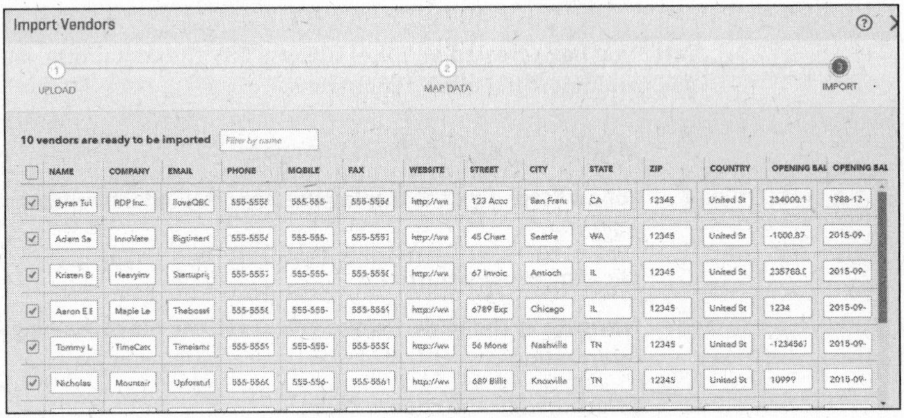

FIGURE 4-6:
The records QBO
will import from
your data file.

9. **Review the records QBO proposes to import to make sure the information is correct.**

   You can make changes to the information in any field by clicking that field and typing. You also can uncheck any row to avoid importing the information in that row to QBO.

10. When you are satisfied that the information is correct, click the Import button in the lower right corner of the screen (not shown in Figure 4-6).

TIP

If the Import button is grayed out and unavailable, that means that some portion of the data cannot be imported. Look for a field highlighted in red to identify information that can't be imported. If the problem isn't apparent, contact Intuit Support for help.

QBO imports the information and displays a message that identifies the number of records imported. The list you imported appears on the appropriate page (see Figure 4-7).

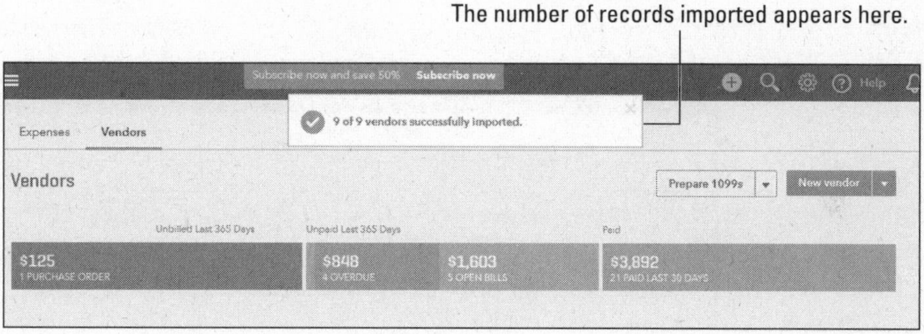

The number of records imported appears here.

Subscribe now and save 50%	**Subscribe now**				⊕ Q ⚙ ⑦ Help ⌕
	✓ 9 of 9 vendors successfully imported.	✕			
Expenses **Vendors**					

Vendors
Prepare 1099s ▾   New vendor ▾

	Unbilled Last 365 Days	Unpaid Last 365 Days		Paid
$125 1 PURCHASE ORDER		**$848** 4 OVERDUE	**$1,603** 5 OPEN BILLS	**$3,892** 21 PAID LAST 30 DAYS

FIGURE 4-7:
The Vendors page after importing vendors using an Excel file.

Adding New People to a List

You use the Sales, Expenses, and Workers links in the Navigation bar to work with your customers, vendors, employees, and contractors. The steps are basically the same to set up a new customer, vendor, employee, or contractor; you just start by clicking the appropriate link in the Navigation bar — Sales for customers, Expenses for vendors, and Workers for employees and contractors. Read on to learn how to set up a new customer.

Creating a new customer

I've chosen to show you how to set up a new customer because customers have the most options to establish. For example, for customers, you can create sub-customers and you can create and assign customer types; these features aren't available for vendors, employees, or contractors.

Follow these steps to set up a new customer in QBO:

REMEMBER

If you have determined that your company needs to use the Multicurrency feature, turn it on before you start creating people so that you have available the fields you need to establish each person's currency. See Chapter 3 for details on the Multi-currency feature.

1. **Click Sales in the Navigation bar and then click Customers to display the Customers page shown in Figure 4-8.**

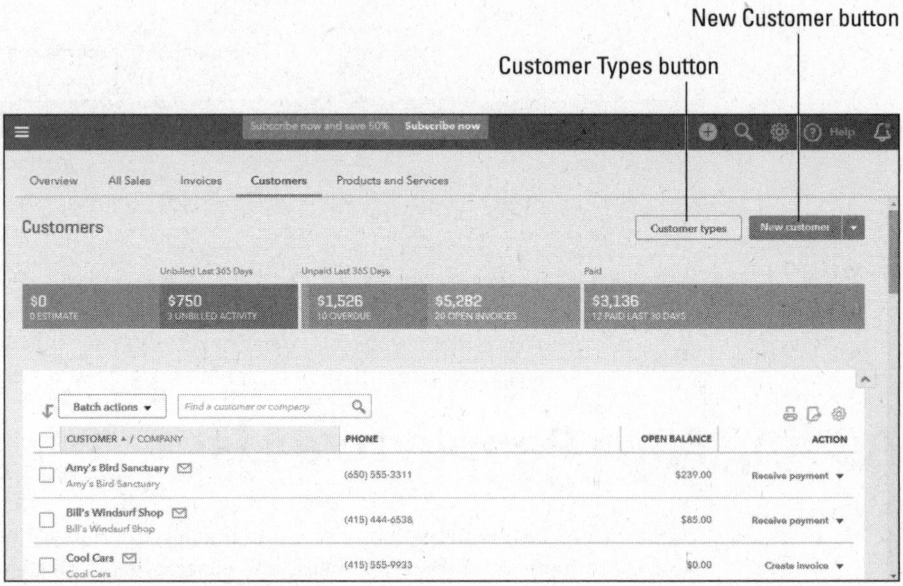

Customer Types button   New Customer button

FIGURE 4-8:
Start from the appropriate page when you want to create a list entry for a new person.

2. **Click the New Customer button in the upper right corner of the page.**

   If you see the page shown earlier in Figure 4-1, you can click the Add a Customer button at the bottom of the page.

TIP

   QBO displays the Customer Information dialog box shown in Figure 4-9.

3. **Type the requested information.**

   For details on creating and assigning customer types, see the next section, "Using customer types."

   If you need to set up a sub-customer (and wonder what that is), see the section "Adding sub-customers."

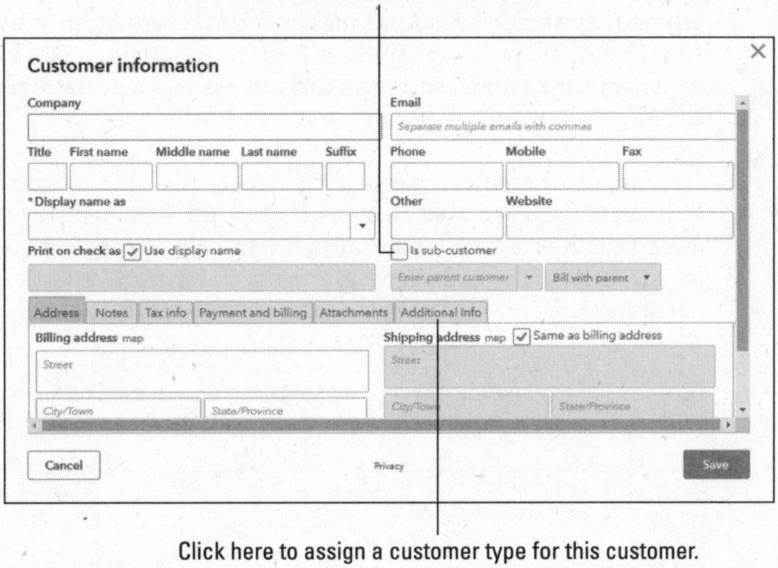

Click here to create a sub-customer.

Customer information

Company

Title First name Middle name Last name Suffix

*Display name as

Print on check as ☑ Use display name

Email
Separate multiple emails with commas

Phone Mobile Fax

Other Website

☐ Is sub-customer

Enter parent customer ▾ Bill with parent ▾

| Address | Notes | Tax info | Payment and billing | Attachments | Additional Info |

Billing address map

Street

City/Town State/Province

Shipping address map ☑ Same as billing address

Street

City/Town State/Province

Cancel Privacy Save

FIGURE 4-9:
Use this dialog
box to enter
information for a
new customer.

Click here to assign a customer type for this customer.

4. **Click Save.**

   QBO saves the customer and displays the customer's page showing transaction information specific to that customer — and, of course, because you just added the customer, you won't see any transactions. You also can view and edit the details you just established for the customer if you click the Customer Details tab. To redisplay the complete list of Customers, click Sales in the Navigation bar and then click Customers.

TIP

You can make any customer, vendor, or contractor inactive as long as the associated person has a $0 balance. I'll discuss employees in Chapter 9. To make a person inactive, click the Action down arrow at the right edge of the appropriate list beside the entry. In the list that opens, click Make Inactive.

Using customer types

You can create customer types to group otherwise unrelated customers; for example, perhaps you offer special discounts at certain times of the year to some customers. You can use a customer type to help you identify the customers to whom you'll offer the discount (keep this one in mind if you intend to take advantage of the pricing rules feature in QBO, covered in more detail later in this chapter).

To create customer types, click the Customer Types button in the upper right corner of the Customers page (refer to Figure 4-8). Then, type a name for your customer type and click Save; repeat this process for each customer type you want to set up.

To assign a customer type to a customer, click the customer's name on the Customers page and then click the Customer Details tab (see Figure 4-10). Click the Edit button at the top or on the right side of the Customer Details page to redisplay the dialog box shown previously in Figure 4-9. Click the Additional Info tab in that dialog box to assign a customer type to the customer.

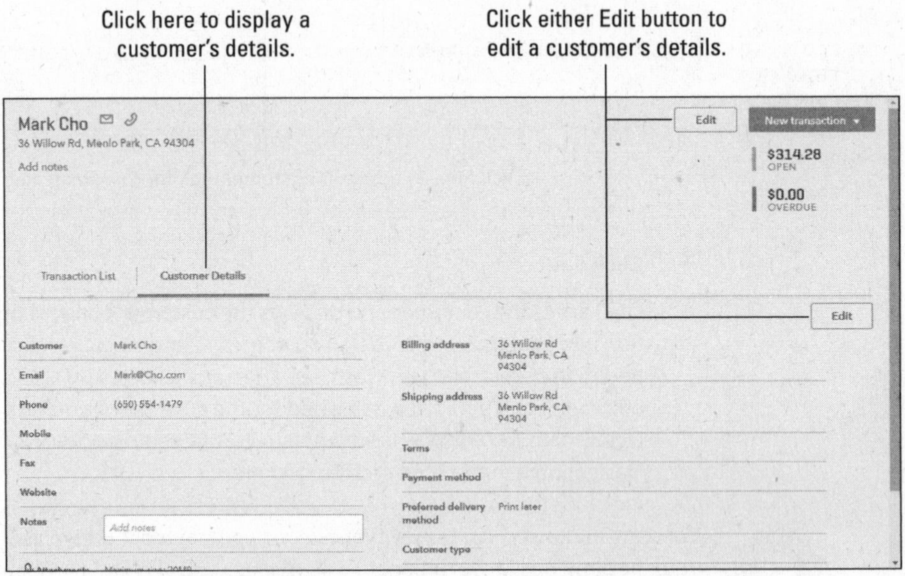

Click here to display a
customer's details.

Click either Edit button to
edit a customer's details.

FIGURE 4-10: You edit the details of a customer's information from the Customer Details tab for the customer.

To save yourself some time, be aware that you don't need to assign the customer type to each individual customer; instead, you can simultaneously assign the same customer type to a group of customers you select. See the section "Working with a batch of people" later in this chapter.

TIP

To see your customers by customer type, use the Sales by Customer Type Detail report, the Sales by Customer Detail report grouped by customer type, and the Customer Contact List customized to include a column for the customer type. You can read more about running reports in Chapter 10.

Adding sub-customers

Sub-customers are a way for you to create a hierarchy for customers, and you can use sub-customers pretty much any way you want. For example, if you're an architect, sub-customers might represent jobs or projects for a particular client (called the "parent customer" in QBO). If you're an attorney, sub-customers could represent different matters for the same client.

If you set up sub-customers, you can choose to bill either the parent or the sub-customer. Sub-customers' balances are included in the parent customer's balance. Transactions for sub-customers appear in the sub-customer's register as well as the parent customer's register. You can create as many sub-customers as you want, but, for any given customer, you can only assign sub-customers up to five levels deep, including the parent customer.

WARNING

If you have any thoughts about using the Projects feature in QBO, be aware that you can easily convert first-level sub-customers to projects if you establish the billing for the sub-customer separately from the parent customer. That is, select Bill This Customer as you set up the sub-customer if you think you might want to convert sub-customers to projects. See Chapter 6 for details on the Projects feature in QBO.

To create a sub-customer, follow the steps in the section "Creating a new customer" and check the "Is Sub-Customer" box on the right side (in the middle) of the Customer Information dialog box (refer to Figure 4-9).

Searching Lists for People

You can use the Customers, Vendors, and Employees pages in a variety of ways. The Contractors page is more limited than the rest; from it, you can search for contractors and prepare 1099s. From the Customers, Vendors, or Employees pages that list all the people in those categories, you can sort the people in the list, export the list to Excel, and perform actions on a selected group of people on the list.

You also can print a basic report by clicking the Print button on any list page; the Print button appears just above the Action column.

Working with a particular person

You can select a particular customer, vendor, or employee and view the transactions associated with that person as well as the person's details, and you can attach files to the person. For this section, I'll work with customers.

To search for a particular person, type some characters that match the person or company name in the Search box that appears above the list of people (see Figure 4-11).

Type here.

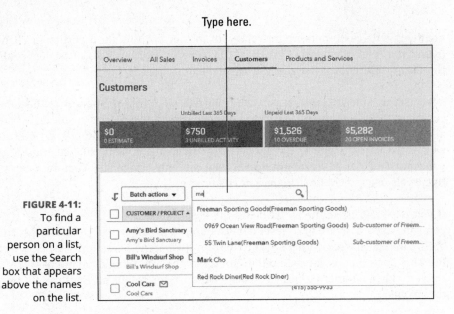

FIGURE 4-11:
To find a
particular
person on a list,
use the Search
box that appears
above the names
on the list.

When you select any person from the list, QBO displays the page specifically associated with that person. The page has two tabs; in Figure 4-12, you see the Transaction List tab; the Customer Details tab appeared earlier in figure 4-10.

TIP

If you have enabled the Projects feature in your company, QBO displays a third tab called the Projects tab, which lists any projects you have created in your QBO company. You can read more about Projects in Chapter 6.

FIGURE 4-12:
The Transaction
List tab shows
transactions in
QBO associated
with the selected
person.

From either tab, you click the Edit button to edit information about that person, and you click the New Transaction button to add a transaction associated with that person.

From the details page of a person, shown earlier in Figure 4-10, you can attach files to keep track of important financial information. For example, you can attach a vendor's 1099 document, a customer's contract, or an employee's receipts. You're not limited to text documents; you also can attach photos. Simply drag and drop the item into the Attachments box at the bottom left side of the appropriate details page; if you prefer, you can click the box and a standard Windows Open dialog box appears so that you can navigate to and select the document you want to attach.

Each attachment can be no larger than 25MB. To view documents you've already attached to a person, click the Show Existing link below the Attachments box and QBO opens a pane on the right side of the page showing the linked attachments.

You also can add attachments to a transaction, as you'll see when you create transactions in Chapters 5, 6, 7, and 9. To view transactions that have attachments, you add the Attachments column to the table that appears on the person's Transaction List page. Display the person's Transaction List page (see Figure 4-13) and then click the table Gear button above the Action column. From the list that appears, click Show More. Show More changes to Show Less and a check box for Attachments appears; click it and the Attachments column appears as part of the table grid. You can identify it as the column heading with a paper clip. Displaying the Attachments column for one person displays it in the Transaction List table for all persons of that type. If attachments exist for any particular transaction, you'll see the number of attachments in the column. Clicking the number lists the transaction's attachments; clicking an attachment in the list opens that attachment.

REMEMBER

You add attachments to the various transactions as you create them; only attachments associated with transactions appear on the various Transaction List pages, and attachments associated with a person appear on the associated person's page.

When you finish working with one person, you can easily switch to another in that list using the list's Split View list pane.

You can click the Split View icon (refer to Figure 4-13) to display a pane listing the people stored in the list (see Figure 4-14).

From the list in the Split View pane, you can scroll down to find a person, or you can type a few letters of the person's name or company name in the Search box at the top of the list to find that person in the list. Or, you can sort the list by name or by open balance. Click a person to switch to that person's page.

To add a new person to the list, click the plus (+) symbol at the top of the list in the Split View pane to see the dialog box shown earlier in Figure 4-9. To display the Customers page shown earlier in Figure 4-8, click Customers at the top of the Split View list or click Sales in the Navigation bar and then click Customers.

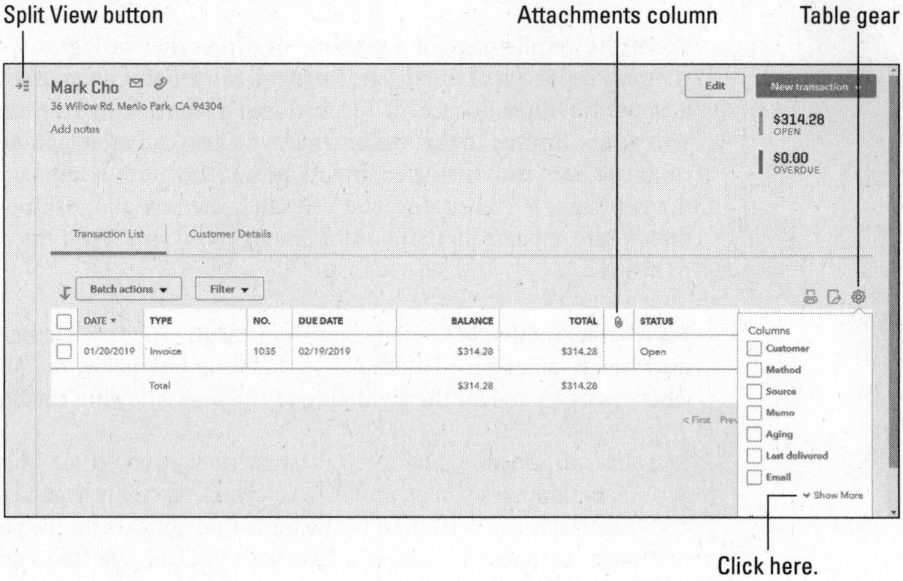

Split View button   Attachments column   Table gear

FIGURE 4-13:
Adding the
Attachments
column to the
table on the
Transaction List.

Click here.

To close Split View, click the Close Split View button (refer to Figure 4-14).

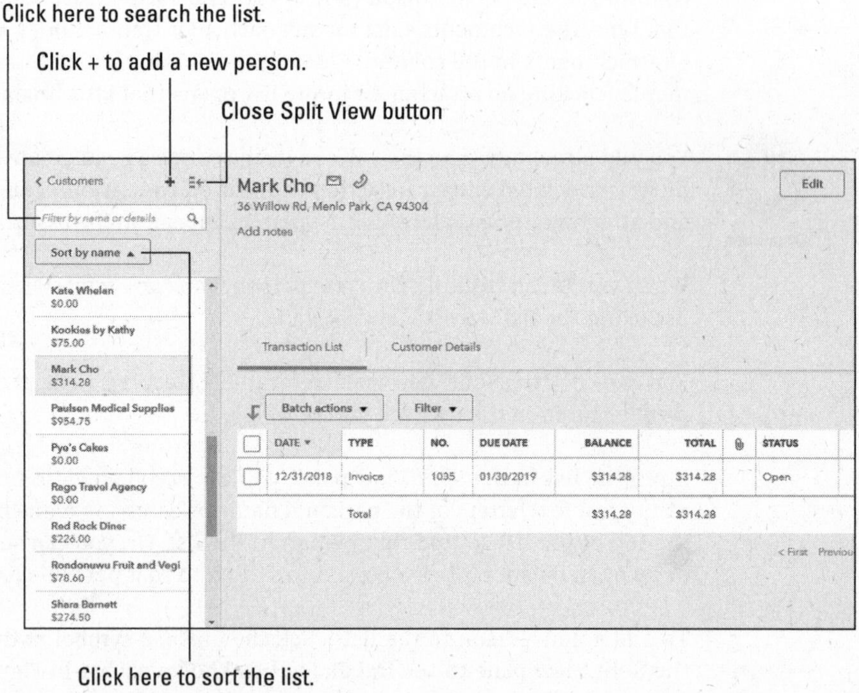

Click here to search the list.

Click + to add a new person.

Close Split View button

FIGURE 4-14:
Displaying a list's
Split View.

Click here to sort the list.

Sorting a list

In addition to sorting in Split View, you can sort the lists on the Customers and Vendors page by name or open balance. By default, QBO sorts the entries on these pages alphabetically by name in ascending order.

TIP

You can sort employees in alphabetical order and reverse alphabetical order, by pay method, or by status (active or inactive). You can't sort contractors; QBO, by default, sorts them in alphabetical order.

To change the sort order for the Customers or Vendors lists, click Sales or Expenses in the Navigation bar and then click Customers or Vendors to display the appropriate page; for this example, I use the Customers page.

Next, click the heading for the column by which you want to sort. If you click the Customer/Company column heading, QBO displays the customers in descending alphabetical order. If you click the Open Balance column heading, QBO sorts the list in Open Balance order, from lowest to highest.

Exporting a list to Excel

You can export a list of your customers or vendors to Excel.

TECHNICAL
STUFF

In this section, I assume you have a copy of Excel on your computer; otherwise, downloading your list to an Excel file wouldn't make much sense. If you don't have a copy of Excel on your computer, you can download and use the free mobile version of Excel.

Click the appropriate link in the Navigation bar (Sales or Expenses) to subsequently display either the Customers page or the Vendors page; I use the Vendors page in this example. At the right edge of the page, just above the Action column, three buttons appear. Click the middle button, and QBO exports the list to an Excel file; a button for the file appears at the bottom of the screen in Chrome (see Figure 4-15).

Click the button at the bottom of the screen, and Excel opens the file. You can edit the file if you click the Enable Editing button in the yellow bar at the top of the window. And, for those of you using Excel mobile, you need to sign in using your Microsoft account to edit the file.

Click here to export the list.

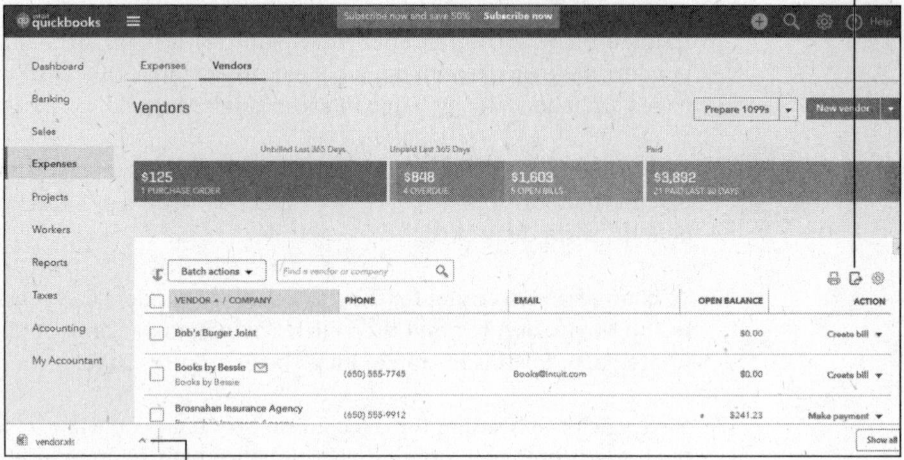

FIGURE 4-15:
Exporting a
vendor list to
Excel.

Click here to open the Excel file.

Working with a batch of people

When you work with customers or vendors, you can take certain actions simultaneously for a group of people. For example, you can select specific vendors by clicking the check box beside each name and then send the same email to those vendors, pay bills online for the selected vendors if you are using the `Bill.com` add-on with QBO Essentials, Plus, or Advanced, or make the selected vendors inactive.

TIP

You can use the Bill.com add-on to pay bills online from QBO; there is a full-service Bill.com app, but here, I'm talking about the add-on to QBO. You'll find the Bill.com app available in the Intuit App Center. You can visit the store by choosing Apps from the Navigation pane. There is no monthly subscription fee for Bill.com, but there is a per transaction fee for each payment you process.

For customers, in addition to sending email, you can create and send statements to them, assign the selected customers to a customer type (you use customer type to group customers; you can read about setting up customer types earlier in this chapter, in the section "Using customer types"), and make the selected customers inactive.

To use one of these actions for a group of people, click the appropriate link in the Navigation bar — Sales or Expenses — followed by the appropriate list page to display the associated page. For this example, I used the Customers page.

Next, click the check box beside the names you want to include in your action and then click the Batch Actions button (see Figure 4-16). Select the action you want to take, and then follow the prompts onscreen to complete the action.

Click here to assign batch actions.

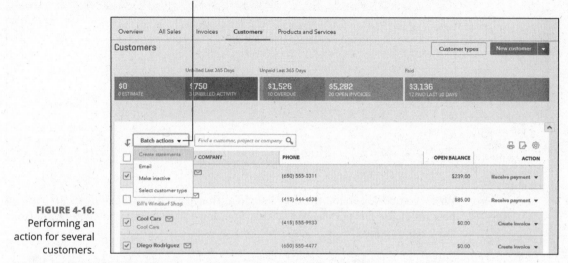

FIGURE 4-16:
Performing an action for several customers.

Changing Settings for People Lists

You can, to some extent, control the appearance of the lists on the Customers page, the Vendors page, and the Employees page. For example, you can opt to show or hide street address, attachments, email, and phone number information, and you can opt to include or exclude inactive entries in the list. You also can control the number of entries displayed on each page, as well as adjust those entries' column widths.

REMEMBER

The elements you can show or hide depend on the list you're using; for example, you can show or hide address information on the Customers and Vendors lists but not on the Employees list or the Contractors list.

Click the appropriate link in the Navigation bar — Sales, Expenses, or Employees — to display the associated page; for this section, I worked on the Vendors page.

To control the information displayed in the list, click the table Gear button above the Action column at the right edge of the page (see Figure 4-17). Then select or deselect check boxes to display or hide information. Click outside the list when you finish.

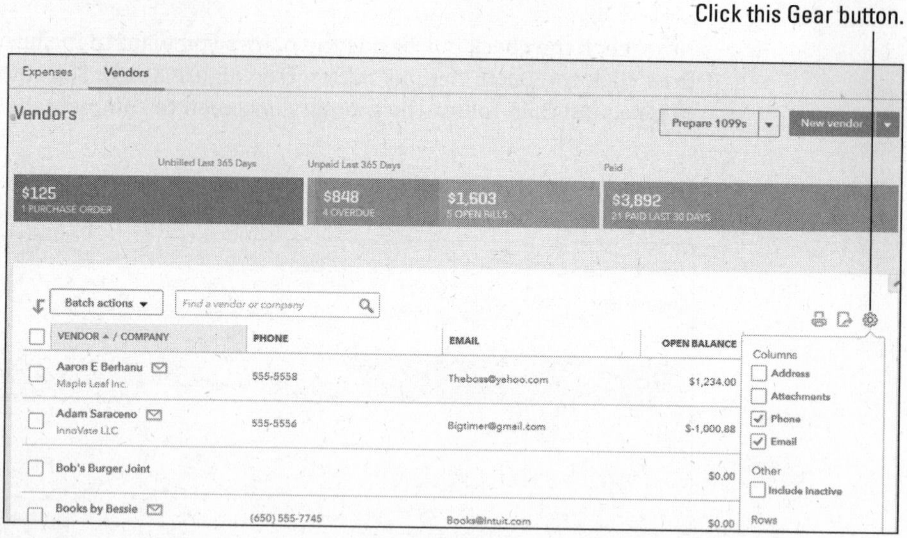

Click this Gear button.

FIGURE 4-17:
Controlling the
information
that appears
in the list.

TIP When you click outside the list, I suggest that you click in the empty area at the bottom of the Navigation bar so that you don't accidentally navigate away from the current page.

To adjust the width of any column, slide the mouse pointer into the row of column heading labels above the list and place it over the right edge of the column you want to adjust. When the mouse pointer changes to a pair of vertical lines and a pair of horizontal arrows pointing outward, drag the mouse. When you start to drag, the mouse pointer reverts to a pointer and a vertical bar appears, guiding you in resizing the column (see Figure 4-18). Release the mouse button when you're satisfied with the column width.

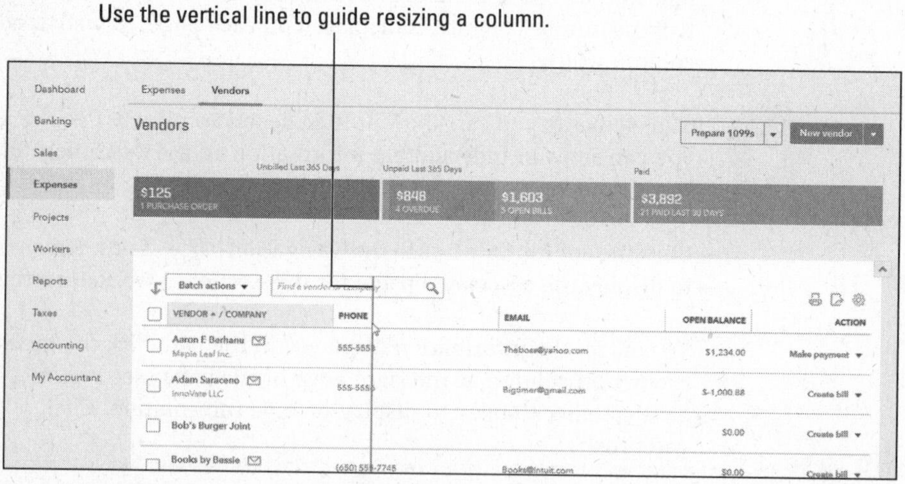

Use the vertical line to guide resizing a column.

FIGURE 4-18:
Adjusting the
width allotted to
the vendor's
name on the
Vendors page.

TIP

QBO remembers column width adjustments you make in registers and on pages like the Customers and Vendors pages, even after you sign out of QBO and then sign back in again.

Working with Products and Services Items

Inventory tracking is available in the QBO Plus edition, and you need to turn on the feature. Choose Gear⇨Account and Settings. In the Account and Settings dialog box, click Sales and, in the Products and Services section, click Track Inventory Quantity On Hand.

REMEMBER

QBO Plus can support inventory tracking capabilities, but, if you're looking for inventory capabilities to support manufacturing, you'll be happier in QuickBooks Desktop Premier or Enterprise versions.

The Products and Services list, shown in Figure 4-19, is the QBO equivalent to the QuickBooks Desktop product's Items list. You display the Products and Services list by choosing Gear⇨Products and Services. In Figure 4-19, I used the compacted view of the list so that you could see more products; you select the compacted view from the table gear on the right side of the page.

You use the Products and Services list pretty much the same way you use the Customer and Vendor lists; for example, you can search for an item by its name, SKU, or sales description. You can identify the columns you can use to sort the list if you slide your mouse over the column heading; if the mouse pointer changes to a hand, you can click that column to sort the list using the information in that column.

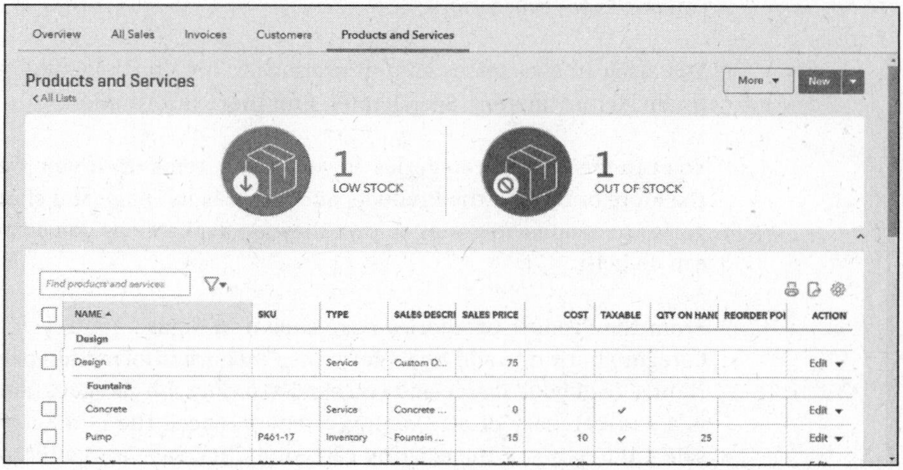

	NAME ▲	SKU	TYPE	SALES DESCRI	SALES PRICE	COST	TAXABLE	QTY ON HAND	REORDER POI	ACTION
	Design									
☐	Design		Service	Custom D...	75					Edit ▾
	Fountains									
☐	Concrete		Service	Concrete ...	0		✓			Edit ▾
☐	Pump	P461-17	Inventory	Fountain ...	15	10	✓	25		Edit ▾

FIGURE 4-19:
The Products and
Services list.

Products and Services

1 LOW STOCK

1 OUT OF STOCK

REMEMBER

Enabling the Multicurrency feature, described in Chapter 3, has no effect on inventory item valuations; QBO assesses and reports inventory item values in home currency units, regardless of the currency used by the vendor who sold you the items. For that reason, the Products and Services list shows no distinctions related to currency.

You can import and export items using an Excel or CSV file, the same way you import and export people information. See the sections "Importing People into a List" and "Exporting a list to Excel" earlier in this chapter. The importing and exporting processes include the information about the item's taxability.

Establishing categories

Categories replace sub-items and are available to all subscriptions that use sub-items except for those who migrate from QuickBooks Desktop. You can use categories to organize what you sell and, using various Products and Services reports, hopefully help you better understand what people are buying from you. Categories do not affect your accounting or your financial reports, and you cannot assign categories to transactions.

You also can use classes and/or locations to help further catalog transactions and financial information. See Chapter 3 for more information.

You can create new categories as you create items or, if you prefer, you can click the More button on the Products and Services list page and choose Manage Categories to create categories so that they are available as you create items. Yes, you can do both.

From the Product Categories page shown in Figure 4-20, you can click the New Category button to add a category; the Category Information panel appears on the right side of your screen and you simply supply the category name. If the category is a sub-category of an existing category, check the Is a Sub-Category box and select the name of the existing category. Click Save at the bottom of the panel to set up your category.

TIP

You can create sub-categories up to four levels deep. That is, you can create a category called Clothing and then create a sub-category of Clothing called Shoes. For the Shoes sub-category, you can create a sub-category called Women's Shoes, and, for the Women's Shoes category, you can create one last sub-category called Sneakers. You can't create a sub-category for Sneakers, but you can create another sub-category for Women's Shoes called Dress Shoes.

Product Categories	
‹ Products and Services	
	⚙
NAME	**ACTION**
Design	Edit ▾
Fountains	Edit ▾
Landscaping	Edit ▾
Sprinklers	Edit ▾
Pest Control	Edit ▾
	Previous 1-5 Next

FIGURE 4-20: The Product Categories page.

If necessary, you can edit an existing category; click the Edit link beside the category you want to modify in the table on the Product Categories page. Once again, the Category Information panel appears, displaying the category's current information. Make changes and click Save; alternatively, you can click Remove to remove a category.

REMEMBER

The effect on items of removing a category depends on whether you remove a sub-category or a category. If you remove a sub-category, QBO moves the items assigned to it up one level. If you remove a category (with no sub-categories) QBO reclassifies the items as uncategorized.

Setting up sales taxes

Don't freak out; this is a lot easier than you might be imagining. QBO contains a wizard that literally walks you through the process, asking you easy questions such as your address and whether you need to charge sales tax outside your state.

"But," you say, "this chapter is supposed to be about lists, and sales taxes aren't lists." Right you are, but setting up sales taxes *before* you set up items makes your life easier. Why? Because QBO uses the sales tax information you supply as you set up items. If you don't set up sales taxes before you set up items, you'll have to go back and edit all your items for taxability. Yuk!

QBO tracks and reports sales tax automatically for companies operating on the Accrual basis of accounting. Further, QBO automatically calculates sales tax on transactions if you set your QBO company accounting basis to Accrual.

So, what should you do if your company operates on the Cash basis of accounting? Set your company accounting method to Accrual before you set up sales taxes (click Gear⇨Account and Settings⇨Advanced). Then, set up sales tax and *then* change your accounting method back to Cash. Be aware that the Sales Tax Center will track your sales tax liability on the Accrual basis, but you can use the Sales Tax Liability reports to identify the correct amount of sales tax to pay.

The first time you click Taxes, QBO prompts you to set up sales taxes. Click the Setup Sales Tax button. If you haven't already entered your company's address in QBO, the wizard prompts you to supply your address. If you have already entered your address, QBO displays it onscreen for you to verify. Click Looks Good when your address is correct, and then click Next.

The wizard then asks if you need to charge sales tax outside your home state; choose No or Yes, as appropriate; if you click Yes, you identify the additional states where you charge sales tax. Click Next.

QBO next asks you when your current tax year starts, how often you file sales tax returns, and the date you started collecting sales tax for your taxing agency. Click Got it!, and that's it — your sales taxes are set up.

As part of QBO's set-up process, it marks all existing customers as tax-paying customers. If you have any customers who don't have to pay tax, such as government agencies, schools, and charities, edit those customers (Sales⇨Customers⇨Edit) and, on the Tax Info tab of the Customer Details dialog box, uncheck the This Customer is Taxable check box and supply exemption details such as the reason the customer is exempt from sales tax and the customer's exemption certificate ID. You might also want to attach a copy of the exemption certificate to the customer on the Customer Details page in QBO.

REMEMBER

Because many small business owners rely on their accountants to handle sales tax reporting, you can find more information about reporting and paying sales taxes in Chapter 15 in the QBOA portion of this book.

Adding service and non-inventory items

You can create inventory, non-inventory, and service items, and you can edit batches of items to change their type; I'll show you how to change an item's type after I show you how to add an item to the list.

1. **To display the Products and Services list, choose Gear ⇨ Products and Services.**

2. **Click the New button.**

   QBO displays the Product/Service Information panel on the right side of your screen (see Figure 4-21) where you select whether you're creating an inventory item, a non-inventory item, a service, or a bundle.

   You can read more about inventory items and bundles later in this chapter.

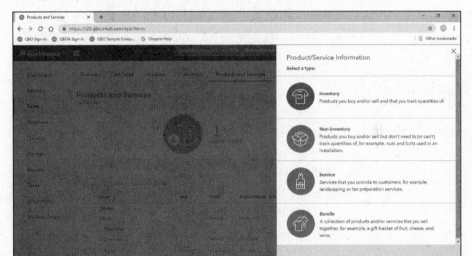

FIGURE 4-21:
Select a type of
item to create.

3. **Click a type to select it.**

   For this example, I chose Non-inventory item. You create a service item the same way you create a non-inventory item, supplying the same kind of information shown in these steps. See the next section, "Creating an inventory item," for details on the additional information you supply when creating an inventory item, and see the section "Working with bundles" for details on creating bundles.

   QBO then displays the panel for the type of item you chose; Figure 4-22 shows the Non-inventory panel.

4. **Supply a name for the item and, if appropriate, a stock keeping unit (SKU).**

   You also can select the item's category.

   You can upload a picture of the item by clicking the Upload button and navigating to the location where you store the picture.

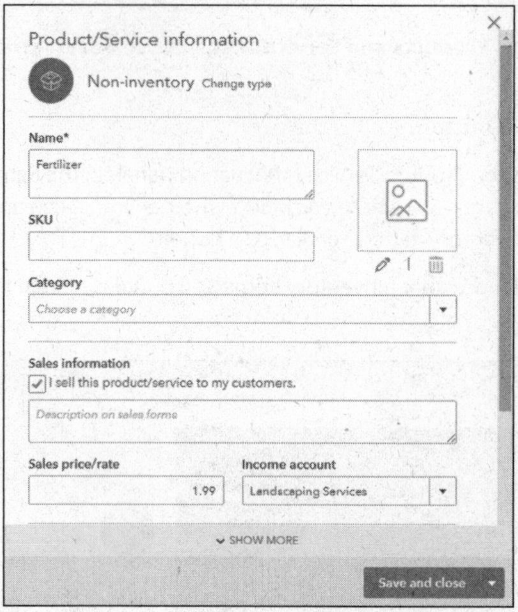

FIGURE 4-22:
Use this window
to create a
non-inventory
item.

5. **In the Sales Information section, you can**

    a. Select the I Sell This Product/Service to My Customers check box and supply a default description,

    b. Supply the price you charge when you sell this item, and

    c. Select the income account associated with the item; if necessary, you can establish a new account.

    QBO uses this information when you select this item on sales transactions.

6. **Make sure a check appears in the Is Taxable check box if appropriate, and choose one of the predefined entries that appear in the Sales Tax Category and What You Sell lists.**

7. **To display the Purchasing Information section (see Figure 4-23), place a check in the I Purchase This Product/Service From a Vendor check box and then, if necessary, click the Show More link at the bottom of the window.**

8. **Supply a default description, the cost you pay when you purchase the item, the expense account associated with the item, and, if you want, the vendor from whom you prefer to purchase the item.**

    QBO uses this information when you select this item on expense transactions.

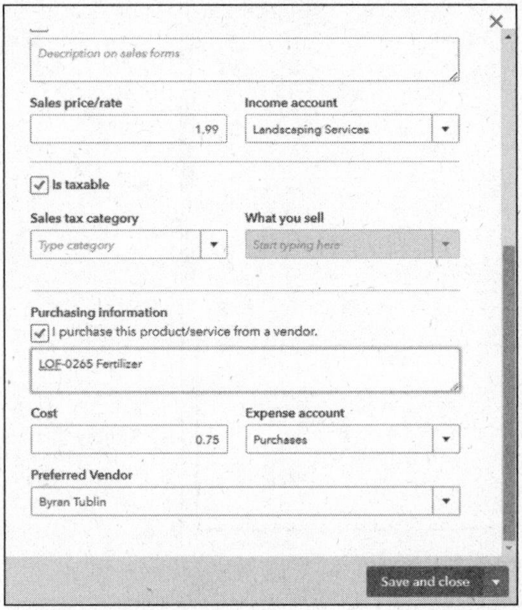

![Figure 4-23 screenshot showing the Add purchasing information form]

Description on sales forms

Sales price/rate | **Income account**
1.99 | Landscaping Services ▼

☑ Is taxable

Sales tax category | **What you sell**
Type category ▼ | Start typing here ▼

Purchasing information
☑ I purchase this product/service from a vendor.

LOF-0265 Fertilizer

Cost | **Expense account**
0.75 | Purchases ▼

Preferred Vendor
Byran Tublin ▼

Save and close ▼

FIGURE 4-23:
Add purchasing information for the item.

9. **Click Save and Close.**

   QBO saves the item and redisplays the Products and Services list; the new item appears in the list.

Creating an inventory item

Creating an inventory item has a few additional types of information you need to supply (see Figure 4-24).

Supply the quantity you have on hand and the date on which you determined the quantity on hand. You must supply an As Of date or QBO won't let you save the item. If you intend to enter historical transactions that use the item you're setting up, make sure that you enter an As Of date early enough to accommodate those transactions — typically the beginning of your fiscal year.

REMEMBER

Remember, before you can sell an item, you must own some of it. If you don't own any at the time you create the item, you'll probably buy some of it using an expense transaction, and that will update your quantities for you.

If you're using QBO Plus, you can supply a reorder point. Define your reorder point as the minimum quantity you judge that you need on hand at any given point in time. QBO uses the reorder point you establish to monitor the quantity of the item in stock, and when the quantity on hand falls equal to or below the established reorder point, QBO reminds you to order more.

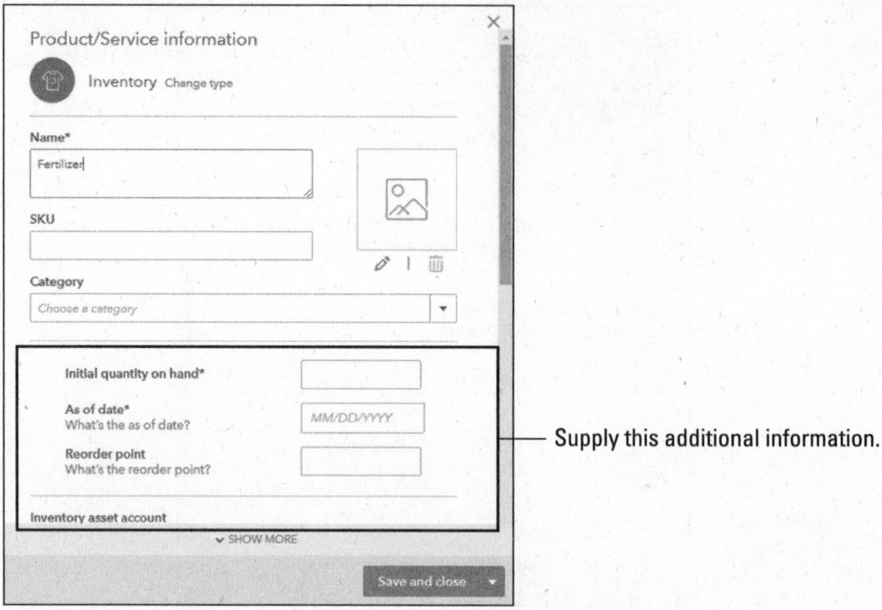

Product/Service information

Inventory Change type

Name*

Fertilizer

SKU

Category

Choose a category

Initial quantity on hand*

As of date*
What's the as of date?   MM/DD/YYYY

Reorder point
What's the reorder point?

Inventory asset account

✓ SHOW MORE

Save and close

FIGURE 4-24:
Supply quantity
on hand and
inventory asset
account
information for
inventory items.

Supply this additional information.

You can set a reorder point after you have created an inventory item; find the item in the Products and Services list and click Edit in its Action column. Then, supply the reorder point and click Save and Close.

You also can use the Products and Services list to see the items for which you have specified reorder points that are low or out of stock. At the top of the list, shown in Figure 4-25, click Low Stock to filter the Products and Services list to show only items for which you have specified a reorder point that are also low on stock. Click Out of Stock to view items for which you have specified a reorder point that you don't have and should consider ordering.

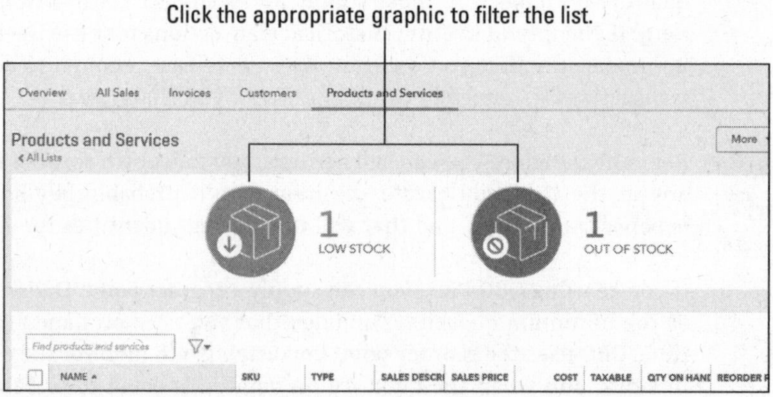

Click the appropriate graphic to filter the list.

FIGURE 4-25:
Use these
graphics to filter
the Products and
Services list to
show only Low
Stock or only Out
of Stock items for
which you have
specified a
reorder point.

Overview   All Sales   Invoices   Customers   **Products and Services**

Products and Services
‹ All Lists   More

1
LOW STOCK

1
OUT OF STOCK

Find products and services   ▽▾

☐   NAME ▲   SKU   TYPE   SALES DESCRI SALES PRICE   COST   TAXABLE   QTY ON HANE REORDER P

QBO defines "low stock" as an item for which you have specified a reorder point and for which you have one or fewer on hand.

To order a low-stock or an out-of-stock item, click the arrow in its Action column and choose Reorder from the drop-down list that appears. QBO creates a purchase order with the item's information filled in. Complete the purchase order and send it to the supplier. Be aware that QBO creates only one purchase order for the items you select. To send purchase orders to multiple vendors, select the items to reorder for a single vendor, click Batch Actions — which appears above the Action column after you select an item — and then choose Reorder. Then, repeat the process for items to reorder from a different vendor.

You can easily cancel the filter for Low Stock or Out of Stock items. Once you select one of these filters, an X appears in the upper right corner of the filter graphic. Click that X, and QBO redisplays the complete Products and Services list.

Working with bundles

If you are using QBO Essentials or QBO Plus, you can create *bundles* to group items that you often sell together. If you were a QuickBooks Desktop user, think of a bundle as a *group item* in the desktop product.

REMEMBER

A bundle is *not* an assembly; QBO doesn't create a bill of materials for a bundle, nor does QBO track a bundle as a separate item with a quantity and separate cost. That means QBO doesn't track quantity on hand for bundles.

If you weren't a QuickBooks Desktop user, think of a bundle as a collection of items — both products and services — that a customer buys from you at the same time. For example, assume you run a landscaping business that sells water features as well as lighting, trimming, and fertilizing services. If a customer buys a water feature, you typically need to sell the customer the water feature itself, concrete to set up the water feature, and a pump to pump the water through the water feature. You can set up the three items needed to create a water feature — the feature, the concrete, and the pump — as a bundle, because you'll need to sell all three at the same time. The idea behind a bundle is to make selling easier by placing all the items in the bundle on a sales form in one step rather than making you separately add each item that makes up the bundle to various sales documents.

TIP

You can use bundles on Estimates, Invoices, Credit Memos, Sales Receipts, Refund Receipts, Delayed Credits, and Delayed Charges. Bundles aren't available for purchasing documents nor can you add a bundle to a price rule (see the section "Using pricing rules" for details on pricing rules).

To create a bundle, follow these steps:

1. **Choose Gear ⇨ Products and Services to display the Products and Services list.**

2. **Click the New button to display the Select a Type panel shown earlier in Figure 4-21.**

3. **Click Bundle.**

   QBO displays the Bundle panel shown in Figure 4-26.

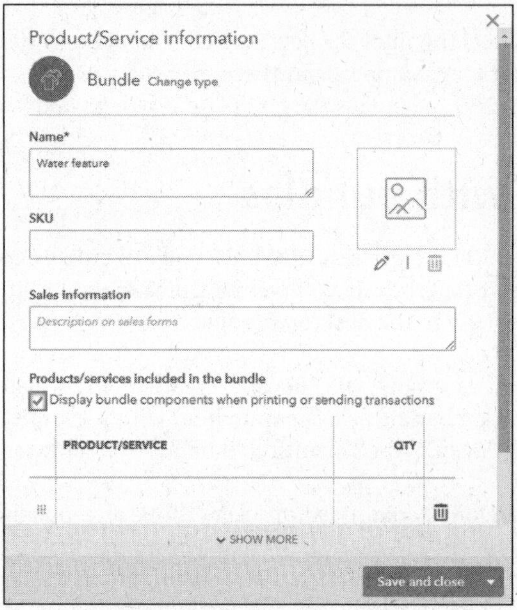

FIGURE 4-26:
The panel where you establish a bundle.

4. **Provide a name, an SKU if appropriate, and a description to appear on sales forms for the bundle.**

5. **In the Products/Services Included in the Bundle section, check the Display Bundle Components When Printing or Sending Transactions check box if you want to list, on sales documents, the components included in the bundle.**

6. **Use the table grid at the bottom of the panel (see Figure 4-27) to identify the products included in the bundle.**

   a. Click Show More to expand the panel so that you can add additional items to the bundle.

   b. Click in the first row of the Product/Service column, and QBO displays a list box you can use to select an item to include in the bundle.

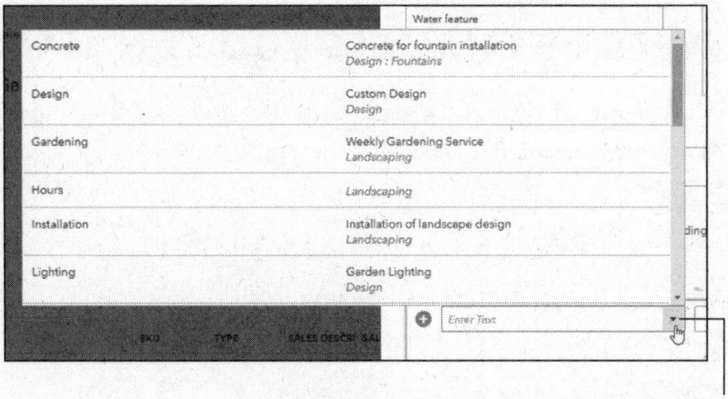

FIGURE 4-27:
Choosing an
item to include
in a bundle.

Click the down arrow to select bundle items.

    c. Supply a quantity for the item.

    d. Repeat Steps b and c for each item you want to include in the bundle.

       A bundle can include up to 50 items. And, you can reorder the items in the bundle by dragging the graphic that appears to the left of each item (the one that looks like nine dots).

    e. When you finish adding items to the bundle, click Save and Close.

REMEMBER

QBO saves the bundle; you'll find it at the bottom of the Products and Services list. To use the bundle, you simply add it to a sales document the same way you add any product or service to a sales document. See Chapter 6 for details on adding products and services to sales documents. And, once you add a bundle to a sales document, you can edit the items included in the bundle, adding or deleting them as needed. The price of a bundle equals the sum of the bundle's components. You can discount a bundle, but you cannot mark up a bundle nor can you track quantity on hand for a bundle; remember, a bundle isn't an assembly.

You can search for bundles the same way you search for any product or service. Use the Search box at the top of the Products and Services list to search by name or SKU.

Changing item types

You can change a service or non-inventory item's type individually, or you can select several items and change their item types simultaneously.

To change any single item's type, edit that item by clicking Edit in the Action column of the Products and Services list; QBO displays the item in the Product/ Service information panel (refer to Figure 4-22). Click the Change Type link at the top of the panel above the item's name.

TYPES OF CHANGES YOU CAN MAKE

Be aware that you can change item types with some limitations. Specifically, you cannot change Inventory items to any other item types. You can make the following types of changes:

- Non-inventory and Service items to Inventory items
- Service items to Non-inventory items
- Non-inventory items to Service items

When changing item types, you change several items at one time only if you are changing Non-inventory items to Service items or Service items to Non-inventory items. If you need to change either a Service item or a Non-inventory item to an Inventory item, you can make the change only one item at a time.

You cannot change a bundle to any other item type because a bundle is a collection of previously defined items. If you make a change to the item type of an item that's included in a bundle, QBO automatically updates the bundle with the new information.

QBO displays a panel very similar to the one shown previously in Figure 4-21; the only differences you'll notice are that Bundle isn't an option, and the current item type contains a check. Click the new item type, and QBO redisplays the Product/Service Information panel using the new item type. Make any other necessary changes and click Save and Close.

Changing the type of a single item using the method just described works well when you only need to change one or two items. But, when you need to change multiple items of the same type to a different type, use a different approach to save time; follow these two steps:

1. **On the Products and Services page, select the check box that appears to the left of each item you want to change.**

   Make sure that you select either Service items or Non-inventory items, but not both. QBO displays two buttons above the table of items (see Figure 4-28).

2. **Click the Batch Actions button and select the new type for the selected items.**

   QBO whirs a bit and then redisplays the Products and Services list, showing the new item types for the items you selected in Step 1.

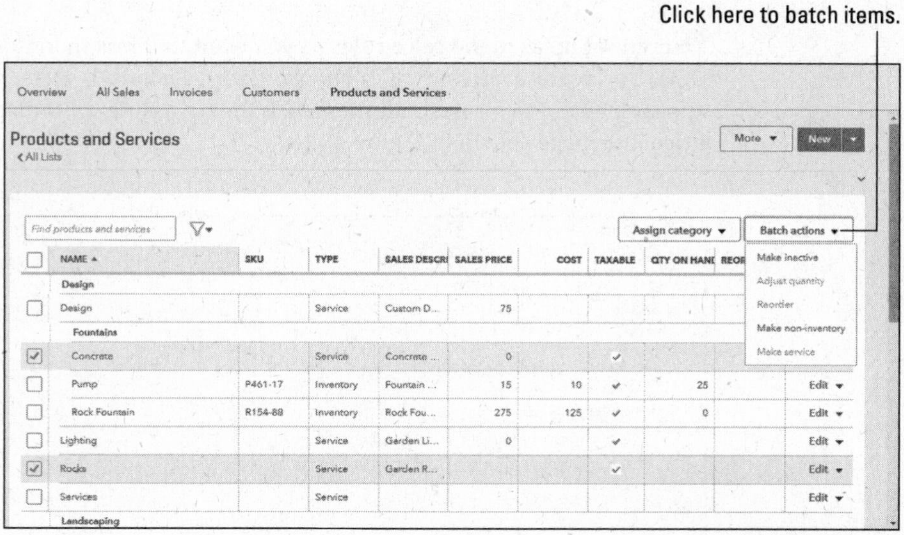

FIGURE 4-28:
Changing
the type of
multiple items
simultaneously.

Overview   All Sales   Invoices   Customers   **Products and Services**

Products and Services
‹ All Lists

More ▼   New ▼

	NAME ▲	SKU	TYPE	SALES DESCRI	SALES PRICE	COST	TAXABLE	QTY ON HAND	REOR	
☐	Design									
☐	Design		Service	Custom D...	75					
	Fountains									
☑	Concrete		Service	Concrete ...	0		✓			
☐	Pump	P461-17	Inventory	Fountain ...	15	10	✓	25		Edit ▼
☐	Rock Fountain	R154-88	Inventory	Rock Fou...	275	125	✓	0		Edit ▼
☐	Lighting		Service	Garden Li...	0		✓			Edit ▼
☑	Rocks		Service	Garden R...			✓			Edit ▼
☐	Services		Service							Edit ▼
	Landscaping									

Assign category ▼   Batch actions ▼

Make inactive
Adjust quantity
Reorder
Make non-inventory
Make service

TIP

Note the Assign Category button at the top of the Products and Services list; this button appears when you select multiple items, and you can use it to simultaneously assign the same category to multiple items.

Using pricing rules

Using pricing rules, currently a feature in beta testing but available in your QBO company if you enable it, you can control product prices. For example, you can

» Offer discounts on specific products.

» Increase the price of specified products.

» Offer special pricing to all or some customers.

» Make special pricing available for a specified period of time.

For former QuickBooks Desktop users, pricing rules are similar to price levels; particularly, QBO doesn't record a price change as a discount but rather as an override of the sale price.

REMEMBER

You can't add a bundle to a price rule, but you can work around this issue if you add items included in a bundle to a price rule. Then, when you subsequently add the bundle to a sales document, the bundle will reflect the price rule pricing.

To use pricing rules, turn the feature on by choosing Gear ⇨ Account and Features ⇨ Sales and editing the Products and Services section to turn on price rules.

You can set up as many price rules as you want, but less than 10,000 works best in QBO. To create a pricing rule, choose Gear➪Lists➪All Lists. On the page that appears, click Price rules and then click Create a Rule. QBO displays the Create a Price Rule page shown in Figure 4-29.

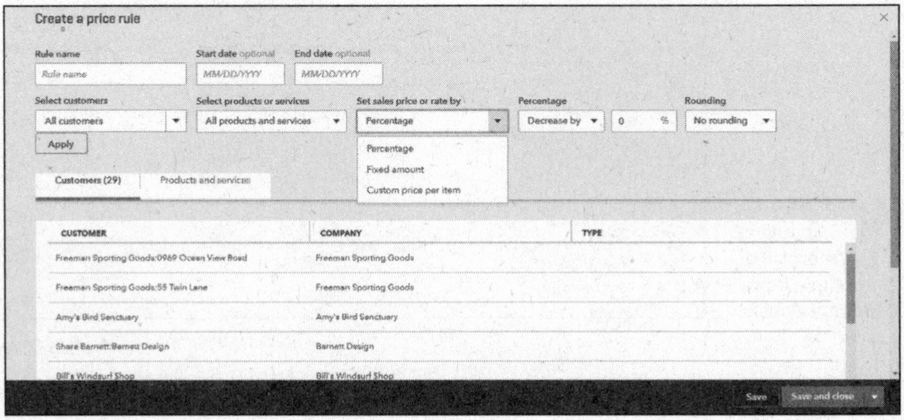

FIGURE 4-29:
Use this page
to create a
pricing rule.

On this page, supply a name for the rule, the start and end dates for the rule, the customers who qualify, and the products or services to which QBO should apply the rule.

Specify how to adjust the price: using a percentage, a fixed amount, or a custom price. Indicate whether the rule is a price increase or decrease and how you want QBO to handle rounding. When you finish, click Save or Save and Close. When you create a sales transaction, QBO automatically applies any appropriate price rule to the transactions.

Adjusting inventory item information

On occasion, you might need to make adjustments to inventory item information. Specifically, you might need to adjust inventory item quantities on hand or starting values.

You can edit any item to change descriptive information, such as its name or description; just click the Edit link in the Action column beside its name on the Products and Services page to view the item's information in the panel shown previously in Figures 4-22, 4-23, and 4-24. In this section, I'm talking about adjusting inventory item information, which encompasses more than editing descriptive information.

Adjusting inventory quantities

You might discover, particularly after physically counting inventory, that you have a different number on hand of an inventory item than reported in QBO. In this case, you need to adjust the quantity in QBO to match what you actually have in stock.

REMEMBER

Use the Physical Inventory Worksheet report in QBO to record item quantities on hand as you count inventory. The report information can help you determine the adjustments you need to make. See Chapter 10 for details on working with QBO reports.

To create an adjustment for a just a few inventory items, follow these steps:

1. **Click the Create menu (+ at the top of the QBO window) and choose Inventory Qty Adjustment (see Figure 4-30).**

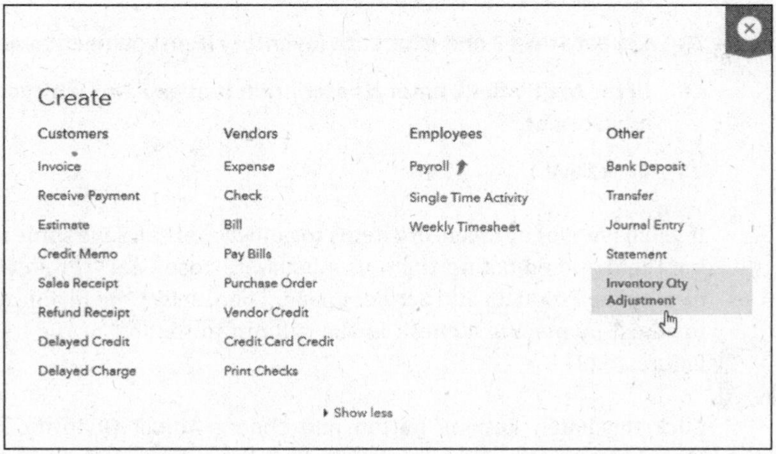

FIGURE 4-30:
Starting an inventory item adjustment for a single inventory item.

QBO displays the Inventory Quantity Adjustment window (see Figure 4-31).

FIGURE 4-31:
You can use this window when you have just a few adjustments to make.

2. **If necessary, change the adjustment date and the Inventory Adjustment Account.**

3. **In the table, click the Product field, click the drop-down arrow that appears, and select an inventory item.**

    QBO fills the inventory item's SKU if available, description, and quantity on hand. QBO also suggests the Qty on Hand value for the New Qty value.

    If you've enabled class and location tracking, you can supply information for those fields as you complete the Inventory Quantity Adjustment window.

REMEMBER

4. **Enter either a new quantity or a change in quantity.**

    Suppose that the Qty on Hand field indicates you own 25 of your item and you need to reduce the quantity you own by 5. You do either of the following:

    a. Enter 20 in the New Qty field, or

    b. Enter -5 in the Change in Qty field.

5. **Repeat Steps 3 and 4 for each inventory item you need to adjust.**

6. **In the Memo field, enter a description that explains why you made this adjustment.**

7. **Click Save.**

If you have a lot of inventory items to adjust, you can save some time by preselecting them and adjusting them as a batch. Choose Gear ⇨ Products and Services to display the Products and Services page. Then, select the inventory items you want to adjust by placing a check in the column to the left of the item name (refer to Figure 4-28).

Click the Batch Actions button and choose Adjust Quantity. QBO displays the Inventory Quantity Adjustment window shown previously in Figure 4-31, but pre-fills the window with the information about the inventory items you selected. Complete Steps 4, 6, and 7 for each item in the window.

Editing an inventory quantity adjustment

If you need to edit an inventory quantity adjustment you previously saved (hey . . . it happens), follow these steps:

1. **Click the Create menu plus sign (+) ⇨ Inventory Qty Adjustment to display the Inventory Quantity Adjustment window.**

2. **In the upper left corner of the window, click the Recent Transactions button (see Figure 4-32).**

    QBO displays recent inventory adjustment transactions.

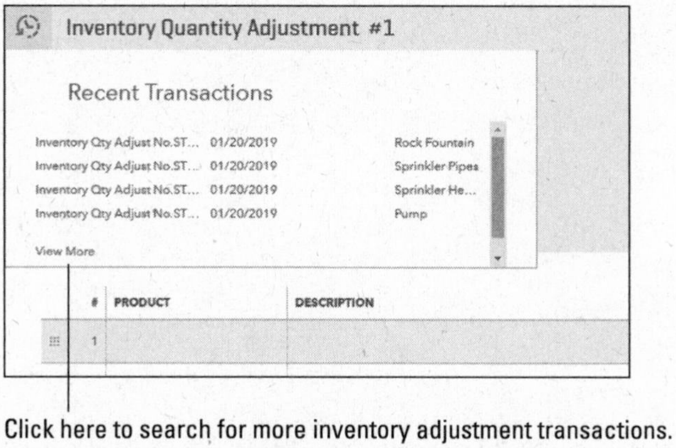

Inventory Quantity Adjustment #1

Recent Transactions

Inventory Qty Adjust No.ST...	01/20/2019		Rock Fountain
Inventory Qty Adjust No.ST...	01/20/2019		Sprinkler Pipes
Inventory Qty Adjust No.ST...	01/20/2019		Sprinkler He...
Inventory Qty Adjust No.ST...	01/20/2019		Pump

View More

	#	PRODUCT	DESCRIPTION
	1		

FIGURE 4-32: Searching for a recent inventory adjustment transaction to edit.

Click here to search for more inventory adjustment transactions.

3. **If the adjustment appears in the list, click it.**

   If the adjustment doesn't appear, click View More to display the Search page, where you can expand your search for the transaction. In most cases, changing the date range will do the trick.

4. **Make the necessary changes.**

   You can remove a line from an adjustment by clicking its Delete button at the right edge of the row.

5. **Click Save and Close in the lower right corner of the window.**

Adjusting an inventory item's starting value

Suppose that you made a mistake when you set up the starting value for an inventory item; you can edit the item's starting value as long as you created the inventory item after the November 2015 QBO release.

> **WARNING**
>
> Changing an item's starting value can have wide-ranging effects, and QBO will display a warning to this effect when you begin an inventory item starting value adjustment. If you're not sure about what you're doing, ask your accountant. Please. She won't mind.

To adjust an inventory item's starting value, follow these steps:

1. **Choose Gear ➪ Products and Services.**

2. **In the Action column beside the inventory item you want to adjust, click the black drop-down arrow and select Adjust Starting Value (see Figure 4-33).**

   QBO displays a warning explaining that changing an inventory item's starting value may affect the initial value of your inventory.

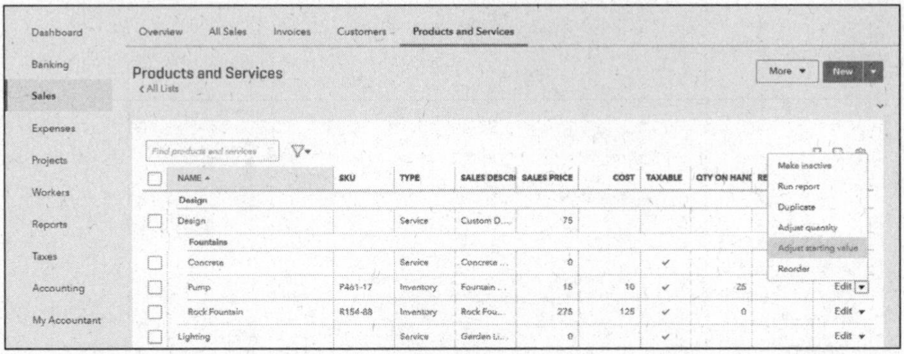

FIGURE 4-33:
Getting ready
to adjust
the starting
value of an
inventory item.

3. **Assuming you've heeded the preceding warning and know what you're doing, click Got it!**

   QBO displays the Inventory Starting Value window (see Figure 4-34).

FIGURE 4-34:
Use this window
to adjust an
inventory item's
starting values.

> **TIP**
>
> If you've enabled class and location tracking, note that you can supply information for those fields along with other fields that affect the inventory item's starting value.

4. **Make the necessary changes.**

> **REMEMBER**
>
> You can't change an item's inventory asset account from the Inventory Starting Value window. To change the item's inventory asset account, display the Products and Services page and click the Edit link for the item to display the item's information in the Inventory Item Product/Services Information panel shown previously in Figure 4-24.

5. **Click Save and Close in the lower right corner of the window.**

A Look at Other Lists

Just as QuickBooks Desktop has other lists besides lists of people and items, QBO also has other lists. To find them, click the Gear icon on the toolbar at the top of the page and, from the menu that appears, click All Lists in the second column from the left. QBO displays the Lists page shown in Figure 4-35.

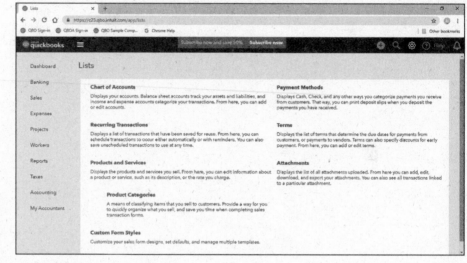

FIGURE 4-35: The Lists page contains links to all available lists in QBO.

Click any list name to open that list and work with it. You can add new entries, select and edit existing entries, and select and delete entries that have never been used. The steps to create any new list element are pretty much the same as the steps discussed in this chapter to create people, items, and product categories.

Chapter 5

Dealing with the Outflow of Money

t's always more fun to make money than to spend it, but paying bills is part of life — unless you're living in *Star Wars: The Last Jedi*, where they have no bills — but, I digress. This chapter explores the transactions you use in QBO to meet your financial obligations.

GETTING UP AND RUNNING

If you start using QBO after you've been in business for a while and have some outstanding bills you haven't yet paid, you can use those bills as a learning tool and enter them as described in this chapter. If you recorded an opening bank account balance back in Chapter 3, be sure to enter into QBO the checks you've written that haven't yet cleared your bank. If you didn't record an opening bank account balance back in Chapter 3, or you recorded a bank account balance as of December 31 of last year, be sure to enter into QBO all the checks you've written this year, even if they have cleared the bank. If you connect your bank account to your financial institution as described in Chapter 8, use the techniques described for the transactions in this chapter to review each transaction to make sure it is properly assigned in QBO.

To record most expense-related transactions, you can choose Expenses from the Navigation bar to display the Expense Transactions page shown in Figure 5-1. Click the New Transaction button to select a transaction type.

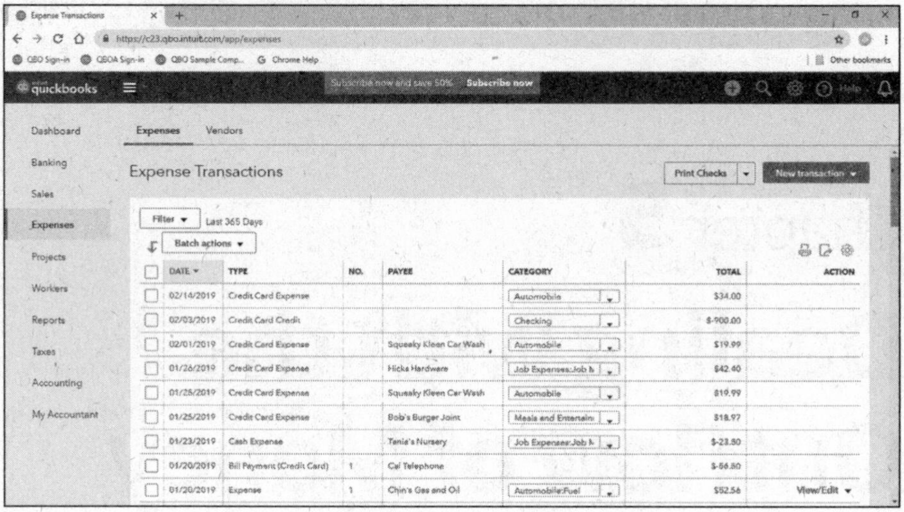

FIGURE 5-1:
The Expense
Transactions
page.

If the transaction type you want to record isn't available, click the Create plus sign (+) icon at the top of QBO and choose the type of transaction you want to record from the Create menu that appears; the Create icon changes to an X when you open the menu, and expense-related transactions show up in the Vendors column (see Figure 5-2).

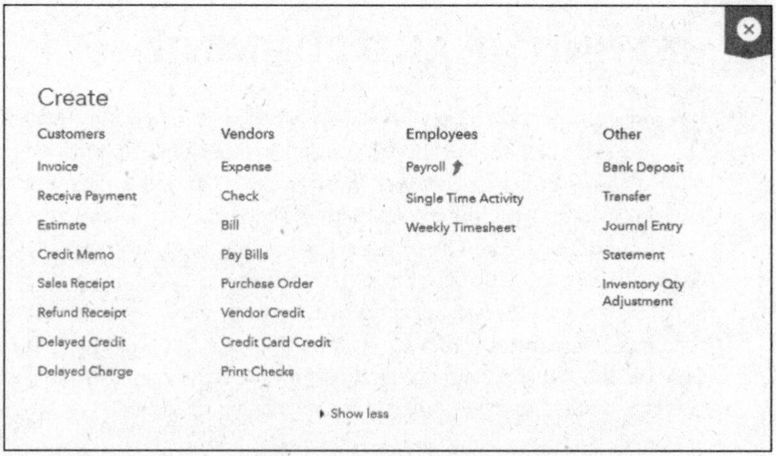

FIGURE 5-2:
Expense
transactions
appear in
the Vendors
column of the
Create menu.

Writing a Check

Typically, you enter a Check transaction when you intend to print a check to pay for an expense. Suppose that the UPS guy has just made a delivery for which you owe money and you want to give him a check: Use the Check transaction. You can print the check immediately or at a later time.

Assigning a check to accounts or items

When you write a check, you need to assign the expense for which you're writing the check to either an account or an item, and you can assign one check to both accounts and items. Follow these steps to enter and print a check:

1. **On the Expense Transactions page, click the New Transaction button.**

2. **From the list that appears, click Check.**

   QBO displays the Check window, which is divided into four sections:

   - **The Header section:** Shown in Figure 5-3, this section displays the balance in the selected checking account, the selected payee and the payee's mailing address, the payment date, the check amount and number, and the option to print the check later. If you opt to print the check later, the check number changes to "To Print" (refer to Figure 5-3).

   - **The Category Details section:** Shown in Figures 5-3 and 5-4, you use this table when the expense is not related to an item you've defined.

   - **The Item Details section:** You use this table when you're writing a check to pay for a product or service you purchased. If you don't see this table, its preference isn't enabled. To display the table, choose Account and Settings ⇨ Expenses ⇨ Bills and Expenses and edit the Show Items Table on Expense and Purchase Forms option.

REMEMBER

   You typically write a check using *either* the Category Details section or the Item Details section, but not both. However, you can use both sections. If you won't be using a section, you can hide it by clicking the downward-pointing arrow beside the section name.

   - **The Footer section:** Not named onscreen, the Footer section contains the check total, the Memo box, and the box you use to attach an electronic document to the check.

3. **Choose a payee and an account from which to make the payment.**

   Along with the payee's address information, QBO displays information from previously entered transactions unless you haven't entered any transactions for that payee yet, or you have disabled the setting to display previously entered transaction information in Account and Settings.

![Check window header]

Check #75   ⑦ Help

| Payee | Bank Account | | AMOUNT |
| Hicks Hardware ▾ | Checking ▾   Balance $1,201.00 | | **$228.75** |

1 linked transaction

Mailing address	Payment date		Check no.
Geoff Hicks Hicks Hardware 42 Main St, Middlefield, CA 94303	01/20/2019		75
			☐ Print later

▾ Category details

#	CATEGORY	DESCRIPTION	AMOUNT	BILLABLE	TAX	CUSTOMER	
⠿ 1		What did you pay for?					🗑
⠿ 2							🗑

Add lines   Clear all lines

FIGURE 5-3:
The Header
section of the
Check window.

TIP

If a pane appears on the right side, it displays transactions you might want to link to the check you're writing — and, if that's the case, see the next section, "Writing a check for an outstanding bill." On the other hand, if the check you're writing has nothing to do with any transaction that appears in the pane, just ignore the pane; you can hide it as described in the next section.

4. **Double-check the payment Date and Check Number, and make an appropriate selection in the Print Later check box.**

5. **Assign part or all of the check to an expense account or an item using the Category Details section or the Item Details section (see Figure 5-4).**
   To assign a portion to an expense account

   a. Click in the Category column and select an appropriate expense account for the check you are recording. You can type characters that appear in the account name and QBO will help you find the account.

   b. In the Description column, describe the expense you're paying.

   c. In the Amount column, supply the amount of the check that you want to apply to the selected account.

![Check window Category and Item details]

Check #75   ⑦ Help

▾ Category details

#	CATEGORY	DESCRIPTION	AMOUNT	BILLABLE	TAX	CUSTOMER	
⠿ 1		What did you pay for?					🗑
⠿ 2							🗑

Add lines   Clear all lines

▾ Item details

#	PRODUCT/SERVICE	DESCRIPTION	QTY	RATE	AMOUNT	BILLABLE	TAX	CUSTOMER		
⠿ 1	Design:Fountains:Rock Founta	Rock Fountain	1	125	125.00				🔗	🗑
⠿ 2	Landscaping:Sprinklers:Sprink	Sprinkler Heads	15	0.75	11.25				🔗	🗑
⠿ 3	Landscaping:Sprinklers:Sprink	Sprinkler Pipes	25	2.50	62.50				🔗	🗑
⠿ 4	Design:Fountains:Pump	Fountain Pump	3	10	30.00				🔗	🗑

FIGURE 5-4:
The Category
Details and Item
Details sections
of the Check
window.

d. If you incurred the expense on behalf of a customer and you want to bill the customer for the expense, check the Billable box — and, if appropriate, the Tax box — and select the customer's name in the Customer column.

e. Repeat Steps a to d to add more lines to the check.

6. **To assign part or all of the check to items or services you have defined, use the Item Details section (refer to Figure 5-4):**

a. Click in the Product/Service column and select an appropriate item for the check you are recording.

You can type characters in the Product/Service column and QBO will help you find the item.

b. Optionally, edit the Description column for the selected item.

c. Use the Qty, Rate, and Amount columns to supply the quantity of the selected item you are purchasing, the rate you're paying for each item, and the amount you're paying. When you supply any two of the Qty, Rate, and Amount values, QuickBooks calculates the third value.

d. If you purchased the item on behalf of a customer and you want to bill the customer for the item, check the Billable box — and, if appropriate, the Tax box — and select the customer's name in the Customer column.

e. Repeat Steps a to d to add more items to the check.

7. **You can scroll down in the Check window to the Footer section to view the check's total, type a message to the payee, and attach an electronic document (such as the payee's invoice) to the check.**

TIP

To attach an electronic document to the check, click in the Attachments box; a standard Open dialog box appears that you can use to navigate to the document. Alternatively, you can drag and drop the electronic copy into the Attachments box.

8. **At the bottom of the window, you can**

- **Cancel your action or clear the window and start again.**

- **Click Print Check to print the check.**

  The first time you print checks, QBO walks you through the process of selecting the type of checks to use and aligning them for your printer.

- **Click Order Checks to visit the Intuit Marketplace and order check stock.**

- **Click Make Recurring to set up the check as a recurring payment you intend to make on a schedule you specify.**

  See the section "About recurring transactions" later in this chapter for details on recurring transactions.

- **Click More to see additional actions, such as voiding the check or viewing its audit history.**

- **Click Save and New to save the check and redisplay the Check window so that you can write another check.**

REMEMBER

The Save and New button is a sticky preference. That means, if you click the drop-down arrow to the right of the button and select Save and Close, the next time you open the window to write a check, the default button will be the Save and Close button.

Writing a check for an outstanding bill

You can use the Check window to write a check to pay a bill you previously entered — something that you cannot do in the QuickBooks Desktop product. Note that you shouldn't use the Check transaction if you're planning on paying several bills. Instead, see the section "Paying bills" at the end of this chapter.

If you select a payee for whom an outstanding bill exists, QBO displays a pane at the right side of the Check window (see Figure 5-5) that shows all transactions linked to the selected payee; each transaction appears as a separate entry. If nothing in the pane applies to your transaction, you can hide the pane by clicking the button shown in Figure 5-5.

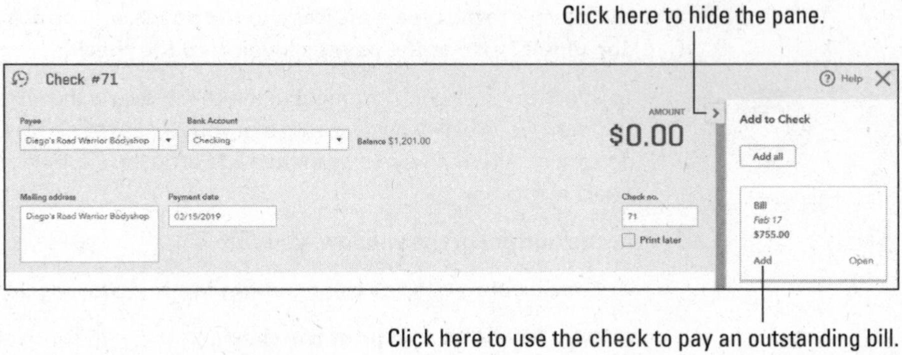

Click here to hide the pane.

FIGURE 5-5:
If you select a payee for whom you previously entered a bill, the outstanding bill appears in the pane on the right side of the Check window.

Check #71
Payee: Diego's Road Warrior Bodyshop
Bank Account: Checking   Balance $1,201.00
AMOUNT $0.00
Add to Check
Add all
Mailing address: Diego's Road Warrior Bodyshop
Payment date: 02/15/2019
Check no. 71
Print later
Bill
Feb 17
$755.00
Add   Open

Click here to use the check to pay an outstanding bill.

If you're writing the check to pay a bill that appears in the pane, click Add in the Bill transaction you want to pay. That way, QBO appropriately applies the check you're writing to the outstanding bill and correctly reduces your outstanding obligations.

WARNING

If you write a check to pay a bill and you *don't* apply the check to the bill, your reports show that you continue to owe the bill amount to the payee, which really messes things up.

When you click Add, QBO adds that bill to the check and switches to the Bill Payment window, essentially converting the check to a bill payment transaction. In Figure 5-6, you see the Bill Payment window after I added an outstanding bill to a check in the Check window. If you compare Figures 5-5 and 5-6, you'll notice that the original check number was 71, and it's still 71 in the Bill Payment window.

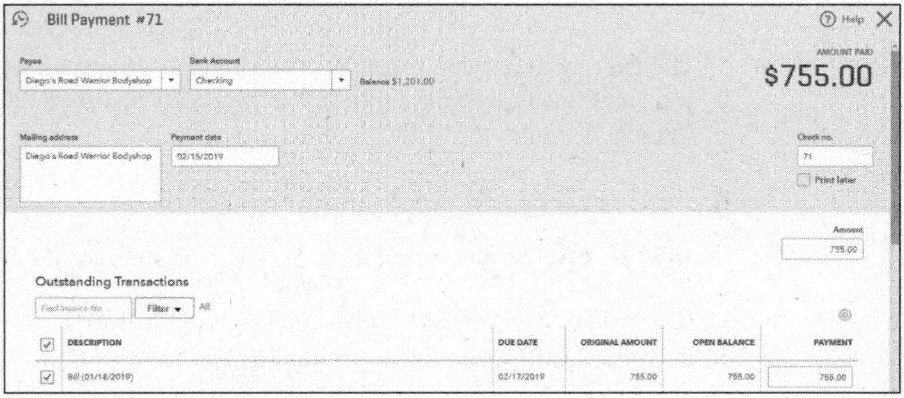

FIGURE 5-6:
The Bill Payment window.

	Bill Payment #71					⑦ Help ✕
	Payee	Bank Account				AMOUNT PAID
	Diego's Road Warrior Bodyshop ▾	Checking ▾	Balance $1,201.00			**$755.00**
	Mailing address	Payment date				Check no.
	Diego's Road Warrior Bodyshop	02/15/2019				71
						☐ Print later
						Amount
						755.00

Outstanding Transactions

Find Invoice No. | Filter ▾ | All

	DESCRIPTION	DUE DATE	ORIGINAL AMOUNT	OPEN BALANCE	PAYMENT
☑	Bill (01/18/2019)	02/17/2019	755.00	755.00	755.00

You complete the Bill Payment transaction the same way you complete a Check transaction; follow Steps 7 and 8 in the preceding section. If you add the wrong bill to a check, you can cancel the Bill Payment transaction without saving it.

Creating an Expense

You use an Expense transaction when you're trying to record an expense-related transaction without printing a check. For example, you record an Expense transaction to account for a payment you make using a credit or debit card. And, you use an Expense transaction if you have manually written a check that you now need to record in QBO without printing it.

The major difference between the Expense transaction window and the Check transaction window is the lack of any tools to help you print an Expense transaction; compare Figures 5-4 and 5-7.

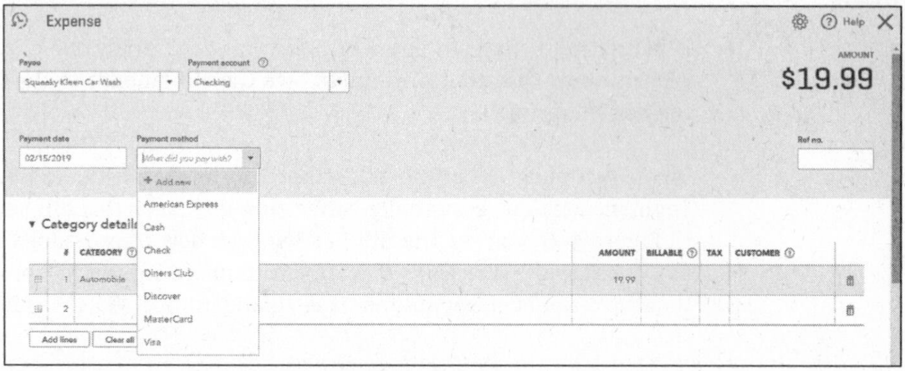

FIGURE 5-7:
You can use the
Expense
transaction
window to
record making a
payment without
writing a check.

The Expense transaction window also contains a Payment Method list box that you don't find in the Check transaction window. Other than those two differences, the windows appear and function the same way.

QBO AND CREDIT CARD TRANSACTIONS

By default, QBO treats credit card transactions as cash transactions, a conservative approach that recognizes expenses as they occur. To account for credit card transactions, set up your credit card company as a vendor and, in your Chart of Accounts, set up a Credit Card account for the credit card. Then, use Expense transactions to record credit card purchases for the credit card vendor. In the header section, select the credit card vendor and credit card account. On the detail lines, assign each credit card transaction to the appropriate account or item for that purchase; that is, if you use your credit card to buy office supplies, select your Office Supplies account in the Category Details section for that purchase. If you need to record a credit card return, use the Credit Card Credit transaction. If you want to download credit card transaction information into QBO, see Chapter 8.

When the credit card bill arrives, you can pay it in a number of ways:

- To pay by check, use the Check transaction, select your credit card company as the vendor, and, in the Category Details section, select your credit card account.

- To pay by transfer (where you transfer money electronically or manually from a bank account to your credit card account, which reduces both accounts), use the Transfer transaction, selecting the bank account you'll use to pay the bill as the Transfer Funds From account and the credit card company/vendor you're paying as the Transfer Funds To account.

- To pay the bill while reconciling the credit card account, follow the steps in Chapter 8 to reconcile the account. When you click Finish, you'll be given the option to write a check to pay the amount due, enter a bill to pay the bill later, or do nothing about paying the bill now (and later, on your own, enter a check or a bill for the amount due).

If you want to recognize credit card expenses when you pay your credit card bill (rather than when you make a purchase using your credit card), *do* set up a vendor for your credit card company, but *don't* set up a credit card account in the Chart of Accounts, and don't enter Expense transactions or Credit Card Credit transactions in QBO for credit card transactions as they occur. Instead, when you receive your credit card statement, enter a Bill transaction for the credit card vendor, as described later in this chapter, and allocate each line on the credit card statement to the appropriate account or item on the bill; record credit card refunds as negative lines on the Bill transaction. QBO then treats your credit card account as an Accounts Payable vendor. And when you're ready to pay the credit card bill, you can write a check, transfer funds, or use the Pay Bills page to pay the credit card statement. Remember, this is the less conservative approach to tracking credit card expenses; if you are a heavy user of your credit card, do yourself a favor and use the first approach so that you can effectively manage your credit card spending.

Entering a Purchase Order

Businesses that order lots of stuff from vendors often use purchase orders to keep track of the items on order. The QBO purchase order feature is available only in QBO Plus and Advanced as a feature you turn on. It is not available in QBO Essentials or QBO Simple Start.

Purchase orders in QBO do not affect any of your accounts; instead, they simply help you keep track of what you order. And, when the order arrives, you can compare the goods that come in the door with the ones listed on the purchase order to make sure they match.

If you plan to use purchase orders, then your ordering process typically happens in the following way:

» You place an order with a vendor and you enter a purchase order in QBO that matches the order you placed.

>> You receive the items you ordered, typically along with a bill for the items; you then match the items you receive to the purchase order and enter a bill for the items. Note that sometimes you receive the bill without the items or the items without the bill.

>> You pay the vendor's bill.

Turning on the purchase order feature

To use purchase orders in QBO, make sure you turn on the feature. Choose Gear ⇨ Account and Settings. Then, click Expenses on the left side of the Account and Settings dialog box that appears, and turn on the "Use Purchase Orders" option. You also can customize the email message QBO sends to your vendors with purchase orders, as shown in Figure 5-8.

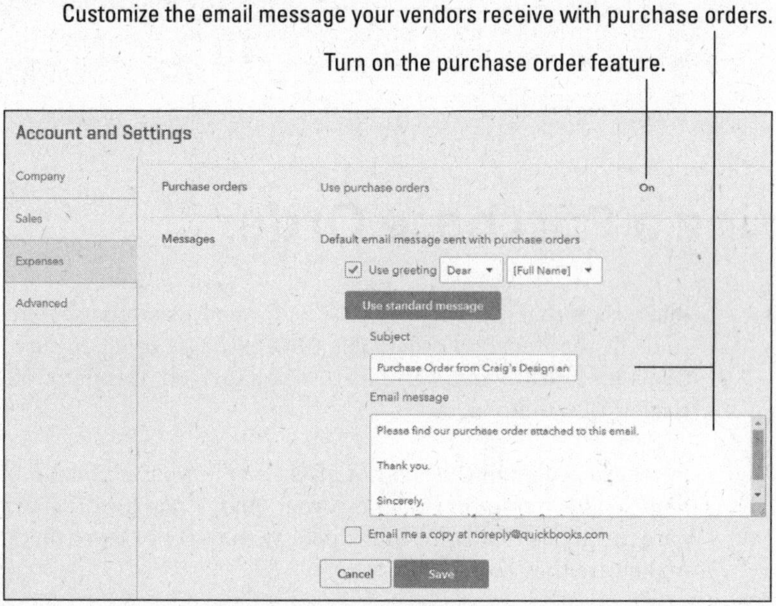

Customize the email message your vendors receive with purchase orders.

Turn on the purchase order feature.

Account and Settings

Company			
Sales	Purchase orders	Use purchase orders	On
Expenses	Messages	Default email message sent with purchase orders	
Advanced		☑ Use greeting Dear ▾ [Full Name] ▾	

Use standard message

Subject

Purchase Order from Craig's Design an

Email message

Please find our purchase order attached to this email.

Thank you.

Sincerely,

☐ Email me a copy at noreply@quickbooks.com

Cancel   Save

FIGURE 5-8: Turn on the Purchase Orders feature and set up a customized message for QBO to include with purchase orders to your vendors.

TIP

You can use your own custom purchase order numbers if you choose Gear ⇨ Account and Settings ⇨ Expenses. Then click in the Purchase Orders section to edit purchase order settings, select the Custom Transaction Numbers check box, and then click Save. You also can convert Estimate transactions to Purchase Order transactions; see Chapter 6 for details.

Creating a purchase order

You enter a purchase order using the Purchase Order transaction window; you can open this window from the Expense Transactions page, the Create menu (the plus sign), or from the Projects Center (for details on projects, see Chapter 6). The header area of a typical purchase order looks like the one shown in Figure 5-9.

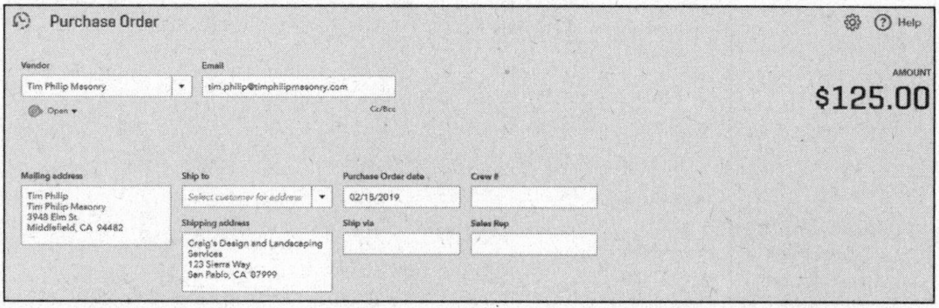

FIGURE 5-9: The header area of the Purchase Order window.

As you fill in the Purchase Order transaction window, QBO assigns a status of Open to the purchase order; the status appears just below the vendor's name in the upper left corner of the transaction window.

When you receive the goods, the vendor's bill, or both, you record a bill as described in the next section, or a check, an expense transaction, or a credit card charge as described earlier in this chapter, showing what you paid (or what you owe) the vendor.

When you select a vendor who has open purchase orders on any of these types of transactions, a pane appears on the right side of the window, showing available purchase orders. You add a purchase order to the transaction the same way you add a bill to a Check transaction: by clicking the Add button in the pane. In Figure 5-10, I've opened a Check transaction and selected a vendor who has open purchase orders.

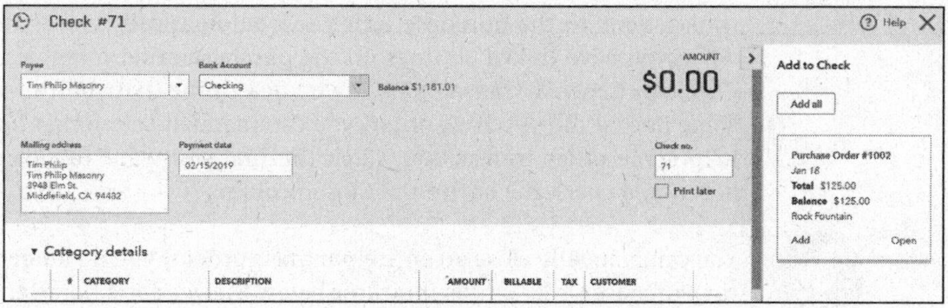

FIGURE 5-10: The Check window, with a vendor selected who has open purchase orders.

When I click Add to add the purchase order to my transaction, QBO adds the purchase order lines to the first available line in the Item Details section of my Check transaction. QBO also indicates, immediately below the vendor name, that the Check transaction has one linked transaction (see Figure 5-11).

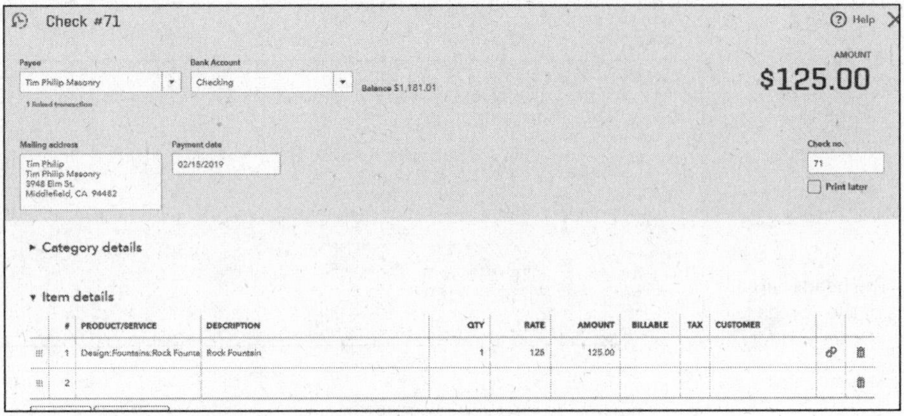

FIGURE 5-11:
A Check transaction after adding a purchase order to it.

If you save the Check transaction and then reopen the purchase order, you find that QBO has changed the purchase order's status from open to closed so that you don't accidentally add the purchase order to another transaction.

TIP

If you add the wrong purchase order to a transaction, you can remove the purchase order line in the Item Details section by clicking the trash can icon at the right edge of the line.

Working with partial purchase orders

Suppose that you receive only part of an order or that you want to pay for only part of an order. No problem. You can add part of a purchase order to a Bill, Check, or Expense transaction and later add more to another bill, check, or expense — and continue in this way until you use the entire purchase order. QBO links multiple transactions to the purchase order and automatically closes the purchase order when you have linked all lines on the purchase order to any combination of Bill, Check, or Expense transactions. If you determine that you're not going to receive some line on the purchase order, you can manually close that line without linking it to some other transaction. Click the line you want to close on the purchase order, and check the box in the Closed column.

TIP

You can manually close an entire purchase order if you no longer need it; just click the Purchase Order status indicator below the vendor's name and change the status from Open to Closed (refer to Figure 5-9 to see the indicator).

Suppose that you've got a purchase order similar to the one shown in Figure 5-12 and that you receive two lines on the purchase order but you're still waiting for the other two lines. You can create a transaction to pay only for those items you have received and leave the rest open on the purchase order. Follow these steps:

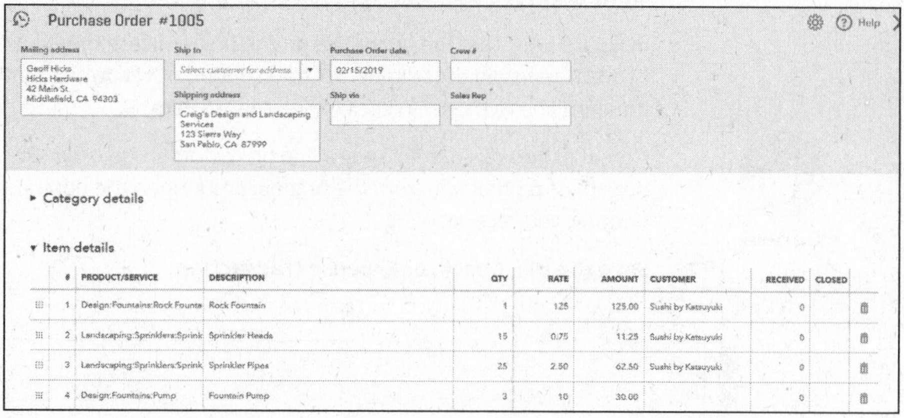

FIGURE 5-12:
A purchase order with multiple lines.

1. **Open the Create menu (the plus sign) and choose Bill, Check, or Expense, depending on the type of transaction you want to use.**

   For this example, I'll use a check.

2. **Select the vendor.**

   Available purchase orders for the selected vendor appear in the panel on the right-hand side of the screen, where you can see some of the lines on the purchase order as well as its original and current amounts (see Figure 5-13).

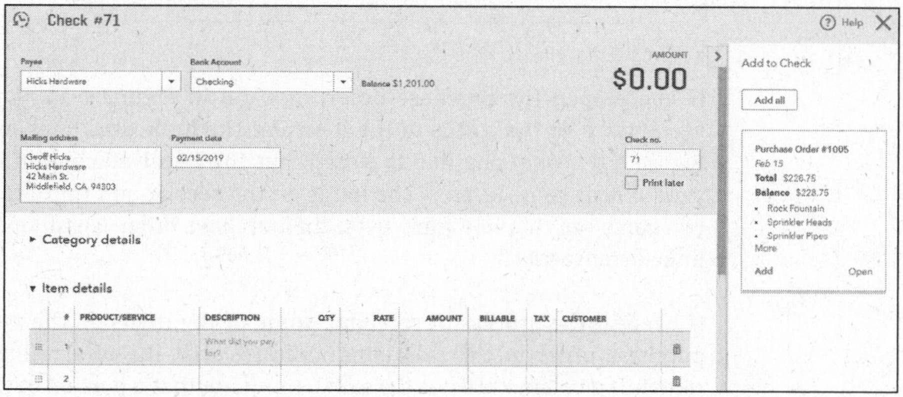

FIGURE 5-13:
A check showing an available purchase order with multiple lines for the selected vendor.

3. **Click Add on the purchase order in the panel.**

   QBO adds all the lines on the purchase order to the Item Details or Category Details section starting at the first available line in the appropriate section.

4. **Edit the quantity or amount for each line to reflect the portion that you want to record as partially received or paid.**

   In Figure 5-14, I set the quantities on the first and last lines to zero to indicate I haven't received those items yet and so am not yet paying for them. I also set the third line to partially receive the ordered item.

   REMEMBER

   Note that you can partially pay a line on the purchase order by changing the quantities on that line from the original amount on the purchase order to the number you receive.

5. **Save the Bill, Check, or Expense transaction.**

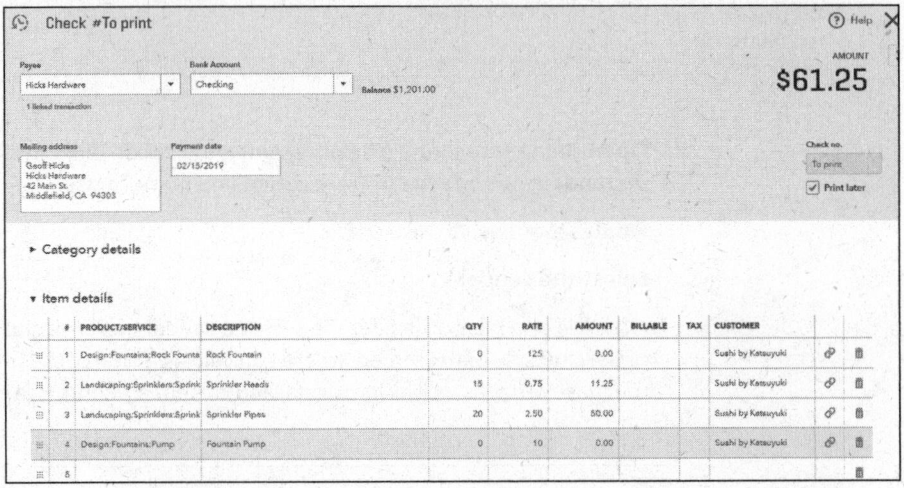

FIGURE 5-14:
Receiving and paying for part of a purchase order.

If you reopen the purchase order, as I did in Figure 5-15, you'll see that QBO keeps track of the status of the items on the individual lines of the purchase. In Figure 5-15, only one line is closed, but the Received column indicates that the vendor sent some or all of the items on the second and third lines. And, although you can't see this in Figure 5-15, the purchase order is still open and shows one linked transaction.

If I repeat the process of receiving some of the items on the purchase order, the purchase order in the side pane indicates that the total value and the current remaining balance are not the same, implying that a portion of the purchase order has been received. And, after I identify additional received items and save the Bill, Check, or Expense transaction, the original purchase shows two linked transactions and, if appropriate, additional closed lines on the purchase order.

FIGURE 5-15:
Reviewing a purchase order after receiving some of the items on it.

Purchase Order #1005 ⚙ ? Help ✕

Mailing address
Geoff Hicks
Hicks Hardware
42 Main St.
Middlefield, CA 94303

Ship to
Select customer for address...

Shipping address
Craig's Design and Landscaping Services
123 Sierra Way,
San Pablo, CA 87999

Purchase Order date
02/15/2019

Crew #

Ship via

Sales Rep

▶ Category details

▼ Item details

#	PRODUCT/SERVICE	DESCRIPTION	QTY	RATE	AMOUNT	CUSTOMER	RECEIVED	CLOSED	
1	Design:Fountains:Rock Founta	Rock Fountain	1	125	125.00	Sushi by Katsuyuki	0		🗑
2	Landscaping:Sprinklers:Sprink	Sprinkler Heads	15	0.75	11.25	Sushi by Katsuyuki	15	✓	🗑
3	Landscaping:Sprinklers:Sprink	Sprinkler Pipes	25	2.50	62.50	Sushi by Katsuyuki	20		🗑
4	Design:Fountains:Pump	Fountain Pump	3	10	30.00		0		🗑

This line is closed.

TIP

Clicking on "linked transactions" under the purchase order's status in the upper left corner of the window displays the linked transaction types, dates, and amounts; you can click any linked transaction to display it.

Wondering how to easily determine how much of a particular purchase order you have received or paid and how much is still outstanding? Use the Open Purchase Orders Detail report shown in Figure 5-16.

FIGURE 5-16:
The Open Purchase Orders Detail report.

OPEN PURCHASE ORDERS DETAIL
February 1-15, 2019

DATE	NUM	VENDOR	PRODUCT/SERVICE	ACCOUNT	QTY	RECEIVED QTY	BACKORDERED QTY	TOTAL AMT	RECEIVED AMT	OPEN BALANCE
▼ Design										
▼ Fountains										
▼ Pump										
02/15/2019	1005	Hicks Hardware	Design:Fountains:Pump	Inventory Asset	3.00	0.00	3.00	30.00	0.00	30.00
Total for Pump					3.00	0.00	3.00	$30.00	$0.00	$30.00
▼ Rock Fountain										
02/15/2019	1005	Hicks Hardware	Design:Fountains:Rock Foun...	Inventory Asset	1.00	0.00	1.00	125.00	0.00	125.00
Total for Rock Fountain					1.00	0.00	1.00	$125.00	$0.00	$125.00
Total for Fountains					4.00	0.00	4.00	$155.00	$0.00	$155.00
Total for Design					4.00	0.00	4.00	$155.00	$0.00	$155.00
▼ Landscaping										
▼ Sprinklers										
▼ Sprinkler Pipes										
02/15/2019	1005	Hicks Hardware	Landscaping:Sprinklers:Spri...	Inventory Asset	25.00	20.00	5.00	62.50	50.00	12.50
Total for Sprinkler Pipes					25.00	20.00	5.00	$62.50	$50.00	$12.50
Total for Sprinklers					25.00	20.00	5.00	$62.50	$50.00	$12.50
Total for Landscaping					25.00	20.00	5.00	$62.50	$50.00	$12.50
TOTAL					29.00	20.00	9.00	$217.50	$50.00	$167.50

TIP

In Figure 5-16, I hide the Navigation pane by clicking the three horizontal bars in the upper left corner of the QBO window; I wanted to give the report more screen real estate.

To run this report, click Reports in the Navigation pane. Then, use the Search box to type "Open Purchase"; you won't need to type more than that — QBO displays the report title in the search results, and you can click it to display the report. You also can use the Open Purchase Order List report. For more on reports, see Chapter 10.

Entering and Paying Bills

You use QBO's Bill transaction to enter a bill from a vendor that you don't want to pay immediately. QBO tracks the bill as a *payable*, which is a liability of your business — money you owe but have not yet paid. Most companies that enter Bill transactions do so because they receive a fair number of bills and want to sit down and pay them at one time, but they don't want to lose track of the bills they receive. They also want to be able to easily determine how much they owe; if you enter Bill transactions, you can print the A/P Aging Summary and Details reports to find that information.

REMEMBER

Depending on the version of QBO that you use, the Bill transaction might not be available to you; if that's the case, pay your bills using the Check or the Expense transaction.

Entering a bill

To enter a bill you receive from a vendor, you use QBO's Bill transaction as shown in the following steps. If you pay a bill on a regular basis, it might be a candidate for a recurring bill; see the next section.

1. **Choose Expenses ⇨ Expenses to display the Expenses list page.**

    REMEMBER

    If you are working with a project, you can choose Projects, select the project, and click Add to Project.

2. **Click the New Transaction button in the upper right corner of the page and select Bill from the menu that appears.**

    QBO displays the Bill transaction window shown in Figure 5-17.

3. **Select the vendor from whom you received the bill.**

    QBO fills in the vendor's mailing address information.

4. **Check and, if necessary, change the bill date and the due date.**

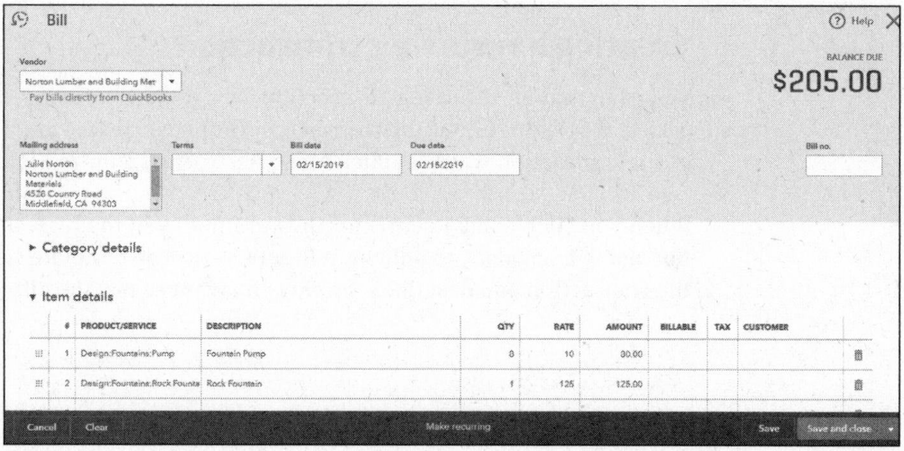

FIGURE 5-17: The Bill transaction window.

5. **Use the Category Details section, the Item Details section, or both to record information about the bill.**

   See the section "Writing a Check" for details on filling out the Category Details section and the Item Details section. Be aware that I hid the Category Details section in Figure 5-17 so that you could see the information in the Item Details section.

6. **Optionally, scroll down to the Footer section (which isn't shown in Figure 5-17) and enter information in the Memo field and attach electronic documents to the bill.**

7. **Click Save.**

About recurring transactions

To help you avoid repeating the same task over and over, you can set up *recurring transactions*. You can set up recurring transactions for bills, invoices, and, well, just about any type of transaction in QBO; in fact, it's easier to tell you that you *can't* set up recurring transactions for bill payments, customer payments, and time activities. Throughout this section, I'm going to use a bill as an example for setting up a recurring transaction.

Typically, recurring transactions work best for transactions with static amounts that you intend to pay on a regular basis; your rent is a perfect candidate for a recurring transaction. Be aware that transactions that occur on a regular basis but with amounts that vary, like your utility bills, are good candidates for recurring transactions as long as you set them up using Reminder for the transaction type, as described in the next section.

Creating a recurring transaction

You can create a recurring transaction in a number of ways; in my opinion, the easiest way is to fill out the transaction in the usual way and then, at the bottom of the transaction window, click Make Recurring (refer to Figure 5-17).

When you click Make Recurring, QBO prompts you to create a recurring transaction using a *template*, as shown in Figure 5-18. The template serves as a model for the transaction and describes the way you want to pay the bill. Follow these steps:

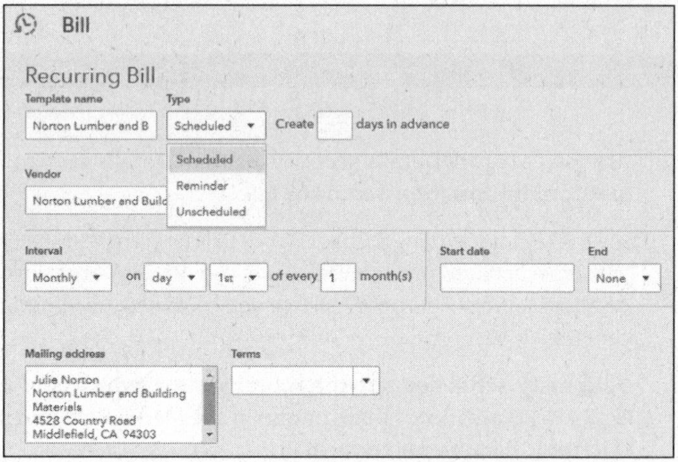

FIGURE 5-18: Setting up a recurring transaction.

Bill

Recurring Bill

Template name	Type		
Norton Lumber and B	Scheduled ▾	Create [ ] days in advance	
	Scheduled		
Vendor	Reminder		
Norton Lumber and Build	Unscheduled		

Interval						Start date	End
Monthly ▾	on	day ▾	1st ▾	of every	1 month(s)	[ ]	None ▾

Mailing address	Terms
Julie Norton Norton Lumber and Building Materials 4528 Country Road Middlefield, CA 94303	[▾]

1. From the Type list, choose one of the following:

- **Scheduled:** If you select this type, QBO automatically creates the transaction and enters it. That is, if you set up a scheduled recurring bill to be entered on the first of each month, QBO automatically enters the bill on the first of each month — without any intervention from you.

REMEMBER

  For some recurring transactions, like invoices, you have the option to automatically send emails. If you select this option, QBO creates the transaction and automatically emails it.

- **Reminder:** If you select this type, QBO displays a reminder for you to complete and then processes the transaction. This option gives you more control over when and how QBO enters a recurring transaction.

TIP

  This type is useful if you want to set up a recurring transaction for a bill, like your utility bills, where the amount changes but the due date doesn't. You can edit the transaction before entering it.

- **Unscheduled:** QBO won't schedule the transaction nor remind you that it's time to use the transaction. Instead, the template will be available to use as you need it.

  For this example, I chose Reminder, because it has basically the same options as Scheduled except that I can control its entry into QBO. For an Unscheduled transaction type, you don't establish the interval, start date, and end date.

REMEMBER

2. **Fill in the number of days before the transaction date that you want QBO to remind you (or schedule the transaction).**

WARNING

Avoid surprises. Be aware that QBO sets the date on the scheduled transaction using the scheduled date, not the date you enter the transaction. But a recurring transaction charges a customer's credit card or ACH payment on the day you record the recurring transaction. So, the charge gets processed on the day it's recorded, but the transaction date could potentially be a future date.

3. **Ensure that the vendor is correct.**

4. **In the Interval section, select the frequency with which you pay the bill, along with the timeframe.**

   - For daily transactions, select the interval in days to pay the bill. You can, for example, opt to pay the bill every 10 days.

   - For weekly transactions, select the interval in weeks and the day of the week to pay the bill. For example, you can pay a bill every three weeks on Thursday.

   - For monthly transactions, select the interval in months and the day of the month to pay the bill. For example, you can pay a bill every month on the last day of the month.

   - For yearly transactions, select the month and day of the year to pay the bill.

   - In the Start Date field, specify the first date on which you want QBO to enter the bill and, if appropriate, the last date to enter the bill. You might set an ending date for a rent bill to coincide with the end of your lease.

5. **Confirm that the mailing date and terms are correct, scroll down the page to confirm that the detail section of the transaction is correct, and add any memo information or attachments to the transaction.**

   If any lines in the detail section have a value of $0, QBO won't save those lines.

6. **Click Save Template in the lower right corner of the window.**

Making changes to recurring transactions

To work with existing recurring transactions, choose Gear⇨Recurring Transactions to display the Recurring Transactions list (see Figure 5-19).

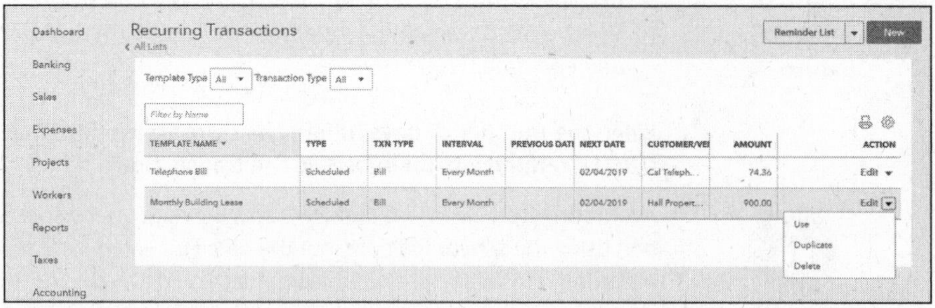

FIGURE 5-19:
The Recurring
Transactions list.

To make a change to an existing transaction, click Edit in the Action column; QBO displays the transaction in the window shown previously in Figure 5-18. Any changes you make to recurring transaction templates are not retroactive; you must manually change transactions already entered to correct them.

REMEMBER

If you make changes to a customer or vendor that will affect an existing recurring transaction — for example, if you change address information — QBO displays a message when you save those changes that tells you that QBO will update related recurring transaction templates.

If you click the down arrow beside Edit in the Action column, you see the options for a recurring transaction, as follows:

>> **Use:** Enter transactions with types of Reminder or Unscheduled. You don't need to enter transactions with a type of Scheduled because QBO does that for you automatically.

>> **Duplicate:** Create additional recurring transaction templates from existing recurring transaction templates. For example, you might use the template for your rent to create another template to pay monthly insurance.

>> **Delete:** Choose this option to remove a recurring transaction template that you no longer need.

Last, you can print a report of your existing recurring transaction templates. Choose Reports in the Navigation bar. Then, click in the Search box and type **recu** (that's all you'll need to type for QBO to find the Recurring Template List report) and click it to display a report like the one shown in Figure 5-20.

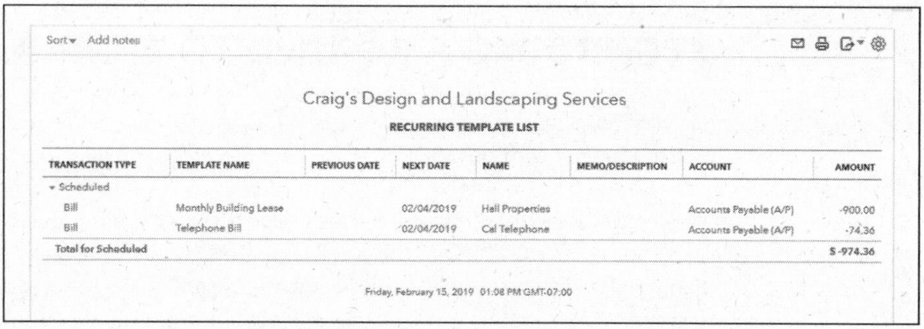

TRANSACTION TYPE	TEMPLATE NAME	PREVIOUS DATE	NEXT DATE	NAME	MEMO/DESCRIPTION	ACCOUNT	AMOUNT
Scheduled							
Bill	Monthly Building Lease		02/04/2019	Hall Properties		Accounts Payable (A/P)	-900.00
Bill	Telephone Bill		02/04/2019	Cal Telephone		Accounts Payable (A/P)	-74.36
Total for Scheduled							$ -974.36

FIGURE 5-20: The Recurring Template List report.

Recording a vendor credit

You enter a vendor credit to record returns to vendors or refunds from vendors. A vendor might supply you with a credit document that indicates you no longer owe the amount stated on the document, or the vendor might issue a refund check to you.

If a vendor issues a credit document, you enter a vendor credit and then apply it when you pay the vendor's bill. If a vendor issues a refund check to you, you still enter a vendor credit, but you also enter a deposit and then link the deposit to the vendor credit.

Follow these steps to enter the vendor credit:

1. **On the Expenses list page, choose New Transaction ⇨ Vendor Credit.**

   QBO displays the Vendor Credit window shown in Figure 5-21.

2. **Select the vendor who issued the credit.**
3. **Enter the date of the credit.**
4. **Enter the credit amount.**

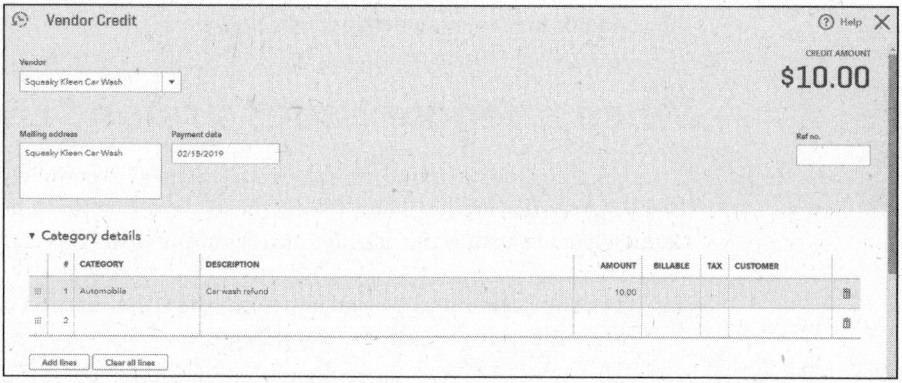

FIGURE 5-21: A Vendor Credit transaction.

RECORDING A REFUND TO A CARD CREDIT

If a vendor issues a credit to your credit card, the way you handle it depends on how you track credit cards in QBO.

If you haven't set up a credit card account and you wait to enter credit card transactions when you receive and record the credit card vendor's bill, enter a line on the Bill transaction using the account associated with the refund and make the amount negative.

However, if you *have* set up a credit card account, record a Credit Card Credit transaction, whether you manually record Expense transactions or download them; when you record a Credit Card Credit, QBO lets you post the transaction to any of your available credit cards. In the Category Details section, select the account associated with the refund. Note that when you download transactions, you'll be able to match both Expense transactions and Credit Card Credit transactions to downloaded information.

5. **In the Category Details section, select the account used on the original bill.**

   If you received the credit because you returned items to the vendor, select the items you returned in the Item Details section.

6. **You can optionally scroll down and attach a digital copy of the credit to the Vendor Credit transaction.**

7. **Click the arrow beside Save and New in the lower right corner of the window and choose Save and Close.**

TIP

   The Save option referenced in Step 7 is called a *sticky preference,* which means that after you select Save and Close, it will appear as the default Save option the next time you display this screen.

If the vendor issued only a credit document, read the section "Paying bills" to learn how to use the vendor credit you just entered to reduce the amount you owe the vendor when you pay the vendor's bill.

When a vendor issues a refund check . . .

If the vendor issues a refund check to you, you need to complete the previous steps to enter a vendor credit. Then, follow these steps to enter a deposit to record the refund check in your bank account and then link it to the vendor credit:

1. **Click the Create plus (+) sign and, from the Other section of the Create menu that appears, choose Bank Deposit.**

   QBO displays the Bank Deposit transaction window shown in Figure 5-22.

FIGURE 5-22:
The Deposit
transaction
window.

Bank Deposit

Account: Checking Balance $48,460.00 Date: 02/15/2019 AMOUNT **$10.00**

Don't see the payments you want to deposit?

▼ Add funds to this deposit

#	RECEIVED FROM	ACCOUNT	DESCRIPTION	PAYMENT METHOD	REF NO.	AMOUNT	
1	Squeaky Clean Car Wash	Accounts Payable (A/P)		Check		10.00	
2							

Add lines   Clear all lines   Other funds total **$10.00**

2. **In the Add Funds to This Deposit section shown at the bottom of Figure 5-22, enter the following information:**

- **In the Received From column, select the vendor who issued the check.**

- **In the Account column, select the Accounts Payable account.**

- **In the Amount column, enter the amount of the check.**

3. **Click the arrow beside Save and New in the lower right corner of the window (not shown in Figure 5-22) and choose Save and Close.**

QBO redisplays the page you were viewing when you started the bank deposit.

REMEMBER

The Save option functions as a sticky preference, and you might not see Save and New because you previously made a different choice.

4. **Click the Create plus (+) sign and, from the Create menu that appears, choose Expense.**

5. **Select the vendor whose refund check you deposited.**

QBO displays available deposits, credits, and bills on the right side of the window (see Figure 5-23).

6. **Click Add in the Deposit transaction.**

7. **Click Add in the outstanding Vendor Credit transaction.**

When you add these two transactions, in this order, to the Expense, QBO creates a Bill Payment transaction with a net value of $0 because QBO applies the deposit to the vendor credit; Figure 5-24 focuses on the Details section of the transaction.

8. **Click the arrow beside Save and New in the lower right corner of the window and choose Save and Close.**

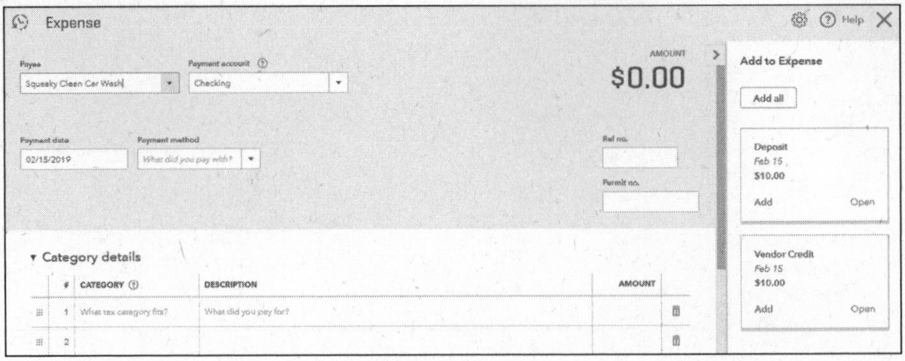

FIGURE 5-23:
Open
transactions
for the selected
vendor appear.

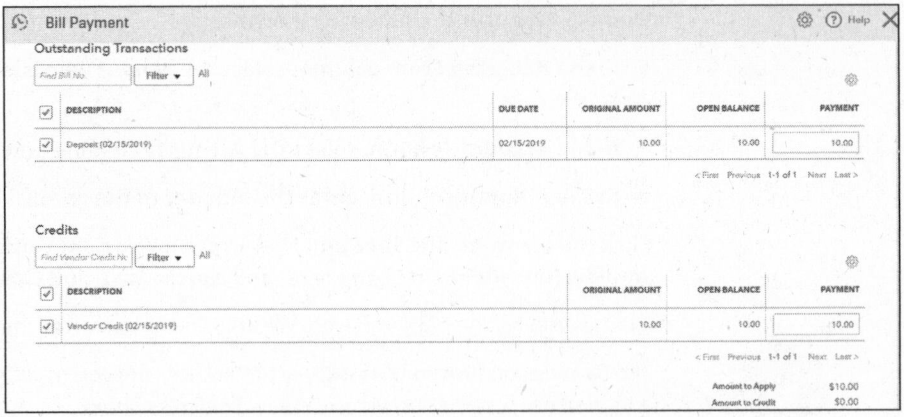

FIGURE 5-24:
Adding the
vendor credit and
the bank deposit
of the vendor's
check results in a
$0 bill payment
transaction.

Paying bills

If you are using QBO Essentials, Plus, or Advanced and want to pay your bills online, skip this section and explore QBO's interface with `Bill.com`. You'll find the Bill.com app available in the Intuit App Store. You can visit the store by choosing Apps from the Navigation pane. There is no monthly subscription fee for Bill. com, but there is a per transaction fee for each payment you process. If you want to pay your bills in QBO without using Bill.com, read on.

If you've been entering bills from vendors, then, at some point, you need to pay those bills. Most people sit down once or twice a month and pay outstanding bills. To pay bills in QBO, follow these steps:

1. **Click the Create plus (+) sign and, from the Create menu that appears, choose Pay Bills in the Vendors column.**

QBO displays the Pay Bills page shown in Figure 5-25. Overdue bills display a red flag.

Pay Bills

	Payment account		Payment date	Starting check no.	
	Checking ▾ Balance $1,201.00		02/15/2019	71	☐ Print later

Pay bills directly from QuickBooks

Filter ▾   Last 365 Days

☐	PAYEE	REF NO.	DUE DATE ▲	OPEN BALANCE
☐	PG&E		01/05/2019 📢	$86.44
☐	Norton Lumber and Buil...		01/20/2019 📢	$205.00
☐	Robertson & Associates		01/20/2019 📢	$315.00
☐	Brosnahan Insurance Ag...		01/23/2019 📢	$241.23
☐	Diego's Road Warrior Bo...		02/17/2019	$755.00

Overdue bills

0 bills selected $0.00

Total payment (USD) 0.00

FIGURE 5-25:
The Pay Bills page lists bills you owe but have not yet paid.

2. **From the Payment Account list, select an account to use to pay the bills.**

For this example, I'll assume you use a Checking account to pay your bills.

TIP

If you find yourself short on cash, you can use the QuickBooks Capital app, a free app available in the Intuit App Center, to apply for a loan. QuickBooks capital uses your QBO data to complete the loan application, and, if approved, you can receive a short-term working capital loan ranging up to $35,000, with six months to repay the loan. Once submitted, you'll receive a decision within two to three days. The app adds a Capital tab to the Navigation bar that you can use to track the loan.

3. **Provide a payment date at the top of the screen.**

4. **Enter the number of the first check you'll use to pay bills.**

REMEMBER

You can select the Print Later check box to identify bills to pay and schedule them to print later; at the time you print the checks, QBO lets you establish the starting check number.

5. **In the Filter list, you can select an option to specify the outstanding bills you want to consider paying.**

By default, QBO displays unpaid bills for the last year, but you can limit what appears onscreen for your consideration by a variety of dates and even for selected payees. Be careful here; remember, limiting what you see might mean missing a bill you need to pay.

By clicking the appropriate column heading, you can opt to sort the listed bills by Payee, Reference Number, Due Date, or Open Balance.

6. **Select the check box in the column at the left side of each bill you want to pay.**

   As you select bills to pay, QBO updates the Payment column and the Total Payment Amount using the bill amount as the default payment amount (see Figure 5-26). You can change the payment amount of any bill by typing in the Payment column.

REMEMBER

   If a vendor credit exists, QBO assumes you want to apply outstanding vendor credits to reduce the amount you owe a particular vendor.

7. **In the lower right corner of the window, click Save and Print (not shown in Figure 5-26), or click the arrow beside Save and Print to choose either Save or Save and Close.**

   Click Save or Save and Close to mark the bills paid without printing any checks. Click Save and Print to print checks and mark the bills paid.

TIP

If you choose to pay the bills using a credit card rather than a bank account, the window looks the same except that no options appear related to printing checks, just as you'd expect.

If you opted, in Step 4, to print checks later, you can print those checks by choosing Create ➪ Print Checks. The Print Checks option appears in the Vendor column of the Create menu.

Chapter **6**

Managing the Inflow of Money

This is where the fun starts. "Why?" you ask. Because this chapter covers stuff related to bringing money into the business, which, from any businessperson's perspective, is the reason you started your business — and therefore the most fun part!

Before diving into preparing various types of forms, you should consider whether you want to take advantage of the Projects feature in QBO, so, I'll start there.

Managing Projects

If your business is oriented toward completing projects for your customers, exploring QBO's Projects feature is in your best interest before I dive into using the various sales transactions. QBO's Projects feature helps you organize, in one centralized location, all the pieces — that is, associated transactions, time spent, and necessary reports — that make up . . . well, a project. And, the reports included in the Projects feature help you determine each project's profitability and keep on top of unbilled time and expenses as well as non-billable time. You'll still complete all the various sales transaction forms described in this chapter in the same way I describe them, with one change: instead of starting from the Sales Transaction list or the Create menu, you'll be able, but not required, to start from the Project tab. If you enable the Projects feature before you enter transactions, your picture of a project's profitability will be clearer.

Turning on projects in QBO

REMEMBER

Be aware that you cannot turn the Projects feature off after you have turned it on. You don't need to use it, but it will remain enabled in your company. If you want to play around with the feature before enabling it in your company, try it out in the QBO sample company. You can read about the sample company in Chapter 11.

If you're using QBO Plus in Canada, the UK, the United States, or Australia, you can take advantage of the Projects feature. To turn on the feature, follow these steps:

1. **Choose Gear ⇨ Account and Settings ⇨ Advanced.**

2. **In the Projects section, click beside Organize All Job-Related Activity in One Place to turn on the Projects feature.**

3. **Click Done to return to your QBO company.**

    A new option, Projects, appears on the Navigation pane (see Figure 6-1). When you click the option, QBO prompts you to set up your first project.

But before you jump in and start creating projects, read on . . .

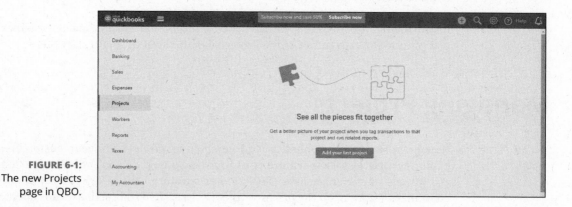

FIGURE 6-1:
The new Projects page in QBO.

Enabling projects in Customer lists

Before you set up any new projects, there's one housekeeping chore you need to complete for the Projects feature to work properly. Choose Sales⇨Customers to display the Customers page. In the table portion of the page, just above the Action column, click the Table Settings gear. Then, place a check in the Include Projects check box (see Figure 6-2). You'll then be able to see projects on the Customers page and in list boxes on transactions, as well as on the Projects Center page.

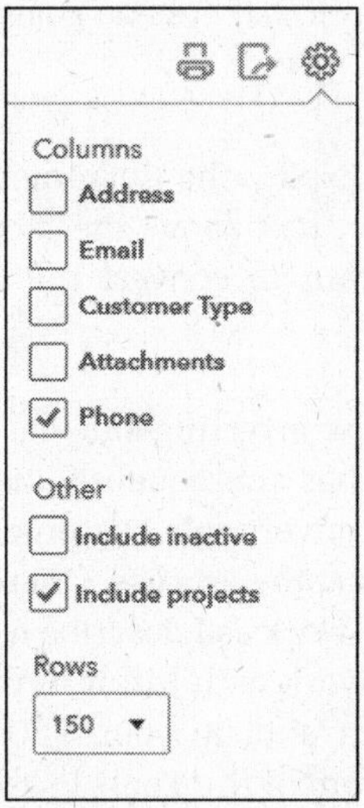

FIGURE 6-2: Enable the Include Projects check box.

Converting sub-customers to projects

You can use — and might have been using up until now — sub-customers to act as projects. So, is QBO blurring the line between sub-customers and projects? Not really. If you use the Projects feature, you'll notice that projects appear in the Project Center, where they will be easier to manage and evaluate using reports. Sub-customers remain only on the Customers list. The benefit of using the Projects feature lies with the fact that the Project Center keeps the information for each project in one place. Sub-customers don't offer this centralization — unless you convert them to projects.

If you've been using sub-customers to serve as projects, QBO can walk you through converting sub-customers to projects. So, before you start adding projects, you might want to consider whether you have created sub-customers that you want to convert to projects. Be aware of the following:

» QBO converts sub-customers to projects only if the sub-customers are set up to be billed with the parent customer. You might need to edit your sub-customers to make this change.

» You don't need to convert all sub-customers to projects simultaneously; QBO gives you the opportunity to select sub-customers to convert.

» Once you convert a sub-customer to a project, there's no going back; QBO will treat the sub-customer as a project.

To convert a sub-customer to a project, display the Customers list by choosing Sales ➪ Customers. On the Customers page, just above the table of transactions, QBO displays a message asking if you want to convert the first level of sub-customers into projects.

WARNING

When I first wrote this, the message about converting sub-customers did appear above the table on the Customers page; it has subsequently disappeared and I've had no luck finding it. So, if you need to convert sub-customers, you'll probably need to contact Intuit to find out how to start the process. I'm relatively confident that the rest of the process will continue to work as I describe it here. You can take advantage of QBO's SmartLook feature to work with Intuit in your QBO company. Phone or chat with QBO technical support and, in your QBO company, choose Gear ➪ SmartLook (you'll find it at the bottom of the Tools list on the Gear menu). QBO displays a number that you supply to your technical support representative, giving permission to share your QBO screen (and only your QBO screen). But remember that you have to be in contact with a technical support representative to use this feature; it's not a bat signal that will make an agent show up.

Click Convert Now in the message, and QBO lets you select eligible sub-customers to convert (see Figure 6-3).

Convert sub-customers to projects   ×

This is a one-time conversion that you can do at any time. We'll move all the linked transactions with it.

| Sub-customers | Projects |
| Which ones do you want to convert? | |

☐ (1 of 2 selected)

Freeman Sporting Goods

| ☑ 0969 Ocean View Road | $ | ⊙ | 0969 Ocean View Road | In progress ▼ |
| ☐ 55 Twin Lane | $ | | | |

FIGURE 6-3:
Converting a sub-customer to a project.

Once you click Convert (not shown in Figure 6-3), QBO displays a message explaining that you're about to convert a sub-customer to a project — and there's no going back. If you're sure you want to do this, click Continue. QBO converts the sub-customer(s), sets the status of the project(s) to "in progress," and offers you the option to go to the Projects Center or redisplay the Customer list.

Setting up a project

Now you're ready to set up a project. Click Projects in the Navigation bar and, if you didn't convert any sub-customers to projects, QBO displays the Add Your First Project button on the Projects Center page (refer to Figure 6-1). If you did convert one or more sub-customers to projects, those projects appear on the Project Center page.

To start a new project, click New Project in the upper right corner of the Projects Center page. A panel appears on the right side of the screen; in the panel, supply a project name, which can be anything you want and should be something you'll easily recognize. Also supply the customer associated with the project and, if you want, any notes about the project. When you finish, click Save, and QBO displays a message to let you know that it set up the project. When you click OK to dismiss the message, a page like the one shown in Figure 6-4 appears.

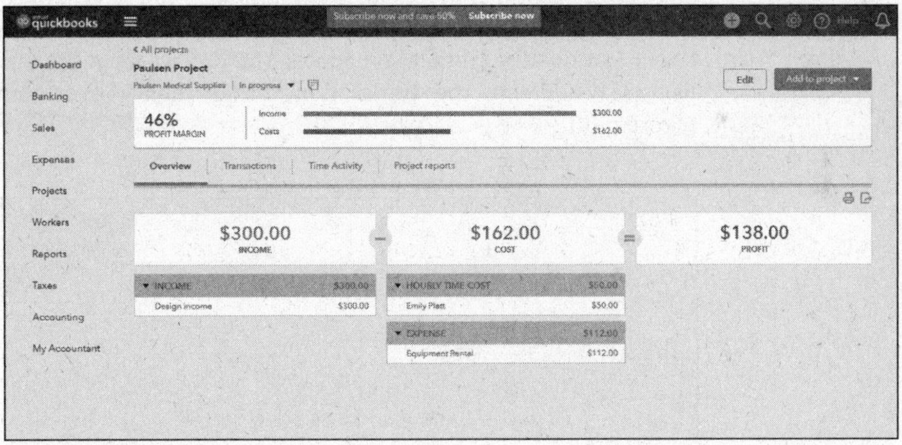

FIGURE 6-4:
The Project Reports page for a project.

The page is divided into two tabs: The Project Reports tab, shown in Figure 6-4, and the Transactions tab — which doesn't have anything on it yet because you just set up the project.

REMEMBER

Even though you select a customer when you create a new project, QBO doesn't automatically pull in existing transactions for the customer to the Projects page. Newly created projects have no transactions — and therefore, logically, the Transactions page is empty and reports contain no information. But, converted sub-customers are a different story. If you convert a sub-customer to a project, you *will* find transactions on the Transactions page; QBO brings them over during conversion so that you can see them in the Projects Center.

WARNING

If you're thinking of changing the customer name on existing transactions to pull those transactions into the project, be careful. Changing the customer can have repercussions throughout QBO. For example, if you try to change the customer assigned to a payment transaction that you have deposited, QBO warns you that you must remove the transaction from the deposit before you can change the customer name. And, that will mess up your deposit unless you remember to re-add the payment to the deposit. So, you see, things can get complicated very quickly. Even though there is a connection between a customer and sub-customer or project, entries on QBO's Customers list are unique list elements. QuickBooks Desktop works the same way in this regard.

Adding transactions to a project

There's no special, secret way to add transactions to a project (this isn't like double, secret probation in *Animal House*). In fact, you have two choices. You can use the techniques described throughout this chapter for the various types of transactions; just make sure that you choose the project from the Customer drop-down list as you create the transaction rather than the customer (as shown in Figure 6-5).

FIGURE 6-5: Creating a new transaction for a project.

Or, you can start many (but not all) your transactions from the Projects Center. Starting your transaction from the Projects Center using the Add to Project button has one added advantage: QBO prefills the project name for you on the transaction. Note that you can't create a Sales Receipt from the Projects page; use the Create menu or the Sales page.

If you can't add a transaction for a project from the Projects Center, just be sure to select the project on the transaction when you create it from either the Create menu or the Customers list page.

Projects and reporting

Once your project collects transactions, reports become meaningful. The Transaction List report shows, by default, exactly what you'd expect: all the transactions assigned to the project.

The Project Profitability report is, essentially, and Profit and Loss report for the project; you see a sample in Figure 6-6.

Filters: Customer ✕

Collapse   Sort ▾   Add notes

Craig's Design and Landscaping Services

PROJECT PROFITABILITY FOR PAULSEN MEDICAL SUPPLIES'S PAULSEN PROJECT (WITHOUT TIME COSTS)

All Dates

	TOTAL
▾ Income	
Design income	300.00
Total Income	$300.00
GROSS PROFIT	$300.00
▾ Expenses	
Equipment Rental	112.00
Total Expenses	$112.00
NET OPERATING INCOME	$188.00
NET INCOME	$188.00

FIGURE 6-6: A sample Project Profitability report.

The Unbilled Time and Expenses report shows you time assigned to the project but not yet billed, and the Non-billable Time report shows you time recorded to the project that you can't bill to the project.

The Project feature also provides you with ways of "disposing" of the project. If you click Project in the Navigation bar and then click the Options button for a particular project, you can opt to mark the project as completed, mark the project as canceled, or delete the project. Note that you can't delete any project that has transactions associated with it; you must mark the project completed or canceled.

Getting Started with Sales Transactions

If you've been in business a while when you start using QBO, and you have some invoices you've issued but customers haven't yet paid, you can use those invoices as a learning tool and enter them as described in this chapter. If you recorded an opening bank account balance back in Chapter 3, be sure to enter into QBO the deposits you've made since your last bank statement. If you didn't record an opening bank account balance back in Chapter 3, or you recorded a bank account balance as of December 31 of last year, be sure to enter into QBO all the deposits you've made this year, even if they have cleared the bank.

To record most sales-related transactions, you can click Sales in the Navigation pane to display the Sales Transactions page shown in Figure 6-7; then click the New Transaction button. If the transaction type you want to record isn't available on the New Transaction menu, open the Create menu by clicking the Create button — the plus sign (+) icon at the top of QBO, which changes to an X after you click it. Then, choose the type of transaction you want to record; sales-related transactions appear in the Customers column (see Figure 6-8).

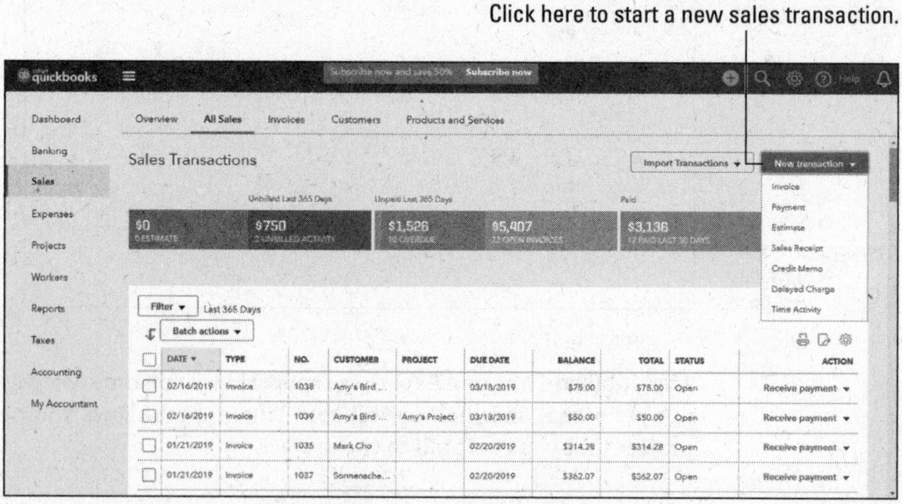

Click here to start a new sales transaction.

FIGURE 6-7:
The Sales
Transactions
page.

Create

Customers	Vendors	Employees	Other
Invoice	Expense	Payroll	Bank Deposit
Receive Payment	Check	Single Time Activity	Transfer
Estimate	Bill	Weekly Timesheet	Journal Entry
Credit Memo	Pay Bills		Statement
Sales Receipt	Purchase Order		Inventory Qty Adjustment
Refund Receipt	Vendor Credit		
Delayed Credit	Credit Card Credit		
Delayed Charge	Print Checks		

▸ Show less

FIGURE 6-8: Sales transactions appear in the Customers column of the Create menu.

Customizing forms to handle subtotals

Before you begin preparing various types of sales forms, you should address a housekeeping task: setting up sales forms so that you can include subtotals on them. If you have no need to subtotal information on your sales forms, you can skip this section and move on to the next one. Or, if you only need subtotals occasionally, you can skip this section and read "Preparing an invoice" to find out how to add a subtotal only when you need it.

REMEMBER

Be aware that you cannot customize forms using any of the mobile apps; you must make your customizations on the web and then you can use your customized form in the mobile app. See `https://quickbooks.intuit.com/community/Help-Articles/Compare-mobile-app-features/m-p/185540` for details on what you can and cannot do using mobile apps.

You can subtotal lines on an invoice, an estimate, or a sales receipt. First, turn on the feature; for this example, I'll turn on the feature for the Invoice form. Follow these steps:

1. **Choose Gear ⇨ Custom Form Styles.**

   The Custom Form Styles page appears, which displays the form styles you have set up.

   REMEMBER

   In Chapter 3, you saw how to customize forms. If you opted not to set up any custom forms, you might not see anything listed on the Custom Form Styles page. In that case, click the New Style button, select a form (Invoice, Estimate, or Sales Receipt), and continue with these steps; for this example, I selected Invoice.

2. **Select a form to customize, and then click Edit in the Action column.**

The Customize Form Style page appears. It contains four buttons across the top left side of the page that you use to display the Design, Content, Emails, and Payments pages. The right side of the page is devoted to previews.

TIP

From the Design page, you can select a template for the form, upload your logo, change the color of the colored portions of the form, select a different font for the form, and print a sample of the form.

3. **From the buttons on the top of page, click Content.**

QBO displays the Content page, with all sections appearing gray and unavailable.

4. **Click in the Table section to edit it.**

The Table section is the section where you see column titles such as Activity, Qty, Rate, and Amount.

QBO makes the content of the Table section visible and available to edit (see Figure 6-9).

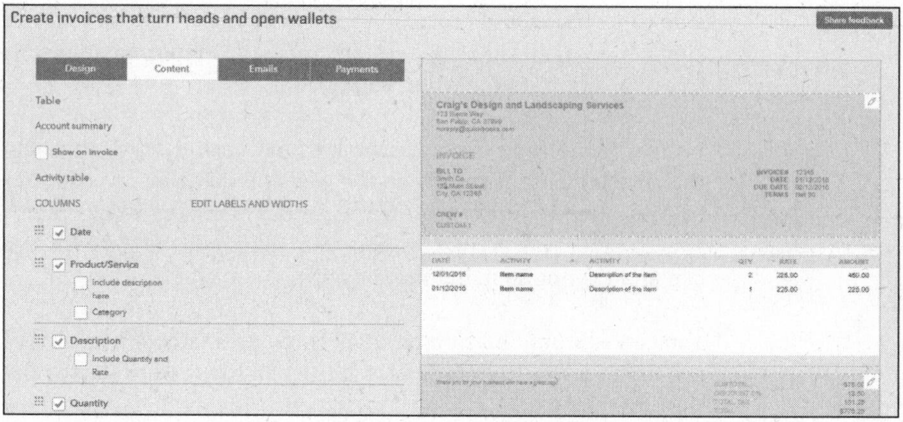

FIGURE 6-9:
The Content page after choosing the Table section to edit.

5. **Scroll down the page and click Show More Activity Options.**

QBO displays additional options for the Table section of the form (see Figure 6-10).

6. **Select the Group Activity By check box and make a selection from the list.**

For my example, I chose Type.

Check this box to enable subtotaling.

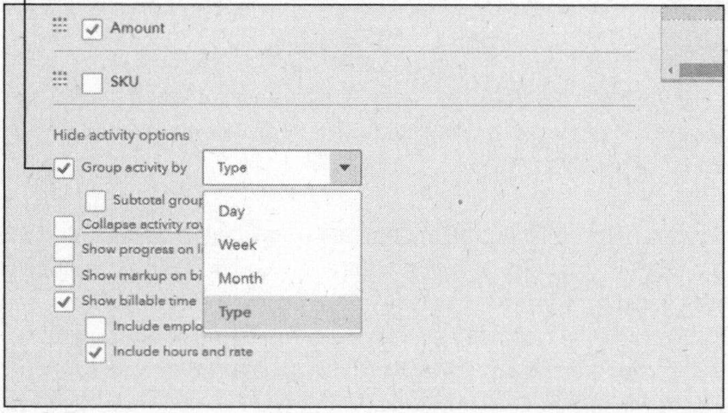

FIGURE 6-10:
Turning on the
setting to enable
grouping on the
selected sales
forms.

| | Amount |
| | SKU |

Hide activity options

☑ Group activity by [Type ▼]

☐ Subtotal grou
☐ Collapse activity rov   Day
☐ Show progress on l
☐ Show markup on bi   Week
☑ Show billable time   Month
☐ Include emplo
☑ Include hours and rate   Type

TIP

TIP

You can select Subtotal Groups if you want QBO to group specifically by the grouping type you select in Settings. Not selecting the option gives you more flexibility on the forms.

If you email progress invoices to customers, you can select the Show Progress on Line Items (Email Only) check box to add an Estimate Summary and a Due column to invoices. The Estimate Summary shows the estimate number and amount, invoices previously created for the estimate, and total amount you have invoiced to date. The Due column shows the amount still due for each line item.

7. **Click Done in the lower left corner of the window to save the settings.**

   If you want to preview the form in a PDF file, click Preview PDF (also in the lower left corner of the window).

You'll need to repeat the preceding steps for each type of form (invoice, estimate, and sales receipt) on which you want to be able to subtotal information.

Preparing an invoice

You enter invoices in QBO to inform customers that they owe you money for goods you sold them or services you performed for them. In QBO, you can prepare invoices and send them using email or using the U.S. Postal Service.

QBO GOOGLE CALENDARS, AND GMAIL

If you record work you perform on your Google Calendar (to later use in invoicing), you can use the Invoice with Google Calendar app, available in the Intuit App Center, to automate the process of pulling event details and descriptions from your Google Calendar onto a QBO invoice.

Once you enable the integration between your Google Calendar and QBO, you simply start a QBO invoice form and click the Google Calendar icon that appears on the form. Using a panel that appears to the right on the invoice form, you set search parameters; that is, you select a Google Calendar and a timeframe and supply a search keyword. QBO searches your Google Calendar for matching events and, when you opt to add events to the invoice, QBO imports event details including title, description, hours worked, and date from your Google Calendar, eliminating the duplicate data entry for you.

You also can invoice directly from Gmail using the add-on app QuickBooks Invoicing for Gmail, offering electronic payment options to your customers. This app has no monthly subscription fee, but it does charge per transaction, and, if you're interested in it, you can install it through QuickBooks Labs (see Chapter 3 for information on QuickBooks Labs).

When you prepare an invoice, you include items on the invoice to provide information about what you're selling to the customer. You create items for both services and products using the Products and Services list, as described toward the middle of Chapter 4. To enter an invoice, follow these steps:

1. **Choose Sales ⇨ All Sales in the Navigation pane to display the Sales Transactions page.**

2. **Click the New Transaction button and, from the list that appears, click Invoice.**

   REMEMBER

   If you are working with a project, you can choose Projects, select the project, and click Add to Project.

3. **Choose a customer.**

   QBO displays the customer's mailing address, payment terms, invoice date, due date, and Send Later option.

   TIP

   If a pane appears on the right side, it displays transactions you might want to link to the invoice you're creating; you can see examples in the sections "Preparing an estimate" and "Creating Billable Time Entries."

4. **Double-check the Invoice Date, Due Date, and Terms, and make an appropriate selection in the Send Later check box.**

   If you want to send invoices via email, you can set up your preferences; from the QBO Dashboard page, click the Gear button beside your company name and choose Account and Settings. Set up your company's email address on the Company page. Set up message preferences in the same Account and Settings dialog box; click Sales and edit the Messages section. In addition to editing the actual message, you can provide email addresses to which you want to send copies — regular and blind — of all sales documents.

5. **Fill in the products and services the customer is buying:**

   a. Click in the Product/Service column and select an item for the invoice you are creating.

      You can type characters in the Product/Service column, and QBO will help you find the item.

   b. Optionally, edit the Description column for the selected item.

   c. Use the Qty, Rate, and Amount columns to supply the quantity of the selected item you are selling, the rate you're charging for each item, and the amount the customer should pay. When you supply any two of these three values, QBO calculates the third value.

   d. If appropriate, check the Tax box.

   e. Repeat Steps a to d to add more items to the invoice.

6. **To add a subtotal in the proper place on the invoice:**

   a. Click the last line on the invoice that should be subtotaled; in Figure 6-11, I clicked the third line of the invoice.

   b. Click the Add Subtotal button, which appears below the lines on the invoice.

      QBO adds a line that subtotals the ones above it. You can continue adding lines to the invoice, as I did in Figure 6-11, and you can add more subtotals.

7. **You can scroll down in the Invoice window, as shown in Figure 6-12, and select a sales tax rate and, if appropriate, a discount amount or percent.**

   You see the Sales Tax Rate option on invoices only if you have turned on the Sales Tax feature by choosing Sales Tax ⇨ Set Up Sales Tax Rates; see Chapter 4 for details on setting up sales taxes.

   You can apply a discount to the invoice if you have turned on the preference to display the Discount box; you can turn on the preference either from the Account and Settings dialog box or, on the invoice form, click the Gear icon and select the Total Discount check box from the panel that appears on the right side of the form.

You also can type a message to the customer; type information in the Statement Memo box — which QBO transfers directly to any statement you create in the future — and attach an electronic document to the invoice.

TIP

You can control whether the discount is a pre-tax or after-tax discount by clicking the switch that appears to the left of the Discount and Sales Tax Rate boxes. Clicking the switch swaps the position of the two boxes; when the Discount box appears on top, the discount is pre-tax.

If you turn on the preference to display the Deposit box at the bottom of the invoice, you can use it to reduce the amount of the invoice by a deposit amount paid by the customer. You can turn on the preference either from the Account and Settings dialog box or, on the invoice form, click the Gear icon and select the Deposit check box from the panel that appears on the right side of the form.

Click the last line to include in the subtotal.   QBO adds the subtotal

#	PRODUCT/SERVICE	DESCRIPTION	QTY	RATE	AMOUNT	TAX
1	Design:Fountains:Rock Founta	Rock Fountain	1	275	275.00	✓
2	Design:Fountains:Pump	Fountain Pump	1	15	15.00	✓
3	Design:Fountains:Concrete	Concrete for fountain installation	50	1	50.00	✓
4					Subtotal: $340.00	
5	Design:Design	Custom Design	2	75	150.00	
6						

Add lines Clear all lines Add subtotal   Subtotal $490.00

FIGURE 6-11:
Click the last line that should be part of the subtotaled group, and then click Add Subtotal.

Click here to add a subtotal.

Click here to control whether a discount is pre- or post-taxable.

#		DESCRIPTION				
4					Subtotal: $340.00	
5	Design:Design	Custom Design	2	75	150.00	
6						

Add lines Clear all lines Add subtotal   Subtotal $490.00

Message on invoice
Thank you for your business and have a great day!

Taxable subtotal $340.00

California ▼ 8% 27.20

Discount percent ▼ $0.00

Message on statement
If you send statements to customers, this will show up as the description for this invoice.

Total $517.20

Balance due $517.20

FIGURE 6-12:
Use the bottom of the Invoice window to handle sales tax, discount information, messages, and attachments.

8. **To attach an electronic document to the invoice, click in the Attachments box and navigate to the document, or drag and drop the electronic copy into the Attachments box.**

9. **At the bottom of the window, you can**

   - **Cancel the invoice or clear the window and start again.**

   - **Click Print or Preview to print or preview the invoice.**

   - **Click Make Recurring to set up the invoice as a recurring invoice you intend to send on a schedule you specify.**

   - **Click Customize to customize the invoice form as described in Chapter 3.**

   - **Click Save to assign an invoice number and save the invoice in QBO.**

   - **Click Save and Send to assign an invoice number, save the invoice, and email a copy to the customer.**

     A window appears, in which you can write an email message or edit the standard message and look at a preview of the invoice. After you send your invoice, the email time and date-stamp information appears in the header. Invoice emails are now mobile-friendly, using a design that makes for easy phone reading. The invoice details also appear in the email so that customers see everything right away without needing to click a link.

TIP

You can click the arrow beside Save and Send and then choose Save and New to save the invoice and start a new one, or choose Save and Close to save the invoice and close the Invoice window. The option you choose will appear the next time you display the Invoice window. In fact, in any transaction window, the choice you make appears the next time you open the window.

Recording a customer payment

Let me start by mentioning that QBO interfaces with QuickBooks Payments, Intuit's online merchant service offering, so that you can accept ACH and credit card payments from your customers and record them directly into QBO. Visit `http://quickbooks.intuit.com/payments` or contact Intuit for details.

In this section, you explore how to record payments in QBO using traditional QBO tools.

When you receive a payment from a customer, you record it in QBO. You can display the Receive Payment window in the following ways:

>> In the Sales Transactions list, you can find the invoice for which you want to record a payment and click Receive Payment in the Action column (see Figure 6-13).

>> You can click the New Transaction button on the Sales Transactions page and select Payment (also shown in Figure 6-13).

>> You can click the Create menu and select Receive Payment.

>> If you are working with a project, you can choose Projects, select the project, and click Add to Project.

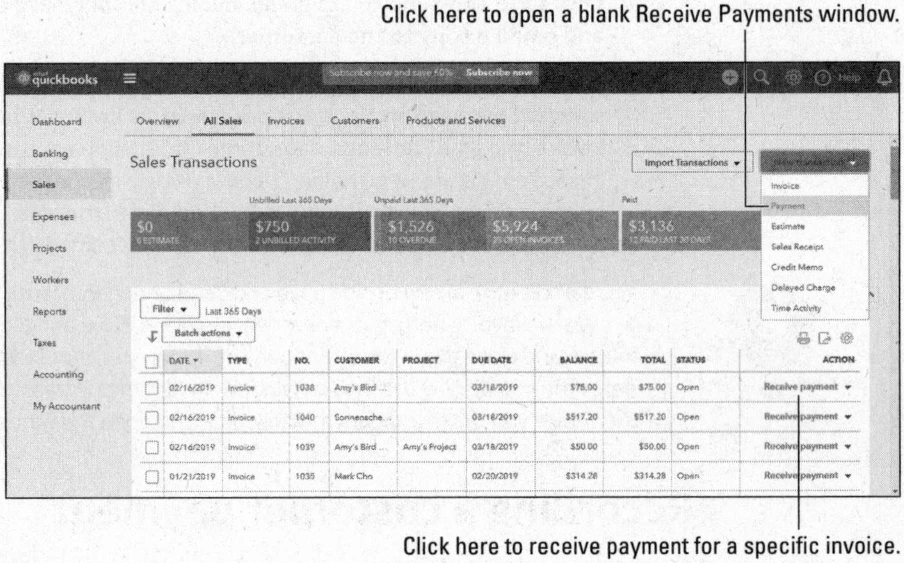

Click here to open a blank Receive Payments window.

FIGURE 6-13:
Opening the
Receive Payments
window from
the Sales
Transaction list.

Click here to receive payment for a specific invoice.

If you choose the first method in the previous list, QBO displays the Receive Payment window, prefilled with the information for the invoice you selected as well as a proposed payment amount.

If you use the second or the third method, QBO displays an empty Receive Payment window. You then select a customer, and QBO displays all the customer's open invoices in the Outstanding Transactions section, at the bottom of the window (see Figure 6-14).

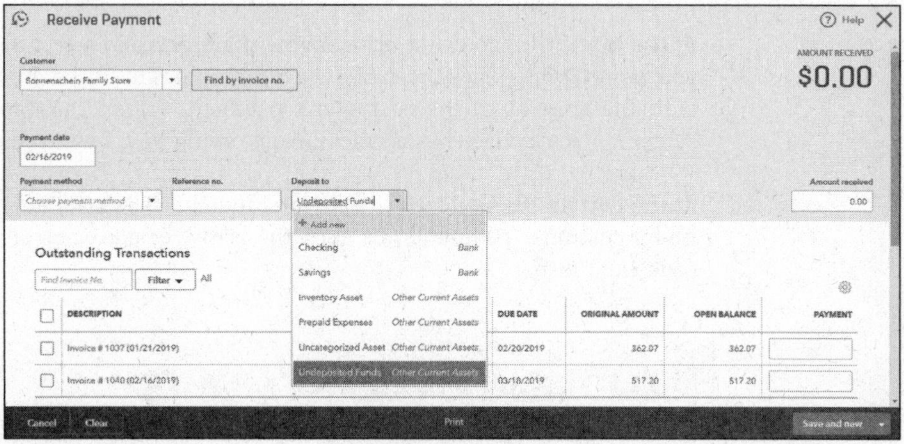

FIGURE 6-14:
The Receive Payment window after selecting a customer with open invoices.

USING THE UNDEPOSITED FUNDS ACCOUNT

If you receive more than one customer payment on any given day, you'll find the Undeposited Funds account a convenient way to handle the money that comes into your business. If you take several checks to your bank on a given day (or your bank receives several checks electronically on a given day), most banks typically don't record the individual checks as individual deposits. Instead, the bank records the sum of the checks as your deposit — pretty much the same way you sum the checks on a deposit ticket you give to a bank teller.

"And why is this important?" you ask. This fact is important because, when you receive your statement from your bank, you need to reconcile the bank's deposits and withdrawals with your own version of deposits and withdrawals. If you track each customer payment you receive as a deposit in the bank, then your deposits won't match the bank's deposits. And, if you don't use the Undeposited Funds account — and instead record customer payments directly into your QBO Bank account — your deposits definitely *won't* match the bank's version of your deposits.

Herald the arrival of the Undeposited Funds account in QBO, which acts as a holding tank for customer payments before you've prepared a bank deposit slip. If you place customer payments in the Undeposited Funds account, you can then use the Bank Deposit feature in QBO to sum up the payments you receive and intend to deposit at your bank simultaneously — and, if you don't go to your bank daily to make deposits, there's no problem. QBO records, as the deposit amount in your QBO Bank account, the amount calculated in the Bank Deposit window, which will match the amount you actually deposit at your bank. Then, your bank reconciliation process becomes quick and easy — well, okay, maybe not quick and easy, but certainly quicker and easier than if you were trying to figure out which customer payments made up various bank deposits.

See Chapter 8 for details on preparing a bank deposit and reconciling a bank statement.

At the top of the screen, select a Payment Method and select the account in which you want QBO to place the customer's payment. Fill in the Amount Received field with the amount of the customer's payment. In the Outstanding Transactions section, place a check beside each invoice being paid by the customer's payment.

At the bottom of the Receive Payment window, click Save and New to enter additional customer payments, or click the arrow beside Save and New and choose Save and Close.

HANDLING OVERPAYMENTS

Although it doesn't happen often, a customer might overpay you. The way you handle the overpayment depends on whether you intend to give the customer a credit or whether you intend to keep the money — as if it were a tip.

Regardless of your intent, make sure that your QBO company is set up to automatically apply credits. Choose Gear ⇨ Account and Settings and then click Advanced on the left side of the Account and Settings dialog box. In the Automation section, make sure that Automatically Apply Credits is turned on. This setting forces QBO to create credits if your customers overpay you. Then, you can choose how to use those credits.

Regardless of how you intend to treat the overpayment, find the invoice in the Sales Transactions list and click Receive Payment. Fill in the full amount you received from the customer, including the overpayment amount, in the Amount Received field. Then, do one of the following:

- To apply the overpayment to an existing invoice, in the Outstanding Transactions section of the Receive Payment window, select the invoices to which you want to apply the payment. Typically, the payment will fully pay at least one invoice and partially pay another invoice. QBO automatically reduces the amount due on the partially paid invoice.

- To apply the overpayment to a new invoice (one you haven't yet created), in the Outstanding Transactions section of the Receive Payment window, select only the overpaid invoice. At the bottom of the Receive Payment window, you can see the amount for which QBO will create a credit when you click Save and Close. When you subsequently create a new invoice for the customer, QBO automatically applies the credit amount to the new invoice.

- If you intend to keep the overpayment as income, create a Tip income account and a Tip service item assigned to the Tip income account. Then, create a new invoice for the customer using the Tip item and the overpayment amount. QBO automatically marks the invoice paid because it uses the overpayment credit it created from the overpaid invoice.

Managing invoice status

If you create and send a lot of invoices, it's really easy to lose track of the status of them. Is an invoice unpaid? Partially paid? Paid but not deposited? You can see where I'm heading here.

QBO has set up the Invoices page to help you track the status of your invoices. If you choose Sales from the Navigation pane and then click Invoices, you see the Invoices page.

At the top of the page, you see graphics that help you determine the dollar amount of your unpaid and paid invoices. The graphic for unpaid invoices breaks down the total into Overdue and Not Due Yet. The graphic for paid invoices breaks down the total into Not Deposited and Deposited (see Figure 6-15).

Click Invoices.   Total unpaid   Total paid

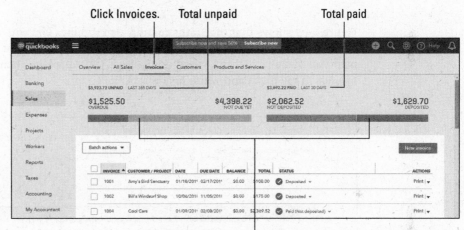

Breakdown of unpaid and paid invoices

FIGURE 6-15: Determining the amount of paid and unpaid invoices in your QBO company.

If you click in the Status column for any transaction, you can see the details behind the transaction. Figure 6-16 shows the status of an invoice that has been paid but the money hasn't been deposited — the transaction's status is Paid, and displaying the details shows you the payment dates and amounts. You can click again the in the Status column for the transaction to hide its details.

A status of Deposited means exactly what you think: You received a payment and you deposited it. And, notice that partially paid invoices appear on separate lines, helping you to track when you received payments for them and the amounts of those payments.

FIGURE 6-16:
Click anywhere in the Status column to see the details for the specific transaction.

Figure 6-17 shows that the Status column also supplies you with additional information; you see invoices that are coming due as well as overdue invoices. And, to help you visually identify overdue invoices, QBO displays them in orange (not obvious in my black and white image).

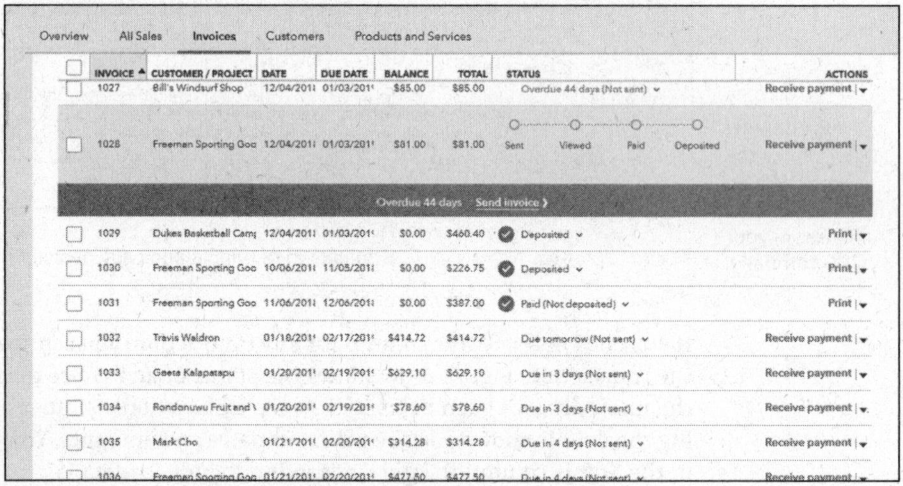

FIGURE 6-17:
In addition to fully and partially paid invoices, you also see which invoices are coming due and which are overdue.

If an invoice's status shows that you haven't sent it yet, you can click the invoice in the Status column to display an option to send it.

Working with estimates

You can use estimates — you might call them quotes or bids — to prepare documents that estimate what you need to charge a client to complete a project; estimates don't update your QBO accounts but do enable you to keep track of proposals you make to customers. If a customer decides to buy, based on your estimate, you can copy the estimate to a purchase order to easily order the items needed to complete the job. You also can copy the estimate to an invoice.

WARNING

You can copy only those estimates with a status of Pending. Copying an estimate to an invoice automatically changes the estimate's status from Pending to Closed. Therefore, if you want to copy an estimate to both a purchase order and an invoice, make sure you copy the estimate to the purchase order first.

NON-POSTING TRANSACTIONS

Estimates and purchase orders are two examples of non-posting transactions. Non-posting transactions don't affect your accounts in any way, but they are helpful because they enable you to enter potential transaction information you don't want to forget. In addition to the estimate and the purchase order, QBO Essentials and Plus also enable you to record two other non-posting transactions: the Delayed Charge and the Delayed Credit.

You can use a Delayed Charge transaction pretty much the same way you use an estimate. The Delayed Charge transaction records potential future revenue, and you can convert a Delayed Charge to an invoice in the same way you convert an estimate to an invoice. For details, see the section "Converting an estimate to an invoice."

The Delayed Credit transaction enables you to record a potential future credit memo. When you prepare an invoice for a customer for whom you've entered a Delayed Credit transaction, QBO displays the Delayed Credit in the pane on the right side of the Invoice window, and you can add the credit to the invoice. A Delayed Credit transaction differs from a Credit Memo transaction because a Credit Memo transaction updates your accounts when you enter it, but a Delayed Credit transaction updates your accounts only when you include it on an invoice.

You fill out both forms the same way you create an invoice; for details, see the section "Preparing an invoice."

Preparing an estimate

Before you prepare an estimate, think about whether the estimate is related to a project; that is, decide whether you want to use QBO's Projects feature. When you use projects, you can see all transactions related to the project in one place. For more information on projects, see the section in this chapter "Managing Projects."

You prepare an estimate in much the same way you prepare an invoice. To display the Estimate window, click the Create menu and choose Estimate. Or, if you prefer to work from the Sales Transactions page, choose Sales⇨All Sales in the Navigation bar, click the New Transaction button, and, from the menu that appears, click Estimate. QBO displays the Estimate window (see Figure 6-18).

REMEMBER

If you are working with a project, you can choose Projects, select the project, and click Add to Project.

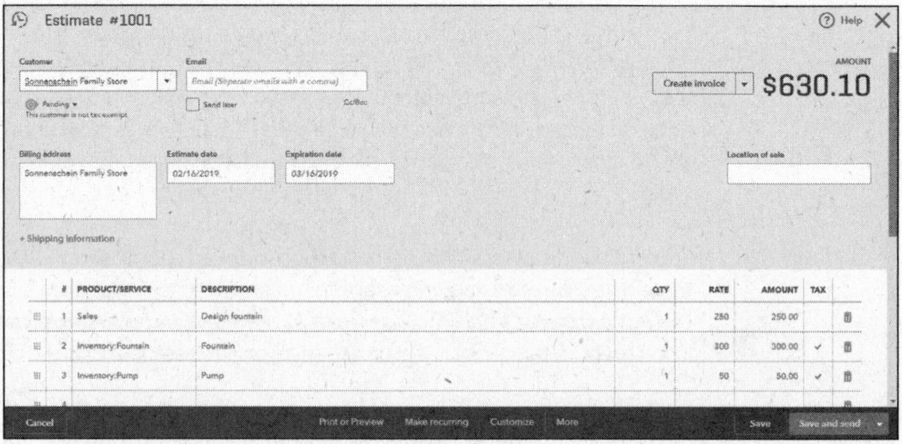

FIGURE 6-18:
Creating
an estimate.

Choose a customer, and QBO displays the customer's address information and the estimate date. You supply the estimate's expiration date and optionally select the Send Later option.

REMEMBER

QBO sets an estimate's status as Pending as long as the estimate is open and has not expired or been converted to an invoice. The status appears just above the customer's billing address.

To fill in the products and services the customer is considering for purchase, click in the Product/Service column and select an item. You can type characters in the Product/Service column and QBO will help you find the item. QBO fills in any default information stored about the item. You can change the description, quantity, rate, amount, and taxable status of the item. Repeat this process to add more items to the estimate.

If you scroll down in the Estimate window, you see the additional fields shown in Figure 6-19.

Click here to control whether a discount is pre- or post-taxable.

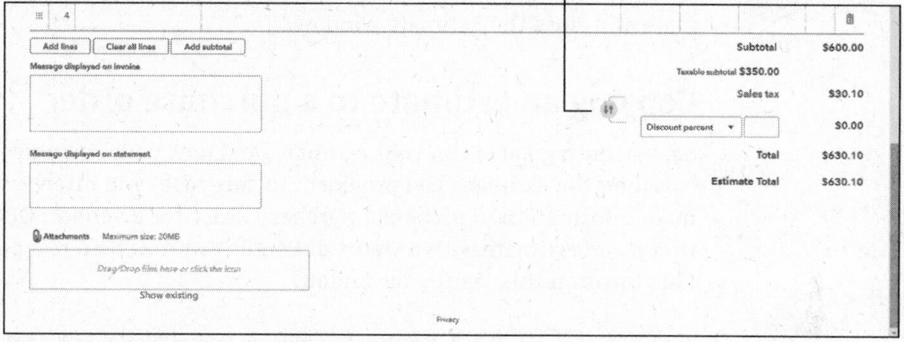

	4			🗑
Add lines	Clear all lines	Add subtotal	Subtotal	$600.00

Taxable subtotal $350.00

Message displayed on invoice

Sales tax | $30.10

Discount percent ▼ | $0.00

Message displayed on statement

Total | $630.10

Estimate Total | $630.10

🔗 Attachments   Maximum size: 20MB

Drag/Drop files here or click the icon

Show existing

Privacy

FIGURE 6-19:
The bottom of the Estimate window.

You can select a sales tax rate, apply a discount percentage or dollar amount to the estimate if you have the company preference turned on to display the Discount box, type a message to the customer, type information in the Memo box, and attach an electronic document to the estimate.

TIP

To attach an electronic document to the estimate, click in the Attachments box and navigate to the folder on your hard disk where you store the document, or drag and drop the electronic copy into the Attachments box.

REMEMBER

You control whether the discount is a pre-tax or post-tax discount by clicking the switch that appears to the left of the Discount and Sales Tax Rate boxes. Clicking the switch swaps the position of the two boxes; when the Discount box appears on top, the discount is pre-tax.

At the bottom of the window, you can

» Cancel the estimate or clear the window and start again.

» Click Print or Preview to print or preview the estimate.

» Click Make Recurring to set up the estimate as a recurring estimate you intend to send on a schedule you specify.

» Click Customize to set up a custom form style for the estimate.

» Click Save to assign a number to the estimate and save it in QBO.

» Click Save and Send to assign a number to the estimate, save it, and email a copy to the customer. A window appears, in which you can write an email message and look at a preview of the estimate. After you send your invoice, the email time and date-stamp information appears in the header.

TIP

You can click the arrow beside Save and Send and then choose Save and New to save the estimate and start a new one, or choose Save and Close to save the estimate and close the Estimate window.

Copying an estimate to a purchase order

So, you did a good job on your estimate, and now your customer wants to purchase based on the estimate you provided. In this case, you often want to use the estimate information to prepare a purchase order for a vendor. QBO Plus enables you to copy an estimate with a status of Pending or Accepted to a purchase order; QBO Plus turns on this feature by default.

WARNING

An estimate's status determines whether it can be copied. If the estimate is open and has not expired or been converted to an invoice, the estimate's status is either Pending or Accepted — the estimate's status changes from Pending to Accepted after your customer approves the estimate. Converting an estimate to an invoice automatically changes the estimate's status to Closed. So, if you intend to copy an estimate to a purchase order, do so before you convert the estimate to an invoice.

Be aware that QBO includes on purchase orders only those items for which you have selected the "I Purchase This Product/Service from a Vendor" option. If you include items on the estimate for which you have not selected this option, those items won't copy to the purchase order. To solve this problem, you can edit your items and make sure you select the option.

You can copy any estimate with a Pending or Accepted status to a purchase order; follow these steps:

1. **Create and save a new estimate using the steps in the preceding section, "Preparing an estimate," or open an existing pending estimate.**

2. **At the top of the Estimate window, click the down arrow beside the Create Invoice button and choose Copy to Purchase Order (see Figure 6-20).**

   You might see the message that explains that some items on the estimate might not carry over to the purchase order. The message appears because some items on the estimate are set up without the "I Purchase This Product/Service from a Vendor" option selected.

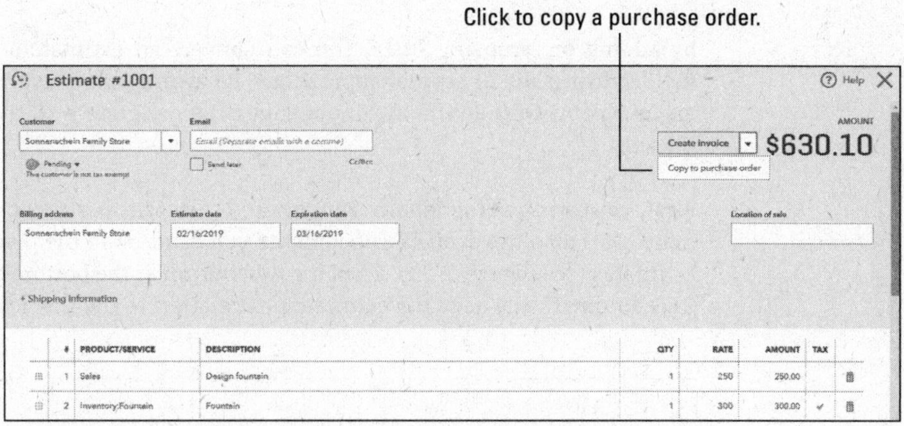

Click to copy a purchase order.

FIGURE 6-20:
Getting ready to copy an estimate to a purchase order.

3. **If the message appears, click OK to dismiss it.**

   QBO creates a purchase order using the information from your estimate and displays it in the Purchase Order window (see Figure 6-21).

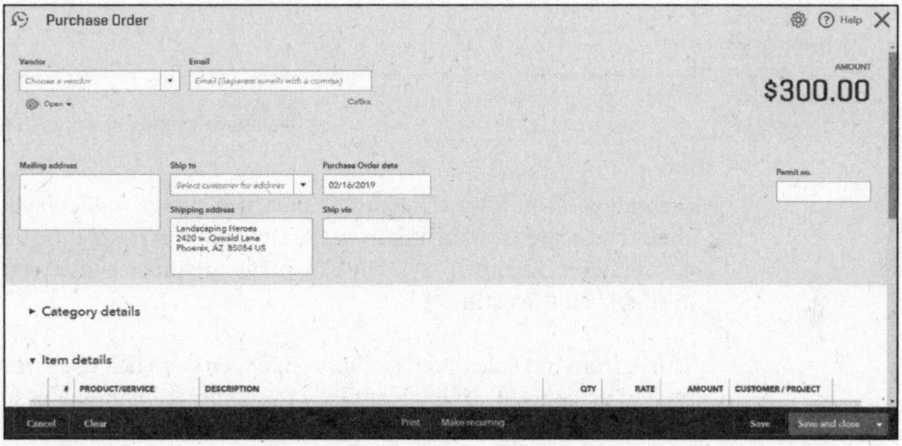

FIGURE 6-21:
A purchase order QBO created from an estimate.

4. **Edit the purchase order as necessary, selecting a vendor and adding any more items to the purchase order.**

5. **Save the purchase order.**

Converting an estimate to an invoice

When you're ready to prepare an invoice for a customer based on an estimate you previously created, save yourself some time and effort and convert the estimate's information to an invoice. You can, if necessary, make adjustments to the invoice by adding or removing lines. You can convert an estimate's information to an invoice using any of several approaches. Be aware that converting an estimate to an invoice in QBO automatically changes the estimate's status from Pending to Closed.

First, you can open the Invoice window and select the customer with the open estimate. QBO displays available documents you can link to the invoice, including any estimates (see Figure 6-22). Click the Add button at the bottom of an estimate, and QBO automatically adds the estimate information to the Invoice window.

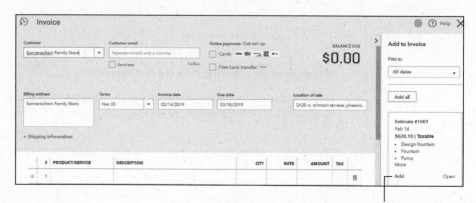

FIGURE 6-22: Converting an estimate to an invoice from the Invoice window.

Click here to add estimate information to the invoice.

Second, you can filter the Sales Transactions page to display only estimates, and click the Create Invoice link in the Action column beside the estimate you want to convert (see Figure 6-23). QBO displays an invoice that contains all the lines available on the estimate.

Third, from the Sales Transactions page, you can click the estimate to open it (and review its content, if you want). In the Estimate window of any estimate with a status of Pending or Accepted, you'll find a Create Invoice button (refer to Figure 6-18); click that button, and QBO displays the Invoice window containing all the information from the estimate.

Regardless of the method you use, after you have converted an estimate on an invoice, QBO changes the estimate's status from Pending or Accepted to Closed. Be aware that QBO closes the estimate even if you don't invoice the customer for all lines on the estimate. Also be aware that you can change an estimate's status from Closed to Pending, but, if you do, you are making all lines on the estimate available for invoicing — and you could then accidentally invoice your customer twice for the same goods. So, if your customer buys only some lines on the estimate but intends to buy other lines at a later point in time, your best bet to ensure that you have the right information available for a future invoice is to let QBO close the original estimate and create another estimate for only the lines the customer didn't yet buy.

Filtering to view only estimates

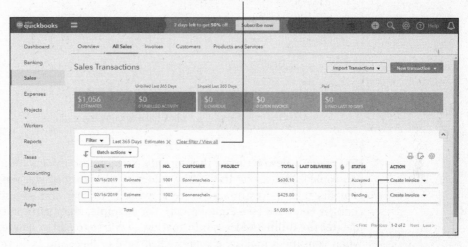

Click this link to start an invoice based on an estimate.

Copying an existing estimate

Suppose that you have an existing estimate — even one you've already converted to an invoice — and you want to create a new estimate using most of the information on the existing invoice. You can make a copy of the existing estimate, edit the copy as needed, and then save the new estimate. Making a copy saves you time because you don't need to reenter a lot of information.

On the Sales Transactions list, click the estimate you want to copy to open it in the Estimate window. Notice that, in Figure 6-24, I've displayed an estimate with a status of Closed.

At the bottom of the window, click the More button and, from the menu that appears, click Copy.

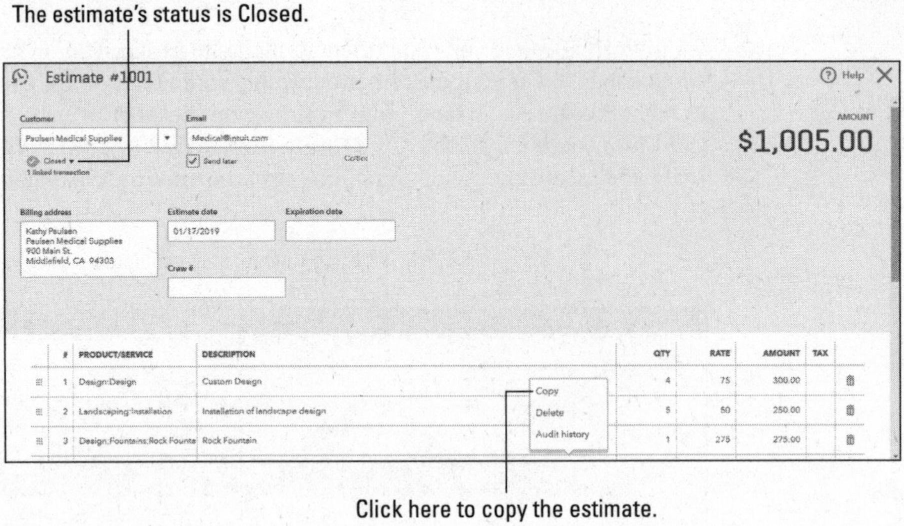

The estimate's status is Closed.

FIGURE 6-24:
Click Copy to duplicate an estimate, even if it's closed.

Click here to copy the estimate.

QBO opens a new estimate that already contains the information of the estimate you copied. Just above the Billing Address information, you see a message that explains that the estimate you're viewing is a copy and you should make any changes you need (see Figure 6-25). For example, change the customer, and QBO updates the Billing Address information. Feel free to add or delete lines as needed. When you finish making changes, click Save or Save and Send in the lower right corner of the window, as appropriate.

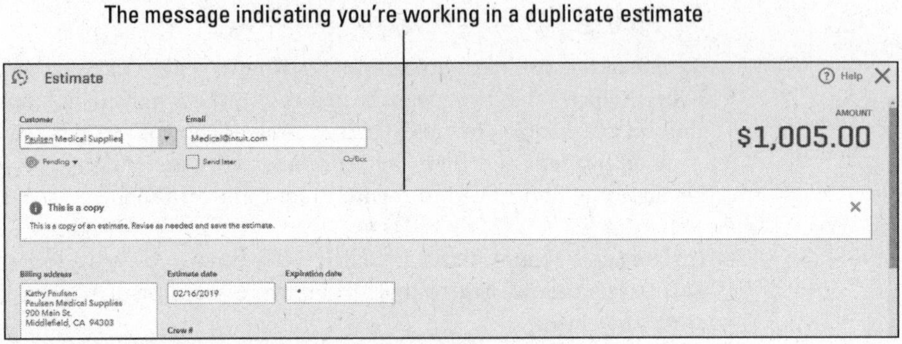

The message indicating you're working in a duplicate estimate

FIGURE 6-25:
Edit the duplicated estimate and save it.

Creating a progress invoice

Suppose your business requires that your work for a customer stretches out over a lengthy period of time — say six months or even a year or more. If you have to wait until you complete the work to collect any money, you'd have a hard time staying in business because you wouldn't have the money to pay your bills.

So, you probably work out arrangements with your customers so that you're paid at various intervals. It's called *progress invoicing*.

TIP

Progress invoicing often goes hand in hand with project work; you can read more about using the Projects feature in QBO earlier in this chapter in the section "Managing Projects." Be aware that you don't need to use the Projects feature to prepare and send progress invoices; but if you *do* intend to use projects, you might want to get them set up before you enter any transactions related to the project. That way, you'll be able to effectively see the transactions affecting the project, including estimates and progress invoices.

Progress invoicing lets you send invoices to your customers at varying intervals that you and your customer establish. QBO uses an estimate you create to enable you to create multiple invoices that account for portions of the estimate until you have entirely invoiced the estimate.

To create progress invoices, you need to turn the feature on in QBO; choose Gear⇨Account and Settings⇨Sales. Then, click in the Progress Invoicing section so that you enable the feature.

Next, create an estimate that you want to use as the foundation for each of your progress invoices. When you're ready to invoice your customer for a portion of the estimate, display the estimate onscreen and click the Create Invoice button. QBO displays the window shown in Figure 6-26.

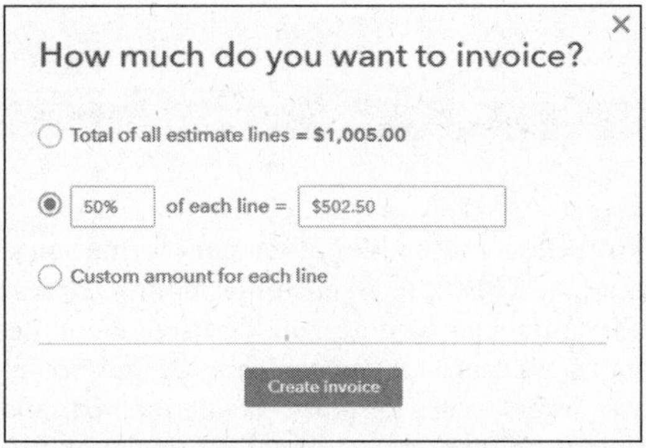

How much do you want to invoice? ✕

○ Total of all estimate lines = $1,005.00

◉ `50%` of each line = `$502.50`

○ Custom amount for each line

[Create invoice]

FIGURE 6-26:
Use this window to establish the amount of a progress invoice.

Based on the choice you make in this window, QBO creates the designated invoice with appropriate values filled in and updates the estimate's value. If you opt to create an invoice using custom amounts for each line, QBO displays the invoice with no amounts filled in so that you can supply them. You create additional progress invoices for the estimate as appropriate until QBO closes the estimate.

Working with sales receipts

You use invoices when you need to track money that a customer owes you but hasn't yet paid. But suppose that your customer pays you at the time you sell goods or render services. In these situations, you don't need to enter an invoice; instead, you can enter a sales receipt. And, if you're shipping the items to the customer, you can print a packing list, which shows the quantities of the items the customer purchased without price information.

Entering a sales receipt

To enter a sales receipt, choose Create ➪ Sales Receipt or, from the Sales Transactions page, choose New Transaction ➪ Sales Receipt to display the window shown in Figure 6-27.

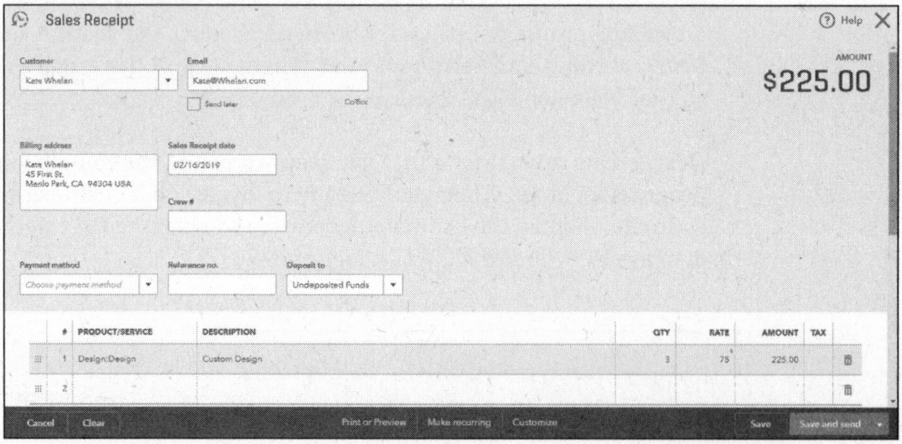

FIGURE 6-27: A sales receipt.

The sales receipt form closely resembles other sales forms you see in this chapter: You select a customer, and QBO fills in customer billing address information and assigns today's date to the transaction. You identify Cc and Bcc email addresses for the sales receipt as appropriate; you can send Cc and Bcc emails for invoices, estimates, purchase orders, sales receipts, credit memos, and refund receipts. Then, enter a payment method and optional reference number, and select the account into which QBO should place the funds. See the sidebar in this chapter "Using the Undeposited Funds account" for information on selecting an account from the Deposit To list.

You fill out the rest of the Sales Receipt transaction the same way you fill out an invoice transaction; if you scroll down in the window, you'll find the same fields at the bottom of the Sales Receipt window as the ones that appear at the bottom of the Invoice window.

Printing sales receipts and packing slips

You can print both the sales receipt and, if appropriate, a packing list. To print either document, click the Print or Preview button at the bottom of the Sales Receipt window. If QBO and your browser — Chrome, in this case — can create a preview of the document, you'll see it onscreen and you can right-click the preview to print the document. If QBO and your browser can't render a preview, you'll see a screen like the one shown in Figure 6-28. You can click the Open button in the middle of the screen, or you can click the Click Here to Download the PDF if You Are Unable to View It Below link; the results of either choice depends on the PDF viewer installed on your computer. For some PDF viewers, the document will appear in a print preview mode. For other PDF viewers, your browser downloads a PDF file. If you're using Chrome, the downloaded PDF file is represented by the icon that appears in the lower left corner of Figure 6-28. You can click the PDF document shown in the lower left corner to display it in the PDF viewer stored on your computer. Figure 6-29 shows the PDF document in Nitro Reader, a free PDF viewer available for download from the Internet.

Notice that the sales receipt displays all pertinent information, including the prices of items.

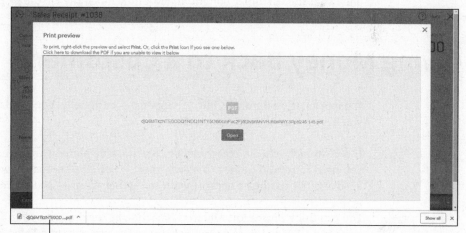

FIGURE 6-28:
The Print Preview window for a sales receipt.

Click here to open the downloaded document QBO creates.

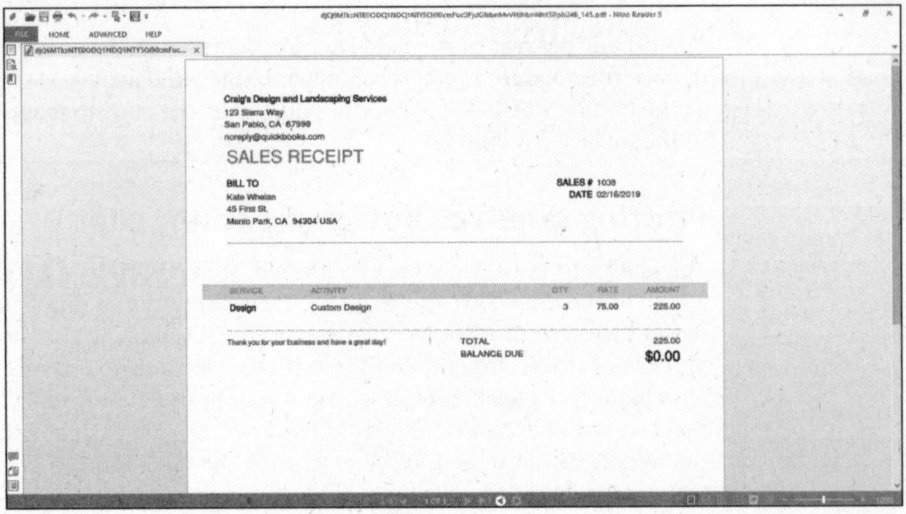

Figure showing a PDF document in Nitro Reader displaying a sales receipt:

Craig's Design and Landscaping Services
123 Sierra Way
San Pablo, CA 87999
noreply@quickbooks.com

SALES RECEIPT

BILL TO
Kate Whelan
45 First St.
Menlo Park, CA 94304 USA

SALES # 1038
DATE 02/16/2019

SERVICE	ACTIVITY	QTY	RATE	AMOUNT
Design	Custom Design	3	75.00	225.00

Thank you for your business and have a great day!

TOTAL 225.00
BALANCE DUE **$0.00**

FIGURE 6-29:
The PDF version of the sales receipt QBO creates.

REMEMBER

You can dismiss the Print Preview window using the X in the upper right corner of the screen or, if you see it onscreen, the Close button at the lower left corner of the Print Preview window.

If you opt to print the packing slip, QBO again saves the sales receipt if you haven't already saved it. Then, QBO downloads the document and displays a preview window like the one shown previously in Figure 6-28. When you click the downloaded PDF document, it opens in your computer's PDF viewer; the difference between the sales receipt and the packing slip is that the packing slip displays only what the customer bought and not how much the customer paid.

Giving Money Back to a Customer

It happens. It's a bummer, but, it happens. Occasionally, you need to return money you have received from a customer.

If a customer returns merchandise to you, issue a credit memo. Alternatively, if you need to refund money to a customer — perhaps because goods arrived damaged and the customer doesn't want to reorder them — issue a refund receipt.

TIP

You can think of a Credit Memo transaction as the opposite of an Invoice transaction, and a Refund Receipt transaction as the opposite of a Sales Receipt transaction. The look and feel of a Credit Memo transaction is similar to an Invoice transaction, but has the opposite impact. Similarly, the look and feel of a Refund Receipt transaction is similar to a Sales Receipt transaction but (again) has the opposite impact.

Recording a credit memo

If a customer returns goods previously purchased or if you and your customer agree that the customer's outstanding or future balance should be reduced, record a credit memo in QBO.

TIP

By default, QBO automatically applies credit memos to outstanding or future invoices. If you want to change that behavior, open the Account and Settings dialog box (choose Gear menu ⇨ Account and Settings) and click Advanced on the left. Scroll down to the Automation section on the right, and click the Automatically Apply Credits option.

You enter a Credit Memo transaction pretty much the same way you enter an invoice; to display the Credit Memo window shown in Figure 6-30, you can click the Create menu button and choose Credit Memo or, from the Sales Transactions page, you can click the New Transaction button and choose Credit Memo.

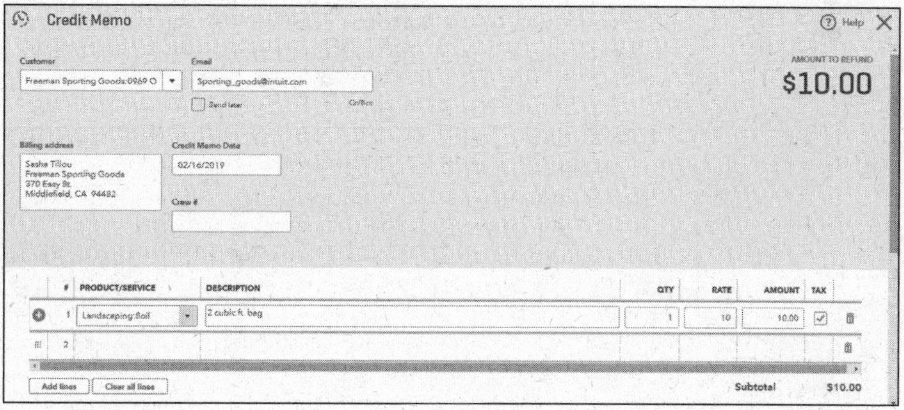

FIGURE 6-30:
Entering a credit memo.

Select the customer, fill in the products or services for which you are issuing a credit memo, fill in the bottom of the Credit Memo window with appropriate information, and save the transaction. This transaction window is very similar to the Invoice transaction window; see the section "Preparing an invoice" for details.

You can enter a credit memo for a customer even if that customer currently has no outstanding invoices; when you enter the customer's next invoice, QBO automatically applies the credit memo to the invoice.

When you enter a credit memo for a customer who has outstanding invoices, QBO applies the credit memo to an outstanding invoice; if you view the Sales Transactions list for that particular invoice, you'll notice that its Status is Partial, meaning that the invoice is partially paid (see Figure 6-31).

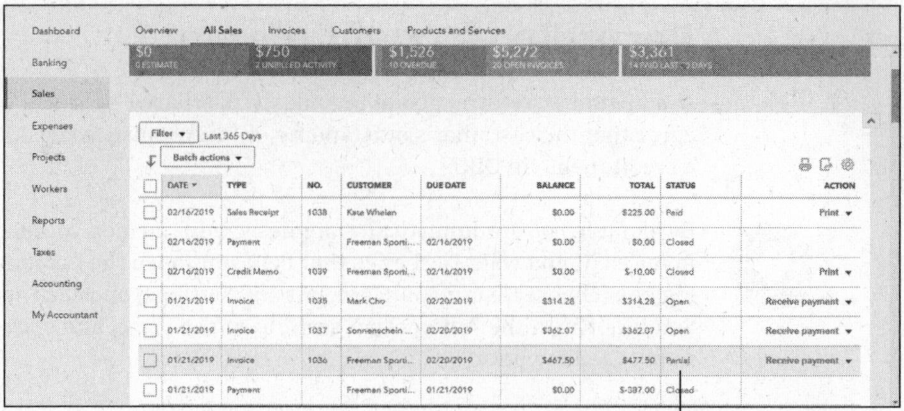

FIGURE 6-31:
An invoice to which QBO has applied a credit memo.

Invoice with a credit memo applied

If you click the invoice to view it, you'll see a link just below the outstanding balance that indicates a payment was made (and the amount of the payment). And, if you scroll to the bottom of the invoice, you'll see the credit amount on the Amount Received line at the bottom of the invoice (see Figure 6-32).

FIGURE 6-32:
By default, QBO applies credit memos to an existing outstanding invoice.

The credit amount appears here.

Issuing a refund to a customer

Use QBO's Refund Receipt transaction if you need to refund money to a customer instead of reducing an outstanding or future balance. In this example, I'm going to issue a refund check to a customer, which will deduct the amount of the refund from a Bank account and reduce an Income account. The customer didn't return any items.

TIP

To account for refunds you issue when a customer doesn't return an item, first set up an account called something like Returns and Allowances, and assign this account to the Category Type of Income and a Detail Type of Discounts/Refunds Given. Then set up a service on the Products and Services list and call it something like Customer Refunds or even Returns & Allowances. Do *not* select Is Taxable for the service. Assign the service to the Returns and Allowances account and don't assign a default Price/Rate.

Filling in the Refund Receipt window is very similar to filling in the Sales Receipt window, so, if you need more details than I supply here, see the section "Working with sales receipts." To display the Refund Receipt window shown in Figure 6-33, click the Create button — the plus (+) sign — and choose Refund Receipt in the Customers column. Select a customer, and QBO fills in related customer information.

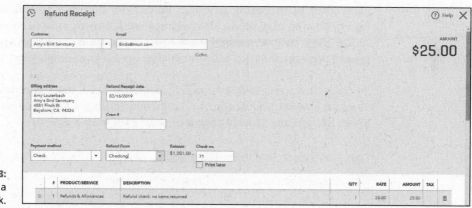

FIGURE 6-33: Issuing a refund check.

Select a payment method and an account; if you select a Bank account like I did, QBO lists the Bank account's current balance and the next check number associated with the account. If you want, click the Print Later check box.

In my example, the customer isn't returning any items, so I selected the Refunds & Allowances service. If your customer is returning items, select the item that the customer is returning in exchange for the refund in the Product/Service column, and don't select the Refunds and Allowances service shown in Figure 6-33.

You can scroll down to the bottom of the Refund Receipt transaction window and fill in all the same information available at the bottom of an invoice. You can also save and send copies of refund receipts to your customers.

Creating Billable Time Entries

This section of *QuickBooks Online For Dummies* focuses on the time-tracking tools that are native to QBO.

TIP

If your business has serious time-tracking needs and you need more power than QBO offers by default, consider using T-Sheets, an app that fully integrates with QBO and easily enables your employees to track time using their mobile devices; any time they record syncs automatically to QBO, with all the appropriate customer, job, and employee information. For more information, visit the Intuit App Center (click the Apps link in the Navigation pane) or visit apps.intuit.com, the direct link at the time I wrote this.

Your employees might work directly for you on activities needed to run your company (such as preparing customer invoices or entering accounting information into QBO), and they might also perform work directly related to your customers. In the latter case, you might want to track the time employees spend on client-related projects and then bill your customers for your employees' time.

To track time using tools available by default in QBO, make sure you turn on Time Tracking options. Choose Gear ⇨ Account and Settings ⇨ Advanced (see Figure 6-34). Then, in the Time Tracking section, enable these two options:

» Add Service Field to Timeslips, and

» Make Single-Time Activity Billable to Customer.

Account and Settings				? Help ✕
Company				
Usage	Projects	Organize all job-related activity in one place	On	✎
Sales	Time tracking	Add Service field to timesheets	On	✎
Expenses		Make Single-Time Activity Billable to Customer	On	
Advanced	Currency	Home Currency	United States Dollar	✎
		Multicurrency	Off	
	Other preferences	Date format	MM/dd/yyyy	✎
		Number format	123,456.00	
		Customer label	Customers	
		Warn if duplicate check number is used	On	
		Warn if duplicate bill number is used	Off	
		Sign me out if inactive for	1 hour	

FIGURE 6-34: Enable time-tracking options in QBO.

You use either the Time Activity window or the Weekly Timesheet window. Regardless of the window you use, QBO tracks the time entered and, when you prepare an invoice for a client for whom time was recorded, QBO prompts you to add the time to the invoice.

In this section, you learn to enter time using both the Time Activity window and the Weekly Timesheet window, and you see how QBO prompts you to include the billable time on a customer's invoice. Note that a time entry that you can bill back to a customer is called, cleverly, *billable time.*

Entering a single time activity

To open the Time Activity window, follow these steps:

REMEMBER

1. **Click the Create plus (+) sign button to open the Create menu.**

   If you are working with a project, you can choose Projects, select the project, and click Add to Project.

2. **In the Employees column, click Single Time Activity.**

   QBO displays the Time Activity window shown in Figure 6-35.

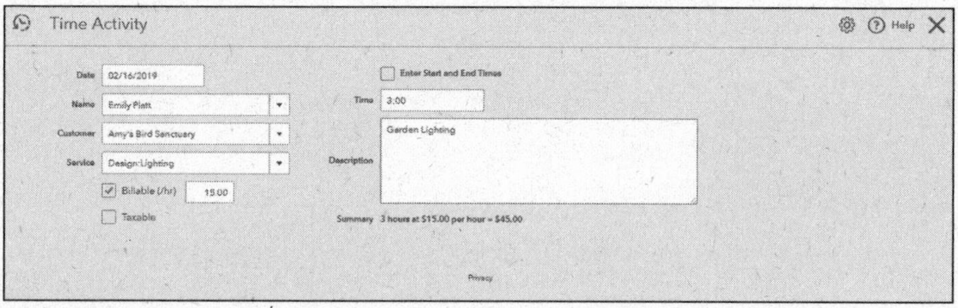

FIGURE 6-35:
The Time Activity
window.

3. **From the Name list, select the employee or vendor who performed the work.**

4. **Enter the date the work was performed.**

5. **From the Customer list, select the customer for whom the work was performed.**

6. **From the Service list, select the service that was performed.**

7. **Place a check in the Billable box, which changes to the Bill At box, and supply an hourly rate.**

8. **If the work performed is subject to tax, place a check in the Taxable box.**

9. **In the Time box, enter the amount of time spent on this activity.**

   You can enter start and end times, including any break time, by checking the Enter Start and End Times box; QBO calculates the time spent and displays it below the Description box.

10. **Enter a description of the work that will appear, by default, on an invoice.**

You can change the description after adding the time entry to the invoice.

11. **In the lower right corner of the window, click Save to save the entry or Save and New to enter another time activity.**

If you click the arrow beside Save and New, you can choose Save and Close.

Using a timesheet to record time

If you prefer to enter time in a grid format that shows the days and dates for a week, then the Weekly Timesheet, shown in Figure 6-36, is for you. To enter time using this window, follow these steps:

1. **Click the Create button — the plus (+) sign — to open the Create menu.**

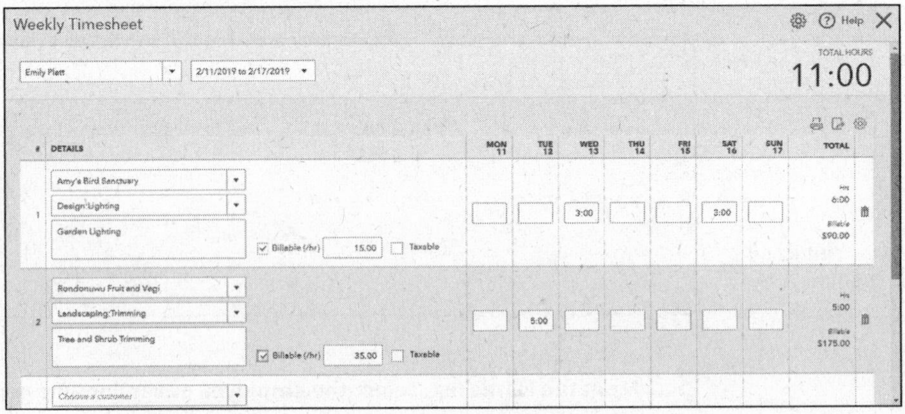

FIGURE 6-36: The Weekly Timesheet.

2. **In the Employees column, click Weekly Timesheet.**

3. **Select the name of the person whose time you're recording.**

4. **Select the week for which you want to record time.**

5. **In the Details section, select a customer name, a service item, and, if appropriate, supply a description.**

6. **To bill the time back to a customer, select the Billable check box and provide a rate at which to charge the time.**

7. **Fill in the time worked on the appropriate day.**

8. **In the lower right corner of the window, click Save, Save and New, or click the arrow beside Save and New and select Save and Close.**

Adding a Billable Expense to an Invoice

You can add billable expense entries, including billable time entries, to an invoice in a couple of ways. For example, if you view any customer's page, QBO displays a list of outstanding transactions, as shown in Figure 6-37. In the Action column of any billable entry, QBO displays a Create Invoice button that you can click to start an invoice to the customer and include the billable expense on the invoice. To view a customer's page, click Sales in the Navigation bar, click Customer on the page that appears, and then click a customer's name.

REMEMBER

If you are working with a project, you can choose Projects, select the project, and click Transactions to view available billable expenses.

Click here to display your customer list and select a different customer.

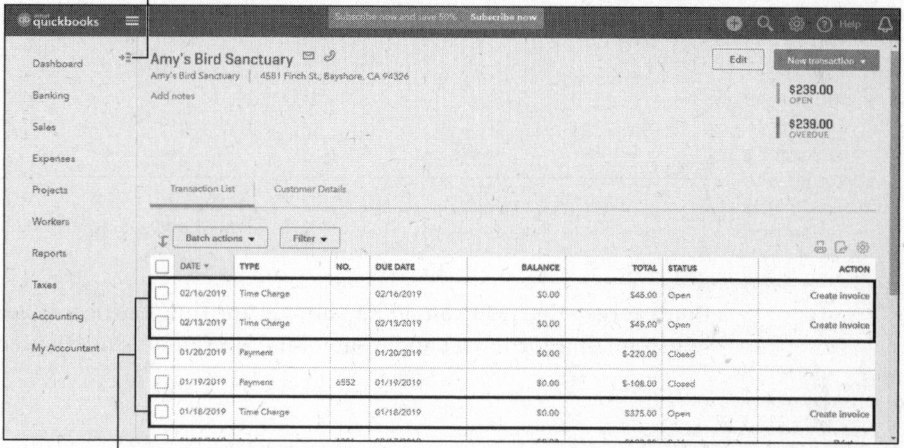

FIGURE 6-37:
Viewing a customer's page in QBO.

These lines contain billable expenses.

But you don't need to go looking for billable time entries. QBO prompts you to add them to any invoice you create for a customer for whom billable entries exist. Start an invoice (from the Create menu — the plus sign — click Invoice) and select a customer. If the customer has billable expense entries, they appear in the pane on the right side of the screen (see Figure 6-38).

Use the Filter options to limit the billable time entries that appear. Then, click the Add button in each billable time entry that you want to add to the invoice. Or, to add all the entries, click the Add All button at the top of the pane on the right. QBO enters each billable time entry's information on a line on the invoice, filling in the service, description, quantity, rate, and total amount. By default, QBO lists time entries individually on the invoice, but you can opt to group time entries by service type. You can edit any information on the invoice as needed. Fill in the rest of the invoice as described in the section "Preparing an invoice," adding other lines that might not pertain to time entries.

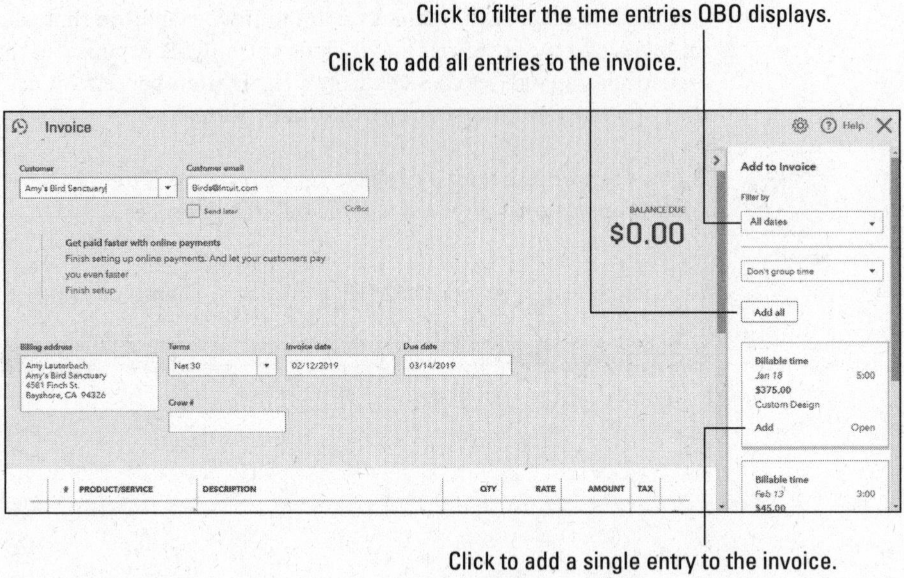

Click to filter the time entries QBO displays.

Click to add all entries to the invoice.

FIGURE 6-38:
Creating an invoice for a customer with billable time entries.

Click to add a single entry to the invoice.

Don't forget that you can add a subtotal for time entries, if you choose. See the "Customizing forms to handle subtotals" section of this chapter for details.

Chapter **7**

Working in Registers

C hapters 5 and 6 show you how to enter transactions such as checks, sales receipts, invoices, and customer payments using various QBO transaction windows. You also see ways to find and filter for certain transactions.

But transaction windows and lists aren't the only way to work with transactions in QBO. You also can use registers. Some people are more comfortable entering transactions, particularly checks, into a register.

And many people find it easy to use a register to quickly view the transactions that affect a particular account and find particular transactions, as described at the end of this chapter.

Understanding Registers

You use registers to see every transaction that affects a particular account. Registers in QBO contain much of the same information you find in the paper registers that banks give you along with handwritten checks. To view the register for a particular account, choose Gear ⇨ Accounting ⇨ Chart of Accounts. Note that the first time you view the Chart of Accounts, you might need to click the See Your Chart of Accounts button before your Chart of Accounts appears. Then, use the View Register link in the Action column to display the register of a particular account (see Figure 7-1).

Chart of Accounts

‹ All Lists

Run Report | New ▾

| Filter by name | | | | | ✎ 🖶 ⚙ |
NAME	TYPE	DETAIL TYPE	QUICKBOOKS BALANCE	BANK BALANCE	ACTION
Checking	🏦 Bank	🏦 Checking	1,201.00	-3,621.93	View register ▾
Savings	🏦 Bank	🏦 Savings	800.00	200.00	View register ▾
Accounts Receivable (A/R)	Accounts receivable (A/R)	Accounts Receivable (A/R)	5,281.52		View register ▾
Inventory Asset	Other Current Assets	Inventory	596.25		View register ▾
Prepaid Expenses	Other Current Assets	Prepaid Expenses	0.00		View register ▾

FIGURE 7-1:
Use the Chart of Accounts page to open a particular account's register.

Click to view a register.

Figure 7-2 shows a Bank account register in QBO. The register page displays the name of the account — in this case, Checking, with the bank balance beside the bank account name — and its ending balance in QBO at the top right side of the register.

Account balance at the bank   Table Gear Settings button

‹ Back to Chart of Accounts

Bank Register | Checking ▾ | Bank Balance
$-3,621.93

ENDING BALANCE
$1,201.00   Reconcile

Go to: 1 of 1 ‹ First Previous 1-44 of 44 Next Last»

▽ ▾ All   🖶 ⬓ ⚙

DATE ▾	REF NO. TYPE	PAYEE ACCOUNT	MEMO	PAYMENT	DEPOSIT	✓ ⬓	BALANCE
Add check ▾							
02/06/2019					$900.00		$1,201.00
	CC-Credit	Mastercard					
01/26/2019		Tania's Nursery		$23.50			$2,101.00
	Cash Purch	Job Expenses:Job Materials:Plants and...					
01/23/2019	76	Pam Seitz		$75.00			$2,124.50

FIGURE 7-2:
A typical Bank account register.

Account balance in QBO

Because the Bank account register shown in Figure 7-2 is electronically connected to its counterpart at a banking institution, you also see the balance in the account as that financial institution reports it — and in this case, the balance at the bank is negative.

TIP

By default, QBO displays the latest transaction first, but you can make changes to the way QBO displays register information, as described later in this section and at the end of this chapter, in the section "Other Things You Can Do in a Register."

One rule you need to remember about registers: They are *not* available for all accounts. You'll find that registers are available for all *balance sheet* accounts except Retained Earnings. Balance sheet accounts fall into the following QBO account category types:

» Bank

» Accounts Receivable

» Other Current Assets

» Fixed Assets

» Other Assets

» Accounts Payable

» Credit Card

» Other Current Liabilities

» Long Term Liabilities

» Equity

You see these account category types when you add a new account to the Chart of Accounts or when you view the Chart of Accounts page in QBO.

TIP

If you use account numbers, then, typically, all asset accounts begin with 10000, all liability accounts begin with 20000, and all equity accounts begin with 30000. This numbering scheme is *not* carved in stone, but most accountants recommend that you follow these guidelines when you assign numbers to the accounts in your Chart of Accounts.

Within the register, you see column headings that identify the information contained in each column for every transaction and, at the right edge of a register page, you see a running balance for the account. All the transactions in a Bank account register affect a Bank account — along with some other account, as dictated by the rules of accounting (*double-entry bookkeeping,* a founding principle of accounting, means that every transaction affects at least two accounts). The amount shown in the Balance column is a running balance for the account as long as the register is sorted by date.

TIP

At the end of this chapter, in the section "Other Things You Can Do in a Register," you learn how to sort a register so that it appears in some order other than the default transaction date order. Be aware that, if you sort by any column other than the Date column, the Balance column won't display any information because the information wouldn't make any sense.

By default, the latest transactions appear at the top of the register, but, if you prefer, you can change the appearance of the register to use Paper Ledger Mode, as shown in Figure 7-3. In Paper Ledger Mode, QBO lists transactions from earliest to latest — similar to the way transactions appear when you use a paper bank account register. In a paper register, you enter your transactions as they occur, so the earliest transactions appear at the top of the register and the latest transactions appear at the bottom of the register.

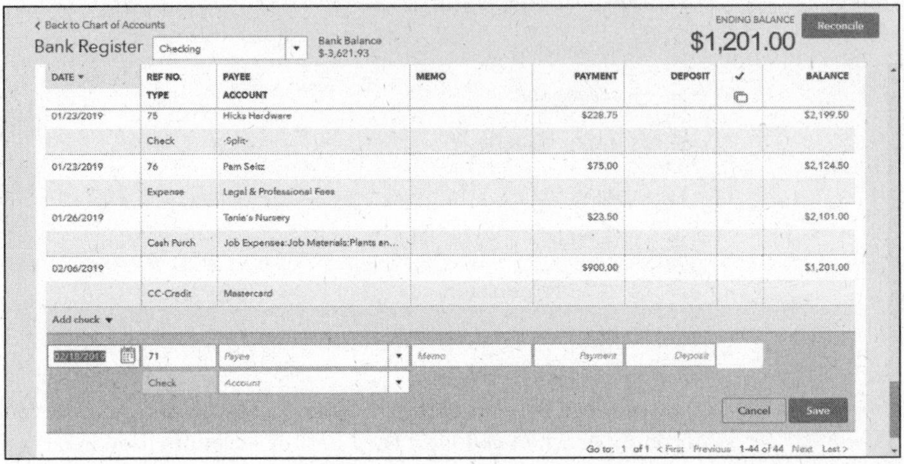

FIGURE 7-3:
A Bank account register in Paper Ledger Mode.

When you switch to Paper Ledger Mode, QBO assumes you want to enter a new transaction, as described later in this chapter in the section "Entering a transaction," and automatically displays a new transaction window at the bottom of the register page.

REMEMBER

To switch to Paper Ledger Mode, follow these steps:

1. **Click the Table Settings gear above the Balance column.**

   You can see the Table Gear Settings button in Figure 7-2.

2. **From the drop-down menu that appears, click Paper Ledger Mode to select it.**

   QBO reorders the transactions in the register so that they appear in date order from oldest to newest.

   In addition, QBO displays a new transaction window at the bottom of the register — ready for you to use, as you can see in Figure 7-3.

To switch back to the register's regular appearance, repeat the preceding steps; when you remove the check beside Paper Ledger Mode, QBO reorders the transactions in the register in date order with the latest transaction at the top of the register page.

In addition to using Paper Ledger Mode, you can control the appearance of a register in a few other ways; you can

» Change the size of columns.

» Control the number of rows on a page in your QBO company.

» Reduce each register entry to a single line.

TIP

QBO remembers the setting you select for the register's appearance even after you navigate away from the register; if you choose to display the register in Paper Ledger Mode, the next time you display any register, QBO displays it in Paper Ledger Mode. Further, if you open a different register, QBO applies your adjustments to that register.

To change the size of any column, slide the mouse pointer into the column heading area on the right boundary of the column. In Figure 7-4, I'm resizing the Memo column. Drag the mouse pointer when the pointer changes to a pair of left- and right-pointing arrows connected to a pair of vertical bars. Dragging to the left makes the column narrower, and dragging to the right makes the column wider. As you drag, a solid vertical line like the one in Figure 7-4 helps you determine the size of the column. Release the mouse button when the column reaches the size you want.

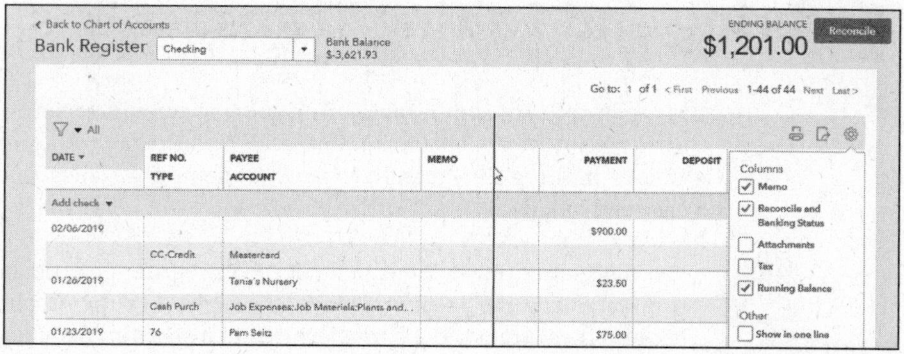

FIGURE 7-4:
Resizing a
column.

If resizing columns doesn't satisfy your viewing needs, you can save space horizontally by removing columns from the register. To do so, you use the options on the Table Settings gear. Click the Gear button above the Balance column at the right edge of the page. In the Columns section (refer to Figure 7-2), remove the checks beside any options you don't need to view; by default, QBO displays the Memo, Reconcile and Banking Status, and Running Balance columns. Remove the checks beside these options and QBO removes their columns from the register. You also can add columns of information such as transaction attachments to a register.

To save space vertically, place a check mark in the Show in One Line box and change the number of rows that appear on a page. You can display 50 rows, 150 rows, or 300 rows. Figure 7-5 shows a register displaying a single line for each transaction. By default, if you opt to display a single line for each transaction in the register, QBO hides the Memo and the Reconcile and Banking Status columns.

FIGURE 7-5:
A register displaying one line for each transaction.

DATE ▾	REF NO.	TYPE	PAYEE	ACCOUNT	PAYMENT	DEPOSIT	BALANCE
Add check ▾							
02/06/2019		CC-Credit		Mastercard	$900.00		$1,201.00
01/26/2019		Cash Purch	Tania's Nursery	Job Expenses:Job ...	$23.50		$2,101.00
01/23/2019	76	Expense	Pam Seitz	Legal & Professional...	$75.00		$2,124.50
01/23/2019	75	Check	Hicks Hardware	-Split-	$229.75		$2,199.50
01/23/2019		Deposit		-Split-		$868.15	$2,428.25
01/22/2019		Cash Purch	Chin's Gas and Oil	Automobile:Fuel	$63.15		$1,560.10
01/22/2019	108	Expense	Tania's Nursery	Job Expenses	$46.98		$1,623.25
01/22/2019	45	Bill Payment	Tim Philip Masonry	Accounts Payable (A...	$666.00		$1,670.23

Bank Register — Checking — Bank Balance $-3,621.93 — ENDING BALANCE $1,201.00 — Reconcile

‹ Back to Chart of Accounts

Go to: 1 of 1 ‹ First Previous 1-44 of 44 Next Last ›

Entering and Editing Transactions

Many people are comfortable using a Bank account register to enter a check, a sales receipt, or a bill payment. But, even if you're not comfortable entering transactions in a register, many people find viewing a transaction in a register very easy and helpful.

REMEMBER

You can't enter transactions in all of QBO's registers; particularly, you can't enter transactions in the Accounts Receivable register or the Accounts Payable register because these transactions must be tied to a specific customer or vendor.

Entering a transaction

Because checks are the transaction most often entered using a register, I'm focusing the discussion in this section on Bank account registers. After you click the View Register link of a bank account, you can enter a transaction into the register.

If you need to add attachments to transactions you enter, display the Attachment column in the register; choose Table Gear Settings ➪ Attachments. You can identify the Table Gear Settings button in Figure 7-2 (shown previously). Displaying the Attachments column automatically gives you the option to add an attachment as you enter a transaction.

By default, QBO helps you enter the most logical transaction for the open register. That might be a check, a deposit, a journal entry, and so on, depending on the register you open; in the case of a Bank account register, QBO displays the Add Check link. To enter the type of transaction QBO suggests, click the Add link below the Date column heading. If you are working in Paper Ledger Mode, the Add link appears at the bottom of the Date column.

But suppose you want to enter a different type of transaction in a bank register. To start a new transaction and enter it, open the appropriate register and follow these steps:

1. **Click the down arrow beside the Add Check button.**

QBO displays the list of available transaction types for the account (see Figure 7-6).

For you keyboard fans, you can press Ctrl+Alt+N to open the Add list box. For a complete list of keyboard shortcuts, see this book's Cheat Sheet.

QBO displays only those types of transactions available in the account register you opened. For example, you can record a customer payment in a Bank account register, but you cannot enter a customer invoice. Similarly, you can record a check or a bill payment in a Bank account register, but you cannot enter a vendor bill.

2. **From the list that appears, select the type of transaction you want to enter; for this example, I selected Sales Receipt.**

QBO fills in today's date and displays lines so that you can complete the transaction (see Figure 7-7).

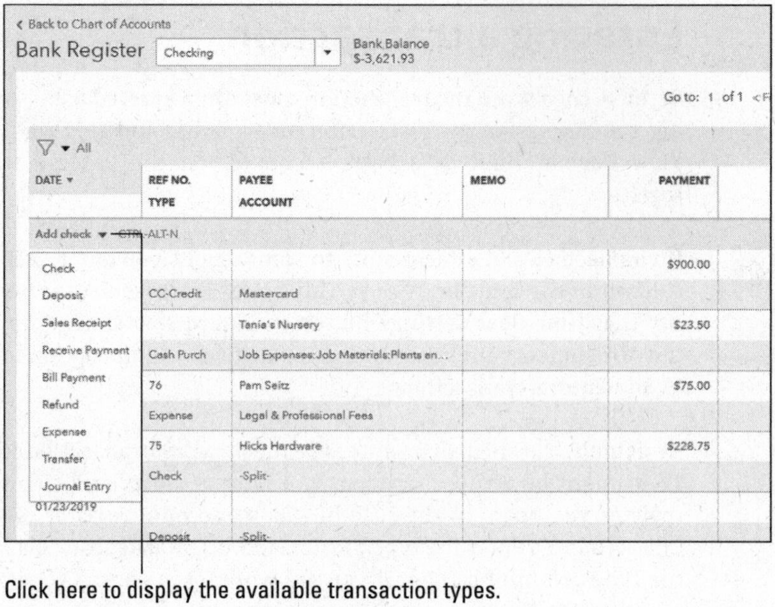

FIGURE 7-6:
Select the type of transaction you want to enter.

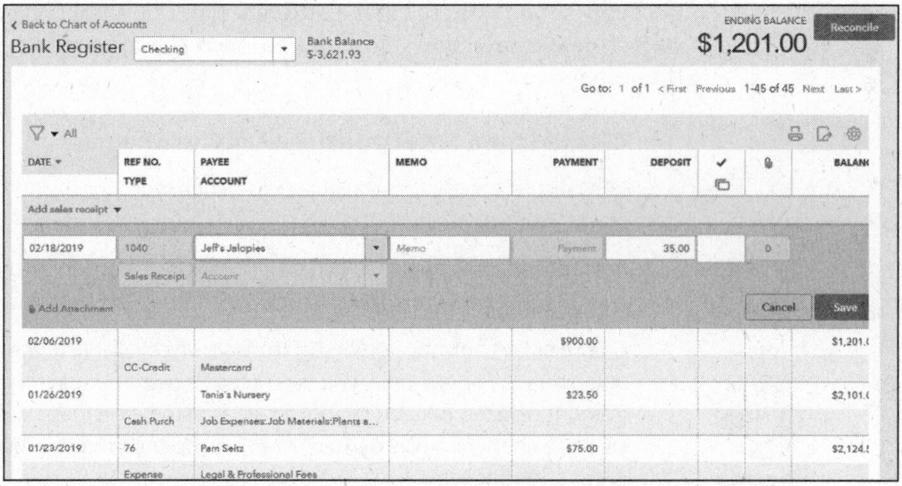

Click here to display the available transaction types.

FIGURE 7-7:
Entering a sales receipt in a Bank account register.

3. **If necessary, change the transaction date.**

4. **Press Tab and, if appropriate, change the reference number for the transaction.**

You can change the reference number only for some types of transactions — and the Sales Receipt isn't one of them.

5. **Press Tab and supply a name.**

For example, if you're recording a payment you received from a customer, select the customer's name. If you're writing a check, select the check recipient's name.

6. **Press Tab and, in the Memo column, supply any memo information you want to record for the transaction.**

7. **Press Tab and, in the appropriate column, provide the amount of the transaction.**

In a Bank account register, record a payment you're making in the Payment amount box and an amount you're depositing in the Deposit amount box. The type of amount you can record (payment or deposit) depends on the type of transaction you're entering; for example, you can record a deposit for a Sales Receipt, but you can't record a payment for a Sales Receipt.

8. **Press Tab.**

QBO places the mouse pointer in the Reconcile and Banking Status column. This column displays a character representing the status of the transaction: C for Cleared or R for Reconciled. When the column is blank, the transaction is neither cleared nor reconciled. Typically this column is updated when you download or reconcile transactions.

If the account is also connected electronically to your financial institution, this column also indicates whether a transaction was added or matched when transactions were downloaded via the account's bank feed.

WARNING

Don't be tempted to adjust the reconciliation status of a transaction from this screen because doing so adjusts the account's reconciled balance, but the adjustment doesn't show up on reconciliation reports. You'll have a mess on your hands if you modify the reconciliation status outside the reconciliation process.

9. **Press Tab.**

QBO's placement of the insertion pointer depends on the type of transaction you're entering. For example, if you're entering a Sales Receipt, a Receive Payment, a Bill Payment, or a Refund transaction, QBO places the insertion point in the area where you can save or cancel the transaction.

If, however, you're entering a Check, a Deposit, an Expense, a Transfer, or a Journal Entry transaction, QBO places the insertion point in the Account column. Select the other account affected by the transaction (in addition to the account whose register you have opened). For example, if you're entering a check, select an Expense account. Then, press Tab to move the insertion point into the area where you can save or cancel the transaction.

TIP

To add an attachment to the transaction, use the Table Gear Settings button to add the Attachment fields. Then, click the Add Attachment button in the lower left corner of the transaction window. QBO opens a standard "Open" dialog box, where you navigate to the electronic document you want to attach to the transaction. Once you find it, click it and click Open to attach it to the transaction.

10. **Click the Save button that appears in the transaction.**

Keyboard fans, press Ctrl+Alt+S.

QBO saves the transaction and starts another of the same type. You can click Cancel to stop entering transactions.

Editing a transaction

You can edit a transaction in the register by clicking the transaction and then making changes. Or, if you prefer to use the transaction window for the type of transaction you selected, click the transaction and then click the Edit button. For example, if you opt to edit an Expense transaction in an account register, QBO displays the transaction in the Expense window. If you opt to enter a Check transaction, QBO displays the transaction in the Check window. See Chapter 5 for examples of transaction windows.

Other Things You Can Do in a Register

Registers wouldn't be all that useful if you could only add and edit transactions. You need to be able to find transactions easily. And, it's always helpful to be able to print a register.

Sorting transactions

After a while, the number of transactions in a register can make the Register page very long, especially in a Bank account register. Looking for a transaction by skimming through the register — or *eyeballing* — can be a nonproductive way of finding a transaction. Instead, sorting the register can help you find a particular transaction.

You can sort by any column in the register simply by clicking that column heading. In Figure 7-8, the transactions are sorted by date, in descending order from latest to earliest; note the downward-pointing arrow in the Date column heading.

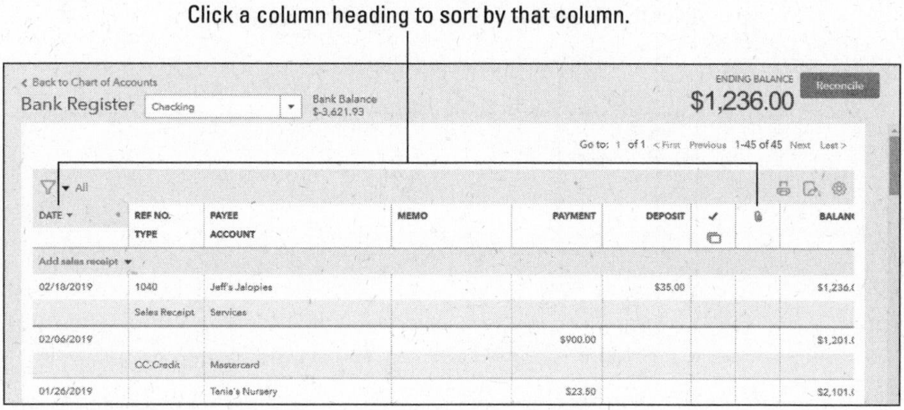

Click a column heading to sort by that column.

FIGURE 7-8:
Sorting
transactions
by date,
from latest to
earliest, is
the default
order QBO
uses to display
transactions.

| | ‹ Back to Chart of Accounts | | | | | | ENDING BALANCE | | Reconcile |
| Bank Register | Checking ▾ | Bank Balance $-3,621.93 | | | | | $1,236.00 | | |

Go to: 1 of 1 ‹ First Previous 1-45 of 45 Next Last ›

▽ ▾ All

DATE ▾	REF NO. TYPE	PAYEE ACCOUNT	MEMO	PAYMENT	DEPOSIT	✓	🔗	BALANCE
Add sales receipt ▾								
02/18/2019	1040	Jeff's Jalopies			$35.00			$1,236.0
	Sales Receipt	Services						
02/06/2019				$900.00				$1,201.0
	CC-Credit	Mastercard						
01/26/2019		Tania's Nursery		$23.50				$2,101.6

To sort the transactions by date from earliest to latest, click the Date column; the arrow beside the column heading name changes direction and points upward.

Or suppose you want to search for transactions for a particular payee. You can click the Payee column heading to sort transactions in alphabetical order by payee, and you can click the column heading a second time to sort in reverse alphabetical order.

WARNING

You can sort by any column heading *except* the Account, Balance, Memo, and Attachment columns. And, if you sort by any column other than Date, the Balance column won't display any information because the information wouldn't make any sense.

Filtering transactions

When sorting seems like the long way to find a transaction, try working with filters to display transactions that meet criteria you set. Click the Filter funnel button that appears just above the Date column, and QBO displays a menu offering a variety of ways you can filter register transactions (see Figure 7-9).

TIP

The current filter appears just beside the Filter funnel button. When you haven't selected any filters, you see "All" beside the Filter funnel button.

If you're looking for a transaction of a certain dollar amount, enter the amount, making sure that you don't forget the currency symbol. When you filter by amounts, use these examples as a guideline:

>> 1234 finds all checks or reference numbers with 1234.

>> $500 finds all transactions that equal $500.

>> >$25 finds all transactions with amounts over $25.

Click the Filter funnel button to view filter options.

Currently selected filter

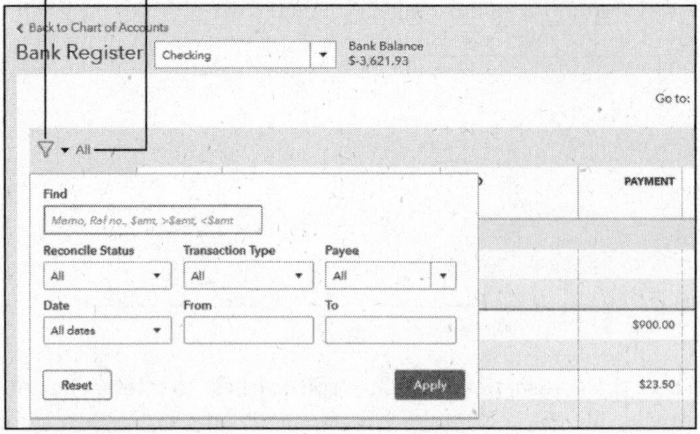

FIGURE 7-9:
Displaying available filters.

To display transactions for a specific transaction date, use the All Dates box to select one of the predefined date ranges (such as Last Week) or use the Date From and To fields to view transactions only within that timeframe.

You also can filter by a transaction's reconciliation status, transaction type, or payee. Just be cognizant that the more filters you apply, the fewer transactions QBO will find.

Any transactions that meet the criteria you specify in the Filter window appear in the register after you click Apply. In addition, the selected filter appears beside the Filter button (see Figure 7-10). You can click the Clear Filter/View All link to clear the filter and redisplay all transactions in the register.

The current filter appears here.

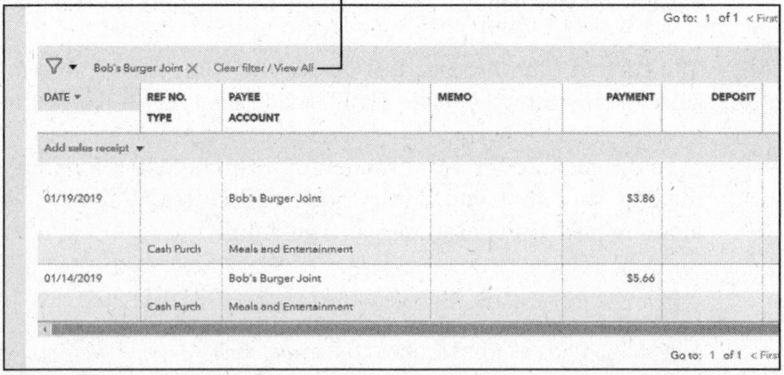

FIGURE 7-10:
A list of transactions QBO found based on criteria specified in the Filter window.

TIP

While viewing a customer or a vendor, QBO displays not only the pertinent transactions, but sums them. If you apply a filter, QBO sums the filtered transactions. If the filter displays more transactions than fit on a single page, QBO displays totals on all pages. And, using the check boxes to the left of the transaction, you can separate or combine certain transactions to see the resulting sum.

Printing a register

When doing research, many people find it easiest to print the information that appears in the register. To do so, click the Print button beside the register's Table Gear Settings button (at the right edge of the register, just above the Balance column). QBO opens a new browser tab — the Print tab — to display your register formatted for printing, along with printing options (see Figure 7-11).

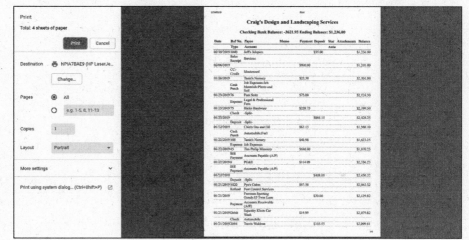

FIGURE 7-11:
Printing a register.

On the left side of the tab, select the printer you want to use and make any other necessary selections, such as the pages to print, the number of copies, and the layout orientation. When you finish selecting settings, click Print. When the report finishes printing, you can close the Print tab to redisplay your register in your QBO company.

TIP

You aren't restricted to printing to paper. For example, you can print the report to a PDF file; click the Change button below the Destination printer and select a PDF option such as Save as PDF or Microsoft Print to PDF. You can even choose Save to Google Docs.

» Connecting QBO Bank and Credit Card accounts to accounts at financial institutions

» Making bank deposits

» Reconciling a Bank account

Chapter **8**

Handling Bank and Credit Card Transactions

The real title of this chapter should have been "Handling Bank and Credit Card Transactions and Other Banking Tasks," but my editors said that title, although accurately descriptive, was too long.

So, in a nutshell, this chapter covers the ways you can connect Bank and Credit Card accounts in QBO to their counterparts at financial institutions. You also find out how to make bank deposits and reconcile your bank statement.

Controlling the Appearance of Bank Accounts

Before diving into using Bank accounts, let's take a look at a few things you can do to make your life easier while working with Bank accounts.

All Bank accounts (and Credit Card accounts) appear on the QBO Dashboard page, and connected accounts also appear on the Banking page. You can control the order in which your accounts appear on these pages. For example, perhaps you'd like your accounts to appear in alphabetical order. Or maybe you'd like them to appear in most used order. Whatever works for you.

On the QBO Dashboard page, click the pencil that appears to the right of Bank Accounts (see Figure 8-1). The pencil changes to the Save button. Then using the icon that appears to the left of an account (nine small dots forming a square), drag up or down to move the account. Once the accounts appear in the order you want, click the Save button. Changes you make will appear on the Dashboard page and, if you have connected accounts, on the Banking page.

Click to change the order in which bank accounts appear.

FIGURE 8-1:
Drag accounts to place them in the order you want.

In addition to changing the order of accounts, you can, to some extent, control the information for connected accounts that appears in the table on the Banking page. After I've show you how to connect accounts, the Banking page will be more meaningful, and I'll show you how to make changes to the information that appears for connected accounts on the Banking page.

Connecting QBO Accounts to Financial Institutions

QBO offers three ways to connect QBO Bank and Credit Card accounts to corresponding accounts at financial institutions:

>> Connect directly if your bank supports a direct connection.

>> Use QuickBooks Web Connect.

>> Import transactions stored in an Excel file.

You have a fourth option: You don't have to connect at all. If you choose this fourth option, skip to the end of this chapter, where I discuss making bank deposits and reconciling bank statements. If you aren't sure whether to connect, read through this section to help you make up your mind.

Connecting . . . or not connecting

I don't think Shakespeare would mind if I paraphrased Hamlet: "To connect or not to connect, that is the question."

In QBO, you might be able to directly connect QBO Bank and Credit Card accounts to their counterparts at financial institutions. I say "might" because not all financial institutions support directly connecting to QBO. If you bank at an institution that doesn't support a direct connection, you can use the QuickBooks Web Connect method to export transactions from the financial institution's website into QBO.

Before I dive into connecting, it's important to understand that you *don't have to connect*. You can work along quite happily in QBO without ever connecting an account at a financial institution to one in QBO. You simply enter transactions that affect the appropriate account and, monthly, you reconcile the accounts.

So, why connect? Most people connect to accounts at financial institutions so that they can electronically verify (by matching) the transactions recorded in QBO with the ones recorded at the financial institution. Connecting is, therefore, primarily a matter of convenience.

REMEMBER

Just a reminder: See Chapters 5 and 6 for details on entering transactions that affect a Bank account. You typically use an Expense transaction to record credit card purchases and a Credit Card Credit transaction to record refunds to a credit card. You also use a Credit Card Credit transaction to record a payment you make to reduce your credit card's balance.

Connecting Bank or Credit Card accounts

After you add a new Bank or Credit Card account, you can opt to connect it to a financial institution — or not. You also can later connect an account you previously created but did not connect even if you use it for a while before deciding to connect. But the whole process starts with you creating a Bank or Credit Card account.

CONNECTING AS A FORM OF DATA ENTRY . . . NOT!

Don't be tempted to use connecting as a method for entering information into QBO. You might think you'll save time because you won't have to fill out transaction windows in QBO, but, in reality, you won't save time. As I discuss later in this chapter, you need to review every downloaded transaction and confirm that it is properly assigned in QBO. And, even if you review transactions daily, you won't have an up-to-date version of your accounting information because you will know about transactions that have not yet cleared your financial institution. That means that the account balances in QBO won't really be up to date unless you enter transactions in QBO and use connecting as a method of confirming that your QBO balances match financial institution balances. Long story short: It's safer to enter transactions and use connected account information to confirm QBO balances.

Setting up a Bank or Credit Card account

In Chapter 3, I show you how to create a new Bank account in QBO, and I don't connect that account to a financial institution. You set up a Credit Card account using the same technique. For example, follow these steps to set up a Credit Card account:

REMEMBER

You might decide later to connect the account, and that's fine. Just remember that you can't connect any account at a financial institution with your QBO data until you set up a corresponding account in QBO using the steps in this section.

1. **Click the Gear button and, from the left side of the menu that appears, choose Chart of Accounts.**

    QBO displays the Chart of Accounts page.

2. **Click the New button on the Chart of Accounts page to open the Account dialog box (see Figure 8-2).**

3. **Open the Account Type list and choose Credit Card.**

    QBO fills in the Detail Type for you.

4. **If you're using account numbers, supply a number for the new account.**

5. **Provide a name for the account and, optionally, a description.**

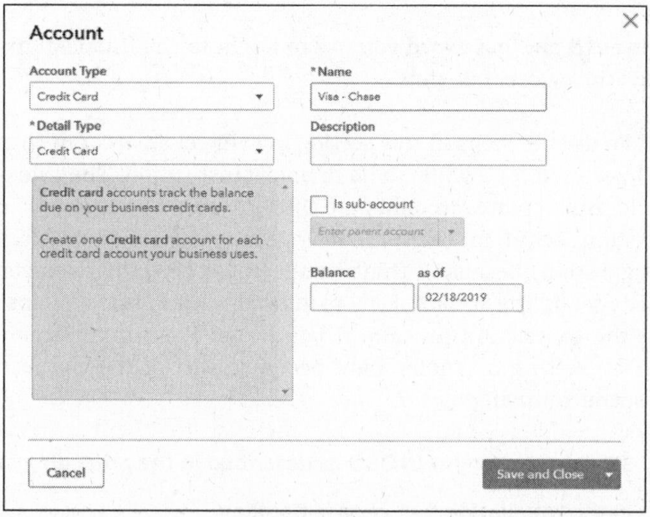

Account   ✕

Account Type   *** Name**
Credit Card   ▼   Visa - Chase

* Detail Type   Description
Credit Card   ▼

Credit card accounts track the balance   ☐ Is sub-account
due on your business credit cards.
                                              Enter parent account   ▼
Create one **Credit card** account for each
credit card account your business uses.
                                              Balance   as of
                                                             02/18/2019

Cancel   Save and Close ▼

FIGURE 8-2:
The dialog box you use to create an account.

6. **Optionally, you can enter your account's balance as it appears on the last statement.**

WARNING

If you enter a balance, QuickBooks updates both the account balance and the Opening Balance Equity account, and your accountant probably won't be happy with you. I suggest that you not enter a balance.

7. **Click Save and Close.**

QBO redisplays the Chart of Accounts page and your new account appears in the list.

REMEMBER

If you don't connect this account to a financial institution, you'll need to enter expense and credit card credit transactions that have occurred since you received the last statement for this credit card account unless you decide to connect the account to its financial institution.

Directly connecting a Bank or Credit Card account

The Banking page in QBO lists accounts you have connected to a financial institution. Before you connect any accounts, the Banking page contains basically a big green Connect button, and you use this button to connect your first account to a financial institution. After you connect an account, the Banking page becomes more meaningful, as you see after you finish the steps in this section. To connect subsequent accounts, you click the Add Account button that appears in the upper left corner of the Banking page.

To create an account that connects directly to a financial institution, assuming your financial institution supports connecting directly to QBO accounts, gather up the user ID and password you use to log in to the financial institution online and follow the next set of steps.

You can use the steps in this section to connect an account that you created earlier and have used for a while to its financial institution. The rule of thumb is that you should first create accounts in QBO's Chart of Accounts as described in the preceding section for each account you intend to connect. This is a "rule of thumb" (a suggestion) because I think you'll find connecting less confusing if you have already set up the accounts you plan to connect to financial institutions before you start the connection process. If you haven't set up an account before trying to connect, setting up the account becomes part of the connecting process, which can seem confusing.

1. **Set up the account in QBO as described in the preceding section.**

2. **In the Navigation bar, choose Banking.**

   QBO displays the Banking page.

3. **If you haven't yet connected any accounts, click the Connect Account button; if you have previously connected an account, click the Add Account button.**

   QBO starts a wizard that helps you connect to a financial institution.

4. **On the first wizard page, shown in Figure 8-3, you either provide your financial institution's website address, or you can click your financial institution's name if it appears on the page.**

   To search for financial institutions, you just need to type a name in the Search box.

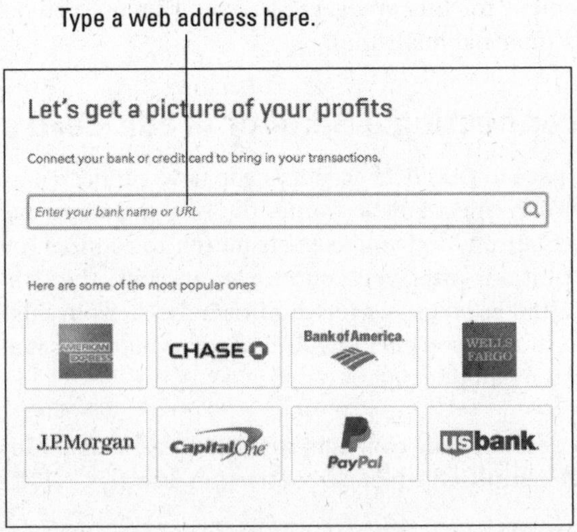

Type a web address here.

Let's get a picture of your profits

Connect your bank or credit card to bring in your transactions.

Enter your bank name or URL

Here are some of the most popular ones

AMERICAN EXPRESS   CHASE ○   Bank of America   WELLS FARGO

J.P.Morgan   Capital One   PayPal   US bank

FIGURE 8-3:
Identify your
financial
institution.

5. On the page that appears, supply your user ID and password and click the Log In button.

QBO might tell you to go to your bank site and sign in; once you do, QBO returns you to the connection process.

To ensure that the connection is secure, QBO might make you walk through a "reCAPTCHA" to confirm that you are not a robot trying to connect to your account. Answer the questions put to you to confirm you are not a robot.

After a few moments, a page appears, displaying the accounts you have at the financial institution and giving you the option to select one or more of those accounts to connect with QBO (see Figure 8-4).

For each account you select, QBO downloads 90 days of transactions or enters a balance transaction on the 90-day "lookback" date to ensure that reconciliation will go smoothly.

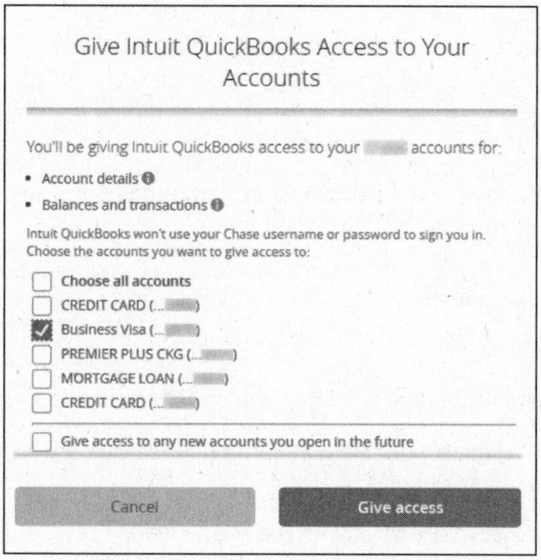

Give Intuit QuickBooks Access to Your Accounts

You'll be giving Intuit QuickBooks access to your ▓▓▓ accounts for:

- Account details ℹ
- Balances and transactions ℹ

Intuit QuickBooks won't use your Chase username or password to sign you in. Choose the accounts you want to give access to:

☐ **Choose all accounts**
☐ CREDIT CARD (...▓▓▓)
☑ Business Visa (...▓▓▓)
☐ PREMIER PLUS CKG (...▓▓▓)
☐ MORTGAGE LOAN (...▓▓▓)
☐ CREDIT CARD (...▓▓▓)

☐ Give access to any new accounts you open in the future

[Cancel]　[Give access]

FIGURE 8-4: Select the accounts you want to connect to QBO and their types.

6. Select the accounts you want to connect to QBO.

7. Click Connect.

Follow any additional onscreen prompts you see to finish setting up the account.

After you connect your first account to a financial institution, QBO changes the appearance of the Banking page to display a list of connected accounts and their related information as downloaded from the bank (see Figure 8-5). In most cases,

QBO automatically downloads activity from your financial institution nightly. For some financial institutions, QBO downloads less frequently.

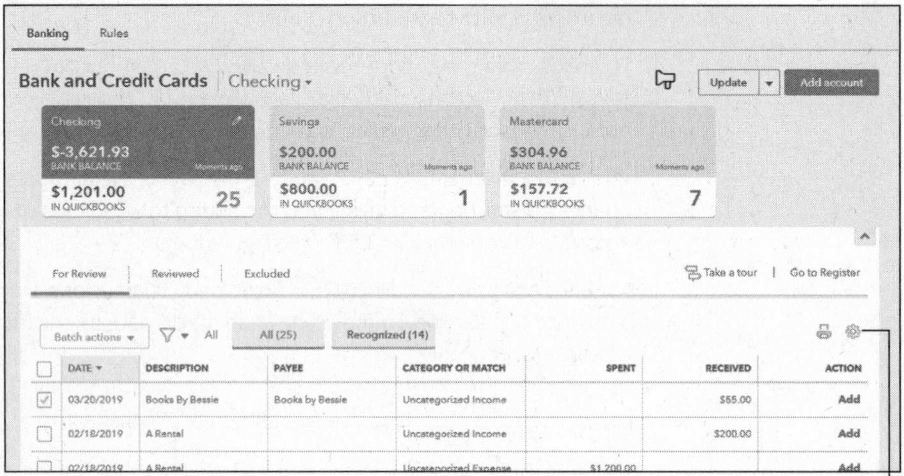

FIGURE 8-5:
After connecting an account, the Banking page displays connected accounts, and you can alter the information in the page's table.

Click to change the table information.

You can make changes to the information that appears in the table on the Banking page; you can opt to:

» Display check numbers.

» Display Payee names.

» Make the date field editable so that you can change it if necessary.

» Display more detailed information about a transaction by displaying information provided by the bank.

» Copy bank detail information into the Memo field.

To change to the page's table, click the Gear button that appears just above the Action column and add or remove check marks to display or hide columns. You also can make adjustments to the column widths in the table on the Banking page, and QBO will remember any column width adjustments you make, even after you sign out of QBO and then sign back in. If you need to display the Memo field in an individual bank register, see Chapter 7.

When you can't connect directly . . .

There are cases where you cannot connect your financial institution to an account in QBO — or, you can connect but transactions don't download. But, all is not lost. You can still update a QBO account with financial institution information using either QuickBooks Web Connect or by importing an Excel file.

Using Web Connect

If you can't connect your account directly to QBO, you can use Web Connect, which has been around for years. If you were previously a QuickBooks Desktop user, you might have used Web Connect. When you use Web Connect, you download transactions from your financial institution's website to your computer, and then you upload the downloaded transactions from your computer to QBO.

WARNING

Because Web Connect files are not encrypted, you should not use a public computer to download information using Web Connect.

To use Web Connect, follow these steps:

1. **In your Chart of Accounts, set up the account into which you will load transactions using Web Connect.**

REMEMBER

You must have an account in your QBO Chart of Accounts before you can load transactions into it, regardless of the connection type. See the section "Setting up a Bank or Credit Card account" earlier in this chapter.

2. **Log in to your financial institution's website and look for a link that enables you to download to QuickBooks.**

Some banks have a Download button associated with each account, and clicking that button enables you to choose the method you want to use to download. Some banks have a "Download to QuickBooks" link or a "QuickBooks Web Connect QBO" link. If you can't find the link, contact your financial institution and let them direct you to the link. After you find it, make note of where it appears on your financial institution's website for future use.

3. **Using the link you found in Step 2, select any of the following file formats:**

- .qbo: QuickBooks

- .qfx: Quicken

- .ofx: Microsoft Money

- Or any file format that references QBO (your bank controls the name of the file formats you see)

In the next section, "Importing transactions via Excel", you'll read about using CSV format.

4. **Select the dates for the transactions you want to download.**

If you download transactions with dates that precede the opening balance you entered for the account in QBO, the account's opening balance will change.

5. **Save the file to a location on your computer where you'll be able to find it later.**

Many people download to the Downloads folder or to their Windows desktop.

6. **To upload the file to QBO, log in to QBO and, in the Navigation bar, choose Banking.**

QBO displays the Bank and Credit Cards page.

- If you have connected other accounts, you'll see the Update and Add Account buttons on the right side of the page (see Figure 8-6).

- If you haven't connected accounts, you'll see the Connect button, and below it, the Upload Transactions Manually button.

7. **Click the Upload Transactions Manually button or the arrow beside the Update button on the right side of the page and choose File Upload.**

QBO starts the Upload File wizard and displays the screen shown in Figure 8-7.

The Update and Add Account buttons

FIGURE 8-6:
Click the arrow beside the Update button and select File Upload.

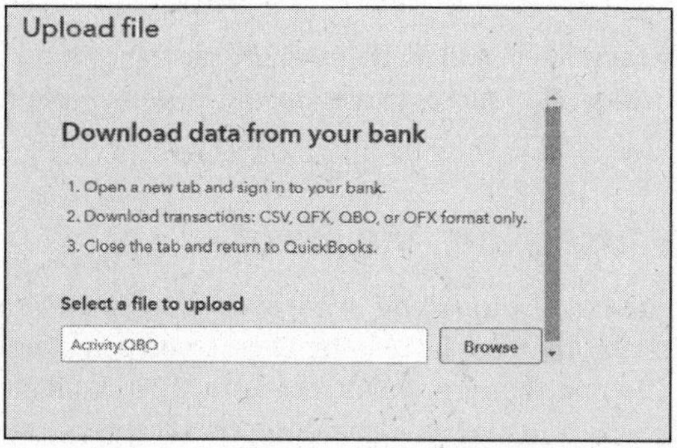

FIGURE 8-7:
Use this screen
to navigate to the
transactions you
downloaded from
your financial
institution.

Upload file

Download data from your bank

1. Open a new tab and sign in to your bank.
2. Download transactions: CSV, QFX, QBO, or OFX format only.
3. Close the tab and return to QuickBooks.

Select a file to upload

Activity.QBO   Browse

8. **Click the Browse button, navigate to the location where you saved the transactions you downloaded in Step 5, and select the downloaded file.**

9. **Click Next in the lower right corner (not shown in Figure 8-7).**

   QBO displays a screen where you select the QBO account into which you want to upload the transactions.

10. **Select the QBO account where the transactions should appear and click Next (see Figure 8-8).**

    QBO uploads the transactions to the selected QBO account. (The process can take a few minutes.)

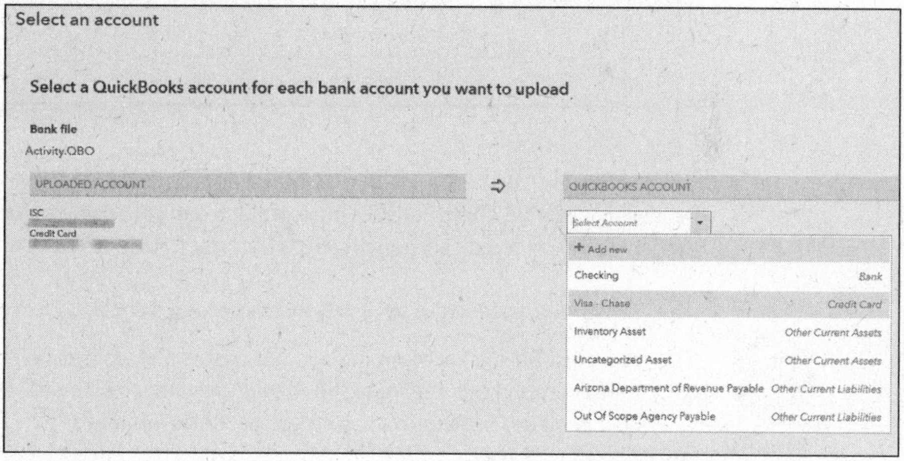

Select an account

Select a QuickBooks account for each bank account you want to upload

Bank file
Activity.QBO

UPLOADED ACCOUNT		QUICKBOOKS ACCOUNT	
ISC	⇒	Select Account ▼	
Credit Card		+ Add new	
		Checking	Bank
		Visa - Chase	Credit Card
		Inventory Asset	Other Current Assets
		Uncategorized Asset	Other Current Assets
		Arizona Department of Revenue Payable	Other Current Liabilities
		Out Of Scope Agency Payable	Other Current Liabilities

FIGURE 8-8:
Select the
account where
QBO should place
the transactions
from your bank.

11. **When you see the confirmation screen that explains your next step (to accept your transactions), click Let's Go.**

To handle the transactions you loaded into QBO, see the section "Managing Downloaded Activity." After you successfully upload a Web Connect file, you should delete it because it is not encrypted and contains your account information.

Importing transactions via Excel

If your bank supports downloading transactions to a CSV format (a *comma-separated values* format that can be read by Excel), you can download your banking activity to a CSV file and then import it into your QBO Bank account. First, log in to your bank's website and save your banking transactions using the CSV format. QBO can import CSV files formatted in either three or four columns, as shown in Tables 8-1 and 8-2.

TABLE 8-1

An Acceptable Three-Column Format

Date	Description	Amount
1/1/2019	Example payment	-100.00
1/1/2019	Example deposit	200.00

TABLE 8-2

An Acceptable Four-Column Format

Date	Description	Credit	Debit
1/1/2019	Example payment	100.00	
1/1/2019	Example deposit		200.00

Open your CSV file using Excel and make sure it matches one of these formats; if necessary, edit it. Then, follow these steps to import the transactions; these steps are very similar to the steps you use when importing a Web Connect file:

1. **Set up the account in your QBO Chart of Accounts.**

   You must have an account in your QBO Chart of Accounts before you can load transactions into it, regardless of the connection type. See the section "Setting up a Bank or Credit Card account" earlier in this chapter.

2. **Choose Banking in the Navigation bar.**

3. **Click the arrow beside the Update button and, from the menu that appears, click File Upload.**

   The Upload File page, shown earlier in Figure 8-7, appears.

4. **Click the Browse button, select the CSV file you downloaded from your bank's website, and click Next in the lower right corner.**

5. **Select the account into which you want to import transactions and click Next in the lower right corner.**

6. **On the Map CSV Columns screen that appears, match the fields in QBO to the fields in your CSV file and then click Next (see Figure 8-9).**

   The transactions you can import from your CSV file appear, with a check box to the left of each transaction. To avoid importing a particular transaction, select its check box.

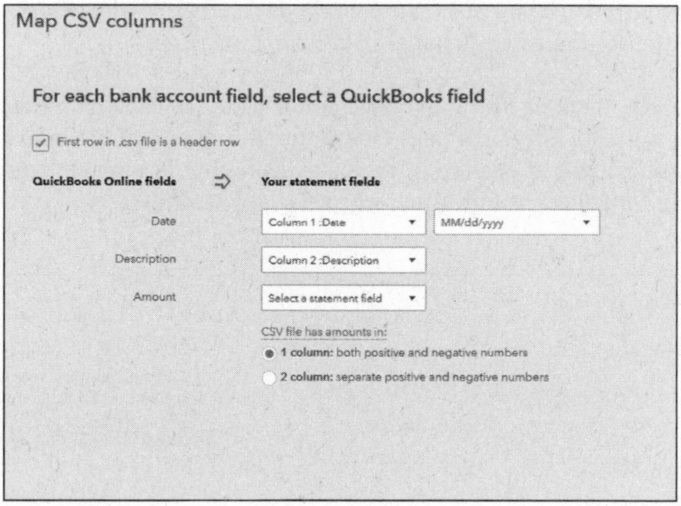

Map CSV columns

For each bank account field, select a QuickBooks field

☑ First row in .csv file is a header row

QuickBooks Online fields	⇨	Your statement fields
Date		Column 1 :Date ▾	MM/dd/yyyy ▾
Description		Column 2 :Description ▾
Amount		Select a statement field ▾

CSV file has amounts in:
● **1 column:** both positive and negative numbers
○ **2 column:** separate positive and negative numbers

FIGURE 8-9:
Match QBO fields to the fields in your CSV file.

7. **Click Next.**

   QBO displays the transactions it will import and gives you the option to exclude transactions.

8. **Deselect transactions if appropriate, then click Next.**

   QBO displays the number of transactions it will import and asks if you want to import the transactions.

9. **Click Yes to import the transactions.**

   When QBO finishes importing the transactions, a confirmation screen appears.

10. **Click Let's Go.**

    QBO redisplays the Bank and Credit Cards page.

To handle the transactions you loaded into QBO, see the section "Managing Downloaded Activity."

Managing Downloaded Activity

Downloading transactions from a financial institution and importing them into QBO is the first part of the process. Regardless of the download method you use, you need to evaluate each transaction and, as appropriate, update QBO with the downloaded transactions. From the Bank and Credit Cards page, you match, exclude, or add transactions downloaded from a financial institution to your QBO company.

REMEMBER

Don't worry; if you make a mistake, you can fix it, as described later in this chapter in the section titled (what else?) "Fixing mistakes."

Choose Banking from the Navigation pane, click Banking again to display the Bank and Credit Cards page (see Figure 8-10), and, if necessary, select an account by clicking it at the top of the page. Note that you match transactions the same way for Bank accounts and for Credit Card accounts.

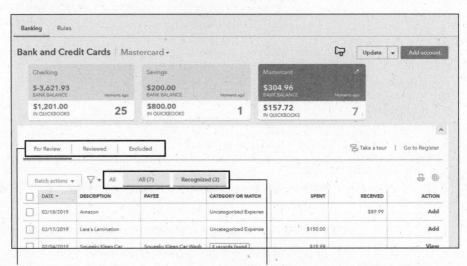

FIGURE 8-10:
Use this page to specify how QBO should handle each downloaded transaction.

Transaction Status tabs   Tabs for viewing and filtering downloaded transactions

Just below the accounts, QBO displays three transaction status tabs:

» If you click For Review, transactions appear that you have downloaded but have not yet specified how you want to handle.

» If you click Reviewed, transactions appear that you have downloaded and added to QBO.

>> If you click Excluded, transactions appear that you have downloaded and decided not to include in QBO.

To view the transactions you need to consider, click For Review. QBO displays a button you can use to take batch actions — I discuss that button in a moment — and two additional tabs:

>> The All tab lets you view all downloaded transactions for the selected account.

>> The Recognized tab displays downloaded transactions that QBO thinks it knows how to handle.

Both the All tab and the Recognized tab display the same information; think of the Recognized tab as a filtered version of the All tab.

In the Category or Match column, QBO suggests a way to assign each transaction. Using both information from other businesses like yours and your past behavior, QBO tries to identify downloaded transactions that potentially match transactions you entered in QBO. If you have previously accepted a transaction from a vendor, QBO assumes that you want to assign the same category to subsequent transactions for that vendor. And, if you change the payee on a transaction, QBO will suggest that change the next time a transaction appears for that payee.

TIP

Although the suggestions are helpful, after a while, you might find yourself wishing that QBO would stop suggesting and just record the transaction — and you can use *auto-add rules* to accomplish that behavior. See the section "Establishing rules to accept transactions" later in this chapter for details.

QBO sorts transactions for review into three basic groups (see Figure 8-11):

>> When QBO finds no matches, the words "Uncategorized Expense" or "Uncategorized Income" appear in the Category or Match column, and the word "Add" appears in the Action column.

>> When QBO finds only one possible match, QBO assumes the match is accurate and suggests a match accordingly; transactions like these appear in green in the Category or Match column, and QBO displays "Match" in the Action column. Be aware that you can still make changes to the transaction before you accept it.

>> If QBO finds multiple possibilities, it doesn't actually assign information to the transaction, but notifies you of possible matches by displaying the number of records found in the Category or Match column and the word "View" in the Action column.

Read on to learn how to handle these situations.

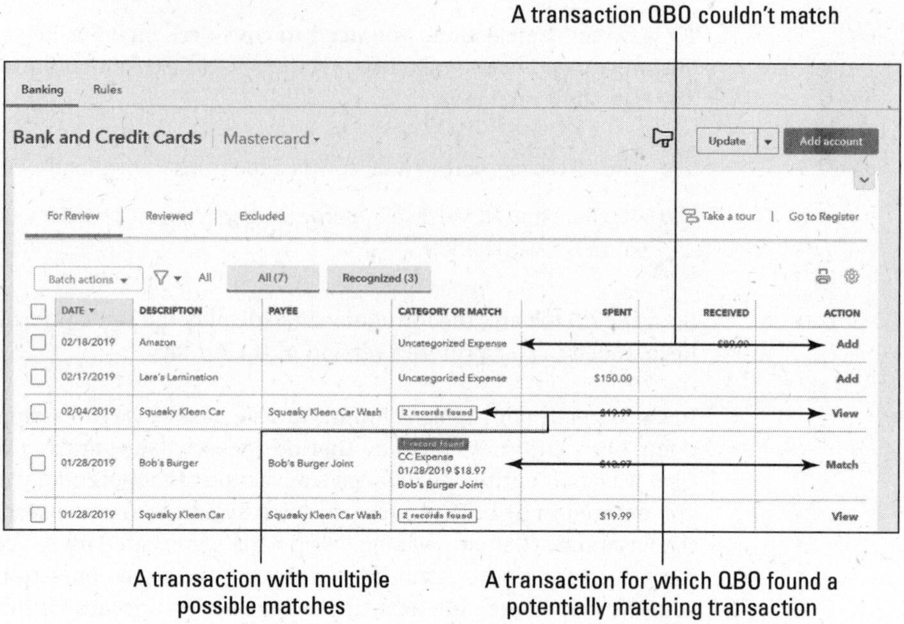

A transaction QBO couldn't match

FIGURE 8-11:
The Category or
Match column
and the Action
column help
you identify
transactions
QBO matched
and transactions
QBO couldn't
match.

A transaction with multiple possible matches

A transaction for which QBO found a potentially matching transaction

Excluding transactions

Time to look at that Batch Actions button now. As you evaluate new transactions, you need to decide first whether they belong in QBO. I suggest that you identify transactions to exclude and then exclude them before you deal with transactions you intend to include in QBO. That way, you quickly eliminate transactions that need no further consideration. When might you exclude a transaction from QBO? Suppose that you accidentally used a business credit card to pay for groceries. This transaction is not a business expense and shouldn't be part of your QBO transactions. So, you can exclude the transaction from QBO. Just remember, when you reconcile your statement, the statement balance will include all transactions, not just those you included in QBO.

To exclude a transaction, follow these steps:

1. **On the For Review tab, select the check box on the left side of each transaction you intend to exclude.**

2. **Click the Batch Actions button above the list of transactions.**

3. **From the menu that appears, click Exclude Selected.**

   QBO moves the selected transactions to the Excluded tab on the Bank and Credit Cards page; the tab appears above the table grid, along with the For Review tab and the Reviewed tab.

Including transactions

The remaining transactions fall into two categories: those that don't have an obvious matching transaction in QBO and those that do. And, you can identify the category into which a transaction falls using the Action column. If you see Add in the Action column, QBO couldn't find an obvious matching transaction; if you see Match or View in the Action column, QBO did find one or more potentially matching transactions (refer to Figure 8-11). QBO makes its best guess for adding or matching transactions, but it isn't perfect.

When QBO guesses correctly . . .

You need to confirm or change each transaction before you include it in QBO. If the listed transaction information is correct, you don't need to individually add or match transactions as described in the rest of this section. Instead, you can follow the steps in the preceding section except, in Step 3, click Accept Selected.

If you need to make the same change to a number of transactions, select those transactions and choose the Modify Selected option in the Batch Actions list.

When QBO doesn't know . . .

QBO might not know how to handle a transaction, or QBO might simply guess wrong. In these cases, you need to change the transaction before you accept it.

Transactions QBO thinks you should add . . .

You can easily identify a transaction that QBO isn't sure how to handle because QBO displays an Add link in the Action column and, in the Category or Match column, you see the words "Uncategorized Expense" or "Uncategorized Income."

When you click one of these transactions (you don't need to click the Add link; you can simply click the line for the transaction), QBO expands the transaction information so that you can change the details of the transaction (see Figure 8-12).

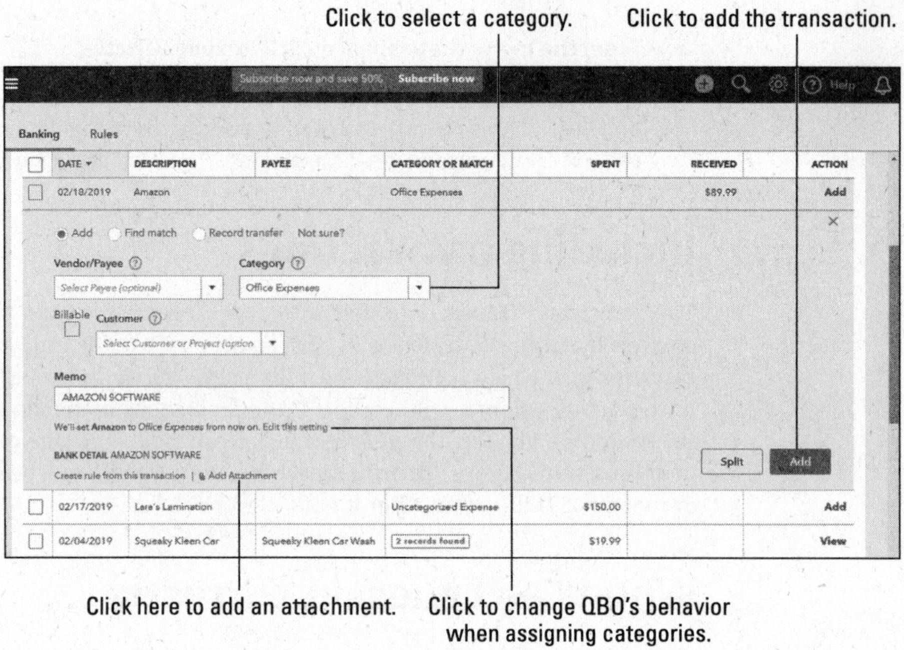

Click to select a category.   Click to add the transaction.

Click here to add an attachment.   Click to change QBO's behavior when assigning categories.

FIGURE 8-12: When you click a transaction that displays the Add link in the Action column, QBO displays transaction details so that you can assign the transaction to an appropriate category.

For example, you can use the option buttons above the transaction information to specify whether you want to add the transaction, search for a matching QBO transaction, or transfer the transaction information to another account. If you opt to add the transaction, you can (and probably should) change the category QBO suggests to one you deem more appropriate; in Figure 8-12, I changed the category from Uncategorized Expense to Office Expenses. You also can click the Split button on the bottom right side of the transaction information to distribute the transaction among multiple categories.

If you're working with a Bank account transaction, be aware that you can change the check number if needed.

If you change the transaction's category, QBO will assume, in the future, that all transactions for the selected vendor should be assigned to the category you choose. You can change this behavior by clicking the Edit This Setting link just below the memo. When you click the link, you can choose to leave future transactions uncategorized or to create a custom rule; I talk about rules in the next section, "Establishing rules to accept transactions."

You also can add attachments to any transaction using the Add Attachment link at the bottom of the expanded transaction information window. After you make your changes, you can click the Add button to add the transaction to QBO.

Transactions QBO thinks it can match . . .

Again, you can easily identify these types of transactions; a Match link appears beside them in the Action column. When you click a downloaded transaction that QBO suggests you match to an existing QBO transaction, QBO displays a different set of details (see Figure 8-13). You can

>> **Select the correct matching transaction:** In the Records Found section, click a link beside any possible match to display the transaction in its transaction window, where you can identify the category to which that possible match was assigned. If that category is appropriate for the transaction QBO downloaded, cancel the transaction window to return to the Banking page and select the correct match in the Records Found section and click the Match button.

>> **Search for other matching transactions:** If none of the Possible Matches is applied in QBO the way you want to apply the downloaded transaction, you can click the Find Other Records button to search for additional possible matches.

>> **Add the transaction (and supply account information for it):** If you can't find a similar transaction already recorded in QBO, you can click the Add option button in the upper left corner of the details for the transaction and then add the transaction as described in the preceding section.

>> **Transfer the transaction to a different account:** Click the Record Transfer option button in the upper left corner of the details for the transaction and then select a new account for the transaction — and click the Transfer button that replaces the Match button shown in Figure 8-13.

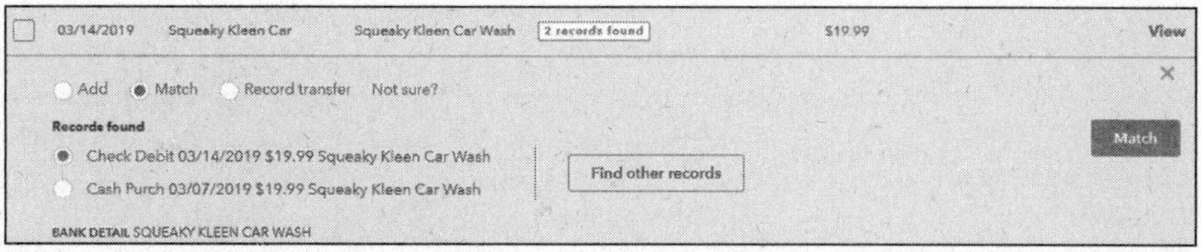

FIGURE 8-13:
The transaction details QBO displays when you click a transaction you plan to match to an existing QBO transaction.

Repeat the process of adding and matching until you've handled all downloaded transactions. Each transaction that you add or match disappears from the For Review tab on the Bank and Credit Cards page and appears on the Reviewed tab; see the section "Fixing mistakes" for more information on using the In Quick-Books tab.

Establishing rules to accept transactions

I've already established that QBO tries to learn your habits as you review downloaded transactions; you can help the process along by establishing rules for QBO to follow. When you set up rules, you speed up the review process because, effectively, you tell QBO in advance how to treat certain types of transactions.

How rules work

Suppose, for example, that you purchase gas for business-use cars from Shell gas stations and you always pay using a credit card you've connected to a financial institution in QBO. Effectively, you want to categorize all transactions at Shell stations to your Fuel expense account.

THE ORDER OF RULES

The order of the rules you establish matters. QBO uses your rules in the order they appear on the Rules page and applies only one rule to any particular transaction. To ensure that QBO applies the correct rule to a transaction, you can reorder the rules. Drag the waffle icon that appears to the left of the rule on the Rules page.

Drag here to reorder rules.

Suppose that you set up two rules in the following order:

- Rule 1: Categorize all transactions under $10 as Miscellaneous Expenses.
- Rule 2: Categorize all McDonald's transactions as Meals & Entertainment.

If a $12 dollar transaction from McDonald's appears, QBO applies Rule 2. But if a $7.50 transaction from McDonald's appears, QBO applies Rule 1.

You can manually assign the category to one of these transactions and wait for QBO to "learn" your preference, or you can set up a rule for QBO to follow. When you establish a rule, you stipulate information such as the accounts and the types of transactions (money in or money out) to which the rule should apply. Note that you can create rules that affect all accounts or rules that affect specific accounts.

You then identify criteria that individual transactions should meet before QBO acts on the transactions. Last, you specify the information QBO should assign to transactions that meet the criteria. For example, you can specify a transaction type and a category.

The rules you establish can work in one of two ways:

» QBO can use your rule to suggest changes to downloaded transactions that you then review and approve. Or,

» You can opt to have QBO automatically apply the rule to all transactions that it determines match the rule's conditions and add those transactions to QBO.

When you use the first approach, QBO identifies, on the For Review tab of the Bank and Credit Cards page, transactions for which it finds and expects to apply a rule. You can identify these transactions because, in the Category or Match column, they display a Rule icon.

TIP

QBO uses different icons to identify transactions matched by rules but not yet added to your company and transactions added automatically by rules; you can read more about these icons in the section "Fixing mistakes."

The second approach — letting QBO automatically apply a rule — might seem risky, but it really isn't. Even though QBO automatically applies the rule, you can still make changes to transactions that QBO automatically accepts.

Creating a rule

You set up either type of rule — the one that suggests changes and you must review them, and the one that automatically adds transactions based on a rule — using the same steps. There's only one step where you do things differently; I'll point out that step when I get there.

1. **Choose Banking from the Navigation pane.**

   The Bank and Credit Cards page appears.

2. **Click Bank Rules above the list of bank and credit cards.**

   QBO displays the Bank Rules page shown in Figure 8-14.

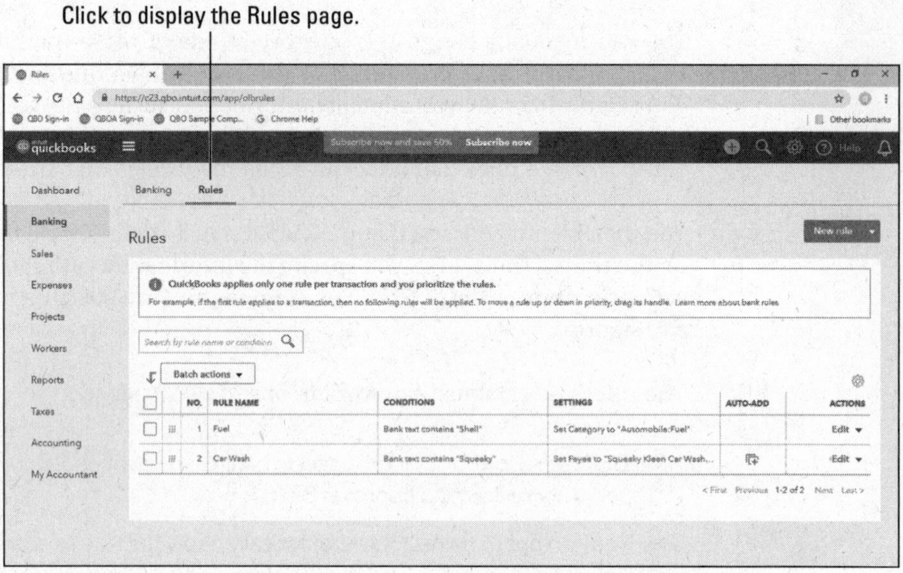

Click to display the Rules page.

FIGURE 8-14:
The Bank
Rules page.

3. **Click the New Rule button in the upper right corner of the Bank Rules page.**

   QBO displays the Rule dialog box shown in Figure 8-15.

4. **Assign the rule a name — one that will be meaningful to you.**

   You can't use special characters like the apostrophe (') in a rule name.

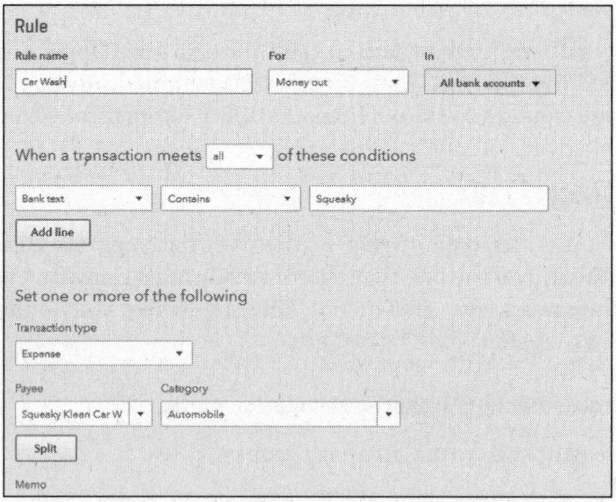

FIGURE 8-15:
The Rule dialog
box, where
you set the
information
you want QBO
to apply to
transactions
when it uses
the rule.

5. **Identify whether the rule applies to money coming into QBO or money flowing out of QBO, and select the accounts to which you want the rule to apply.**

6. **Use the "When a Transaction Meets" section of the Rule page to set criteria QBO should use when examining downloaded transactions to determine whether to apply the rule to them.**

   You can set multiple criteria using the Add Line button, and you can specify that a transaction should meet all or any of the criteria. Specifying "all" is more stringent and QBO is more selective about applying the rule.

   TIP

   The first list box in the section enables you to specify whether QBO should compare the transaction description, the bank text, or the transaction amount to a condition you set. For those inquiring minds out there, Description (the transaction description) refers to the text that appears in the Description column of the Bank and Credit Cards page. The Bank Text option refers to the Bank Detail description the bank downloads; you can view the Bank Detail description if you click any downloaded transaction. The Bank Detail description appears at the bottom left of the transactions being edited back in Figure 8-13.

7. **At the bottom of the Rule dialog box, shown in Figure 8-16, set the information you want QBO to apply to transactions that meet the rule's criteria.**

   You can choose one or more of the following:

   a. Select the Transaction Type QBO should assign to the transaction.

   b. Select the Payee and one or more categories to apply to transactions that meet the rule's conditions.

   c. Optionally, add a Memo to each transaction that meets the rule's conditions.

   For more on ways to use the Memo field, see the sidebar "The Memo field and transaction rules."

   d. Select the Automatically Add to My Books check box if you want QBO to automatically add transactions that meet the rule's conditions to your company.

   REMEMBER

   This is the "different" step I referred to in the introduction to these steps. If you select this box, you don't need to approve transactions to which QBO applies this rule. But, you can always make changes to automatically added transactions.

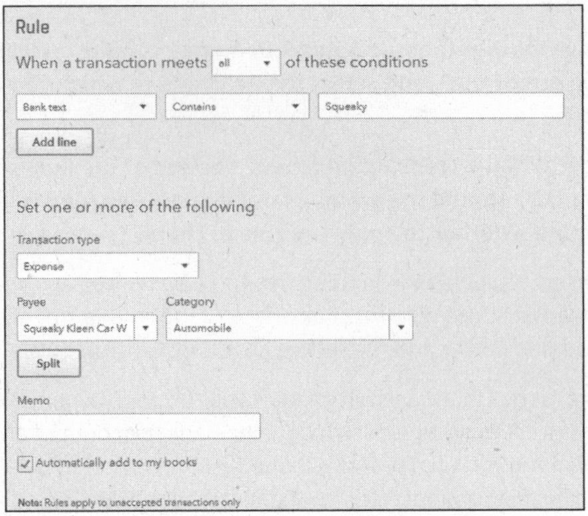

FIGURE 8-16:
Provide the
information
QBO should use
on transactions
that meet the
rule's criteria.

8. **Click Save in the lower right corner of the Rule page (the Save button doesn't appear in Figure 8-16).**

Once you create a rule or rules, you can use the Actions column of the Rules page to copy them (so that you don't have to create similar rules from scratch) and to delete rules you no longer want. And, if you need to edit a rule, click the Edit link in the Actions column to reopen the Rule dialog box and make changes.

TIP

Accountants, you can help your clients and save some time if you create a set of rules in one company and then export and import rules between QBO companies. See Chapter 13 for details.

THE MEMO FIELD AND TRANSACTION RULES

QBO uses different special icons to identify transactions added using rules and transactions automatically added using rules. And QBO "remembers," in QBO registers, transactions added using rules. But, at the present time, you can't filter a register to show you only those transactions added by a rule (automatically or not).

You can, however, filter registers using the Memo field. So, if you anticipate needing to filter a register for transactions added by rules and transactions added automatically by rules, use the Memo field in the Rule dialog box to distinguish them. You might include text such as, "Added by Rule" and "Added Automatically by Rule" to appropriate rules.

Fixing mistakes

On the Bank and Credit Cards page, you can easily identify transactions to which QBO has applied rules because, in the Category or Match column, QBO uses different icons to identify transactions added by rules and transactions added automatically by rules. And you can see how QBO handles each downloaded transaction in your company when you click the Reviewed tab on the Bank and Credit Cards page (see Figure 8-17).

Click to view accepted transactions.   Click to undo an accepted transaction.

Suppose that you accidentally include a transaction in QBO that you meant to exclude. Or suppose that QBO assigned the wrong category to a transaction. You can easily correct these mistakes using the In QuickBooks tab on the Bank and Credit Cards page.

REMEMBER

The method used to match and add a transaction — manually, through a rule, or automatically through a rule — doesn't matter. You can make changes to any downloaded transaction. Be aware, though, that QBO treats downloaded transactions as having cleared your bank; so, if you edit a downloaded transaction in the register, QBO will ask you if you're sure.

If you include a transaction in QBO that contains mistakes — for example, the transaction was automatically added by a rule to the wrong category — you can undo the action. Undoing an accepted transaction removes it from the register and places it back on the For Review tab, where you can make changes and accept it again as described earlier in this chapter in the sections "Excluding transactions" and "Including transactions."

To undo an accepted transaction, click the Reviewed tab on the Bank and Credit Cards page. Find the transaction and click the Undo link in the Action column. QBO displays a message telling you that "Undo" was successful. Switch to the For Review tab, find the transaction, edit it, and accept it again — or, you can exclude it from QBO, if appropriate, as described earlier in this chapter in the section "Excluding transactions."

Making a Bank Deposit

In Chapter 6, I show you how to record payments from customers, and I suggest that you use the Undeposited Funds account as you record a Receive Payment transaction. So, after receiving a customer payment and placing it in the Undeposited Funds account, your Bank account — where the money will eventually show up — hasn't yet been updated. That updating happens when you prepare a bank deposit.

You can think of the Undeposited Funds account as a temporary holding place until you prepare a bank deposit. "So, why use the Undeposited Funds account?" you ask. "Why not just place the customer payments into the Bank account where they belong?"

Excellent questions. And the answers revolve around making sure that the bank deposits in QBO match the ones at your bank, because if the deposits match, bank statement reconciliation — everybody's least favorite task — becomes quite easy. But if they don't match . . . well, you don't want to go there.

For example, if you receive more than one customer payment on any given day, you'll take several checks to your bank that day. And you'll probably deposit all of them as a single deposit. Most banks typically don't record the individual checks that make up a deposit as individual deposits. Instead, the bank records the sum of the checks as your deposit — pretty much the same way you sum the checks on the deposit ticket you give to the bank teller.

"And why is this important?" you ask. This fact is important because, when you receive your statement from your bank, you need to match the bank's deposits and withdrawals with your own version of deposits and withdrawals. If you track each customer payment you receive as a deposit in the bank, then your QBO deposits *won't* match the bank's deposits. But if you record customer payments into the Undeposited Funds account, your deposits *will* match the bank's version of your deposits because you'll move multiple checks from the Undeposited Funds account to create a single deposit to your bank account.

So, assuming that you're following my advice and using the Undeposited Funds account before you prepare a bank deposit slip, you then use the Bank Deposit feature in QBO to sum up the payments you receive and intend to deposit simultaneously at your bank. QBO records, as the deposit amount in your QBO Bank account, the amount calculated in the Bank Deposit window, which will match the amount you actually deposit at your bank. Then, your bank reconciliation process becomes quick and easy — okay, maybe not quick and easy, but certainly quicker and easier than if you were trying to figure out which customer payments make up various bank deposits.

To set up a bank deposit, follow these steps:

1. **Click the Create button — the plus (+) sign — and, from the Create menu, select Bank Deposit.**

QBO displays the Bank Deposit transaction window shown in Figure 8-18. Existing payment transactions appear at the top of the window in the Select the Payments Included in This Deposit section. You can use the lines in the Add Funds to This Deposit section to add new payment transactions that are not associated with an outstanding invoice.

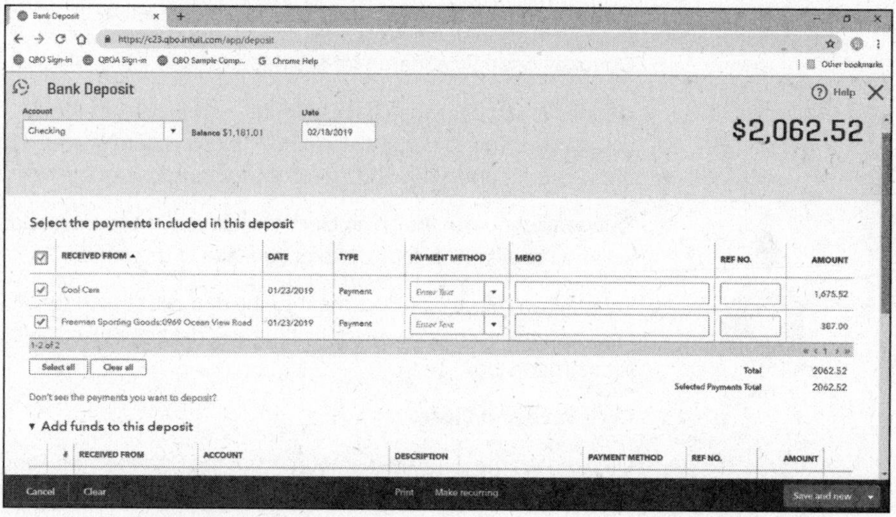

FIGURE 8-18:
Use the Bank Deposit window to select payment transactions to deposit.

WARNING

Don't try to record a payment from a customer for an outstanding invoice in the Add Funds to This Deposit section. QBO is unlikely to match the line on the Bank Deposit transaction to the outstanding invoice. Instead, record the Receive Payment transaction; the transaction then appears in the Select the Payments Included in This Deposit section of the Bank Deposit transaction window.

2. **At the top of the window, select the account into which you plan to deposit the payments.**

3. **In the Select the Payments Included in This Deposit section, click the check box beside each transaction you want to include on the deposit.**

4. **For each transaction you intend to deposit, select the Payment Method.**

TIP

Credit card companies often deposit credit card transaction receipts into your Bank account, and most of them make a daily deposit. To keep bank statement reconciliation as simple as possible, I suggest that you record separate QBO deposits for each credit card you accept. You can group the checks and cash payment methods on the same deposit. If you're using Intuit Payments, it automatically makes the deposits when credit card transactions are funded. A third section appears on the Deposit screen called QB Payments that will be collapsed by default so as not to confuse people with additional funds to deposit.

5. **Optionally, you can supply a memo and a reference number.**

The total of the selected payments — and the amount you intend to deposit unless you add entries in the Add Funds to This Deposit section — appears below the Select the Payments Included in This Deposit list.

6. **Scroll down the Bank Deposit transaction window.**

Optionally, supply a memo for the deposit.

Optionally, supply a cash back amount — money from the deposit total that you don't intend to deposit — along with an account in which to place the cash back amount and a memo to describe the purpose of the cash back amount.

Optionally, you can attach an electronic document to the deposit, such as a scanned copy of the deposit ticket you take to the bank.

TIP

To attach an electronic document to the deposit, click in the Attachments box and navigate to the document or drag and drop the electronic copy into the Attachments box.

7. **Click Save and Close.**

QBO moves the deposited amount from the Undeposited Funds account to the account you selected in Step 2.

All that's left to do is take a trip to the bank. Or if you're mobile-savvy, you might be able to remotely deposit checks via your cellphone; talk to your banker.

Reconciling a Bank Account

Most people's least favorite task is reconciling the bank statement. But, if you're diligent about entering transactions in QBO and recording bank deposits as described in the preceding section, reconciling your bank statement should be a fairly easy process. Get your last bank statement and follow these steps:

1. **Click the Gear button and, from the Tools portion of the menu that appears, click Reconcile.**

2. **From the Reconcile page that appears, select the account you want to reconcile (see Figure 8-19).**

   Note that you should also reconcile credit card statements.

   REMEMBER

   You might see a Reconcile an Account button on the Reconcile page; click it, and a dialog box appears that summarizes, in roadmap-like style, the reconciliation process. Click Let's Do It to continue and display the page shown in Figure 8-19.

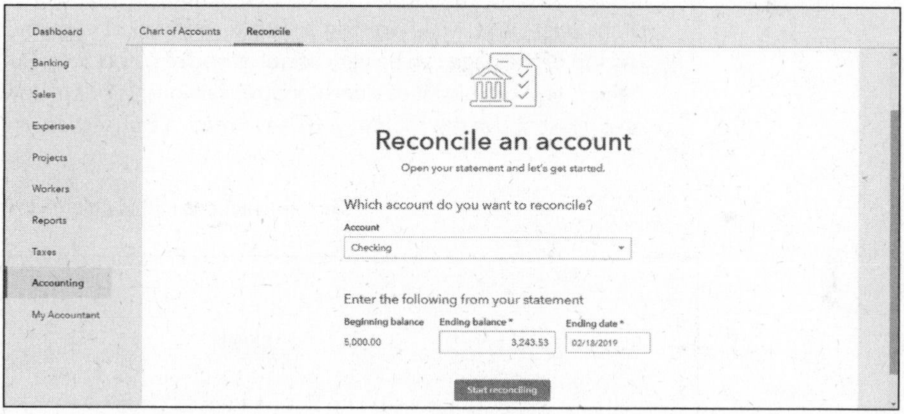

FIGURE 8-19:
Enter information found on your bank statement.

Reconcile an account

Open your statement and let's get started.

Which account do you want to reconcile?

Account

Checking

Enter the following from your statement

Beginning balance	Ending balance *	Ending date *
5,000.00	3,243.53	02/18/2019

Start reconciling

3. **Enter the ending date and balance found on your bank statement, and then click Start Reconciling.**

   QBO displays the Reconcile page shown in Figure 8-20.

4. **Select each transaction that appears on your bank statement and on the Reconcile page by clicking in the rightmost column.**

   TIP

   Paychecks deposited in two bank accounts will show up as two distinct transactions in QBO, so they should be easy to match during reconciliation.

By selecting a transaction, you're marking it as having cleared the bank. Your goal is to have the Difference amount at the bottom of the Reconcile window equal $0. If your account is connected to your bank, many transactions might already display a check mark in the rightmost column because the transaction has been downloaded from the bank and matched to a transaction in QBO.

By default, QBO filters the Reconciliation page to display all uncleared transactions dated before the statement ending date, but you can click Payments to view only payments and Deposits to view only deposits, similar to the way most bank statements are organized. Also by default, QBO hides transactions with dates later than the statement ending date. If, after selecting all the transactions you see, the Difference amount isn't $0, then click the X beside Statement Ending Date to look for additional transactions to mark as cleared. You also can take advantage of the Filter funnel to filter the transactions in a way that works best for you. And, be sure to compare the totals QBO lists for payments and deposits to the corresponding numbers on the bank statement; that can help you track whether you're missing a payment, a deposit, or both.

TIP

If you need to view the register of the account you're reconciling, you can click the "register" link in the upper left corner of the page. When you finish viewing the register, click the Reconcile button that appears in the upper right corner of the page. And, while working on the Reconciliation page, the information at the top of the page can be very useful as you're reconciling. But, if you don't need it, you can hide it to view more transactions; click the upward pointing arrow just above the column you use to mark a transaction as reconciled.

Click transactions in this column to mark them as cleared.

FIGURE 8-20: Match transactions found on your bank statement with those shown on the Reconcile page in QBO.

Chart of accounts > Bank register > Reconcile

Reconcile   Checking
Statement ending date: February 18, 2019

| $3,243.53 | | $4,980.01 | | | $-1,736.48 |
| STATEMENT ENDING BALANCE | − | CLEARED BALANCE | | | DIFFERENCE |

| $5,000.00 | | $19.99 | | $0.00 |
| BEGINNING BALANCE | − | 1 PAYMENT | + | 0 DEPOSITS |

Edit info   Save for later

Show me around

Payments   Deposits   All

DATE	CLEARED DATE	TYPE	REF NO.	ACCOUNT	PAYEE	MEMO		PAYMENT (U	DEPOSIT (US	○
10/21/2018		Bill Paym...	10	Accounts Payabl...	Robertson &...			300.00		○
10/29/2018		Receive ...	1053	Accounts Receiv...	Bill's Windo...				175.00	○
11/12/2018		Expense	12	Legal & Professi...	Robertson &...			250.00		○
12/04/2018		Check	4	Automobile.Fuel	Chin's Gas a...			54.55		○
12/10/2018		Sales Ta...		- Split -		Q1 Payment		38.50		○
12/10/2018		Sales Ta...		- Split -		Q1 Payment		38.40		○
12/13/2018		Expense	9	Job Expenses:J...	Tania's Nurs...			89.09		○
12/13/2018		Check	12	Legal & Professi...	Books by Be...			55.00		○

5. **When the Difference amount equals $0, click the Finish Now button (see Figure 8-21).**

   QBO displays the Success message and gives you the opportunity to view the Reconciliation report by clicking View Report. The Reconciliation report looks like the one shown in Figure 8-22. The report is broken into a summary section that you can see in Figure 8-22 and a detail section, not visible in Figure 8-22, that lists all checks and deposits you cleared.

Click to complete reconciliation.

FIGURE 8-21:
The goal of reconciliation is to make the Difference amount equal $0.

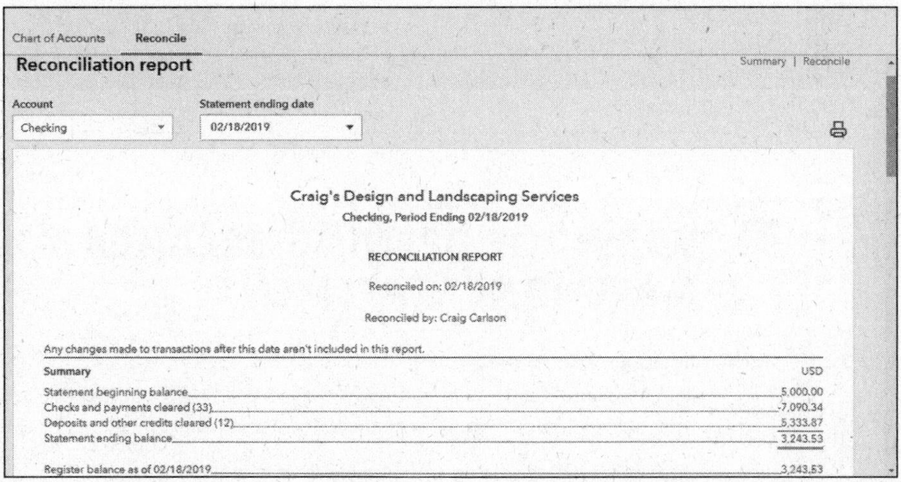

FIGURE 8-22:
A typical reconciliation report.

You can click any transaction on the report to view it in the window where you created it. And to produce a paper copy, click the Print button in the upper right corner of the report window.

You can view the Reconciliation report at any time. Just redisplay the Reconcile page shown previously in Figure 8-19 (choose Gear ➪ Reconcile) and click the History by Account link that appears in the upper right corner of the page (not shown in Figure 8-19). When you click the link, which appears only after you have reconciled an account, QBO displays the History by Account page, which lists prior reconciliations (see Figure 8-23) for an individual account. Click the View Report link beside any reconciliation on this page to see its Reconciliation report.

To view reconciliations for other accounts, use the Account list box to select a different account.

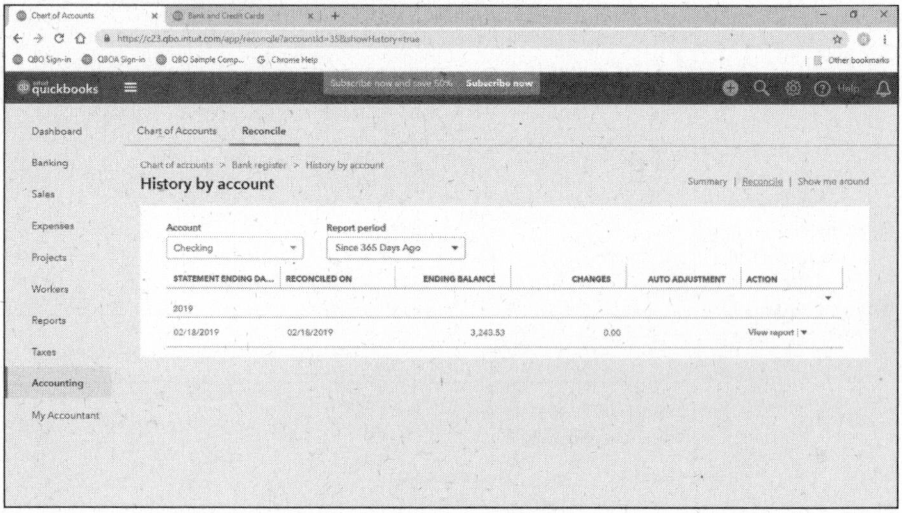

FIGURE 8-23:
Prior Reconciliation reports you can view.

WHEN THE OPENING BALANCE DOESN'T MATCH THE STATEMENT

It happens sometimes. You go to reconcile an account and its opening balance doesn't match the ending balance of the prior reconciliation period. You need to fix the beginning balance before you can reconcile the account.

Good news, here . . . QBO provides tools that help you fix the problem — in the form of a Reconciliation Discrepancy report that lists transactions associated with the erroneous beginning balance. When you select an account to reconcile that has a beginning balance problem, QBO displays a message that identifies the amount by which the account beginning balance is off, and offers a "Let's Resolve This Discrepancy" link. When you click the link, QBO displays a Reconciliation Discrepancy report that lists the transactions affecting the erroneous beginning balance. Typically, the report contains transactions that were changed after they were reconciled or were not reconciled when they should have been. The Reconciliation Discrepancy report also contains a "Difference" amount — and your goal is to make that amount be $0. You accomplish that by handling the transactions QBO displays on the Reconciliation Discrepancy report.

If you want to explore what happened to the listed transactions that made them cause the discrepancy, you can click the View link of the transaction — it appears in the right column of the report — and QBO will show you an Audit report for the transaction that details the changes that were made to the transaction.

To correct a transaction, click it on the report and QBO gives you ways to correct the transaction. Once you correct the transaction on the Reconciliation Discrepancy report, the account is ready to reconcile.

Chapter **9**

Paying Employees and Contractors

As an employer, you have a responsibility to pay both your employees and any contractors who work for you. In this chapter, I explore both responsibilities.

It's important to understand that QBO users can prepare payroll in one of two ways: using QBO with Self Service Payroll (which I call QBOP for QBO Payroll) or using QBO with Full Service Payroll. Although both of these options work in QBO, this chapter explores using QBOP, where you use QBO to do the work yourself. There isn't much point for me to describe QuickBooks Online with Full Service Payroll because Intuit does the work for you if you choose that plan.

REMEMBER

If you opt to use Full Service Payroll, Intuit does the work and is also responsible for penalties. So, if you aren't confident in your abilities to handle payroll, consider starting with Full Service Payroll and, when you're comfortable, switch the service to QBOP.

At the end of this chapter, I explore the ways QBO users typically pay — and report on paying — contractors, who are vendors who perform work for a company but do not qualify as employees.

Understanding the Employee Payroll Process

Just so you understand the job you're undertaking, be aware that running payroll is more than just issuing paychecks to your employees (although your employees will tell you that's the most important part of payroll). Yes, you first need to prepare accurate paychecks that account for withheld payroll taxes, deductions for benefits such as health insurance, and company contributions to, for example, retirement plans. But then, after you've prepared paychecks, you also need to electronically deposit withheld payroll taxes, remit amounts withheld for deductions and benefits to the appropriate parties, and file payroll tax returns with the appropriate taxing authorities. And all this work needs to be done according to a timetable that the IRS has established based on the size of your business's payroll tax liability.

Getting Started with QBO Payroll (QBOP)

When you prepare payroll, the process involves setup work so that you can accurately calculate payroll checks. You must also account for payroll taxes withheld from each employee's paycheck. You will remit federal and state payroll taxes to the appropriate tax authorities. You will also remit any required deductions and contributions that affect each employee's paycheck to appropriate agencies.

This section examines the payroll setup process in QBOP and assumes that you are just starting out in business and have not paid any employees yet.

TIP

SEASONED EMPLOYERS AND ENTERING PAYROLL HISTORY

If you're a seasoned employer who's been in business for a while and using QuickBooks for Windows Desktop, you might want to import your company into QBO as described in Chapter 12. In that case, your employees will appear in QBO; but, assuming you intend to use QBOP, you'll have some setup work to complete, much of which is similar to the work described in this chapter — and, as you'll see, the Payroll Setup wizard walks you through that work. Entering payroll history is where things differ for you; the "newly in business," at whom this chapter is aimed, don't have any payroll history to enter, so the treatment for entering payroll history is light.

Switching mid-year can cause confusion; I recommend (and your accountant will agree) that you plan to switch at the start of a new year or, at the very least, at the start of a quarter. You can enter history as of the last day of the preceding quarter, and the only additional information you need to enter would be information that has an impact on an annual form, such as the employee's W-2.

But for those who have been recording payroll in QuickBooks Desktop, you'll find the QuickBooks Desktop Payroll Summary report most useful because it contains all the information the Payroll Setup wizard requests to establish your payroll history information. Using the information on the Payroll Summary report, you enter, for each employee for the current year, total wages, deductions, and taxes for prior quarters. Using the same report, enter the same information for the Year-to-Date as of Today column presented by the Payroll Setup wizard. Last, seasoned employers enter prior payrolls, totaled for all employees, once again using the Payroll Summary report from QuickBooks Desktop.

You enter the total payroll for each pay period in the current quarter. As you enter these numbers, you are entering information paid to *all* employees (not individuals) for the date — which makes the task less onerous because there's less data entry. Similarly, you enter total taxes paid by tax for that pay period.

And, because you've been paying employees, you'll also need to enter information about prior payroll tax payments you made during the current payroll year to reconcile the payroll tax history.

You can use the details in this article to help you complete your company's setup after you import it: https://community.intuit.com/articles/1274215-what-to-do-after-completing-an-import-to-quickbooks-online-from-quickbooks-desktop-mac-windows-us. And the steps you see in this chapter will also help you set up QBOP.

Turning on QBOP

QBOP uses a wizard to walk you through the payroll setup process. You start by first turning on payroll in QBO. Then, the wizard walks you through setting up your company so that you can pay your employees.

REMEMBER

Be aware that you can set up employees without turning on payroll. You will be able to enter payroll later, going back as far as the date on which you started your payroll subscription. Also note that not turning on payroll immediately doesn't save you any money. You are charged for your subscription from the time you sign up for the service less any trial time even if you don't pay any employees. I suggest that you plan to set up payroll as soon as you subscribe so that you don't spend months paying for a subscription you're not using.

Click the Workers link in the Navigation bar, and then click Employees. On the page that appears, click the Get Started button. The Payroll wizard starts. On the first page, shown in Figure 9-1, you choose between Self Service Payroll — the choice for this chapter — and Full Service Payroll. Because this chapter is about using QBOP, I chose the Try Self Service Payroll option — and if you want to use QBOP, you too should choose this option. The QBO Employees page reappears; click the Get Set Up button to start the payroll setup process.

WARNING

Following the Payroll Setup wizard in order eliminates the vast majority of errors and costly setup issues that tend to surface at the year end, when you least need the trouble. It's best to not skip a step in the name of getting started.

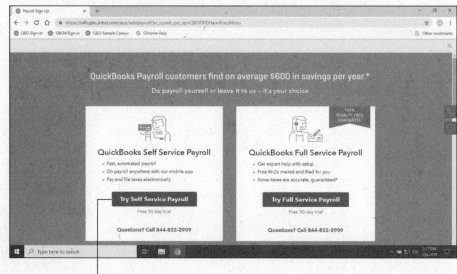

FIGURE 9-1: Choosing an option for payroll.

Click to start payroll setup.

TIP

At the time I wrote this, the Employees page stated that I was signed up for Enhanced Payroll, the previous name for Self Service Payroll. So, if you see Enhanced Payroll, don't panic. You've got the correct payroll subscription.

On the first page of the Get Ready for Payroll wizard, QBO displays the information you provided when you initially set up your company.

Double-check the information and click the Continue button in the lower right corner of the screen. On the next screen of the wizard, you indicate whether you've been paying employees during the current year or whether you are about to start paying employees for the first time.

If you indicate that you have previously done payroll and are now switching to QBOP, the wizard displays additional questions for you to answer concerning the method you used to pay employees prior to subscribing to QBOP. Answer the questions and click the Continue button in the lower right corner of the screen. If you indicate that you've not previously paid employees, no additional questions appear, so you can just click Continue in the lower right corner of the screen.

As I mentioned in the beginning of this chapter, I'm going to assume that you've not previously paid any employees. If you have been using QuickBooks for Windows Desktop to prepare payroll, you can enter payroll history information for each employee and each payroll using information you find on the Payroll Summary report from the QuickBooks Desktop program.

The next page of the wizard prompts you to add employees (see Figure 9-2).

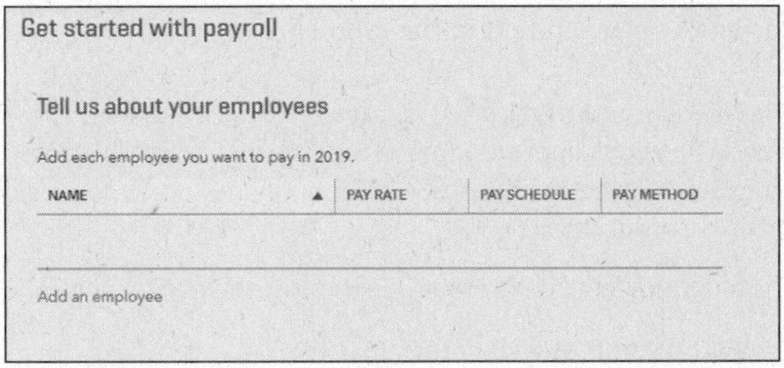

Get started with payroll

Tell us about your employees

Add each employee you want to pay in 2019.

NAME		PAY RATE	PAY SCHEDULE	PAY METHOD

Add an employee

FIGURE 9-2:
The Payroll Setup wizard helps you add current employees.

Click Add an Employee, and the wizard displays a fairly lengthy screen for you to complete about the employee. On the first part of the screen, shown in Figure 9-3, provide the employee's name and hire date.

QBO offers to let you invite the employee to fill in the employee information, including W-4 information, using a secure portal. If you want the employee to provide the information, provide the employee's email address and click Send Email. Alternatively, choose No, I Want to Enter the Info Myself.

REMEMBER

W-4 forms are the Internal Revenue Service's form that employees complete to specify their withholding allowance. If you need to complete Form W-4 for any employee, you can visit www.irs.gov and click the W-4 link in the Forms & Instructions section to display editable PDF forms.

For this example, I'm going to assume you want to provide the information yourself.

FIGURE 9-3: Fill in the basic information about the employee.

Scroll down the page and fill in the following information:

» The frequency with which you pay the employee and the next expected pay date. When you supply pay frequency information, QBO creates a pay schedule that you can apply to subsequent employees you create. Figure 9-4 shows a typical pay schedule.

» The amount you pay the employee (hourly, salaried, or commission only).

» Whether the employee has any deductions.

» Form W-4 withholding information, which includes, as you can see from Figure 9-5, the employee's address, social security number, marital status, and withholding amount. State payroll tax information appears at the bottom of the screen and is not shown in Figure 9-5. These requirements vary from state to state, but QBOP prompts you to supply information for the state in which your business operates.

TIP

TIP

To identify your state's payroll tax requirements, visit your state's website and search for *payroll taxes*.

>> The method you want to use to pay the employee (such as paper check or direct deposit). If you choose Direct Deposit, specify the bank account information for the employee (account type, routing number, and account number).

For Direct Deposit checks, you can choose to deposit the paycheck in its entirety in a single account, deposit the check into two accounts, or deposit a portion of the check directly and pay the balance as a paper check.

What's Josh's pay schedule?

How often do you pay Josh?

Every Other Week ▼

When's the next payday?

02/22/2019

When's the last day of work (pay period) for that payday?

02/20/2019

What do you want to name this pay schedule?

Every Other Friday

☑ Use this schedule for employees you add after Josh

Next four pay periods (based on dates you entered)

PAY PERIODS	PAYDAY
02/07/2019 – 02/20/2019	02/22/2019
02/21/2019 – 03/06/2019	03/08/2019
03/07/2019 – 03/20/2019	03/22/2019
03/21/2019 – 04/03/2019	04/05/2019

FIGURE 9-4: A typical pay schedule.

Payroll Taxes Setup and Compliance

What are Josh's withholdings?

Need blank W-4 forms?

W-4 Employee's Withholding Allowance Certificate **2019**

1. First name* M.I. Last name*
   Josh   Bergen

2. Social Security number*

Home address*

City or town*   State* ZIP code*
   AZ ▼

3. ⦿ Single
   ○ Married
   ○ Married, but withhold at higher Single rate
   ○ Do Not Withhold

4. Total number of allowances you are claiming 4. 0

5. Additional amount, if any, you want withheld from each paycheck . . . .   5. $ 0.00

FIGURE 9-5: Information required to complete a Federal Form W-4.

When you finish supplying the employee's information, click Done, and QBO displays the My Payroll page, listing active employees (see Figure 9-6). From this page, you can edit existing employees (click the employee to edit the information), you can add more employees, and you can start a payroll — and you probably should go ahead at this point and add the rest of your employees.

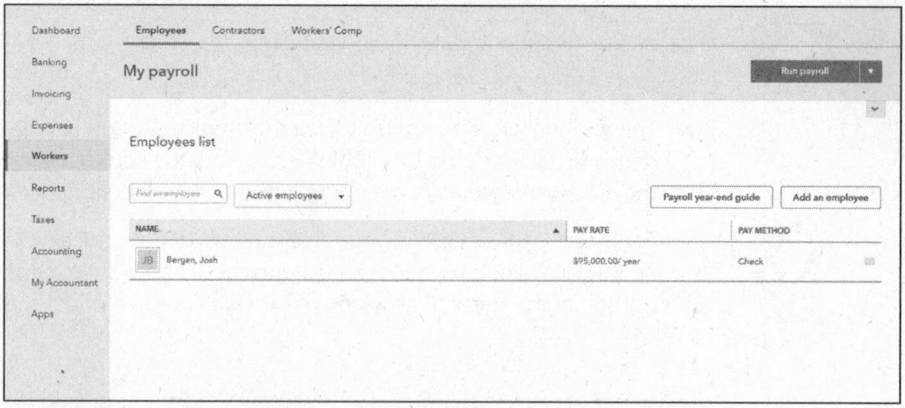

FIGURE 9-6:
Add or edit
employees.

Setting payroll preferences

In addition to adding employees, you should review payroll preferences and set up payroll taxes.

To review payroll preferences, click the Gear button. From the menu that appears, click Payroll Settings (in the Your Company column) to display the Preferences page shown in Figure 9-7. The page contains a series of links that you can click to review or establish various settings related to payroll. Understanding this page might make you feel less overwhelmed by what you see.

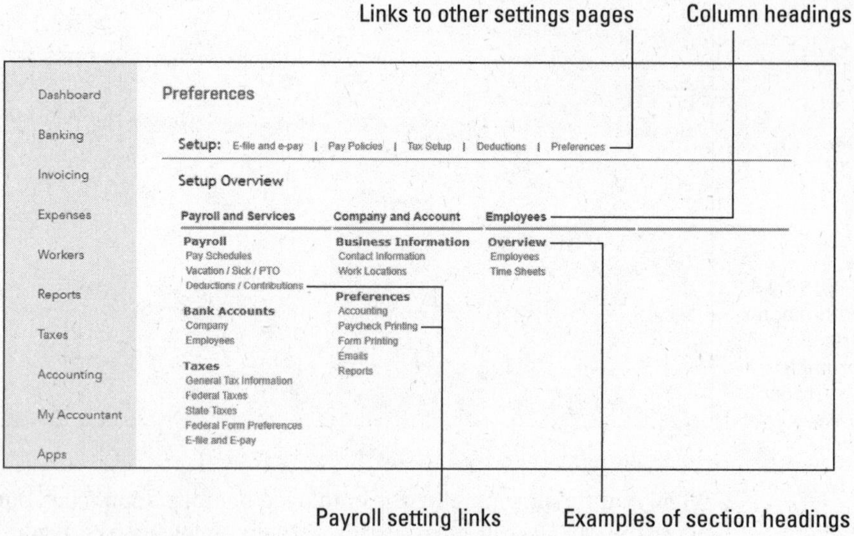

Links to other settings pages   Column headings

FIGURE 9-7:
The Payroll
Preferences page.

Payroll setting links   Examples of section headings

The Setup Overview page is divided into three columns: Payroll and Services, Company and Account, and Employees. Within each column, you find additional headings — I refer to these additional headings as *section headings* — that summarize the types of settings you find as you click each link in that section. For example, under the Company and Account column, you find section headings for Business Information and Preferences. In the following bullets, I describe the kind of information you find as you click the links under each section heading on the Setup Overview page.

In addition, links appear above the Setup Overview heading; good news here — these aren't additional settings that you need to review. Instead, these links lead to the same pages as some of the links listed in the columns and section headings on the Setup Overview page. For example, the E-file and E-pay link at the top of the page displays the same page as the E-file and E-pay link in the Taxes section under the Payroll and Services column heading. And clicking the Pay Policies link displays the same page as clicking the Pay Schedules and Vacation/Sick/PTO links in the Payroll section under the Payroll and Services column heading.

In the bullets that follow, you find a description of the pages that appear as you click the links beneath each section heading:

» In the Payroll section (under Payroll and Services), you can set up additional pay schedules; establish vacation, sick, and paid time off policies; and define deductions and contributions used by your company during payroll.

» In the Taxes section, you establish general company tax information (such as your company's legal organization); set up your federal tax ID number and your filing and tax deposit schedule requirements; set up your state's payroll requirements, which vary from state to state; and designate whether you have a third-party or paid form preparer. You also can enroll in electronic services for filing and paying payroll taxes. To identify your state's payroll tax requirements, visit your state's website and search for *payroll taxes*.

» Use the Business Information section to ensure that your contact information is accurate.

» Use the Preferences section to establish the following:

- Wage and tax accounts for payroll

- Paycheck and W-2 form printing settings

- Payroll-related email preferences such as receiving reminders about preparing payroll, making tax payments, and filing tax forms

- Report settings to identify reports you want available after you prepare payroll

>> In the Overview section, the Employees link takes you to the Employees page; clicking Employees on the Preferences page has the same effect as clicking Employees in the Navigation bar.

>> Use the Time Sheets link in the Overview section to establish the way you want to enter employee hours.

Setting up payroll taxes

Before you start using payroll, you should use the wizard in QBOP to set up payroll tax form and filing information. The wizard asks you for federal and state tax details such as your federal Employer ID Number (EIN) and your corresponding state account number, how often you're required to remit payroll taxes, and whether you want to file and pay taxes electronically or manually using paper coupons. Choose Taxes in the Navigation bar and then click Payroll Tax to display the Payroll Tax Center before you set things up (see Figure 9-8).

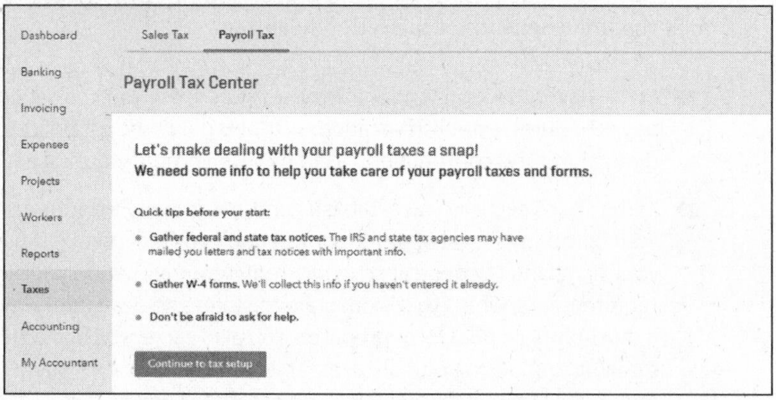

FIGURE 9-8: The Payroll Tax Center before you establish settings for payroll tax forms and payments.

Click Continue to Tax Setup, and the wizard displays the Business Details page. Confirm or change information the wizard supplies about your business, including the address you use when filing tax forms, the first time you'll be running payroll using QBOP, and the timeframe during which you hired your first employee. If workers' compensation insurance is required in your state, QBO notifies you and asks you if you'd like a quote on a policy that integrates with QBOP. After making your choices, click Continue. If you indicate that you are a new employer, the wizard displays a list of the items it will set up for you; click OK.

TIP

The date you start using QBOP determines the "as of" date of historical information you need to collect — and determines that date to be the first day of the current quarter. Try to start using QBOP on January 1 of any year — that way, you don't need to enter any historical information. If you can't start using QBOP on January 1, try to start using it on the first day of an accounting period — either on the first day of your company's fiscal year or on the first day of a month. Historical payroll transactions can be summarized prior to that date, but must be entered in detail after that date.

The Payroll Tax setup wizard next displays the Federal and State Tax Details page shown in Figure 9-9. Supply your federal Employer Identification Number (EIN), and confirm the payroll tax form you use and how often you must remit payroll taxes. You should also specify whether your company is a federally recognized non-profit organization that is not required to pay federal unemployment taxes (FUTA). And, indicate whether you want to share your information for the purpose of getting workers' comp insurance offers. For your state, supply your state tax ID number.

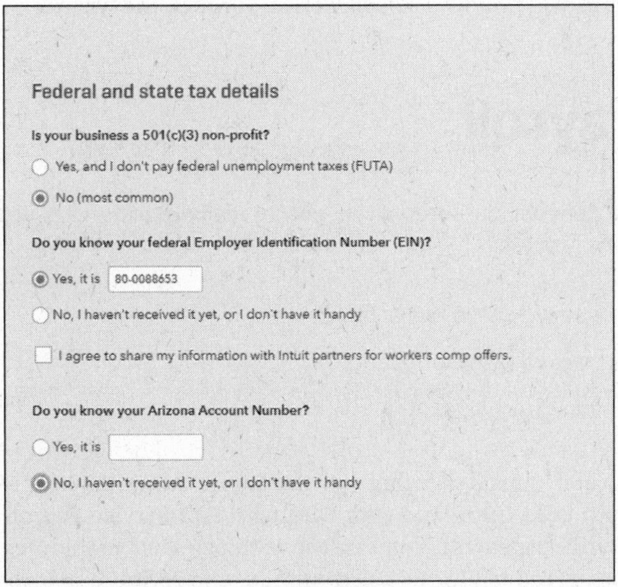

Federal and state tax details

Is your business a 501(c)(3) non-profit?

○ Yes, and I don't pay federal unemployment taxes (FUTA)

◉ No (most common)

Do you know your federal Employer Identification Number (EIN)?

◉ Yes, it is   80-0088653

○ No, I haven't received it yet, or I don't have it handy

☐ I agree to share my information with Intuit partners for workers comp offers.

Do you know your Arizona Account Number?

○ Yes, it is

◉ No, I haven't received it yet, or I don't have it handy

FIGURE 9-9:
The Federal and State Tax Details page.

Click Save, and QBOP displays the E-pay and E-file Setup page, where you specify whether you want to file and pay payroll taxes electronically or manually, using paper coupons. If you opt to file and pay electronically, you then supply information about the bank account from which you want to pay, including your routing and account number.

When you finish supplying information about how you want to file and pay your taxes, click Next. QBO confirms that you've finished setting up your payroll taxes. Click Done, and QBO redisplays the Payroll Tax Center screen (see Figure 9-10).

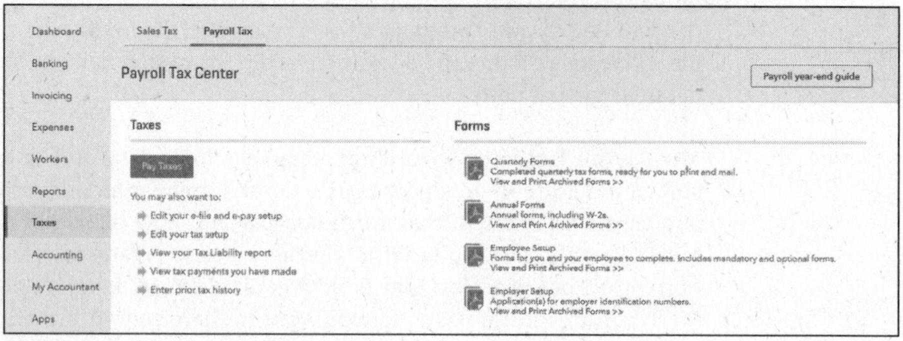

FIGURE 9-10:
The appearance of the Payroll Tax Center screen now that you've finished setting things up.

You can use the links on the Payroll Tax Center screen to make changes to any of the settings you provided as you worked through the wizard.

Preparing Payroll

Once you get past the setup work, you're ready to process payroll — essentially a three-step process:

>> Record paycheck information.

>> Review paycheck information.

>> Generate paychecks.

TIP

Mobile users: Consider trying out the Intuit Online Payroll Mobile app, which works with both QBOP and with QBO with Full Service Payroll (as well as other Intuit payroll products). You can use it to pay your employees and your payroll taxes, file payroll tax forms electronically, and review employee information and paycheck history. Data syncs automatically between the mobile app and your Intuit payroll account. Download the mobile app from the Apple App Store or from the Google Play Store; it's free with a payroll subscription.

Recording payroll information

To start preparing paychecks, click the Workers link in the Navigation bar and then click Employees to display the My Payroll page. Then, click the Run Payroll button on the top right side of the page.

QBOP starts the Run Payroll wizard by displaying the window shown in Figure 9-11, which lists all your employees (I have only four employees in this company, so my list is short). If you use multiple pay schedules, QBO prompts you to choose a pay schedule before showing you the page in Figure 9-11.

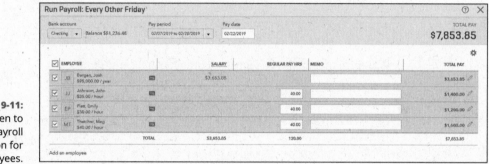

FIGURE 9-11: Use this screen to enter payroll information for your employees.

At the top of the window, select the bank account from which you'll pay employees and double-check pay period and pay date information. By default, QBO places a check mark to the left of each employee scheduled to be paid, but you can remove the check if appropriate. For each employee paid on an hourly basis, supply the hours worked during the pay period.

TIP

If you have lots of employees and want to see more of them onscreen, click the gear on the right side of the screen above Total Pay in the table and choose Compact. QBO reduces the amount of screen real estate it allots to each employee.

Reviewing and generating payroll checks

Once you finish entering hours and, if appropriate, memos for each employee you plan to pay, click the Preview Payroll button in the lower right corner of the Run Payroll window (shown previously in Figure 9-11). The Run Payroll wizard displays the Review and Submit page, similar to the one shown in Figure 9-12.

TIP

LETTING EMPLOYEES USE TIMESHEETS

If you use QBO Plus, you can set up *time-tracking users* who can log in with limited privileges that enable them to complete timesheets (and do nothing else).

To add a time-tracking user, follow these steps:

1. **Click the Gear button at the top of the Dashboard page and, from the menu that appears, click Manage Users in the Your Company column.**
2. **Click the Add User button and, from the window that appears, click Time Tracking Only.**
3. **Click Next and select the employee (or vendor) you want to fill out timesheets.**
4. **Supply the employee's (or the vendor's) email address.**
5. **Click Next and then click Finish.**

QBO sends to the user an email containing a link that he clicks to complete the Time Tracking Only setup process. If the user already has a QBO sign-in name and password, he can use it. Otherwise, he needs to create a sign-in name and password.

Once the user has signed in, the Single Activity Time Sheet screen appears; if the employee prefers to use the Weekly Timesheet screen, she can click the tab at the top of the screen. Because most employers don't pay their employees based on hours reported on timesheets — employers instead use timesheets to bill clients for time spent on client projects or to track labor costs associated with a project — see Chapter 6 for details on entering time.

You can view hours entered on timesheets by time-tracking employees. Before you start payroll, click the Create (+) button at the top of QBO, select Weekly Timesheet, and then select the employee. If you prefer, you can print information: Run a Time Activity by Employee report (click the Reports link in the Navigation bar and then search for "Time Activities by Employee Detail." Then, customize the report to display the payroll timeframe. For information on reports, see Chapter 10.

And don't forget that, if tracking time is important to your business, you can subscribe to TSheets Time Tracking, the add-on app that integrates with QBO and enables time tracking from any mobile device.

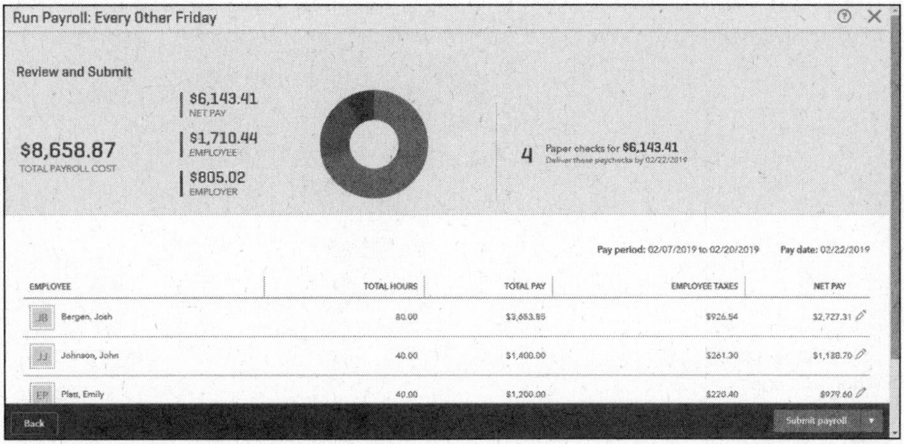

FIGURE 9-12:
Reviewing
paychecks before
generating them.

Run Payroll: Every Other Friday					
Review and Submit					
$8,658.87 TOTAL PAYROLL COST	**$6,143.41** NET PAY **$1,710.44** EMPLOYEE **$805.02** EMPLOYER			4	Paper checks for **$6,143.41** Deliver these paychecks by 02/22/2019

Pay period: 02/07/2019 to 02/20/2019   Pay date: 02/22/2019

EMPLOYEE	TOTAL HOURS	TOTAL PAY	EMPLOYEE TAXES	NET PAY
Bergen, Josh	80.00	$3,683.85	$926.54	$2,727.31
Johnson, John	40.00	$1,400.00	$261.30	$1,138.70
Platt, Emily	40.00	$1,200.00	$220.40	$979.60

Back   Submit payroll

When you're satisfied with the information on this page, click the Submit Payroll button in the lower right corner of the screen. If you're unsure about the payroll or you don't have time to complete it now, click the down arrow beside the Submit Payroll button and choose Save for Later to save the work you've done so far.

TIP

You can click the pencil at the right edge of the line for any employee to see the details associated with the employee's paycheck. If necessary, you can make changes to some paycheck details; for example, for hourly employees, you can change the hours an employee worked and the federal and state income tax amounts.

QBO displays the last screen of the Run Payroll wizard, which confirms that you've completed payroll. If you don't directly deposit paychecks for your employees, QBO gives you the option to print paychecks and stubs. You can supply a starting check number and click Print Pay Stubs to preview paychecks and stubs and print them (see Figure 9-13).

TIP

If you pay your employees by direct deposit, expect 24-hour turnaround. You can submit a payroll request up until 5pm PT the day before payday. The confirmation screen displays when the funds will be withdrawn from your bank account and deposited into the employee's bank account.

On the last screen of the Run Payroll wizard, click the Finish Payroll button in the lower right corner (and not shown in Figure 9-13) to record the payroll information in QBO.

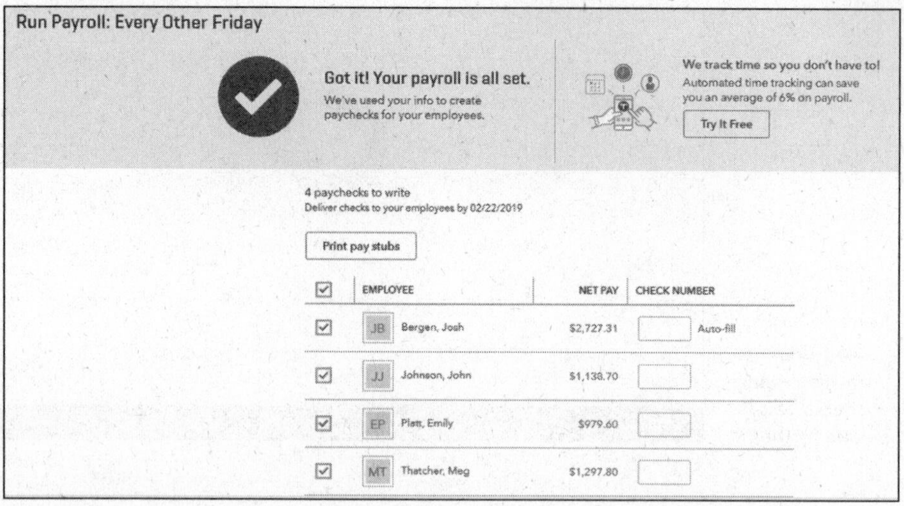

FIGURE 9-13: When you don't directly deposit paychecks, you'll see a page like this one.

Correcting payroll exemptions (without calling Tech Support)

It happens. You pay an employee, perhaps several times, and then discover that the employee should have been exempt from State Unemployment Insurance. Or you discover that the employee was set up as exempt and shouldn't have been exempt. You can fix this issue yourself, without calling Intuit Technical Support. And, once you've updated the employee's settings, QBO will adjust payroll information and, if appropriate, set up a reimbursement for the employee. You might need to pay additional taxes based on the change, and you will probably need to deal with your state to amend tax returns you filed and arrange for payments or credits to future taxes due, as needed.

In the United States, it doesn't matter where you live; QBO makes adjustments for all 50 states and the District of Columbia. In general, when you change the exempt status for SUI for an employee, QBO will, *for the current calendar year only:*

>> Recalculate employee paid taxes (such as CA SDI).

>> Pay amounts owed to employees on the next check.

>> Recapture amounts owed from employers on the next check.

>> Recalculate federal unemployment tax (FUTA) to 6%.

WARNING

Although you also can change exemption status for Social Security/Medicare and for FUTA, QBO will *not*, at this time, adjust your books for erroneously withheld Social Security/Medicare and FUTA the way it will make adjustments for erroneously withheld SUI. To adjust your books (and tax liabilities) for Social Security/Medicare and FUTA, you will need to talk to your accountant or to Intuit Technical Support. Watch for additional payroll-related changes that you'll be able to make without calling Intuit Technical Support as QBO advances over time.

Here's how you change an employee's SUI exemption settings in QBO:

1. **Click Workers in the Navigation pane, click Employees, and click the name of the employee whose status you need to change.**

2. **In the Pay section of the Employee Details page that appears, click the pencil icon to edit the employee's pay information (see Figure 9-14).**

FIGURE 9-14: Click the pencil icon in the Pay section to edit pay information.

Click to edit information.

3. **On the page that appears, click the pencil icon under the withholdings question (see Figure 9-15).**

4. **On the Payroll Taxes Setup and Compliance page that appears, scroll down and click Tax Exemptions (see Figure 9-16).**

5. **Click the state tax to be exempted.**

   In the figure, I clicked AZ SUI and JTT.

6. **Click Done in the lower right corner of the page.**

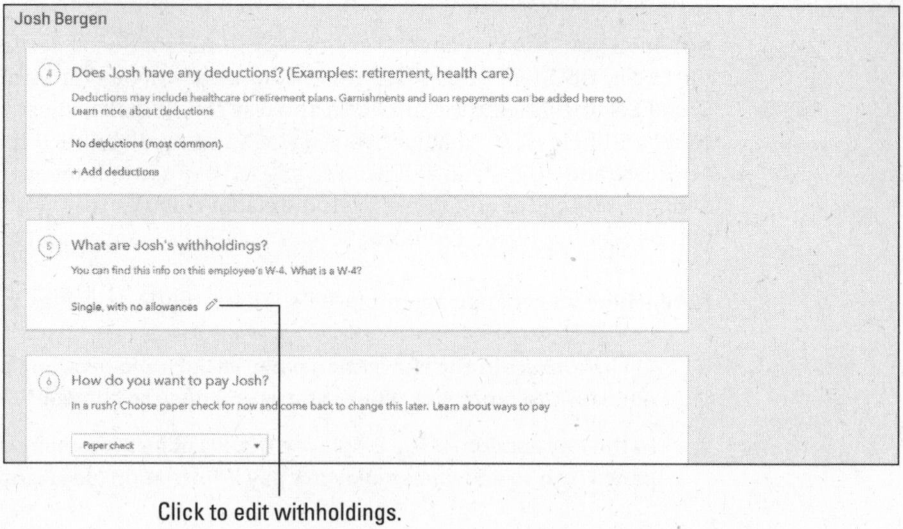

FIGURE 9-15: Click the pencil icon in the withholdings question to edit the employee's withholdings.

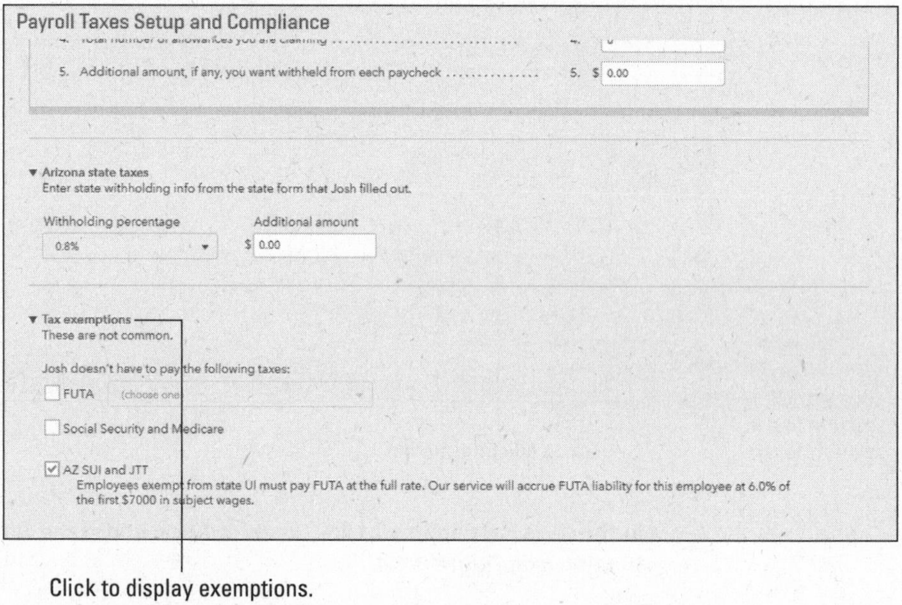

Click to edit withholdings.

FIGURE 9-16: Click Tax Exemptions to display taxes for which an employee might be exempt.

Click to display exemptions.

QBO displays a message like the one in Figure 9-17, explaining what's going to happen when you click Continue. After you click Continue, the page you saw in Figure 9-15 appears, with a message at the top explaining that you successfully updated tax exemptions and, if appropriate, QBO adjusted for FUTA and SUI employer taxes. The message contains a link to the Payroll Tax Center, where you find details of additional payroll tax payments you might need to make; don't forget to file amended tax returns. And, QBO will ensure that the employee's next paycheck includes any appropriate reimbursements if you added exemptions or deductions if you removed exemptions.

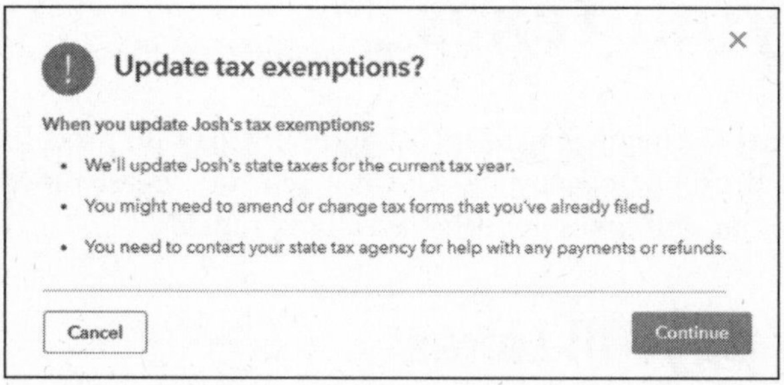

> ⚠ **Update tax exemptions?**   ✕
>
> When you update Josh's tax exemptions:
>
> - We'll update Josh's state taxes for the current tax year.
> - You might need to amend or change tax forms that you've already filed.
> - You need to contact your state tax agency for help with any payments or refunds.
>
> Cancel   Continue

TIP

Do you need to void or delete a paycheck? Display the list of paychecks you've issued by clicking Paycheck List in the upper right corner of the Employee page, just below the Run Payroll button (click Employees in the Navigation pane). Select the paycheck you need to void or delete and click the Void or Delete button above the list. QBO will walk you through a series of questions that helps you get the job done.

Printing payroll reports

Once you complete payroll, you might want to print payroll-related reports. Click the Reports link in the Navigation bar to display the Reports page. Scroll down the page listing Standard Reports to find the Payroll reports (see Figure 9-18).

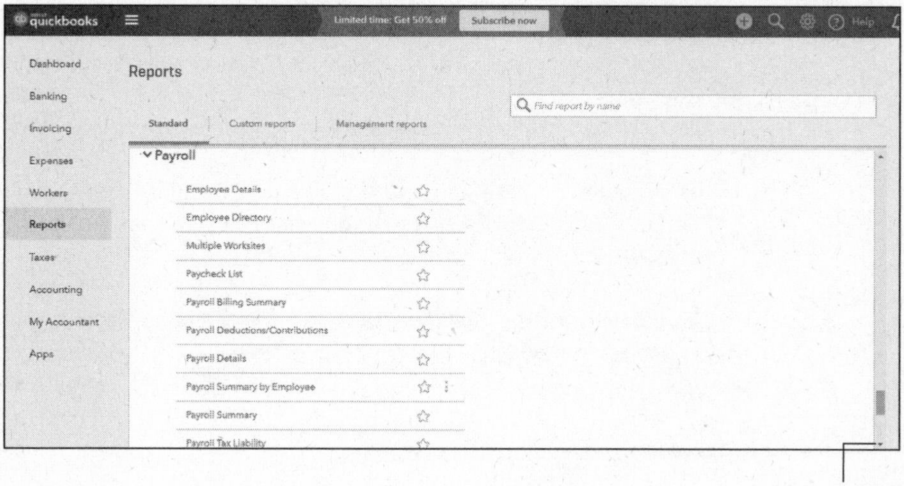

FIGURE 9-18:
From the Reports page, display all reports.

Click to scroll.

You can click any payroll report to print it to the screen and, subsequently, to your printer. To customize reports, see Chapter 10.

Managing Payroll Taxes

As I mention at the beginning of this chapter, the payroll process doesn't end with preparing and producing paychecks. On a schedule determined by the IRS, you need to remit payroll taxes and file payroll tax returns.

Paying payroll taxes

Using rules established by the IRS, most QBO users pay payroll taxes semi-weekly or monthly, depending on the amount you owe (called your *payroll tax liability*).

PAYROLL-RELATED DUE DATES

Payroll and unemployment tax payments are due on a different schedule than the corresponding tax forms. To summarize, payroll tax payments for most QBO users are due semi-weekly or monthly, depending on the size of your payroll tax liability. The payroll tax form (Federal Form 941) is due quarterly.

Federal unemployment tax payments are typically due quarterly, but the federal unemployment tax return (Federal Form 940) is typically due annually.

If you do business in a state that imposes a personal income tax, then you also have state payroll tax obligations. In addition, most states impose an unemployment tax.

And, localities within any given state might also impose payroll tax obligations.

The due dates for these state and local payments and their corresponding returns vary from state to state; to determine the due dates for your state and locality, check at the state's website.

Last, but not least, the listed due dates in QBO might be earlier than the actual due dates to accommodate E-file and E-pay processing.

You must make federal tax deposits by electronic funds transfer. Most people make federal tax deposits using the Electronic Federal Tax Payment System (EFTPS), a free service provided by the United States Department of Treasury. QBOP does not make use of the EFTPS; instead, QBOP pays directly on your behalf through your E-file and Pay portal. For this reason, you need to complete and sign Form 8655 before you can set up E-file and Pay.

To pay your payroll taxes, choose Taxes ⇨ Payroll Tax to display the Payroll Tax Center (shown in Figure 9-19). Once you've paid employees, the Payroll Tax Center displays taxes that are due, along with their due dates and e-payment cutoff dates. You can preview how much you owe by printing the Payroll Tax Liability report; click the View Your Tax Liability Report link on the Payroll Tax Center page.

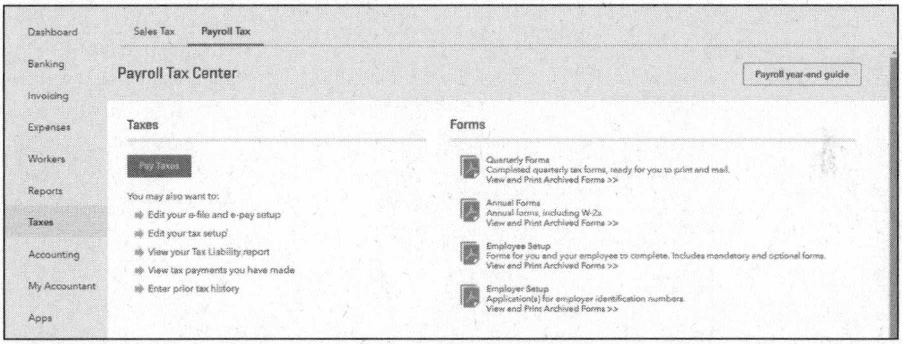

FIGURE 9-19: The Payroll Tax Center after you have recorded payroll information.

When you click the Pay Taxes button, QBO displays the Pay Taxes page (see Figure 9-20), which shows payroll tax amounts that you owe; if you owe money to more than one payroll tax authority, QBO separates your liabilities by payroll tax authority and displays appropriate due dates.

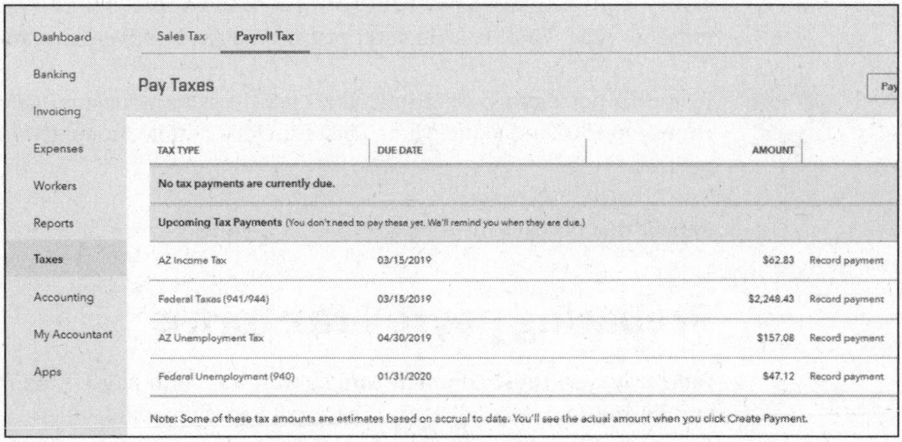

FIGURE 9-20: Your payroll tax liabilities.

If you expand the Upcoming Tax Payments line, QBO displays estimated amounts of your upcoming liabilities.

When you click the Record Payment link beside a line, QBO shows you the amount you owe, allocated by tax item (see Figure 9-21). At the top of the screen, you can opt to pay the liability electronically using EFTPS or make the payment yourself.

I'm working in a sample company, so I deliberately did not set up electronic payment capabilities. Therefore, you don't see, in Figure 9-21, any reference to paying manually or paying electronically.

Approve Payment	⑦ ✕
Federal Taxes (941/944)	**$2,248.43**

Enter the payment date. Once you click Record payment, QuickBooks Online Payroll provides specific instructions about how to pay this tax.

Liability Period	Due Date
02/01/2019 to 02/28/2019	03/15/2019
Bank Account	Payment Date
Checking ▼ Balance $42,644.64	Earliest ▼ 02/19/2019

TAX ITEM	AMOUNT
Federal Income Tax	$1,046.79
Social Security	$486.94
Social Security Employer	$486.94
Medicare	$113.88
Medicare Employer	$113.88
	$2,248.43

Cancel	Delete	Record payment ▼

FIGURE 9-21:
A payroll tax payment.

When you finish reviewing the details for the payment, including the bank account from which you'll make the payment, and the payment date, click the E-pay button or the Record Payment button (depending on whether you're paying electronically or making the payment yourself) in the lower right corner of the screen. QBO displays a payment confirmation window that describes the payment method, type, liability, due date, payment date, and payment amount.

If you're not paying electronically, click the arrow beside Record Payment and choose Record and Print. Then, QBO provides detailed instructions for making the payment.

Repeat this process for each payroll tax liability currently due.

Preparing payroll tax forms

Quarterly, you must complete and submit a federal payroll tax return using Federal Form 941, which identifies the total wages you paid, when you paid them, and the total taxes you withheld and deposited with appropriate taxing authorities throughout the quarter. The IRS permits you to file the form electronically or to mail the form.

If you live in a state that imposes a personal income tax, then you typically must also file a similar form for your state; check your state's website for the rules you need to follow for payroll tax reporting. Your state probably has a state unemployment form you need to prepare and submit as well.

When you click Quarterly Forms on the Payroll Tax Center page (refer to Figure 9-19), QBOP displays the reports you need to prepare and submit (see Figure 9-22).

FIGURE 9-22: The payroll tax returns you need to prepare and submit appear on the Quarterly Tax Forms page.

Sales Tax	Payroll Tax

‹ Payroll Tax Center

Quarterly Tax Forms

Employer's Quarterly Tax Return
File this form each quarter to report federal taxes withheld, paid, and owed in the previous quarter. (Does not include FUTA.) 941 ›

Arizona Quarterly Withholding Tax Return
File Form A1-QRT quarterly with the Department of Revenue. AZ A1-QRT ›

Arizona Quarterly UI Form
File Form UC-018 with your UI tax payment each quarter. AZ UC-018 ›

Want to view or print a form you already saved or e-filed? View and Print Archived Forms.

Click the link to the right of each form, and QBOP displays a page where you can opt to file the form electronically and preview the form in a PDF viewer. Click the View button to preview the form, and it appears prefilled with information in your PDF viewer. As you scroll to the bottom of the form, filing instructions appear.

Repeat the process of reviewing and printing each form as appropriate.

Paying Contractors

Paying contractors is pretty much a straightforward experience. You can wait until you receive a bill from a contractor, enter it, and subsequently pay it as described in Chapter 5.

But, to ensure that you can accurately report payments you made to contractors, you need to ensure that they are set up as vendors who will receive Form 1099-MISC; I'll call these people "1099-eligible contractors" going forward.

REMEMBER

I use the term "1099-eligible" because, while you might hire someone as a contractor, if you don't pay that person at least $600.00 — the threshold established by the IRS — then technically, you don't have to produce a 1099 for that contractor. Further, if you don't pay a contractor more than $600.00, QBO does not show payments to that contractor on reports.

1099-eligible contractors are people who work for you but who are not your employees. Specifically, the IRS distinguishes between 1099-eligible contractors and employees based on whether you, the employer, have the means and methods of accomplishing the work or if you simply have the right to control and direct the result of the work. If you have the means and methods to accomplish the work, the person working for you is an employee, not an independent, 1099-eligible contractor. If you can't decide, ask your accountant.

In this section, I focus on setting up 1099-eligible contractors, paying them (without using direct deposit), reporting on 1099 payments you've made, and preparing 1099s for those of your contractors who need them.

TIP

If you use QBOP, you can pay contractors (as well as employees) via Direct Deposit. You must first turn on and complete Direct Deposit setup for your company's payroll subscription, which involves you supplying your banking (routing and account) information from which contractors and employees will be paid. Then, to set up a contractor as a Direct Deposit recipient, click Worker⇨ Contractors. On the page that appears, click the Check It Out button and follow the onscreen directions to add a contractor's banking information and initiate payment within QBO the same way you would for employees. Direct Deposit for Contractors costs you a per-month fee to issue as many direct deposit checks as you want.

Setting up 1099 contractors

You can set up 1099-eligible contractors in two different ways, and the end result is the same:

>> You can use the information in Chapter 4 to set up a new vendor and make sure that you check the Track Payments for 1099 box.

>> You can use the Contractors page to set up a contractor; QBO automatically sets up any contractor you add from this page as a 1099-eligible contractor.

Because you saw how to set up new people in Chapter 4, I'll focus on using the Contractors page to create a new contractor; follow these steps:

1. **Click Workers ⇨ Contractors.**

   QBO displays the Contractors page, which lists currently established contractors.

2. **Click the Add a Contractor button.**

   QBO displays the dialog box shown in Figure 9-23,

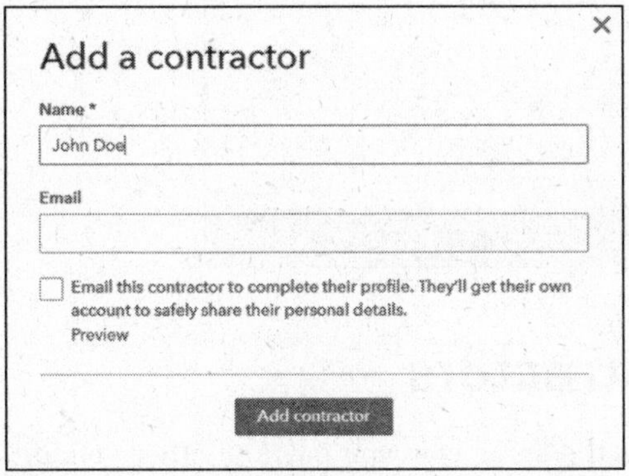

Add a contractor

Name *

John Doe

Email

☐ Email this contractor to complete their profile. They'll get their own account to safely share their personal details.
Preview

Add contractor

FIGURE 9-23: Setting up a new contractor.

3. **Provide the contractor's name and, if you want the contractor to complete his or her profile, you can provide an email address.**

   If you provide the contractor's email address, Intuit contacts the contractor and get the contractor's 1099 information for you, including the contractor's signature on the W-9 form the IRS requires you to keep on file. Intuit uses the form information to populate the contractor's record and leave a PDF of the W-9 form for you in the Contractors page, under Documents.

   TIP

4. **Click Add Contractor.**

   QBO adds the contractor and displays the contractor's details page, where you can click Add to provide details about the Contractor Type (see Figure 9-24). QBO uses this information when you prepare 1099s for the year.

5. **Click Save.**

   QBO redisplays the contractor's details page showing the details you just provided.

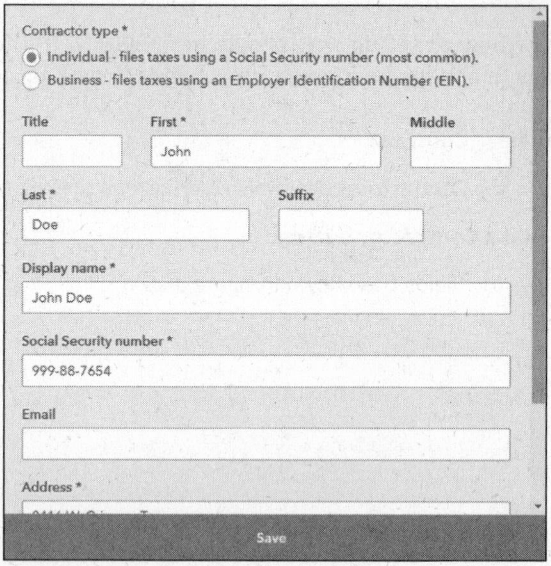

FIGURE 9-24:
Provide the Contractor Type information QBO needs to eventually prepare 1099s.

Paying contractors

You pay contractors the same way you pay any other vendor; see Chapter 5 for details on entering bills, expense transactions, and checks. If a contractor sends you a bill, you can enter it and pay it when appropriate. The most important point to remember about paying contractors is to categorize them using the appropriate account on your Chart of Accounts. In my examples in this section, I've assigned all contractor payments to an expense account I named "Contractors."

Reporting on 1099 vendor payments

Here comes the tricky part. QBO contains a 1099 Contractor Summary and 1099 Contractor Detail report, but both reports show information only on outstanding bills — *not* on bills you have paid. You can think of these reports as Accounts Payable reports for contractors.

To view payments you have made to 1099–eligible contractors, you need to

>> Make sure that you have set up your company to be ready to prepare 1099s.

>> Prepare the 1099 Transaction Detail report, which shows contractors to whom you have paid more than $600.00, the IRS-specified threshold for reporting payments to contractors.

REMEMBER

The report excludes payments you make to contractors using a credit card because you aren't responsible for providing a 1099-MISC for credit card payments; instead, the contractor's payment processor will provide the contractor with a 1099-K.

To make sure that you have set up your company to prepare 1099s, you walk through most of the process of, well, preparing 1099s. Follow these steps:

1. **Choose Workers ⇨ Contractors.**

   QBO displays the Contractors page, listing the 1099-eligible contractors you have set up.

2. **Click the Prepare 1099s button in the upper right corner of the page.**

   QBO displays a page explaining what will happen as it walks you through this process.

3. **Click Let's Get Started.**

   QBO asks you to review, and, if necessary, edit your company's name, address, and tax ID number.

4. **Click Next.**

   QBO asks you to categorize payments you made to your contractors (see Figure 9-25).

TIP

   In most cases, you'll check Box 7, Nonemployee Compensation, and then select an account from your Chart of Accounts list where you assigned your 1099-eligible contractor payments; in my example, I chose the Contractors account.

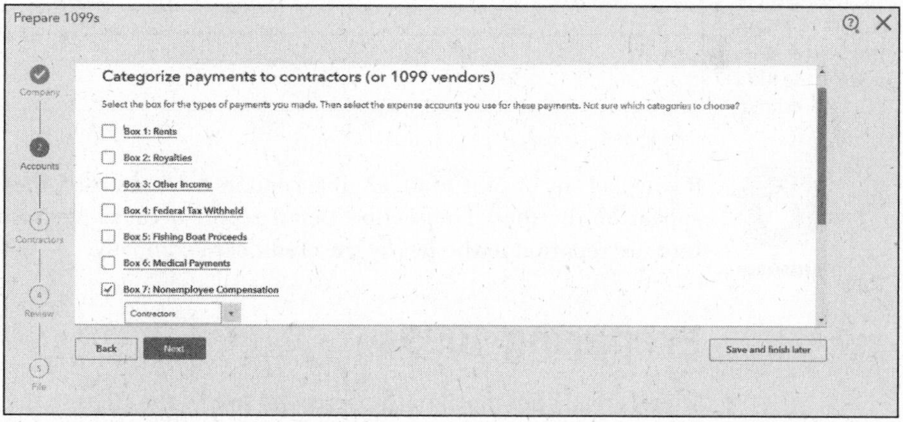

FIGURE 9-25:
Select the boxes on the Form 1099 that apply to the payments you made to your 1099-eligible vendors.

5. **Click Next.**

   QBO displays a page where you can review information about the contractors you've set up; only contractors who meet the $600.00 minimum threshold appear on this page. You review the contractor's address, tax ID, and email if provided, and you can click Edit in the Action column if you need to make changes.

6. **When you finish reviewing contractor information, click Next.**

    QBO next displays the total of payments you've made to each contractor for you to review; you can print the information shown on the page, but you don't need to do so because you can print a report of the information.

7. **You've now set up your company sufficiently to view reports on 1099 information; assuming that you are not ready to prepare 1099 forms, click Save and Finish Later.**

At any time, you can now print the 1099 Transaction Detail report shown in Figure 9-26. This report gives you detailed information about the amounts you've paid to 1099-eligible vendors who have met the IRS's $600.00 threshold. Choose Reports in the Navigation bar and, on the Reports page, scroll down to find the 1099 Transaction Detail report.

Add notes

Landscaping Heroes
1099 TRANSACTION DETAIL REPORT
January - December 2018

DATE	TRANSACTION TYPE	NUM	MEMO	1099 BOX	ACCOUNT	SPLIT	AMOUNT	BALANCE	TAX ID
▾ Amy Reilly									
12/12/2018	Check	2		Box 7	Contractors	Checking	1,200.00	1,200.00	542-26-9678
Total for Amy Reilly							$1,200.00		
▾ Linda Morrison									
12/20/2018	Expense	1		Box 7	Contractors	Checking	900.00	900.00	243-56-9876
Total for Linda Morrison							$900.00		
TOTAL AMOUNT							$2,100.00		

Friday, February 8, 2019 02:14 PM GMT-07:00

If you paid any of your 1099-eligible vendors by credit card, those payments won't appear on the 1099 Transaction Detail report because payments made by credit card are reported to the IRS by the credit card company.

Preparing 1099s

There's really not much to say here; you follow the steps in the preceding section except Step 7, where you don't click Save and Finish Later. Instead, you click Finish Preparing 1099s and then follow the onscreen instructions to print for 1099s for you and for your contractors who qualify to receive a Form 1099.

Chapter **10**

How's the Business Doing?

N o big surprise here: To help you measure and evaluate your business's health, you use reports. The reports reflect the information in QBO, so, keeping QBO up to date with your daily activities helps ensure that accurate information appears on the reports you run.

Quickly Review Income and Expenses

When you click Reports on the Navigation bar, you see a page like the one shown in Figure 10-1.

Reports are organized into three tabs (more about that in the next section) and you see the Standard tab by default. As you scroll down the Reports page, you'll find reports organized in the following categories:

» Favorites

» Business Overview

» Who Owes You

Use this scroll bar to scroll down the Reports page.

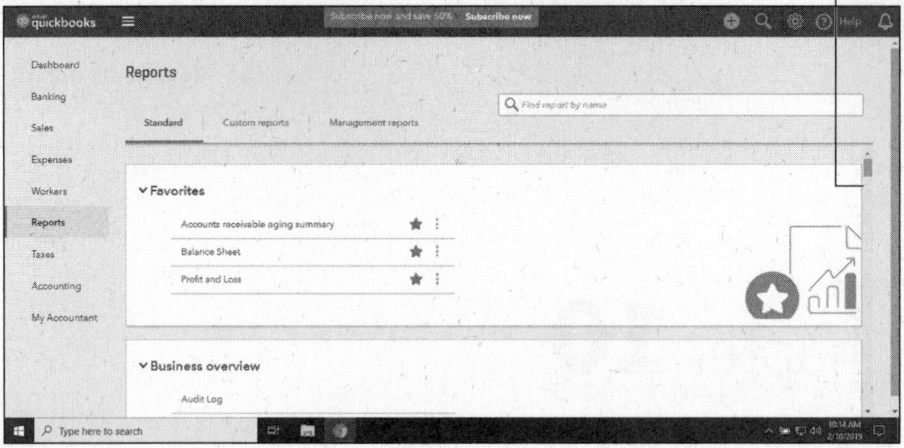

FIGURE 10-1: The Reports page.

- Sales and Customers
- What You Owe
- Expenses and Vendors
- Sales Tax
- Employees
- For My Accountant
- Payroll

REMEMBER

The list of available payroll reports depends on whether you have a payroll subscription. If you don't, you'll see a much shorter list of available payroll reports: an Employee Contact List and two reports related to time tracking.

Finding the Report You Want

Reports in QBO are organized into three categories:

- Standard
- Custom Reports
- Management Reports

These categories appear on the Reports page and function as tabs; that is, you click a tab to see the reports in that category.

Examining standard reports

QBO lists all reports available to you on the Standard tab of the Reports page based on your QBO subscription level, the features you use in QBO, preferences, and add-ons.

TIP

Simple Start subscriptions now have a Trial Balance and General Ledger report. In Figure 10-2, I've scrolled down the Standard tab to show you many of the reports in the Business Overview section of the tab. Remember, the reports I display in the figure might differ from the ones you see when you review standard reports.

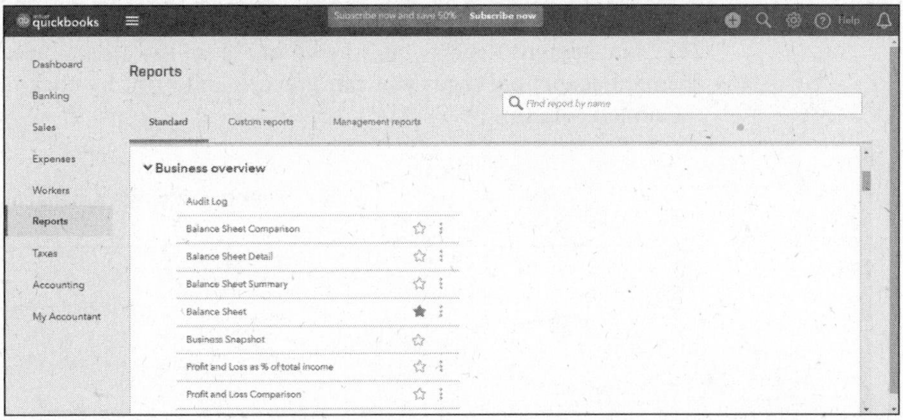

FIGURE 10-2:
Business
Overview reports.

Notice the filled-in star beside the Balance Sheet report. On your screen (and my screen, too) the star is green; in my black and white book, the star appears gray, at best. The filled-in star indicates a report marked as a *favorite* and, if you refer to Figure 10-1, you'll see the Balance Sheet report appears in the Favorites section of the Standard tab.

Use the Favorites section to bring reports you use most often to the top of the default page that appears when you click Reports in the Navigation bar. To make a report into a favorite, simply click the empty star beside it; QBO automatically fills in the star and displays the starred report at the top of the Standard tab in the Favorites group.

Finding reports you customize

The Custom Reports tab lists reports you have printed — whether to your display or a printer — customized, and saved, either as single reports or in a report group. The Custom Reports tab remains empty until you customize and save a report as described later in this chapter in the section "Saving a customized report." In that section, I also show you how to place a customized report into a group, and you get a look at the Custom Reports page after it contains a report saved to a group.

TIP

If you're a former QuickBooks Desktop user, be aware that saving a report in QBO is the equivalent of memorizing a report in the QuickBooks Desktop product, and saving a report to a group in QBO is conceptually the same as creating a memorized report group in the QuickBooks Desktop product.

Taking a look at management reports

The Management Reports tab, shown in Figure 10-3, lists three predefined management report packages you can prepare and print by clicking the View link in the Action column.

Click to customize a management report package.

Reports
Find report by name
Standard
Custom reports
Management reports
NAME
CREATED BY
LAST MODIFIED
REPORT PERIOD
ACTION
Company Overview
QuickBooks
This Year
View
Sales Performance
QuickBooks
This Year
View
Expenses Performance
QuickBooks
This Year
View

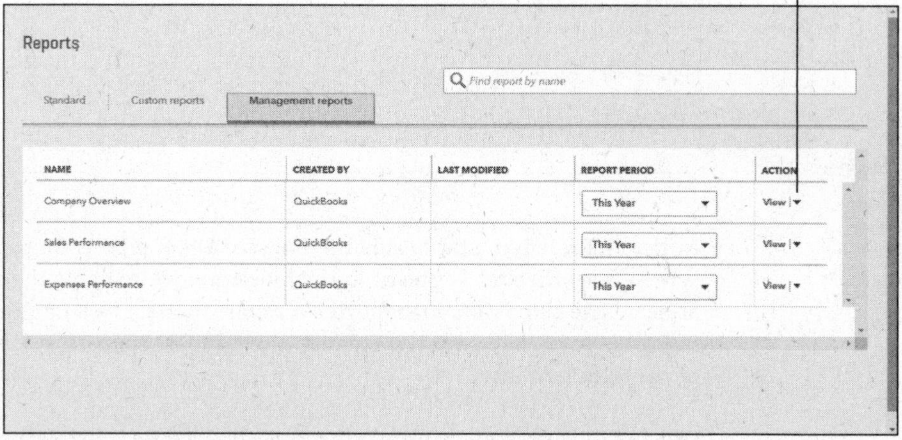

FIGURE 10-3: The Management Reports page.

These report packages are really quite elegant; each package contains a professional-looking cover page, a table of contents, and several reports that relate to the report package's name:

» The Company Overview management report contains the Profit and Loss report and the Balance Sheet report.

» The Sales Performance management report contains the Profit and Loss report, the A/R Aging Detail report, and the Sales by Customer Summary report.

» The Expenses Performance management report contains the Profit and Loss report, the A/P Aging Detail report, and the Expenses by Vendor Summary report.

When you click View in the Action column beside a management report, QBO typically creates a PDF version of a management report. You can click the PDF link at the bottom of the browser or in the Print Preview window that appears to open the report in the PDF viewer you have installed on your computer. You might be able to print the management report directly from QBO, but, if you can't, your PDF viewer will definitely give you the option to scroll through and print the report. In Figure 10-4, I've already downloaded the Company Overview management report into my PDF viewer; you can see the cover page and, in the thumbnail section on the left, the Table of Contents and the Profit and Loss report page.

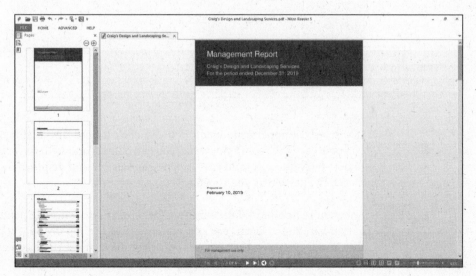

FIGURE 10-4:
An example management report open in a PDF viewer.

You can also customize these reports; click the downward-pointing arrow beside a report to see your choices. If you opt to edit a report package, you can add your logo to the cover page, add more reports to the package, include an executive summary, and add end notes to the package.

If you don't want to mess with the originals, click Copy from the drop-down menu; QBO automatically creates a "-1" version of the report, and you can modify it to your heart's delight.

Searching for a report

You don't need to use the tabs to find a report. Instead, you can click in the Find a Report by Name box at the top right portion of the Reports page and type some portion of the report you want to display; when you do, QBO displays all reports that meet the criteria you supplied, listed alphabetically, in a drop-down list (see Figure 10-5).

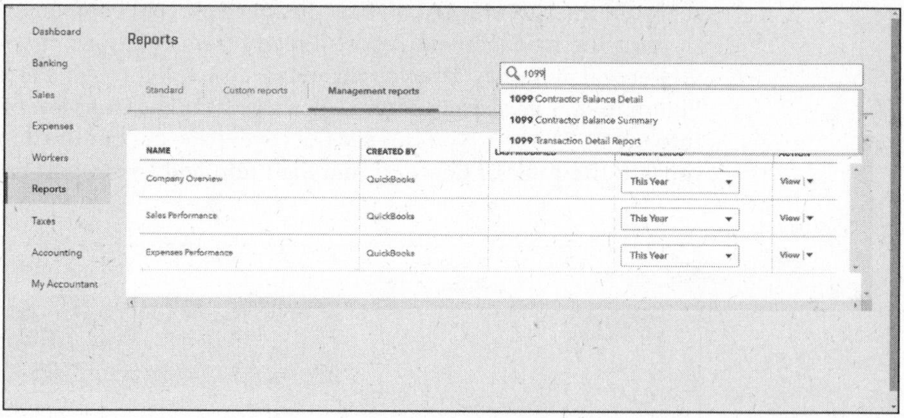

FIGURE 10-5:
Searching for a report.

If you see the report you want, you can click it, and QBO displays it onscreen. If you don't see the report you want, you can change or add to the criteria in the Find Report by Name box, and QBO again searches for and displays report names that match the keywords you typed.

And, you're not limited to searching for reports after clicking Reports in the Navigation bar. You also can use the Search tool at the top of the QBO screen (next to the Gear menu) to search for a report regardless of the page you are viewing.

Printing a Report

To produce any report, simply click the report's title. QBO automatically displays the report using standard settings. To redisplay the Reports page, click the Back to Report List link above the report's settings or click Reports in the Navigation bar.

On most reports, you can *drill down* to view the details behind the report's numbers. For example, from the Profit and Loss report, you can click any Income or Expense account value, and QBO displays the transactions that make up the number on the Profit and Loss report. I clicked the dollar amount for Design income, and QBO displayed the Transaction report shown in Figure 10-6.

Click to redisplay the original report.

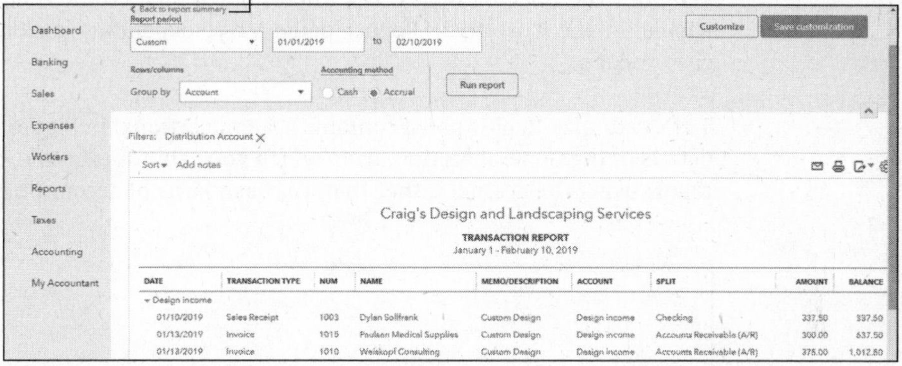

FIGURE 10-6:
The Transaction report that appears after clicking an income account on the Profit and Loss report.

To redisplay the original report — in this case, the Profit and Loss Report — you can click the Back to Summary Report link at the top of the report page.

TIP

If you want to keep the original summary version of the report open and also view the details from drilling down, duplicate the tab containing the summary version of the report before you drill down to view details. When you finish working with the details, you can close the tab containing them. To duplicate a tab in Chrome, right-click the tab and select Duplicate. To duplicate a tab in Firefox, right-click the tab and select Duplicate tab. Or, you can press and hold down the Ctrl key as you click the browser refresh button, which appears at the left edge of the address bar.

Customizing a report

You can customize most reports in a variety of ways. For most financial-based reports, you can opt to run the report using a Cash or an Accrual basis accounting method; list reports aren't financial reports, so you won't see an option to select the accounting method on these reports.

For all reports, you can change the date range covered by the report by opening the Transaction Date list box and making a selection, or by setting specific dates in the From and To boxes. After you make your selection, click the Run Report button to refresh the report and display information only in the date range (or other criteria) you selected.

You can establish more detailed custom settings for any report; throughout this section, I discuss the available customization options in relation to the Profit and Loss Report.

Click the Customize button at the top of the report. QBO displays the Customize panel for the selected report. It's important to understand that the settings that appear in the Customize Report panel vary, depending on the report you are customizing.

The Customize Report panel contains several sections; in Figure 10-7, you see the details of the General section, from which you can, for example, opt to display the report using the accrual rather than the cash basis of accounting.

To view the settings available in the Rows/Columns section, click the right-pointing carat beside the section name. From the Rows/Columns section (see Figure 10-8), you can control the columns and rows that appear on the report. You also can add a variety of comparison columns.

From the Filter section, shown in Figure 10-9, you can control the entries from the Account, Customer, Vendor, Employee, and Product/Service list that QBO includes on the Profit and Loss report.

Figure 10-10 shows the settings you can control in the Header and Footer sections of the report as well as the report alignment.

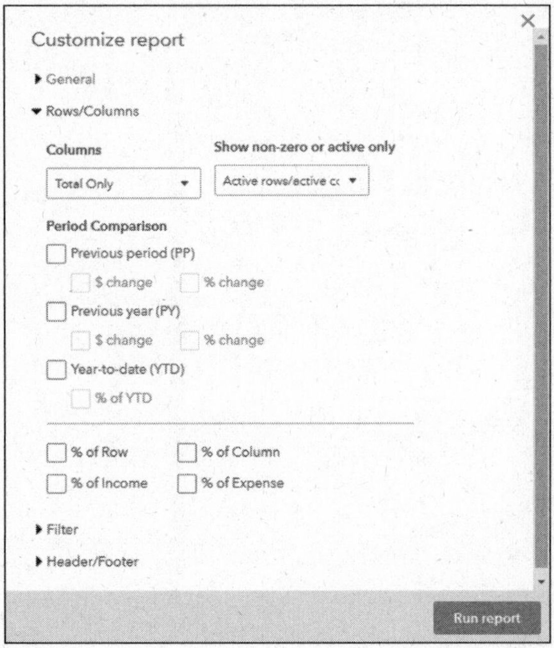

FIGURE 10-8:
Use these
settings to control
the rows and
columns that
appear on the
report.

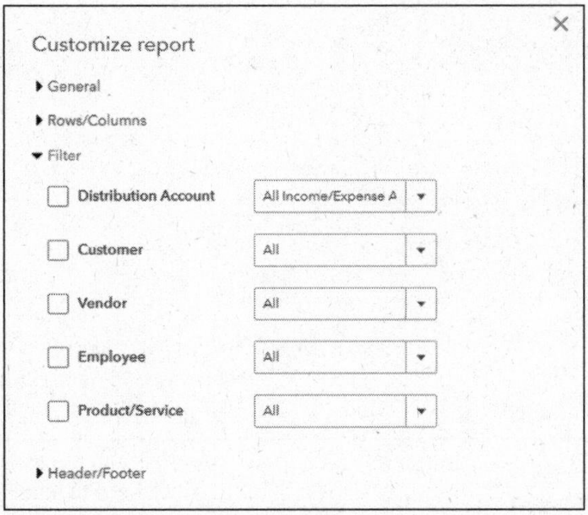

FIGURE 10-9:
The filtering
options you
can control on
the Profit and
Loss report.

When you're finished customizing the report, click Run Report in the lower right corner of the Customize Report panel, and QBO displays the report onscreen using your customized settings (see Figure 10-11). With the report onscreen, you can click the Print button to print the report to paper or to a PDF file. Or, you can click the Email button to email the report or the Export button to export the report to Excel or to a PDF file.

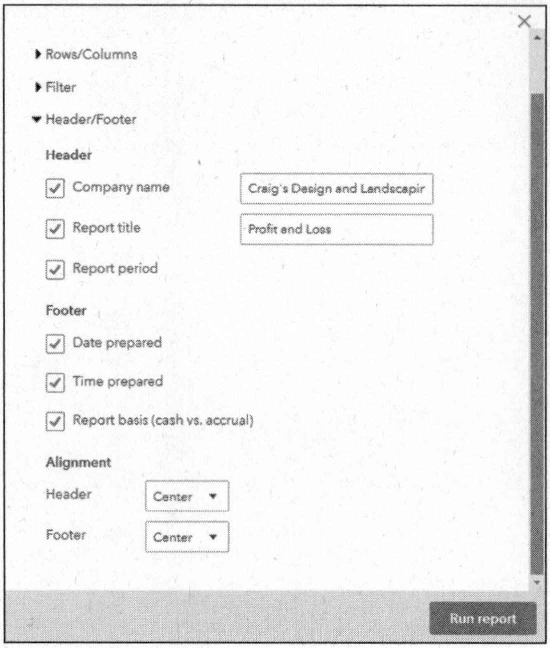

FIGURE 10-10:
The Header/
Footer settings
you can
customize on
the Profit and
Loss report.

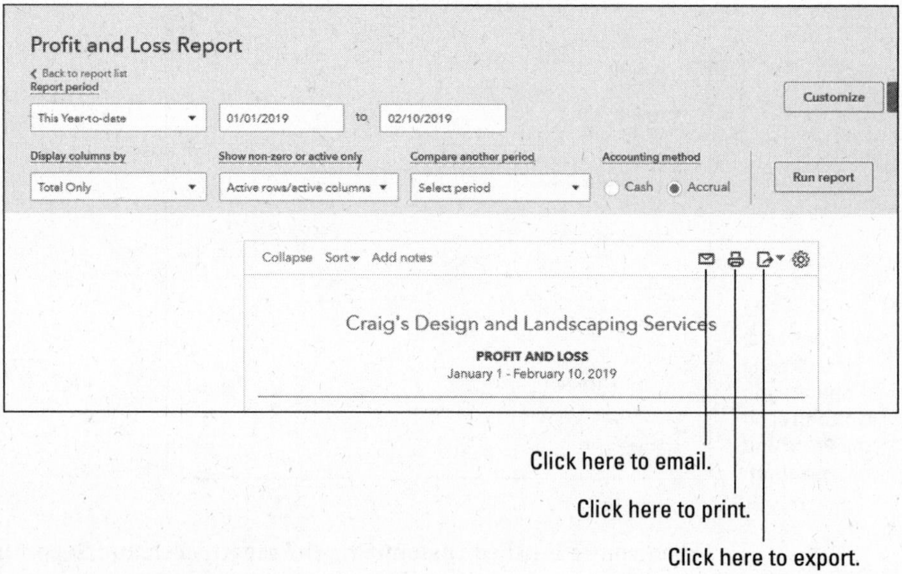

Click here to email.

Click here to print.

Click here to export.

FIGURE 10-11:
The report after
customizing.

REMEMBER

When you use Chrome to export a report to Excel, a button with the report title followed by "xlsx" appears in the bottom left corner of the screen; click that button to open the report in Excel. Be aware, too, that QBO automatically saves a copy of the report to the local hard drive; mine appeared in the Downloads folder. If you don't delete the reports, QBO increments the report name for subsequent reports you export to Excel.

TIP

To find the folder where QBO stores the report, click the up arrow on the right side of the report's button in the lower left corner of the QBO screen and choose Show in Folder.

Saving a customized report

Once the report looks the way you want, you might want to save it so that you don't need to apply the same customizations each time you run the report. Click the Save Customization button at the top of the report page to display a panel like the one shown in Figure 10-12.

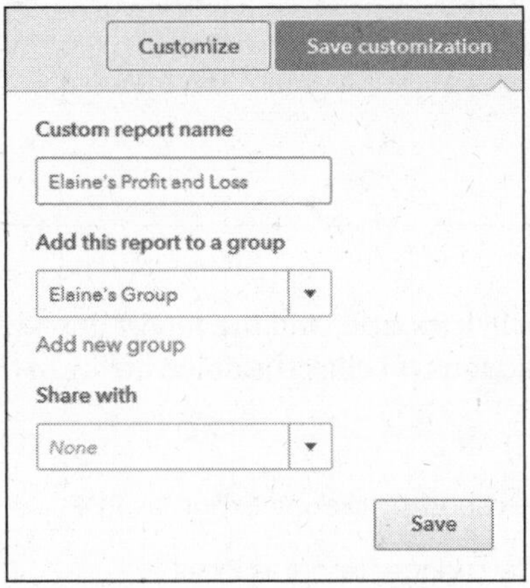

FIGURE 10-12: Use this panel to save a customized report.

Supply a name for the customized report; you can use the QBO name for the report, but you'd be better off including some information in the name that helps you remember the customizations — unlike the one I used in the figure, which really doesn't tell us much other than the report isn't the standard Profit and Loss report.

You can add the report to a group you create; creating a group is useful if you want to email several reports simultaneously. To add a group, click the Add New Group link, which displays the New Group Name box. Then, type the group's name in the New Group Name box and click the Add button. The next time you want to add a report to the group you created, simply select the group name from the Add This Report to a Group list box in the panel.

You also can opt to share the customized report with the other users on your account, and accountants can share with users in their firm; click the Share With list box and select All.

Once you save your settings in the Save Customizations dialog box, the saved report appears on the Custom Reports tab of the Reports page. And, if you created a group, the report appears in that group. In Figure 10-13, my customized version of the Profit and Loss report appears in a group called (uninspiringly) Elaine's Group.

To print any custom report, I click its title, and the report appears onscreen. I also can take any of the following actions if I click the down arrow in the Action column beside the report:

» Create a PDF version of the report by clicking Export as PDF.

» Export the report to Excel by clicking Export as Excel.

» Delete the customized report by clicking Delete.

To change a custom report's name or group, click the Edit link beside the report.

If you click the down arrow in the Action column beside a report group name, you can

» Export the group in PDF format, or

» Delete the group.

WARNING

Be aware that deleting a group has more consequence than just removing a named group from the My Custom Reports page. If you click Delete in the drop-down list in Action column beside a report group name, you delete the report group and all custom reports the group contains.

If you select the Edit link in the Action column beside a report group name, you can change a report group's name or set an email schedule for the report group; QBO displays the report group's settings page shown in Figure 10-14. Toggle the Set Email Schedule button to the On position to display and edit scheduling information.

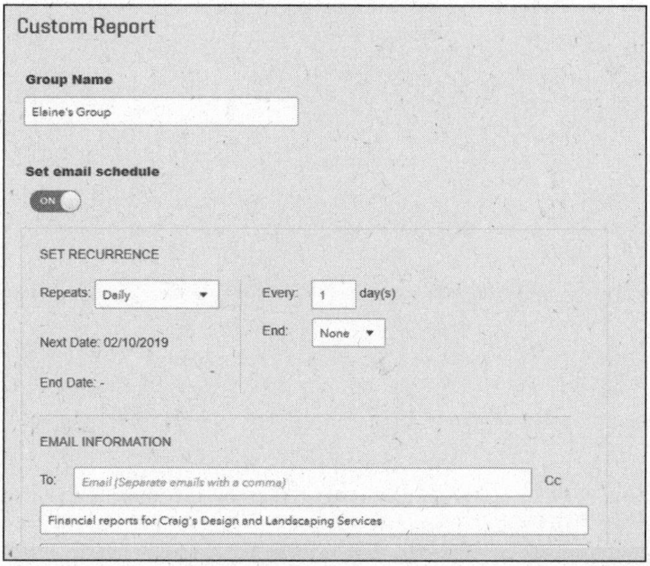

Custom Report

Group Name

Elaine's Group

Set email schedule

ON

SET RECURRENCE

Repeats: Daily   Every: 1   day(s)

Next Date: 02/10/2019   End: None ▾

End Date: -

EMAIL INFORMATION

To: Email (Separate emails with a comma)   Cc

Financial reports for Craig's Design and Landscaping Services

FIGURE 10-14:
Set an email schedule for a report group.

By default, QBO chooses Daily as the email interval, but you can customize the email schedule. Fill in the Email information, separating each email address with a comma (,); QBO uses the same subject each time it emails the report group.

At the bottom of the page, not visible in Figure 10-14, if you select the Attach the Report as an Excel File check box, QBO sends the reports in Excel format; if you don't select this check box, QBO sends the reports in HTML format.

3

Managing the Books for the Accountant

Chapter **11**

Setting Up Shop in QBOA

Part 1 of this book covers the details of QBO, and QBO is the product you use to enter transactions into a company.

Accountants' needs differ from those of a client — for example, accountants need to work in multiple QBO companies, and clients usually work in only one company. Further, accountants have work they need to do in a client's company that the client doesn't need to do — like make journal entries to correctly classify income or expenses and to write off bad debts.

To accommodate the needs of accountants, they use QuickBooks Online for Accountants (QBOA). QBOA provides a front-end interface that acts as a portal you, the accountant, use to open client QBO companies. When you open any particular client's company, you have available to you the features for the client's subscription level: Simple Start, Essentials, Self-Employed, Plus, or Advanced.

REMEMBER

As you see in this chapter, the interface for a client QBO company opened in QBOA varies slightly from the interface your client sees when opening the company.

Signing Up for and into QBOA

Setting up a QBOA subscription account is free, and your QBOA subscription remains free for as long as you use it. You can sign up for the Intuit Wholesale Pricing program and receive discounted QBO rates for each client subscription you manage; contact Intuit for details.

For more information on the Wholesale Pricing program, see the section "Working with Wholesale Billing" later in this chapter.

When you sign up for a QBOA subscription account, you get, as one of the perks, a free QBO company that you can use for your own QuickBooks company.

To create a QBOA account, open your browser and navigate to http://quickbooks.intuit.com/accountants/online. On the web page that appears, click the Sign Up for Free link on the left side of the page and then click QuickBooks Online Accountant (see Figure 11-1).

FIGURE 11-1:
Navigating to the QBOA sign-in page.

Click here.

Once you click QuickBooks Online Accountant, the web page shown in Figure 11-2 appears. If necessary, click the Change link to select the region where you do business if it differs from the one shown onscreen. Then, provide the rest of the requested information, including a password, and then click the Continue button (not visible in Figure 11-2) at the bottom of the page.

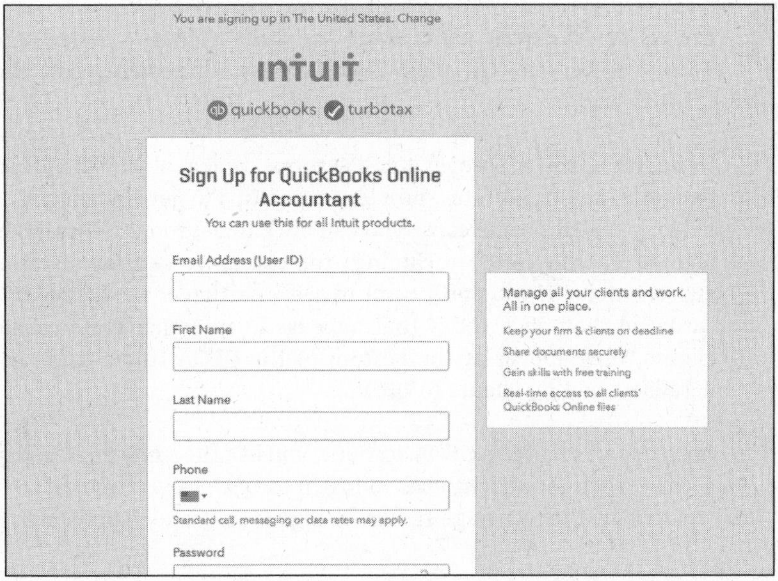

FIGURE 11-2:
Provide a limited
amount of
information to
create a QBOA
account.

On the page that appears, enter your Accounting Firm Name and your firm's zip code. QBOA uses the company name you provide to create the free company you can use to manage the books for your own business. You can read more about this company later in this chapter, in the section "Understanding and Using the Free QBOA Company."

After supplying your firm name and zip code, click Finish. QBOA creates your account, signs you in, and starts a short tour of the QBOA interface. Once you complete the tour, your QBOA Home page looks similar to the one shown in Figure 11-3.

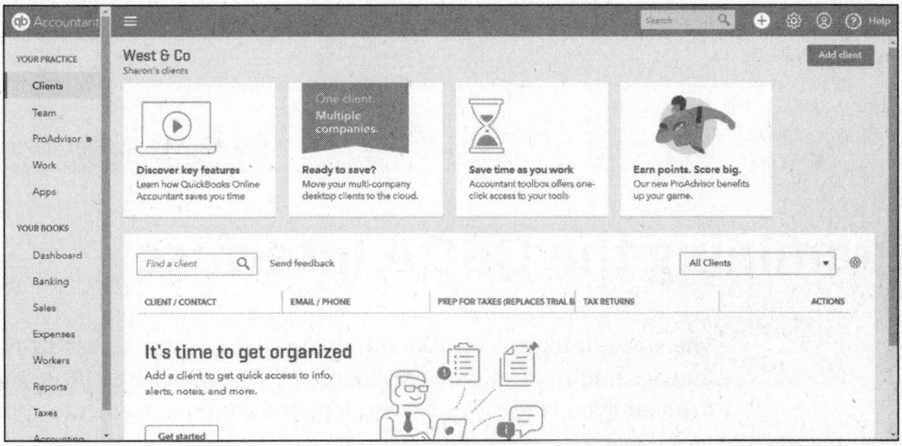

FIGURE 11-3:
A typical QBOA
Home page after
creating a QBOA
account.

Just as you'd expect, by clicking the Finish button, you're agreeing to Intuit's Terms of Service, the End-User License Agreement, and the Privacy Policy for QBOA.

In addition, the "Discover Key Features" video, a tour of QBOA that lasts about two-and-a-half minutes, provides some tips to get you started. In addition to the video, you'll see some cards you can click to get more information on the subjects printed on the cards, including, for example, getting discounts on QBO Plus subscriptions. If you don't want to see a particular card, slide the mouse over the card and then click the X that appears in its upper right corner. After you add clients, they appear at the bottom of the QBOA Home page; see Chapter 12 for details on adding clients to QBOA.

Once you've created a QBOA account, you use the same page to log in to your QBOA account that your client uses to log in to QBO. Navigate to `https://qbo.intuit.com` to view the web page shown in Figure 11-4 and supply your login credentials.

![Sign in page for QBOA showing the Intuit QuickBooks sign-in screen with options to sign in with Google, User ID and Password fields.]

Examining the QBOA Interface

The QBOA interface focuses on giving accountants access to tools they need to manage multiple clients. Although the view in the QBOA interface changes, depending on where you're working, two common elements appear:

>> The Navigation bar runs down the left side of the page.

>> The green QBOA toolbar runs across the top of the page and contains tools on its left and right sides. When you work in a client QBO company, the toolbar across the top of the page is black.

You use the Navigation bar to display the various pages in QBOA. The Navigation bar contains two choices that display different views and affect the choices in the QBOA toolbar: the Your Practice and Your Books views. The following two sections explore the Navigation bar and the QBOA toolbar in each of these views.

Working with the Your Practice view

By default, when you log in to QBOA, the QBOA Home page displays the Clients page of the Your Practice view, as you see in Figure 11-5. The Clients page displays . . . well, a list of your clients. If you wanted to navigate to this page (because you viewed another portion of QBOA and now want to return to the list of your clients), you'd use the Navigation bar to click Clients under Your Practice.

On the Clients page, you can search for a client, see overview information about each client, and open a client's QBO company. You can also control the appearance of the Clients page. See the section "Controlling the Appearance of the Client List," later in this chapter, for details on working with the Clients page.

When you click Team in the Navigation bar, you can set up the users in your firm that will have access to various client companies. For more information, see the section "Setting Up Your Team."

When you click ProAdvisor, you see options you can click that provide information about the benefits and training offered through the Intuit ProAdvisor program. If you weren't previously a member of the ProAdvisor program, QBOA automatically establishes a free Silver membership for you; for details on what that means, visit https://quickbooks.intuit.com/accountants/tools-proadvisor.

When you click Work, you display the area of QBOA that provides practice management support; see Chapter 15 for details on the practice management tools QBOA offers.

And, when you click Apps, you visit the App Center, where you can search for apps that extend the capabilities of QBO and QBOA. You also can view the apps you've already installed.

Across the top of the interface, you find a toolbar with the following buttons, from left to right:

>> **The Accountant button:** This button contains the QuickBooks logo and offers you another way to display the Client List shown in Figure 11-5.

>> **The Menu button:** This button (containing three horizontal lines) acts as a toggle to hide and display the Navigation bar.

>> **The Go to Client's QuickBooks drop-down button:** You can use this list box to display a list of your clients; clicking a client name in the list opens the client's company.

>> **The Search box:** When you click in this box, a list of recent transactions or reports appears; you can type in the box to search for the transaction or report of your choice, or you can click an item in the list.

>> **The plus sign (+) icon:** This button displays the Create menu, which you use to create a client or a user from the QBOA Home page. While working in a client's or your own QBO company, you use the Create menu to create transactions and more.

>> **The Gear button:** Click this button to display the Gear menu (see Figure 11-6). The Gear menu shows the settings you can establish for your own company, your client's company, and your QBOA account.

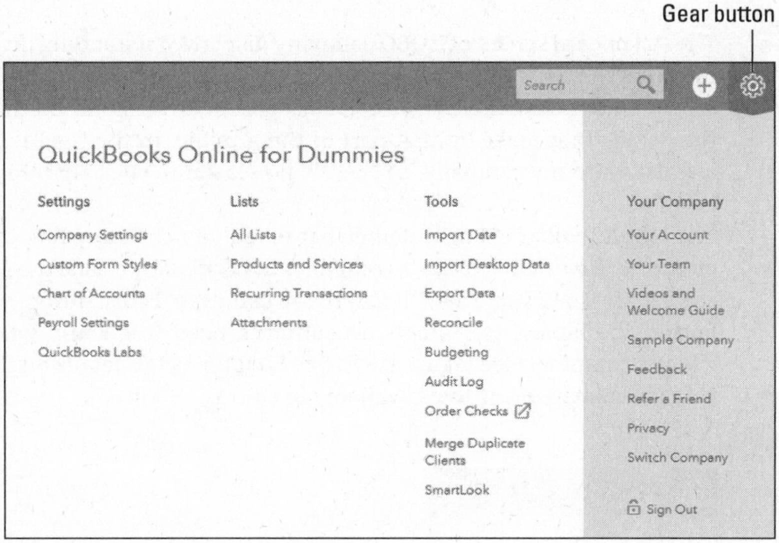

Gear button

QuickBooks Online for Dummies

Settings	Lists	Tools	Your Company
Company Settings	All Lists	Import Data	Your Account
Custom Form Styles	Products and Services	Import Desktop Data	Your Team
Chart of Accounts	Recurring Transactions	Export Data	Videos and Welcome Guide
Payroll Settings	Attachments	Reconcile	Sample Company
QuickBooks Labs		Budgeting	Feedback
		Audit Log	Refer a Friend
		Order Checks	Privacy
		Merge Duplicate Clients	Switch Company
		SmartLook	Sign Out

FIGURE 11-6:
The choices available from the Gear menu.

REMEMBER

You also can open the QBO sample company from the Gear menu; read more about opening and working in the sample company later in this chapter, in the section "Working with the Sample Company."

>> **The ProAdvisor Profile button:** This button, which appears to the right of the Gear button, displays the ProAdvisor Profile page, where you can set up information that Intuit includes in the ProAdvisor directory. Potential clients use the ProAdvisor directory to find you, so, here's the place to toot your horn.

>> **The Help button:** Click this button to open the Help menu so that you can search for help on any topic. Help in QBOA is context sensitive and available from all screens. When you open the Help menu from a transaction screen, the suggested choices that appear are based on the type of transaction you were viewing when you clicked Help.

Working with the Your Books view

When you click Your Books in the Navigation bar, you open the Dashboard page of your own QBO company. The links in the Your Books portion of the Navigation bar match the same links that your client sees when he opens his QBO company.

The view when you open your own company's books in QBOA matches the view you see when you open any client's QBO company from QBOA; the only difference onscreen is the name of the company that appears on the QBOA toolbar.

The Dashboard screen of a QBO company displays outstanding invoice and expense information, a list of your bank account balances, profit and loss information, and sales in interactive filters; you can click part of any graphic on this page to display the details that make up that part of the graphic. In the figure, I haven't entered any data into my company, so there's no reason to click anything.

The QBOA toolbar changes somewhat when you click any link in the Your Books view or you work in a client's company. In particular, beside the Menu button, you see a suitcase button that I'll call the Accountant Tools button; you can click this button to display, well, tools accountants need frequently when working in a client's company (see Figure 11-7). See Chapter 15 for details on these tools and on practice management tools available in QBOA.

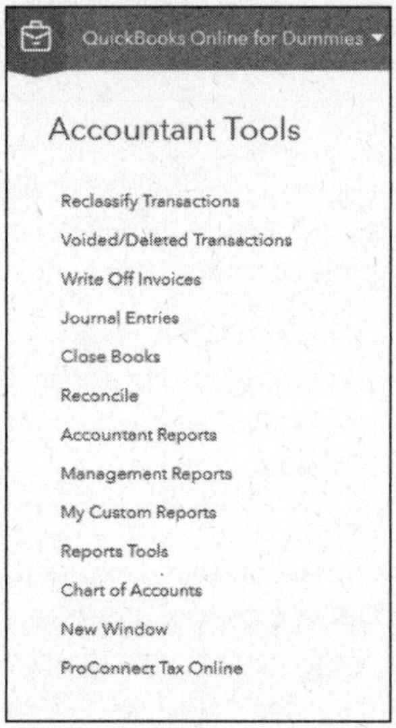

FIGURE 11-7: The tools available to accountants while working in a client company.

Accountant Tools

Reclassify Transactions
Voided/Deleted Transactions
Write Off Invoices
Journal Entries
Close Books
Reconcile
Accountant Reports
Management Reports
My Custom Reports
Reports Tools
Chart of Accounts
New Window
ProConnect Tax Online

The List Box button beside the Accountant Tools button displays the name of the currently open QBO company; when you click Your Books, your company's name appears.

The Search box, Create button (the plus sign), the Gear button, the ProAdvisor Profile button, and the Help button all work the same way in the Your Books view as they do in the Your Practice view.

REMEMBER

While any company is open, you can use the QBOA toolbar to open the list box displaying the company's name to switch to a different client company. Also, you can redisplay the Clients page at any time by clicking the Accountant button on the QBOA toolbar.

Setting Up Your Team

If your accounting firm has more than one person who need access to client QBO companies, the person who creates the QBOA account — called, in QBOA parlance, the *master administrator* — can set up the other users — as many as you need. The other users get their own login credentials and access to those clients that the master administrator specifies; for those clients, the QBOA user can access the Accountant tools described in Chapter 15. The master administrator also specifies the user's level of access to the firm's information; a user can have Basic, Full, or Custom access.

TIP

Using separate QBOA login information helps maintain security in QBOA, because a lot of financial information (product subscriptions and billing information, for example) is tied to login information.

So, what's the difference, status–wise, between basic, full, and custom access?

>> Those users with full access can open and work in the firm's books as well as in client QBO companies and can access the Team page and make changes to any user's privileges.

>> Those users with basic access can access only client QBO companies.

>> Those users with custom access have either basic or full access with at least one privilege set differently from QBOA's defaults for basic or full access.

To set up multiple users in a QBOA account, the master administrator or any firm member with full access privileges to QBOA sets up other members of the firm; during the process, QBOA sends an email to the other firm members whom, for this discussion, I'll call *invitees*. Once an invitee accepts the invitation, QBOA prompts the invitee to set up his own QBOA login credentials. Follow these steps to set up a new user in a QBOA account:

1. **Log in to QBOA.**

2. **Click Team in the Navigation bar.**

   The Team page appears (see Figure 11-8).

3. **Click the Add User button.**

   The three-step Add User wizard begins.

4. **On the first page of the Add User wizard, fill in the name, email address, and title of the team member you want to add.**

   The team member's title is optional.

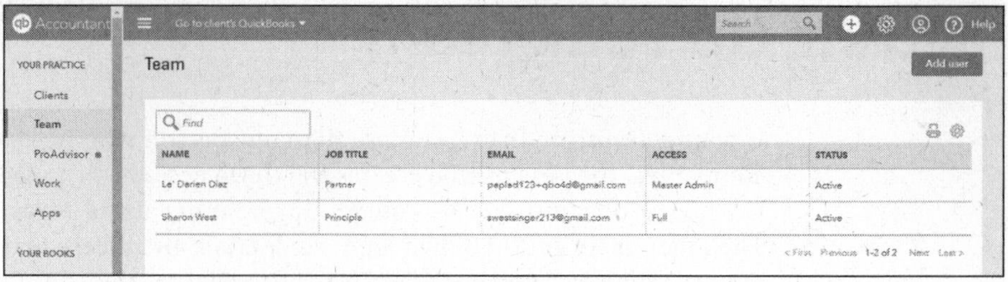

FIGURE 11-8:
View, edit, and add members to your QBOA team.

5. Click Next.

The second page of the Add User wizard appears (see Figure 11-9). On this page, you identify the privileges related to your firm that you want to provide to the team member. In this example, I set up a team member with custom access; this team member has access to the books of certain clients but doesn't have access to the firm's books or to firm administration functions.

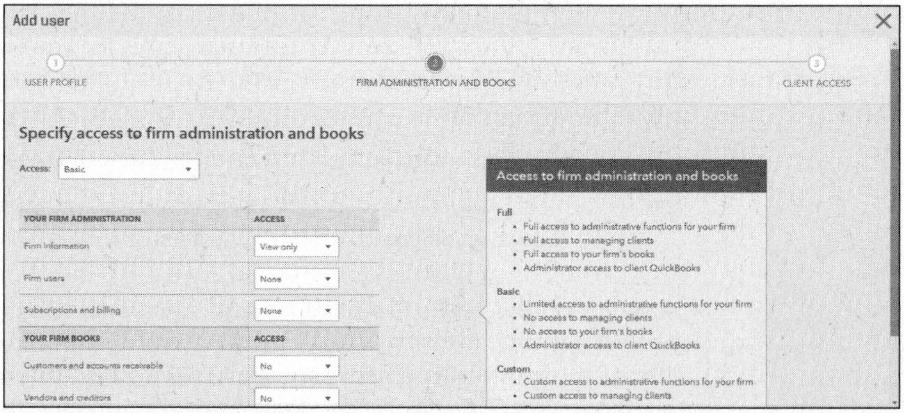

FIGURE 11-9:
Specify the new user's access level to your firm's administration and books.

6. Select the type of access you want to give to the team member.

You can assign Basic, Full, or Custom access; a description of each type of access appears on the right side of the page. Assign Full access to those team members who should have access to your own company's books. Assign Basic access to give a team member access to QBO client companies only.

TIP You can make changes to individual settings; if you do, QBOA sets the team member's access to Custom by default.

7. Click Next in the lower right corner of the page.

The last screen of the Add User wizard appears (see Figure 11-10). On this page, you identify the clients for whom the team member should be able to perform work.

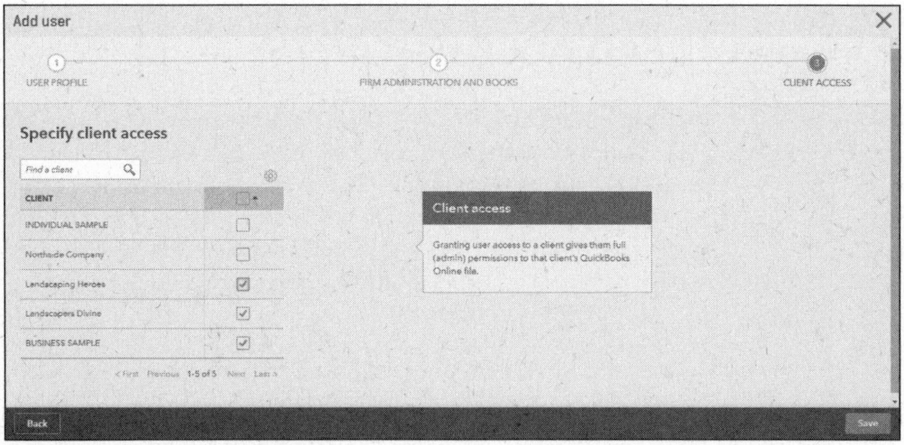

FIGURE 11-10:
You can provide a
team member
access to your
firm's clients on a
selective basis.

8. **Deselect clients as needed.**

9. **Click Save.**

   QBOA adds the new user to your team and assigns a status of Invited to the
   user. In addition, the Status column on the Team screen indicates that QBOA
   sent an email invitation to the user, inviting the user to join your team. After
   the user responds to the QBOA invitation, the user's status changes to Active
   on the Team page in QBOA.

The recipient uses the email invitation that QBOA sends to click the Accept Invite
button, and QBOA displays a page that shows the invitee's user ID or email address
and prompts the invitee to establish a password — and, if being granted full privileges, a security question and answer. Once the invitee supplies the information
and clicks Create Account, QBOA sets up the login information and displays a
Success message, where the invitee clicks Continue. QBOA then logs in the team
member with his assigned privileges and clients; the Home page of a team member with no access to the firm's books looks like the one shown in Figure 11-11.

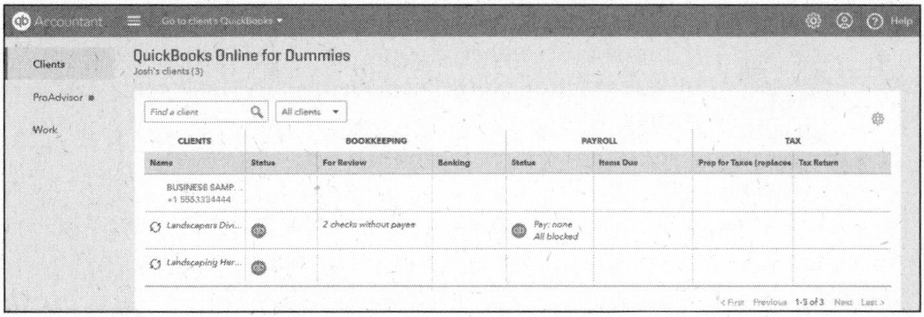

FIGURE 11-11:
The Home page
of an invited
team member
who has limited
privileges in
QBOA.

LEAD ACCOUNTANTS

As you would expect, you add clients using QBO to your QBOA account so that you can work easily with your clients' accounting data (you can read about adding clients to your QBOA account in Chapter 12). For most firms, part of managing clients involves establishing responsibility among firm team members for various clients. To address this need, QBOA uses the "lead accountant" role — the firm member through whom a client has provided access to a QBO subscription.

QBOA assigns the Lead Accountant role when:

- A client invites an accountant: The invited accountant goes through the process of accepting the client invitation and selecting the firm under which the client is assigned. Once the accountant accepts the invitation, the accounting firm has access to the client and the invited accountant — who is a member of the firm — is assigned the Lead Accountant role.

- A firm member creates a client company: When a team member within the firm creates a client company in QBOA, QBOA assigns the Lead Accountant to the team member. Chapter 12 describes how to add clients to your QBOA account.

But, things happen, and a team member with a Lead Accountant role for one or more clients might leave the firm. In this case, you can make the team member inactive (you can't delete users in QBOA) and QBOA will prompt you to assign a new Lead Accountant to the client(s) associated with the (now inactive) team mwwember.

To make the team member inactive, click the Team page (refer to Figure 11-8) and click the team member. QBOA opens the Edit User dialog box; from the Status list box, choose Inactive and save your changes.

To log in to QBOA in the future, the team member navigates to qbo.intuit.com and supplies her login credentials.

If the team member already has a QBO or QBOA login, he clicks the Accept Invitation button. If the team member has no account, he clicks the Create Account button.

Controlling the Appearance of the Client List

You can use the Clients page to open any client's QBO company, and you can control the appearance of the Clients page, shown in Figure 11-12.

Click here to open a client QBO company.

To open any client's QBO company, click the QuickBooks logo in the Status column of the Client List page. Or, if you prefer, open the Go to Client's QuickBooks list box on the QBOA toolbar to select the QBO company you want to open.

REMEMBER

If you click a client's name — rather than the QuickBooks logo — you don't open the client's company. Instead, you see overview details about the client that includes information such as tasks to complete in the client's books, the account watch list, or payroll alerts. To open a client's company, remember to use the QuickBooks logo or the Go to Client's QuickBooks list box.

You can control the appearance of the Client List page. For example, you can use the list box above the table to filter the list to show all clients or only the QBOP clients in your list. And, you can control the columns of information that appear on the Client List page. And, you can opt to hide or display inactive clients; for more information on making a client inactive, see the section "Removing clients from your Wholesale Billing subscription" later in this chapter. Click the Gear button on the right that appears just above the list of clients and make choices from the list that appears (see Figure 11-13).

Click here to control the appearance of the QBOA Client List page.

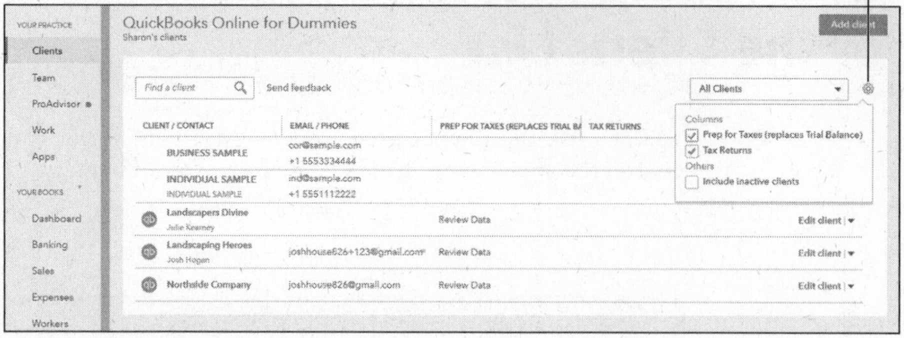

FIGURE 11-13:
Control the
appearance
of the Client
List page.

REMEMBER

QBOA actually contains multiple Gear menus. One of them appears on the QBOA toolbar and is visible from most QBOA pages, even while you work in a client's QBO company; you use that Gear menu to provide information about your QBOA account, establish settings, view lists, and access tools to, for example, import data. On the QBOA Clients page, the other Gear menu appears on the right side just above the list of clients, and you use it to control the information that appears on the page.

Understanding and Using the Free QBOA Company

As I mention at the beginning of this chapter, QBOA users get one free company to use for their own books. To open the company reserved for you, click — yep, you guessed it — Your Books in the Navigation bar, and QBOA opens your company. The interface you see when you open your company looks just like the interface you see when you open any client's QBO company; remember, this interface varies slightly from what a client using QBO sees.

You can use the free QBOA company to enter your own company's information using transactions, or if you've been tracking your business in QuickBooks Desktop, you can, with some limitations, import information from your QuickBooks Desktop company. To enter information using transactions, you can read the chapters in Part 1 of this book, because you as a QBOA user and your clients as QBO users enter transactions in the same way.

TIP

You can import QuickBooks Desktop information, and you can import only list information. For details on importing lists, see Chapter 4. If you want to try importing a QuickBooks Desktop company, see Chapter 12 for details as well as Appendix A, which describe the limitations associated with importing information. Please note that importing into a regular QBO company has time limits, but importing into the QBOA free company doesn't.

REMEMBER

Be aware that the Your Books company is intended to house the firm's data, not a client's data or the data of some other business owned by the QBOA owner. The Your Books company ties into QBOA and updates as clients are added to QBOA. So, if you use it to store the wrong kind of data, that data will be messed up as you add other clients.

Working with the Sample Company

If you've been a QuickBooks Desktop user, you know that QuickBooks Desktop comes with a variety of sample companies that you can use to test company behavior. Like its desktop cousin, QBOA also comes with a sample company.

To open the sample company, follow these steps:

1. **Click the Gear button on the QBOA toolbar.**

QBOA opens the Gear menu.

2. **In the Your Company section, click Sample Company.**

QBOA displays a warning message that you will be logged out of QBOA if you continue.

3. **Click Continue.**

QBOA signs you out of your company and opens the sample company, Craig's Design and Landscaping Services (see Figure 11-14). The interface looks like the QBOA interface you see when you open a client's company. For example, you see the Accountant button in the upper left corner and the QBOA toolbar to the right of the Accountant button. The QBOA toolbar contains the same tools you see while working in a client QBO company.

TIP

To redisplay your QBOA account interface (similar to the one shown previously in Figure 11-12), click the QBOA Go to Client's QuickBooks list box, which currently displays Craig's Design and Landscaping Services, and then choose Back to Your Practice. You'll need to sign back in to your QBOA company.

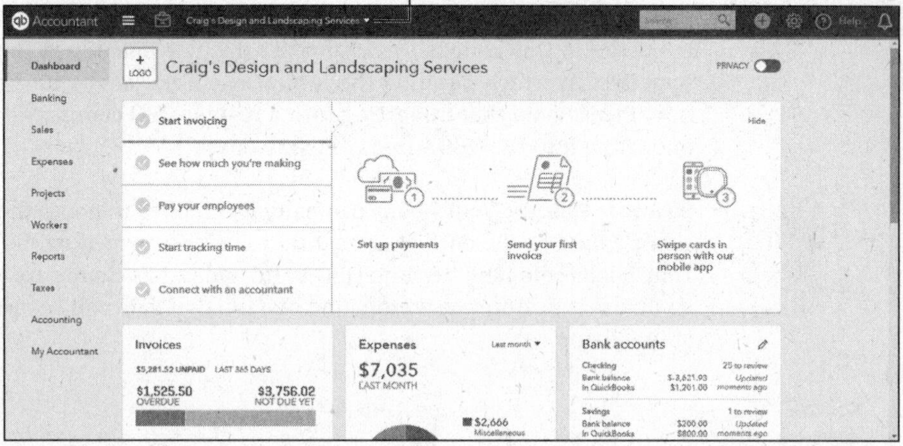

Click here to switch QBO companies or redisplay the QBOA Home page.

FIGURE 11-14:
Craig's Design
and Landscaping
Services, the
QBO and QBOA
sample company.

End users (your clients) also have access to this sample company, but opening it isn't quite as easy as it is for you. Direct your clients to https://accounting. quickbooks.com/redir/testdrive and tell them to click the I'm Not a Robot check box and answer the questions the security verification poses — as I write this, the security verification is a "matching pictures" thing.

Closing Companies and QBOA

When you finish working in a company, you don't close it in QBOA the way you might using QuickBooks Desktop. When you switch from one client QBO company to another, QBOA automatically closes the first client's company.

TIP

To work in two client QBO companies simultaneously, you can use two different browsers, two instances of a single browser, or Chrome's User feature (if you're using Chrome). For more information on working with QBOA in multiple windows, see Chapter 14. For details on using Chrome, see Chapter 17.

Although you don't close QBO companies while working in QBOA, you do close QBOA — by clicking the Gear button on the QBOA toolbar and choosing Sign Out (see Figure 11-15).

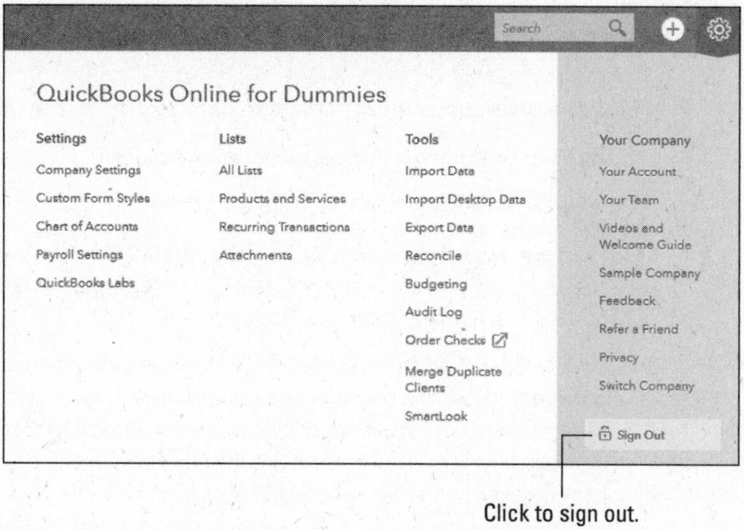

![QuickBooks Online for Dummies menu screen]

QuickBooks Online for Dummies

Settings	Lists	Tools	Your Company
Company Settings	All Lists	Import Data	Your Account
Custom Form Styles	Products and Services	Import Desktop Data	Your Team
Chart of Accounts	Recurring Transactions	Export Data	Videos and Welcome Guide
Payroll Settings	Attachments	Reconcile	Sample Company
QuickBooks Labs		Budgeting	Feedback
		Audit Log	Refer a Friend
		Order Checks ⬈	Privacy
		Merge Duplicate Clients	Switch Company
		SmartLook	🔒 Sign Out

FIGURE 11-15:
Exit from QBOA
by signing out.

Click to sign out.

Working with Wholesale Billing

As I mention in Chapter 2, if you are an accounting professional, you can sign up for the free Wholesale Pricing program. If you manage a client's subscription as part of the Wholesale Pricing program, Intuit sends you the bill for the client's subscription, charging you a reduced rate for the QBO subscription. It is your responsibility to bill the client for the QBO subscription — and QBOA makes that easy for you by providing invoice templates and the ability to bill from within QBOA. The bill you receive from Intuit is a single consolidated bill for all the QBO subscriptions you manage. I'm going to provide only some basic details on the Wholesale Pricing program here; I don't intend to provide detailed information on the ins and outs of the program. If you need more information than I provide here, contact Intuit.

REMEMBER

You don't have to enroll clients as part of the Wholesale Pricing program, but if you do, you can pass the QBO subscription pricing reductions along to your clients, saving them money and making you a hero. The Wholesale Pricing program is often referred to as the Wholesale Billing program; for this discussion, the two terms are interchangeable.

Signing up for Wholesale Billing

Accounting professionals are automatically signed up for the free Wholesale Billing program when they log in to QBOA for the first time. But, the Wholesale Billing program doesn't become active until the accounting professional enters billing information into the Billing Profile in QBOA.

To enter information in the QBOA Billing Profile, follow these steps:

1. **Click the Gear button in the QBOA toolbar to display the Gear menu.**

2. **In the Your Company column, select Your Account.**

   The Your Account page appears, displaying three tabs:

   - The Your Subscriptions tab lists exactly what you'd expect: clients whose subscriptions you are managing, the QBO product (Essentials, Plus, and so on), the subscription price and status.

   - Initially, the Billing Details tab displays payment information you can provide to subscribe to the Wholesale Billing program. Once you have subscribed to the Wholesale Billing program, the Billing Details tab provides key details such as total number of subscriptions, amount you currently owe, and past monthly charges.

TIP

   If you subscribe to the Wholesale Billing program, then, from the Billing Details tab, you can view the details you need to bill clients who are part of your subscription for the portion they owe. No more hand calculations.

   - The Personal Profile tab lists information about your practice, such as the name and the email address of the person who signed up for the QBOA account.

3. **Click the Billing Details tab.**

4. **Fill in all Payment Information fields.**

5. **Click Subscribe.**

   The Your Account page reappears, and the Wholesale Billing status will be active.

Each month, you receive a bill from Intuit that covers the subscription costs of the clients you add to your Wholesale Billing subscription. You'll find the details associated with this bill on the Billing Details tab.

Adding existing clients to your Wholesale Billing subscription

As I discuss in Chapter 12, you can add clients to your QBOA account without using the Wholesale Billing program. That is, you can opt to add retail clients who manage their own QBO subscriptions to your QBOA account. "Why," you ask, "would I have added clients to my QBOA account without adding them to my Wholesale Billing subscription?" Well, to name just two possible examples:

>> You might have added clients to your QBOA account before you joined the Wholesale Billing program.

>> You might have added clients to your QBOA account who wanted to manage their own subscriptions.

Chapter 12 shows you how to add clients to your QBOA account either as retail clients or as part of your Wholesale Billing subscription.

Before you can move an existing client to your Wholesale Billing subscription, you must enter billing information for your Wholesale Billing account in QBOA as described in the preceding section.

LIMITATIONS ASSOCIATED WITH THE WHOLESALE BILLING PROGRAM

You don't have to add a client to your Wholesale Billing subscription; you can still work with clients who pay their own QBO subscription costs. Enrolling a client into Wholesale Billing can save the client money on the cost of the QBO subscription but also makes you responsible for collecting subscription costs. And, the Wholesale Billing program might not be right for all QBO clients. In particular,

- If your client uses QuickBooks Online with Intuit Full Service Payroll (IFSP), no bundle for this combination of products is presently available through the Wholesale Billing program. QBOA is compatible with Intuit Online Payroll (IOP) and QuickBooks Online Payroll (QBOP), so if your QBO clients can use either of those products, those clients can take advantage of any price breaks you might offer for their QBO subscriptions.

- Companies created through the Wholesale Billing program have the ability to transfer master administrator rights. However, *no* accountant can be removed from the company as long as that company is part of your Wholesale Billing subscription, including an accountant who is not associated with the firm housing the company in the Wholesale Billing program.

- If an accounting professional creates a QBO company through QBOA, the company does not come with a 30-day free trial. Instead, at the time the accounting professional creates the company, he must provide a payment method to ensure uninterrupted service.

Further, the client's subscription must be eligible for the Wholesale Billing program. Use the following criteria to determine eligibility:

›› You cannot move clients to your Wholesale Billing subscription on the Wholesale Billing date, which appears on the Your Account page in the Next Bill Date field.

›› The client company's Next Payment Date must be within 33 days of the day you attempt to add the company to the Wholesale subscription. Note: You can find this date in the client company by choosing Gear ⇨ Account and Settings ⇨ Billing & Subscription.

›› Clients must have an active monthly billing subscription and be listed on your the QBOA Clients page. See Chapter 12 for details on adding clients to your Clients page.

REMEMBER

You cannot add annually paid QBO subscriptions to the Wholesale Billing program; the QBO subscriptions must be paid monthly. Further, annual billing subscriptions can be changed to monthly billing subscriptions 30 days before the next annual billing date.

›› Clients must be in the region of QBO that corresponds with your region of QBOA (US, UK, AU, FR, or CA).

›› Clients must be using QuickBooks Online Essentials or QuickBooks Online Plus. QuickBooks Online Simple Start subscriptions CANNOT be added to Wholesale Billing.

›› QBOA users in the United States can add QuickBooks Self-Employed companies to Wholesale Billing subscriptions if the client is subscribed to the Standalone plan.

REMEMBER

Note that Wholesale Billing is not available to QBSE/Turbo Tax bundle users because QBOA has its own default tax software. And, turnaround time for the client to be moved to Wholesale Billing is 24 hours.

So, just how do you go about adding a client to your Wholesale Billing subscription? As mentioned in the preceding set of bullets, you must first add the client to your Client List in QBOA; for details on adding a client to your Client List, see Chapter 12.

Once a client appears on the Clients page, you can add the client to your Wholesale Billing subscription by following these steps:

1. **Click Clients in the Navigation bar.**

2. **Click the Gear in the top right corner of the QBOA toolbar.**

3. **From the drop-down menu, under Your Company, select Your Account.**

   The Your Account window appears.

4. **In the Wholesale Clients section, click the Move Clients to Wholesale button in the Actions column; this button is available only if you have filled in the Billing Details tab.**

   The Move Clients to Wholesale Billing page appears, displaying only those clients not currently part of your Wholesale Billing subscription. No entry appears under Reasons Unable to Move for those clients who are eligible for migration to your Wholesale Billing subscription. If you find you cannot select a particular client to add to your Wholesale Billing subscription, see the sidebar "Why can't I migrate a client?"

5. **Click the check box beside each client you want to move and click Next.**

6. **Review your selections and, when you're satisfied they are correct, click Move Clients.**

   A page appears that identifies clients that migrated correctly and clients whose migration failed.

REMEMBER

WHY CAN'T I MIGRATE A CLIENT?

You might not be able to move a particular client to your Wholesale Billing subscription for a variety of reasons. For example, your client must have an active monthly billing subscription and must appear on your QBOA Client List.

In addition,

- The client QBO company's Next Payment Date must be within 33 days of the day you attempt to add the company to your Wholesale Billing subscription.

- Clients must have an active *monthly* billing subscription and be listed within the QBOA Client List.

  You can change a yearly billing subscription to a monthly billing subscription, but only 30 days before the next annual billing date.

- The QBO client's region (US, UK, AU, FR, or Canada) must match your QBOA region.

- The QBO client must be using QBO Essentials or QBO Plus. You cannot add QBO Simple Start companies to a Wholesale Billing subscription.

TIP

In the Wholesale Clients section, QBOA divides your clients into two sections: The Pending Client Companies section shows clients you have moved to your Wholesale Billing subscription, but which have not yet become active on your Wholesale subscription. The Wholesale Clients section shows clients who have already been fully added to your Wholesale Billing subscription; those are the companies who appear on your Wholesale Billing subscription bill.

A client QBO Wholesale Billing subscription stays active for as long as you maintain a valid form of payment in the QuickBooks Billing Profile. Wholesale QBO companies do not expire.

Removing clients from your Wholesale Billing subscription

Sometimes, things just don't work out between you and a client. If you have previously added that client's QBO company to your Wholesale Billing subscription and you need to part ways, you'll want to remove the client from your subscription. Follow these steps:

1. **Click the Gear in the QBOA toolbar.**

2. **From the drop-down menu, under Your Company, select Your Account.**

   The Your Account window appears.

3. **Scroll down to the Wholesale Clients section and find the company you want remove from your Wholesale Billing subscription.**

4. **In the Actions column, click Transfer Billing to Client.**

REMEMBER

Once you remove a QBO company from your Wholesale Billing subscription, that QBO company is no longer eligible for the wholesale discount, and all previous discounts are removed as well. The client QBO subscriber will be billed the standard rate for his subscription as of the date the subscription is removed unless the client establishes a relationship with another QBOA user. In this case, the client regains the discounts starting from the Wholesale Billing activation date.

Be aware that removing a client from your Wholesale Billing subscription doesn't remove the client from your Client List. And, you can't delete QBO clients. But you can make them inactive, using these steps:

1. **Click Clients in QBOA to display your Client List.**

2. **In the Actions column, click the down arrow beside the name of the client you want to make inactive.**

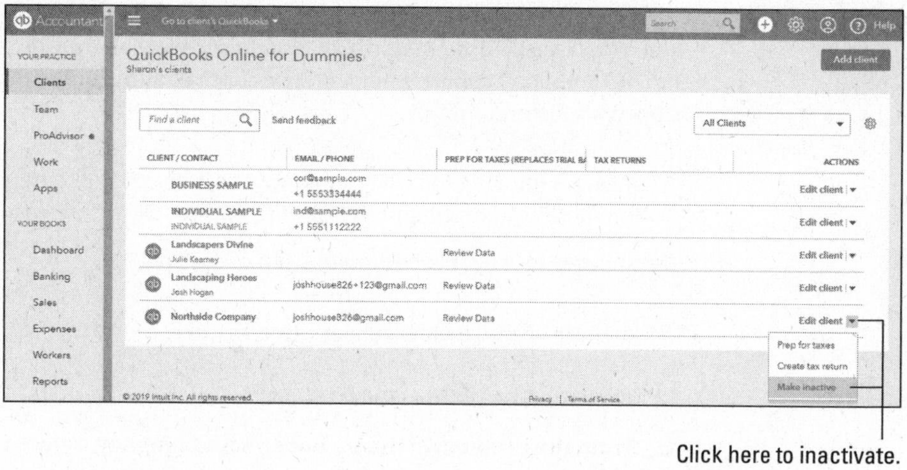

FIGURE 11-16:
Use the Actions
column to make a
client inactive.

Click here to inactivate.

3. **Click Make Inactive.**

QBO asks if you're sure you want to make the client inactive.

4. **Click Yes.**

QBO redisplays the page shown previously in Figure 11-16, but the client no longer appears in the Client list.

TIP

You can change the client's status back to Active if you opt to display inactive clients on the Clients page. Click the Gear button above the Actions column in the table on the Clients page and select the Include Inactive option (refer to Figure 11-13 to see the list). QBO displays all your clients, both active and inactive. To make an inactive client active again, click the Make Active link in the Actions column beside the client's name.

Working with your Wholesale Billing history

You can view and, if you want, download your Wholesale Billing subscription history. Two separate statements are available: one for the QBO subscriptions and one for the Payroll subscriptions. The billing history includes the last six months of bills.

REMEMBER

Be aware that billing statements are available the day after the billing date, not the same day.

Your Wholesale Billing history shows two separate charges for each client: one for the QBO company subscription and one for the Payroll subscription. These charges happen on different dates:

>> Charges for QBO company subscriptions occur on the same date every month, based on when you first entered your billing information.

>> Charges for Payroll occur on the fifth of each month.

Follow these steps to view subscription history:

1. **Click the Gear in the QBOA toolbar.**

2. **From the drop-down menu, under Your Company, select Your Account.**

   The Your Account window appears.

3. **Scroll down to the Wholesale Clients section.**

4. **Click the link for the type of statement you want to see: View QuickBooks Billing History or View Payroll Billing History.**

TIP

You'll also find the option to download your billing history to a comma-separated file that you can view in Excel on this page.

Stop using Wholesale Billing

So, you've decided that you really don't want to participate in the Wholesale Billing program and manage QBO subscriptions for your clients. Although you can't cancel your Wholesale Billing subscription, you can stop using it. There's nothing stopping you from working with clients who manage their own QBO subscriptions.

REMEMBER

You can't cancel your Wholesale Billing subscription because that action would also cancel the QBO subscriptions of the clients assigned to your Wholesale Billing subscription.

To stop using the Wholesale Billing program, you need to remove all the clients currently in your subscription using the steps in the section "Removing clients from your Wholesale Billing subscription."

After you have removed all companies from your Billing Profile, Intuit will no longer bill you because you won't have any QBO clients in your Wholesale Billing subscription.

» **Importing company data from QuickBooks Desktop to QBO**

» **Switching between client QBO company files in QBOA**

Chapter **12**

Adding Companies to the QBOA Client List

After signing up for QBOA and logging in, the next step for the accountant is to populate the Client list with QBO clients, which can happen in a couple of ways. In addition, you might be helping a client set up a QBO company either by creating a new company or by importing information into the QBO company.

This chapter shows you how to add client companies to the Client list and how to import company information from the QuickBooks Desktop product.

TIP

Need to remove a client from your Client list? See Chapter 11 for details on making a client inactive.

Adding a Client's Company to the Client List

You can add a client company to the Client list in two ways:

» By letting your client create his company and then invite you to access it

» By creating a client's company for the client

If you participate in the Wholesale Billing program (also called the Intuit Wholesale Pricing program), you can opt to manage a client's subscription for him. In this case, Intuit bills you for the client's subscription and you then bill your client (see Chapter 11 for more information on the Wholesale Billing program). Alternatively, the client can opt to manage his own QBO subscription but still give you access to his books. At the time this book was written, Intuit was running specials on QBO through its main website. In addition, Intuit was offering discounts for QBO companies managed by accountants using QBOA regardless of whether the accountant or the client created the client's QBO account.

TIP

You're not bound by one choice or the other — that is, managing the client's subscription or not managing the client's subscription. If you participate in the Wholesale Billing program, you can change subscription management at any time.

For details on signing up for the Wholesale Billing program, contact Intuit.

REMEMBER

Once you add a new client to the list, you'll want to start examining their books — and the Client Overview feature described in Chapter 13 can help you sort through the information.

Having a client invite you to be the accountant user

When a client creates his own company, he accepts the responsibility to pay for the company's QBO subscription. Even so, your client can invite you to access the company using the Invite Accountant process in QBO. You can manage any type of QBO subscription in QBOA, including Schedule C and ProConnect Tax Online clients.

Your client should follow these steps:

1. **Have the client open her company in QBO and click the Gear button in the QBO toolbar.**

   QBO displays the client's Gear menu in QBO (see Figure 12-1).

2. **In the Your Company column, have your client click Manage Users.**

   The Manage Users page appears. This page identifies the company's master administrator and enables the client to add users to the QBO subscription (assuming it is not a Simple Start subscription).

3. **Have your client click the Accounting Firms tab (see Figure 12-2).**

   The window shown in Figure 12-3 appears.

Click Manage Users.

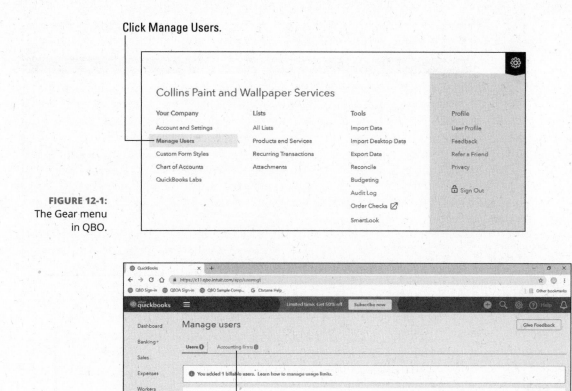

FIGURE 12-1:
The Gear menu
in QBO.

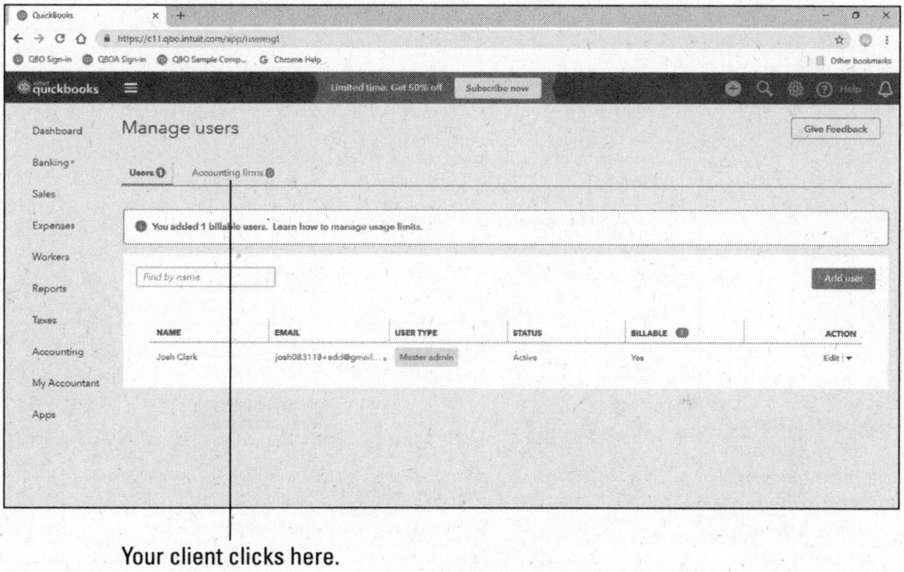

FIGURE 12-2:
The Manage
Users page has
two tabs: Users
and Accounting
Firms.

Your client clicks here.

4. **Have your client provide your email address and click Invite.**

The Accounting Firms tab of the Manage Users page reappears, showing the accountant's email with a status of Invited. QBO sends an email to the accountant that invites the accountant to sign in to the client's company. From this page, if necessary, the client can resend the invitation.

When you receive your client's email, it will look something like the one shown in Figure 12-4.

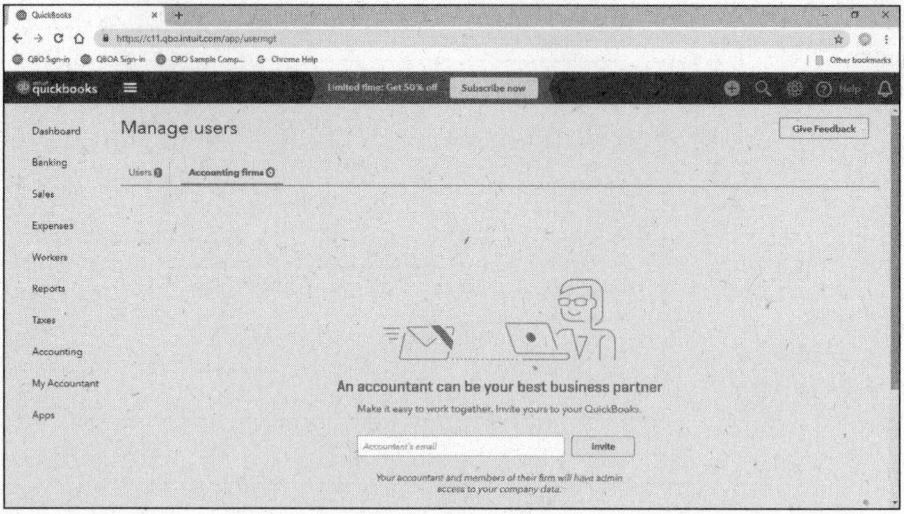

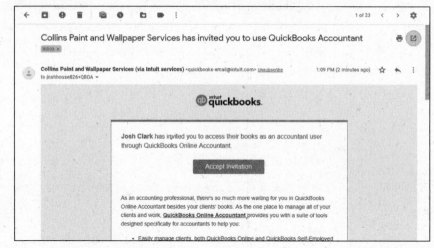

FIGURE 12-3:
The client
fills in the
accountant's
email
information.

FIGURE 12-4:
A sample email
an accountant
might receive
when invited to
access a client's
QBO company.

Click the Accept Invite button, and your default browser opens to the QBOA login page. Fill in your QBOA email or user ID and password, and a Success message appears. Click Continue, and QBOA opens; the new client appears in your list on the Client List page (see Figure 12-5). By default, QBOA gives access to the team member invited by your client and to your QBOA master administrator. You can use the Edit Client page to identify the additional people in your firm who should have access to the client's QBO books. To display the Edit Client page, click the client's name on the Clients page; on the page that appears, click Edit Client in the upper right corner.

You'll also get an email confirmation telling you that the client has been added to your QBOA account.

Inviting a client to your practice

You don't have to wait for clients to invite you to be their accountant; you can issue the invitation.

When an accountant who participates in the Wholesale Billing program adds a client's company to QBOA, billing responsibility becomes a matter of choice:

>> You can pay for the client's subscription and then bill the client back for the cost of the subscription.

>> You can assign billing responsibility to the client.

Further, whether the client will be part of your Wholesale Billing subscription or the client will be assuming billing responsibility, you can opt to be the master administrator or to assign that role to the client. For clients who want to be part of your Wholesale Billing subscription and assume the role of master administrator, you must be an invited accountant in the client's company.

If you retain the master administrator role, you can, at some later time, transfer master admin privileges back to the client. See the section "Transferring master administrator rights back to your client."

At the present time (this could change in the future), if a QBO client wants to remove an accountant, the firm managing the client's Wholesale Billing subscription must first remove the client from Wholesale Billing, even if the accountant the QBO client wants to remove is not affiliated with the firm managing the client's QBO subscription.

To remove a client from your Wholesale Billing subscription, follow these steps:

1. **In QBOA, click Gear ⇨ Your Account.**

   Your Account appears in the Your Company column of the Gear menu.

2. **In the Your Accountant window, scroll down to the Wholesale clients section and click the company you want to remove from Wholesale Billing.**

3. **From the Actions column drop-down, click Remove from Wholesale.**

You can invite any QBO user to your practice except a Simple Start user. Simple Start users must create their own companies and then invite you, the accountant, to their QBO company as described in the preceding section, "Having a client invite you to be the accountant user."

To invite a client to your practice, follow these steps:

TIP

If your client hasn't yet created a QBO account, you can create it for him by using an email address the client supplies to you. Be aware that any QBO company created by an accountant does not get a 30-day trial period. However, ProAdvisor discounts can be applied to companies created through a trial period offer.

1. **Open QBOA.**

2. **Click Clients in the Navigation bar to make sure you're displaying the Client List page.**

3. **From the Client List page, click the Add Client button in the upper right corner above the list.**

   The Client Contact Information page appears (see Figure 12-6).

4. **Select Business or Individual, depending on whether you're adding a business or a self-employed individual.**

5. **Provide a name and an email address for the company.**

   If you provide a name and an email address for which no QBO company exists, a new company will be created. Otherwise, QBOA adds any existing company that uses the name and email address you provide to your QBOA account.

6. **In the QuickBooks Subscription section, choose whether the client is billed directly or whether you want to add the client to your Wholesale Billing subscription.**

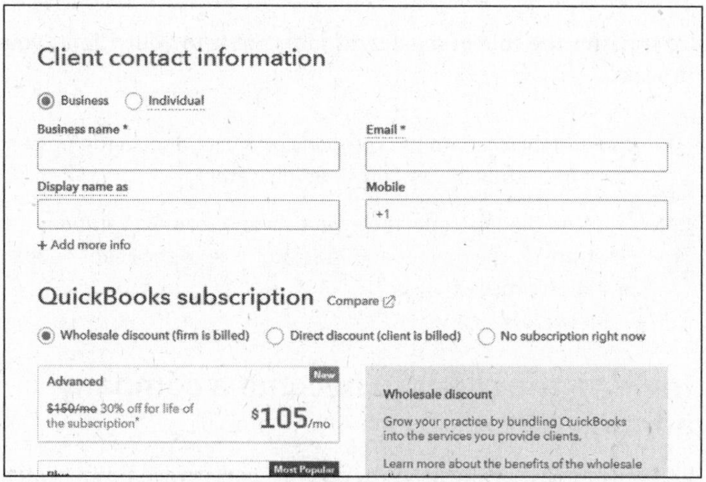

FIGURE 12-6:
The Client
Contact
Information
page of the Add
Client wizard.

7. **Select a type of QBO subscription (Advanced, Plus, Essentials, or Self-Employed).**

8. **Specify whether you should become the client company's master administrator.**

If the client is the master administrator, he receives a link to QBO so that he can sign in.

9. **Identify firm team members who should have access to the client QBO company.**

You can change access privileges later.

10. **Click Save.**

QBOA does some work and creates the company, which appears in the list of companies on the Clients page.

Transferring master administrator rights back to your client

As described in the preceding section, when you add a client QBO company to your QBOA account, you have the option to assign yourself as the master administrator; in this case, QBOA also assigns you as the accountant user for the company. But you can transfer the master administrator role back to your client without affecting your status as the accountant user.

To transfer the role of master administrator to your client, you follow a two-part process:

>> You add the client to the company as a user and, in the process, invite the client to become a company administrator.

>> After the client accepts the invitation to become a company administrator, you transfer the master administrator role to the client — again, using an invitation process.

Inviting the client to become a company administrator

As the first part of the process, create a company administrator for the new company you created when you added the client to your Client list. Follow these steps:

1. **Open the client company using the Go to Client's QuickBooks list on the QBOA toolbar.**

2. **Click the Gear button on the QBOA toolbar and choose Manage Users in the Your Company column.**

   QBO displays the Manage Users page, which initially shows only the accountant user who created the company.

3. **Click Add User.**

   The Add a New User wizard starts.

4. **On the Select User Type page, shown in Figure 12-7, select Company Admin and click Next.**

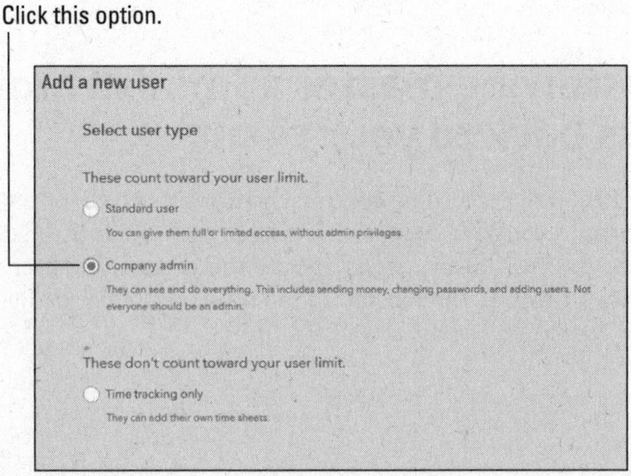

Click this option.

Add a new user

Select user type

These count toward your user limit.

○ Standard user
   You can give them full or limited access, without admin privileges.

◉ Company admin
   They can see and do everything. This includes sending money, changing passwords, and adding users. Not everyone should be an admin.

These don't count toward your user limit.

○ Time tracking only
   They can add their own time sheets.

FIGURE 12-7:
Select Company
Admin.

5. **On the Enter User's Email Address page, provide the client's email address (and optionally, name) and click Save.**

   QBO adds the user to the Manage Users page and a message appears briefly, explaining that QBO will send an email invitation to the user to sign in to the company. The email explains that she must create a QBO user ID unless she already has one. In most cases, if you set up a company for a client, the client doesn't yet have a QBO login.

6. **Click Save.**

   The new user appears on the Manage Users page with an Invited status.

When the client receives the email invitation to become the company administrator, the invitation contains a Let's Go! link.

When the client clicks the link, a QBO login screen appears containing the user's email address filled in — and prompting the user for a password. Typically, the client doesn't have a QBO login yet and so goes through the process of creating a new one; when she finishes filling in the password, she clicks Accept Invitation and she's logged in to QBO. She then receives a message indicating that she successfully accepted the invitation and can access her QBO company.

Transferring the master administrator role to the client

Once the client accepts the invitation to become a company administrator, you're ready to transfer master admin rights to the client. Use QBOA to open the client's QBO company and display the Manage Users page by clicking Gear ⇨ Manage Users. You appear as the master admin, and the client user's status is Active and has a User Type of admin (see Figure 12-8). To transfer the role of master admin to the client, click the down arrow beside Edit in the Action column and choose Make Master Admin.

QBOA displays a message explaining that only one user can serve as the master admin and, by transferring that role to your client, your access changes to admin — you will no longer be the master admin.

QBOA sends an email invitation to your client to become the master administrator, and the client can accept or decline. Assuming the client accepts, he's prompted to log in to QBO. Once he does, he sees a page that explains that the master admin role has been successfully transferred to him and that an email explaining such has been sent to the former master administrator — and that's you.

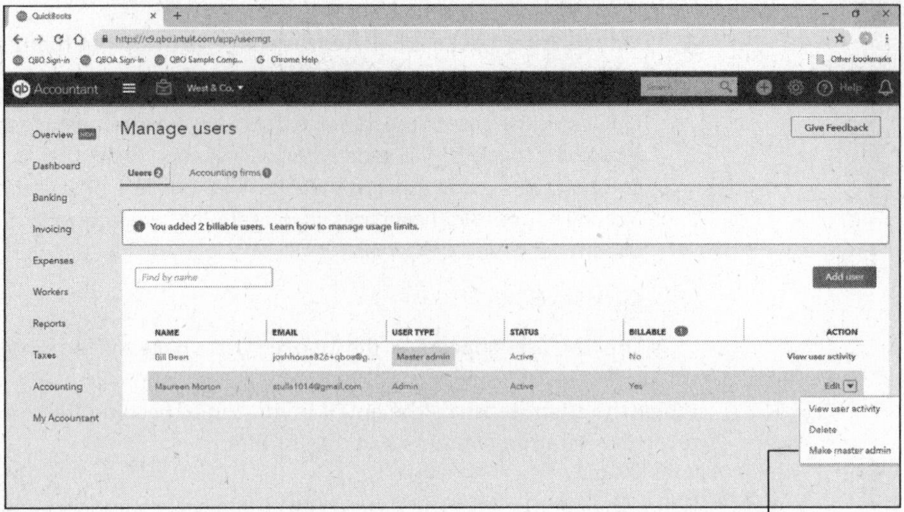

FIGURE 12-8:
Assigning the role of master administrator to the client.

Click here.

If you once again use QBOA to open the client's company and view the Manage Users page, you'll notice that you no longer appear in the Manage Users section and your client is the master administrator for the company. You become a company administrator.

Importing QuickBooks Desktop Information into QBO

If you've been using QuickBooks for the Mac 2013 and higher, QuickBooks Desktop for Windows Pro or Premier 2008 or later in the United States and Canada, and your QBO subscription is less than 60 days old, you can import your company's information into a QBO company. Accountants also can help clients import their QuickBooks Desktop companies into QBO companies. During the conversion process, QBO makes a copy of your QuickBooks Desktop company file and imports it into your QBO company. Your QuickBooks Desktop data remains available for you to use as you need.

Users in countries other than the U.S., Canada, and the UK might be able to import desktop QuickBooks information into QBO with the help of an outside service; contact Intuit for more information. Users of QuickBooks Desktop for Windows 2007 and earlier, QuickBooks for the Mac, and QuickBooks Enterprise should contact Intuit for details on importing their data into QBO. And, accountants importing their own data into the free QBOA company have considerably more time to import: up to 1,060 days of creating the QBOA account.

Assuming that you meet the criteria previously outlined, read on and learn about these five parts of the conversion process:

>> Review general conversion considerations.

>> Examine what won't convert.

>> Update your QuickBooks Desktop software.

>> Perform the steps to export a copy of your QuickBooks Desktop data that QBO uses for importing.

>> Review the tasks you need to complete after converting.

General conversion considerations

It's important to understand several facts about converting QuickBooks Desktop data for use in QBO:

>> As I just mentioned, you can import QuickBooks Desktop data only in the first 60 days you use QBO. Be aware that converting QuickBooks Desktop data does not affect the data in the QuickBooks Desktop product and that you can (and should, at least long enough to confirm that QBO will work for you) continue to use QuickBooks Desktop.

>> Be aware that the process of importing QuickBooks Desktop data into an existing QBO company completely overwrites any list and transaction data already stored in that QBO company.

>> Some information may not be imported when you move your file; see the next section, "An overview of what won't import," for general information and Appendix A for more detailed information. Take the time to familiarize yourself with these import limitations and with the feature differences between QuickBooks Desktop and QuickBooks Online.

>> QBO supports Intuit Online Payroll and QuickBooks Online Payroll (QBOP) to manage payroll. In some cases, your QuickBooks Desktop payroll data will automatically update your year-to-date totals. But, if that data doesn't migrate, and you intend to use QBOP, you will need to enter payroll totals as described in Chapter 9. Don't turn on or set up QuickBooks Online Payroll until after you convert your desktop data. If you've already turned on payroll in your QuickBooks Online company, see the sidebar "Payroll and Desktop Data Conversion."

PAYROLL AND DESKTOP DATA CONVERSION

If you've already turned on payroll in your QuickBooks Online company, don't attempt to import your QuickBooks Desktop file into that QBO company. Instead, you can set up a new empty QBO company file and cancel the subscription for the QBO company in which you turned on payroll; if the QBO company in which you've been working is a trial, you can simply let the trial run out instead of cancelling. The theory here is that you set up the original QBO company (with Payroll) to see how things work, and you'll be fine if you start over and import your QuickBooks Desktop data. If you need to cancel a subscription, do so from the Billing and Subscription tab of the client QBO Account and Settings dialog box (choose Gear ➪ Account and Settings ➪ Billing & Subscription).

>> Make sure all your sales tax filings are current before you export your QuickBooks Desktop data. You might need to make adjustment entries to sales tax filings in QBO after you import the information.

>> Make sure that you are using QuickBooks Desktop 2016 or later; more information on that in the sidebar "Using a QuickBooks Desktop Trial for Conversion."

Before you dive into converting your data, stack the odds for success in your favor by doing some homework. First, examine your QuickBooks Desktop data file to make sure that it will convert. In your QuickBooks Desktop product, open your company and press F2 to display the Product Information dialog box shown in Figure 12-9. In particular, take note of the number of targets listed. If your data file's number of targets falls below 350,000, you can proceed.

REMEMBER

If your data file's number of targets exceeds 350,000, condense your data. If your company's targets still exceed 350,000, consider importing lists only, as described in Chapter 4; QBO offers the option to import lists only. "What's a target?" you ask. Trust me on this; you really don't care. But, if you're dying to know, see https://quickbooks.intuit.com/community/Help-Articles/Targets-vs-Sources-overview/m-p/193286.

Next, using the version of the QuickBooks Desktop product for your country (U.S., Canada, or UK), verify your data file and then condense it so that it includes approximately one year's data. Condensing reduces the size of your data file and removes inactive list entries, and smaller data files tend to convert better. On the File menu, choose Utilities ➪ Condense Data.

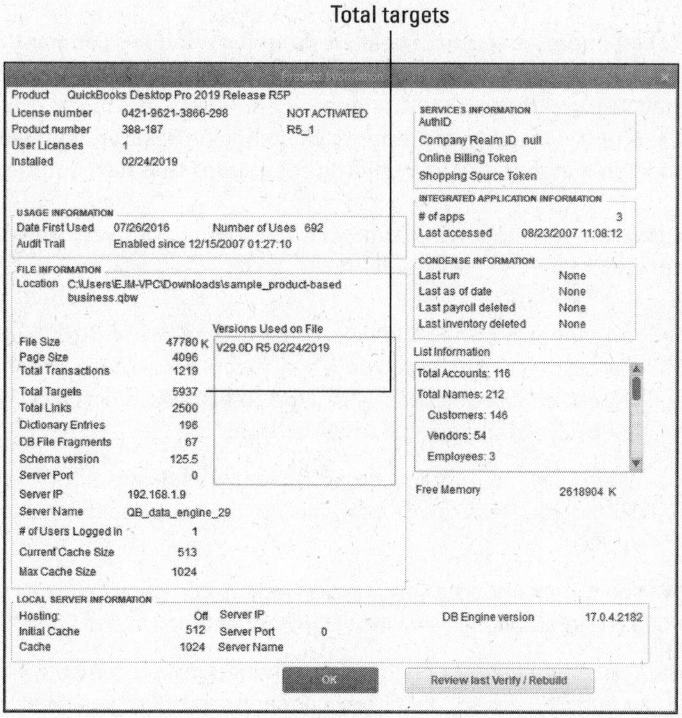

Total targets

FIGURE 12-9:
Check the number of targets in your QuickBooks Desktop company.

WARNING

Before you condense your data, make sure that you back up your data and put the backup in a safe place. That way, you're covered in case something strange happens — not likely, but it's better to be prepared than regretful. Also follow this advice before you export your data to QBO.

If you suspect the QuickBooks Desktop company data isn't in good shape — for example, you get errors while verifying or condensing — you can try rebuilding the data and then rerunning the Condense Data function. If you still get errors, consider importing lists only as described in Chapter 4.

REMEMBER

You should plan to keep your QuickBooks Desktop data file around, if for no other reason than to refer to it for historical data as needed. Many people opt to run QuickBooks Desktop and QBO simultaneously for a month or two to make sure QBO is performing as they expect.

An overview of what won't import

As I mention in the section "General conversion considerations," when you convert a QuickBooks Desktop company to QBO, some data fully converts, some partially converts, and some doesn't convert at all. In addition, QBO contains comparable alternatives for some desktop QuickBooks features and doesn't contain alternatives for others. See Appendix A for details on data conversion considerations.

You can import any QuickBooks Desktop for Windows company or any QuickBooks for Mac company using QuickBooks U.S., including companies with the multicurrency feature turned on, as long as the company meets the target limitation of 350,000. You also can import QuickBooks Desktop companies using UK and Canadian versions, again including companies that have multicurrency turned on.

In general, the following types of files won't convert and therefore can't be imported:

>> You cannot import QuickBooks Desktop data into any QBO company that was created more than 60 days ago, except for accountant company files. You can import QuickBooks Desktop companies into a QBOA company within 1,060 days of creating the QBOA account.

When I say "accountant company files," I'm talking about importing a QuickBooks Desktop company file into the Your Books company available in QBOA.

>> You cannot import a QuickBooks Desktop company into QBO subscriptions using international versions of QBO other than UK and Canadian.

>> You cannot import non-Intuit accounting software company files. If you need to import company data from a non-Intuit product, you need to work with Intuit's full-service team.

>> You cannot directly import accounting data stored in spreadsheet files. You can import these via a third-party app called Transaction Pro Importer, available at http://appcenter.intuit.com/transactionproimporter.

In addition, Appendix A describes the limitations you'll encounter if you import a QuickBooks Desktop company. I suggest you review Appendix A carefully so that you know what to expect. After you've reviewed the general considerations in the preceding section and the limitations for importing found Appendix A, you're ready to import your QuickBooks Desktop company into QBO.

It's important to understand that, even if your company data meets the preceding criteria, some data still won't convert when you import; the list below identifies some of the more visible things that don't convert. For details, see Appendix A:

>> Reconciliation reports: Save your reconciliation reports in QuickBooks Desktop or as PDF files to access them later. In QBO, continue reconciling where you left off. See Chapter 8 for details on reconciling accounts.

>> Recurring credit card charges: At your Merchant Center, cancel each existing automatic credit card recurring charge and re-create it in QBO as a recurring sales receipt. All other recurring transactions convert and import.

TIP

On the good news side, QBO now imports sub-accounts it finds in your Quick-Books Desktop Chart of Accounts — a fairly new development in the QBO export/import process.

» Reports: Find a similar report in QBO and customize it to your preference. See Chapter 10, and you can check out QBO's App Center or the app store at www. Apps.com for a list of reporting apps that can help your business.

» Audit trail: Your desktop audit trail won't come over, but all changes going forward will be captured in the Audit Log within QBO.

» Non-posting transactions or accounts don't convert except for estimates and purchase orders.

USING A QUICKBOOKS DESKTOP TRIAL FOR CONVERSION

If you're using a version of QuickBooks Desktop older than 2016, you shouldn't use your version to export your data to QBO. But, never fear; you can download a free 30-day trial version of the latest edition of QuickBooks available — 2019 at the time I wrote this — and use it to export your data to QBO. Make sure that you pick the right country version of QuickBooks Desktop (U.S., Canada, or UK). And, if you've been using the U.S. QuickBooks Premier Desktop edition, download the trial for U.S. QuickBooks Pro Desktop; you'll be able to open your company in it for the purposes of exporting your data to QBO.

Before you download and install a trial version, remember to open your current version of QuickBooks Desktop, back up your data, and put the backup in a safe place before you install the trial version. Then, download and install a trial version of the latest available QuickBooks Desktop.

Be aware that the trial is good for only 30 days and that you'll be using the trial *only* for the purpose of exporting your QuickBooks Desktop data to QBO. You'll want to keep your older version of QuickBooks Desktop installed so that you can refer to your QuickBooks Desktop data if necessary; the trial installation process gives you the option to keep your older version of QuickBooks and, effectively, install the trial alongside your existing version. To ensure that you retain access to your data, *do not* register or activate the trial version of QuickBooks Desktop. If you try to register or activate the trial, the validation will fail and you'll be locked out. (I have this urge to repeat those last two sentences . . .).

Updating your edition of QuickBooks Desktop

Intuit recommends using the 2016 version of QuickBooks Desktop or later to convert your data to QBO. If you are using a version of QuickBooks Desktop older than 2016, see the sidebar "Using a QuickBooks Desktop Trial for Conversion."

The first step you should take in the process of importing data from a desktop QuickBooks company is to back up your current data and put the backup in a safe place. Then, make sure that your edition of QuickBooks Desktop is up to date. And yes, even if you use a trial version of QuickBooks, you should make sure it's up to date. Follow these steps:

1. **Open the desktop edition of QuickBooks.**

2. **Choose Help ⇨ Update QuickBooks Desktop.**

   The Update QuickBooks window appears.

3. **Click the Update Now tab (see Figure 12-10) and select all updates.**

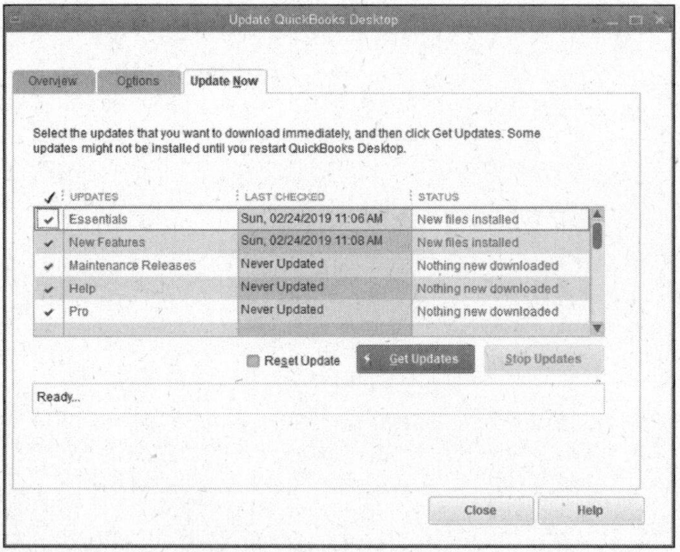

FIGURE 12-10: Select all update areas.

4. **Click the Get Updates button.**

   QuickBooks goes through the process of downloading updates.

5. **Once the updating process finishes, click Close.**

Next, exit from QuickBooks and restart it; if QuickBooks downloaded updates, it prompts you to allow the updates to be installed; make sure you install the updates.

Now, check the following in the QuickBooks Desktop product to help you avoid errors during the export/import process:

>> Make sure you're working in Single User mode: Click the File menu and make sure you see the Switch to Multi-user Mode command. Don't click it; just make sure you see it, because its availability lets you know you're working in Single User mode.

>> Make sure you're logged in to the QuickBooks Desktop data file as the administrator. And, when you log in to QBO to import the data, you'll need to log in as a user with administrator privileges.

>> To eliminate errors that might be introduced by working over a network, move the company file to your local drive.

Okay. You're ready to start the process of exporting a desktop QuickBooks company data and then importing it into a QBO company.

REMEMBER

You can import a QuickBooks Desktop company only during the first 60 days of a subscription with one exception: Accountants can import their own data into the free company that comes with QBOA for up to 1,060 days.

Transferring data from a desktop company into QBO

Before you start the transfer process, don't forget to back up your data and put the backup in a safe place. And, remember, if you turned on payroll in your QBO company, do *not* import into that company. See the sidebar "Payroll and Desktop Data Conversion" for details and suggestions.

During the transfer process, you're given the option to overwrite an existing QBO company or create a new one. In the steps that follow, I set up an empty QBO company before I started and allowed the process to overwrite it. Follow these steps to transfer data from a desktop QuickBooks company into a QBO company:

1. **In QuickBooks Desktop, choose Company ➪ Export Company File to QuickBooks Online.**

QuickBooks Enterprise users should press Ctrl+1 to open the Product Information window and then press Ctrl+B+Q. Then, click OK to close the

Product Information window. QuickBooks Pro/Premier users can also use the keyboard combination if, for some reason, the menu option isn't available.

A wizard starts to walk you through the process of exporting the data.

2. **On the first page of the export wizard, click Start Your Export.**

3. **On the page that appears, sign in to your QBO account as a user with administrative privileges.**

   If you don't have a QBO account yet, you can click Create an Account and walk through the process of supplying a user ID — typically an email address — and a password.

   REMEMBER

   Because you're not signing in from your browser, you might be prompted to authenticate yourself; in this case, Intuit sends a code to your email address and you must check email to be able to supply the code onscreen.

4. **On the page where QuickBooks Desktop displays the Moving-Day Checklist, click Continue.**

5. **Select the appropriate choice for turning on inventory, and then click Continue.**

   If you opt to turn on inventory, select the date you want to use to calculate inventory value using the FIFO method. Intuit recommends that you use the first day following your company's last tax filing period.

   REMEMBER

   Only QBO Plus and Advanced support inventory. If you opt to import inventory, your accounting method changes to FIFO and you need to file Form 3115 with the IRS. If QBO identifies any errors with inventory during the importing process, the process fails and you'll receive an email with instructions on how to fix the items causing the problem. Also be aware that, due to recalculations to FIFO, your Accrual Basis reports and Cash Basis reports will not match. QuickBooks flags any errors with inventory if they appear during import.

6. **Select your QBO company (see Figure 12-11).**

   I selected an existing empty company; choosing an existing company — empty or not — makes QBO overwrite any data already in that company.

7. **Click Continue.**

   QBO makes a copy of your QuickBooks Desktop company file and goes to work creating a file to import into your QBO company. During this process, which may take some time, you really can't use QuickBooks Desktop. Eventually, a message appears, letting you know that you'll receive an email when the process finishes (see Figure 12-12).

8. **Click OK, Got It.**

9. **You can close the QuickBooks Desktop product.**

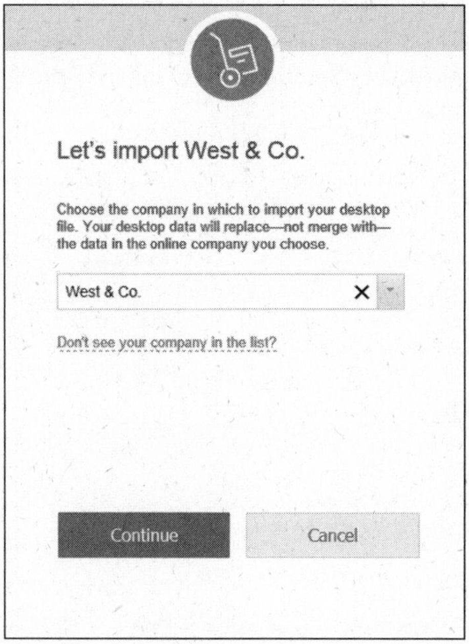

FIGURE 12-11:
Select whether you want to overwrite an existing QBO company or create a new one for your desktop QuickBooks company data.

Let's import West & Co.

Choose the company in which to import your desktop file. Your desktop data will replace—not merge with—the data in the online company you choose.

West & Co.

Don't see your company in the list?

Continue   Cancel

FIGURE 12-12:
This message appears after you finish your part of the export/import process.

We are on it!

We're transferring your data now. When it's done, we'll send a confirmation email with a summary report to

stulls1014@gmail.com

OK, got it

When the email arrives, the message will resemble the one shown in Figure 12-13. You can click the Complete Your Setup button to log in to the QBO company, or you can use the QBO interface.

FIGURE 12-13: A sample of the email message you receive after exporting a desktop QuickBooks company to QBO.

TIP

If you click the Complete Your Setup button in the email, a new browser tab appears displaying the QBO sign-in page.

If the unforgivable happens and your data doesn't convert, you'll receive an email telling you there was a problem and attaching a report for you to review to resolve the issues.

After converting . . .

After conversion finishes, you need to double-check things to make sure that the data looks the way you expected. At this point, I suggest you run and compare the Profit & Loss, Balance Sheet, Accounts Receivable, Accounts Payable, sales tax liability, and, if appropriate, payroll liability reports for both the QuickBooks Desktop company and the QBO company. Be sure you run these reports using the Accrual basis with the dates set to All. Use the Accrual basis because reports run in both products using the Cash basis might not match.

TIP

Need a do-over? During the first 60 days of a subscription, you get a "do-over" on importing data into a QBO company, which can be useful if things don't import as you expect. Just go through the process of importing again.

WARNING

WANT TO "UNDO" AN IMPORT?

Suppose you're not happy with the results of importing and you decide that you simply want to enter data manually into the QBO company. If the client uses Essentials, Plus, or Advanced and the subscription is 60 days old or less, you can clear the data from the QBO company by purging it. Open the company and click Dashboard so that you're viewing the QBO company Home page.

In the browser address bar, change the address to https://qbo.intuit.com/app/purgecompany and press Enter or refresh the page. A page appears that describes what will be deleted (everything), how many days you still have to completely remove the data in the company, and asks if you're sure. Type **yes** in the lower right corner and click OK, and QBO purges the data from your company. If you change your mind and don't want to purge, click Cancel in the lower right corner. Be aware that you can't undo a data purge; once it starts, you must simply wait until it finishes and then you can start using the now-empty company.

Don't try this with the Your Books company; you'll probably cause irreparable damage. If you need to clear data from the Your Books company, contact Intuit Technical Support for help.

And, here's a checklist of things you probably need to do to make the imported QBO company ready for use:

» Set up company users.

» Set up sales tax items.

» Set up payroll, either through Intuit Online Payroll or QBOP.

» Reconcile accounts as needed.

» Review lists and make appropriate entries inactive as necessary.

» Set up recurring transactions to replace desktop QuickBooks memorized transactions.

» Re-create any necessary non-posting transactions, such as purchase orders.

» Review inventory.

» Customize forms and reports and, if appropriate, memorize reports.

» Set up a closing date password.

See Chapter 13 for a discussion of the Client Overview in QBOA, which helps you identify the tasks you need to complete to bring any client QBO company up to snuff.

Switching between Client QBO Companies

If you've worked through Chapters 11 and 12, you might have noticed that client QBO companies don't, by default, open in a separate tab in your browser. So, what do you do when you want to stop working in one client's books and start working in another client's books?

Well, you can click the Accountant button on the QBOA toolbar at any time to redisplay the QBOA interface and your list of clients. From there, you can click the QuickBooks logo beside any client's name to open that client QBO company.

But you really don't need to take two steps to switch between client QBO companies; instead, take advantage of the Go to Client's QuickBooks list box on the QBOA toolbar.

When you're working in a client QBO company, the name of that company appears in the Go to Client's QuickBooks list box; if you click the company name, QBOA displays a list of all your client QBO companies. Just click the name of the company you want to open. No need to worry about saving work; QBO and QBOA do that for you.

Chapter **13**

Exploring a Client's Company from QBOA

A client's QBO company looks a little different when viewed using QBOA. This chapter explores the interface you see when you open a client QBO company from QBOA. It also covers some facets of a client QBO company you might want to review for your client to make sure things flow smoothly for both of you.

Opening a Client's Company

You can open a client's company in QBOA from the Clients page; on the client's line in the list, click the QuickBooks logo (the circle with the letters *q* and *b* in it). Alternatively, you can use the Go to Client's QuickBooks list on the QBOA toolbar, which remains visible at all times, making it easy for you to switch from one client QBO company to another. Simply open the list and select the name of the company you want to open (see Figure 13-1).

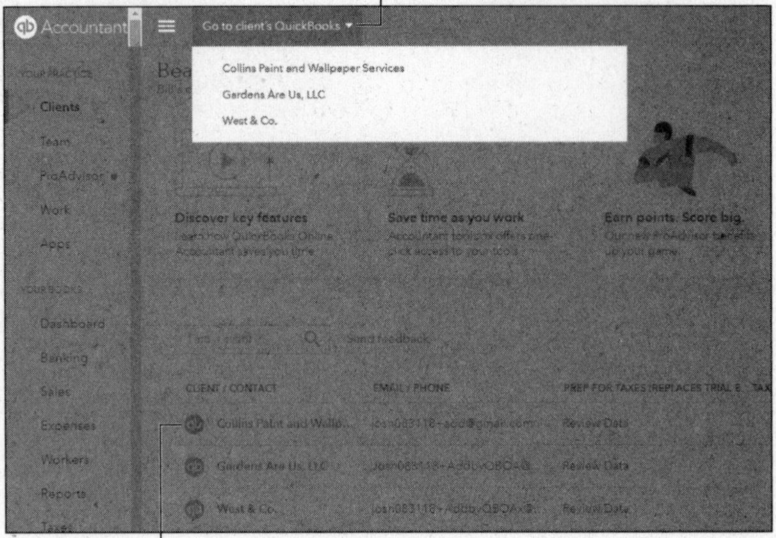

Click this list to open a company.

Click the QB logo to open a company.

FIGURE 13-1:
You can click the
QuickBooks logo
or use the list on
the QBOA toolbar
to open a client's
QBO company.

You don't need to take any special action to close a client QBO company; you can simply open another client QBO company, or you can sign out of QBOA from the Gear menu on the QBOA toolbar.

Reviewing a Client QBO Company

You'll probably want to review the company setup information for client QBO companies to make sure that things are set up properly for your client. You can take advantage of the Client Overview, which provides, well, an overview of the state of the client's QBO company. And, you'll want to review the settings, the Chart of Accounts, and the lists of client QBO companies.

Taking a look at the Client Overview page

This page can help you get a sense of where things stand in your client's QBO company. To display the Client Overview, open the client QBO company using the Go to Client's QuickBooks list box on the QBOA toolbar. Then, click the Overview tab in the Navigation bar. At the top of the Client Overview page (see Figure 13-2), you see information on the client's subscriptions and connected apps.

WORKING IN MULTIPLE WINDOWS

TIP

While working in one client QBO company, you can open different QBO pages. Click the Accountant Toolbox button and, toward the bottom of the list, click New Window. QBOA duplicates the page you are viewing in another browser tab. Using the new tab, navigate to another page in the client QBO company.

All the major browsers let you duplicate tabs; you don't have to use QBOA's New Window command, but it's convenient. To use the browser's duplication capability, right-click any tab and look for a command containing the word "duplicate."

Accountant Toolbox button

Accountant ≡ 📋 Collins Paint and Wallpaper Services ▾

Accountant Tools

Prep for taxes (replaces Trial Balance) NEW
Reclassify Transactions
Voided/Deleted Transactions
Write Off Invoices
Journal Entries
Close Books
Reconcile
Accountant Reports
Management Reports
My Custom Reports
Reports Tools
Chart of Accounts
New Window
ProConnect Tax Online

New Window option.

To access two different client companies simultaneously, you can't just open another browser tab. Instead, you need to use separate browsers. Or, if you're using Chrome, you can sign in to Chrome as a different user. See Chapter 17 for details on Chrome users.

In the middle of the Client Overview page, shown in Figure 13-3, you see information on the client's banking activity; the accounts in the list are set up either as bank accounts or as credit card accounts.

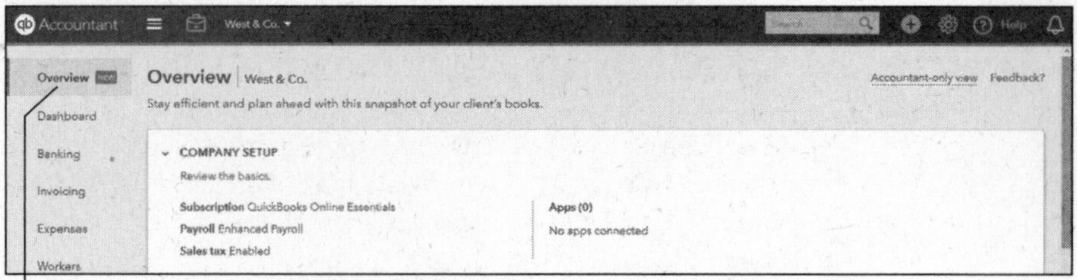

FIGURE 13-2:
In a QBO client company, the top of the Client Overview page shows details of the client's subscriptions and connected apps.

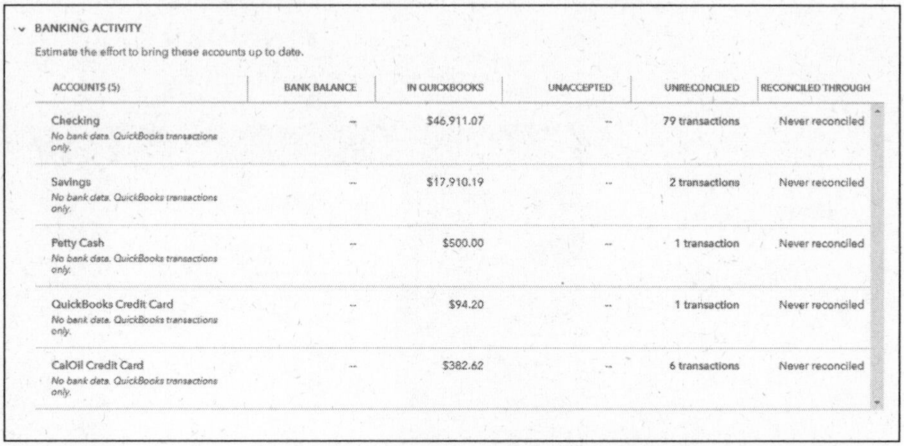

Click here to display the Client Overview page.

FIGURE 13-3:
The Banking Activity section of the Client Overview page.

The bottom of the Client Overview page shows the status of the client QBO company related to issues you commonly find as problems in client QBO companies (see Figure 13-4), giving you leads on information you may need to examine in the client QBO company.

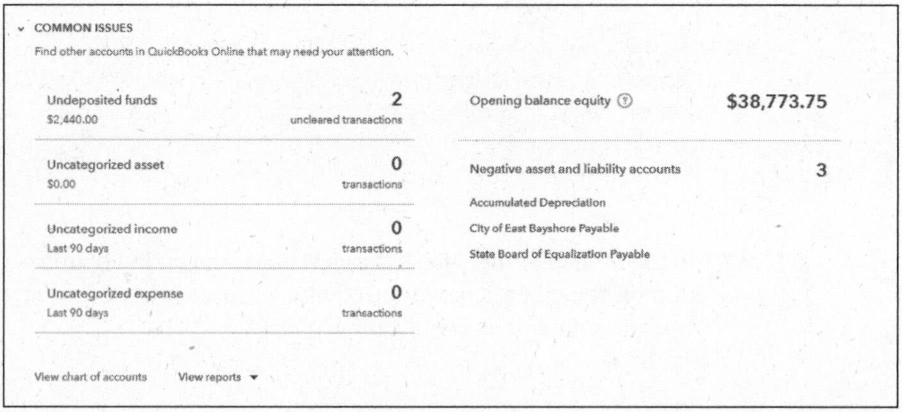

FIGURE 13-4:
The Common Issues section of the Client Overview page.

Be aware that there are no links on the Client Overview page except at the very bottom, where you can click the View Chart of Accounts link, to review the client's Chart of Accounts — which you'll probably want to review, but I suggest that you first review company setup information. Why? Read on. . . .

Examining company setup information

You review company setup information to make sure that the client QBO company uses the correct accounting method, employer EIN, and legal business organization. You also can turn on (or off, but I've never met an accountant who wanted to turn off this option) the option to use account numbers in the Chart of Accounts. To review company settings, follow these steps:

1. **Open the client QBO company you want to review.**

   You can click the QuickBooks logo on the Clients page of QBOA, or you can use the list of clients in the QBOA toolbar.

2. **Click the Gear button on the right side of the QBOA toolbar to display the Gear menu (see Figure 13-5).**

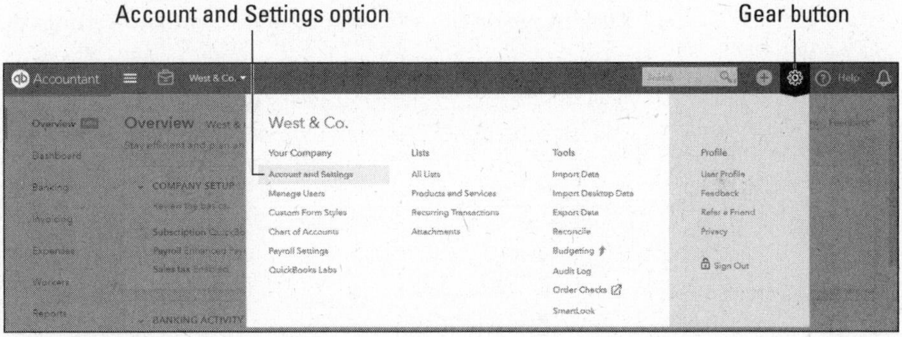

   Account and Settings option   Gear button

FIGURE 13-5:
The Gear menu.

3. **From the Your Company group on the left side of the Gear menu, click Account and Settings.**

   The Company tab (selected on the left side of the Account and Settings dialog box) appears (see Figure 13-6).

   If you set up the company for your client, QBO displays the Company Profile dialog box, requesting the company email, company address, city, state, and zip be filled in. All the fields are required, but you can bypass the dialog box by clicking the X in the upper right corner.

TIP

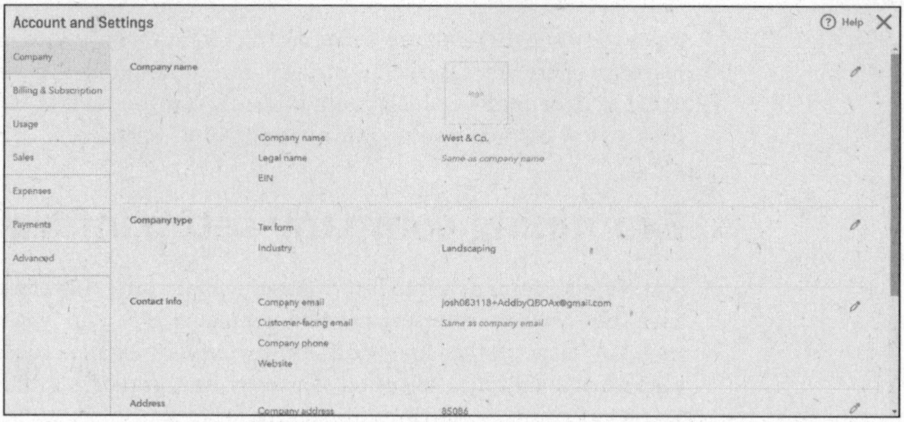

FIGURE 13-6:
The Account and Settings dialog box for a client QBO company.

4. **Review the settings.**

   In particular, set or correct the Company Name, Legal Name, and Employer ID (EIN).

   To make changes, click any setting or click the pencil that appears in the upper right corner of the section of settings. QBO makes the setting options available; make your changes and click Save.

5. **Click Usage on the left side of the Account and Settings dialog box.**

   QBO displays the Usage Limits tab shown in Figure 13-7, where you can review how the client QBO subscription fits within the usage limits Intuit applies to the chosen subscription. I discuss usage limits in Chapter 2.

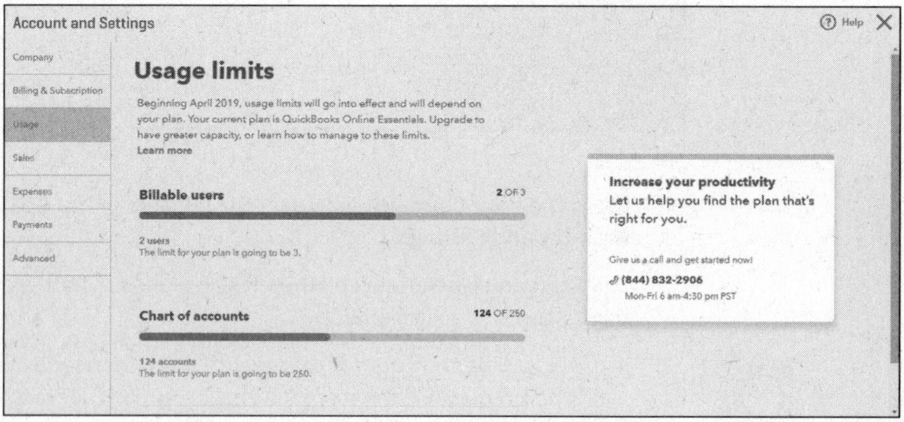

FIGURE 13-7:
Usage limits go into effect in April, 2019.

6. **Click Advanced on the left side of the Account and Settings dialog box.**

The settings on the Advanced page of the Account and Settings dialog box appear (see Figure 13-8).

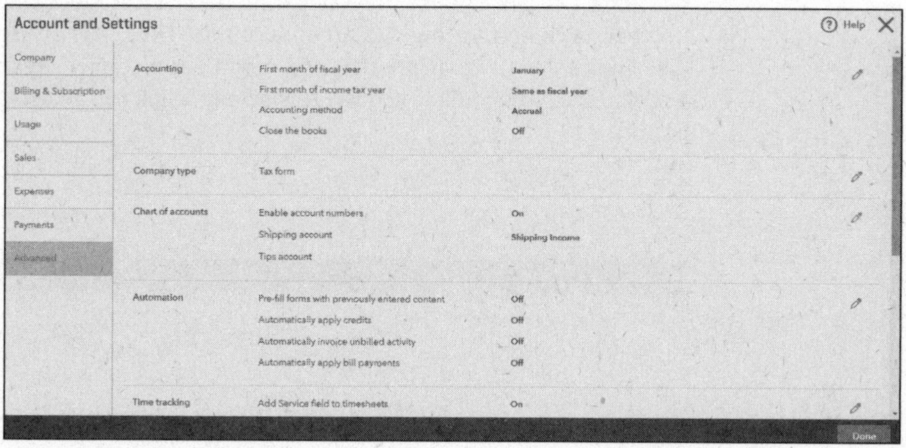

FIGURE 13-8:
Review and, if necessary, make changes to settings on the Advanced tab of the Account and Settings dialog box.

7. **Review the settings.**

In particular, set or correct the following:

- The settings in the Accounting section, which include fiscal and tax year information as well as the QBO company's accounting method.

- In the Company Type section, the tax form setting.

- The settings in the Chart of Accounts section; this is where you control the use of numbers in the Chart of Accounts.

- The settings in the Other Preferences section, which isn't shown in Figure 13-8 but includes displaying warnings when duplicate check numbers and bill numbers are used.

8. **Review any other settings on any of the pages in the Account and Settings dialog box that you feel might need your attention.**

9. **Click Done to save your changes.**

QBO displays a message at the top of the screen indicating that your changes were saved.

Taking a look at the Chart of Accounts

In addition to checking company settings, you'll probably want to review your client's Chart of Accounts to make sure it looks the way you want. You can click the link at the bottom of the Client Overview page to display your client's Chart of Accounts. Or, you can use the Navigation bar: In the client QBO company Navigation bar, click Accounting⇨ Chart of Accounts. The Chart of Accounts page appears (see Figure 13-9). Be aware that you might see a screen suggesting that you take a peek under the hood; if you see this screen, click the See Your Chart of Accounts button.

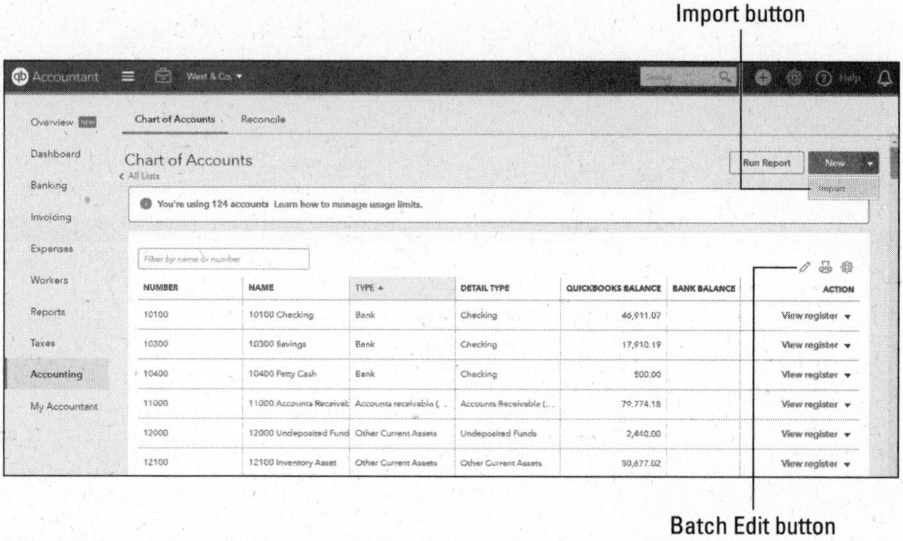

Import button

NUMBER	NAME	TYPE ▲	DETAIL TYPE	QUICKBOOKS BALANCE	BANK BALANCE	ACTION
10100	10100 Checking	Bank	Checking	46,911.07		View register ▾
10300	10300 Savings	Bank	Checking	17,910.19		View register ▾
10400	10400 Petty Cash	Bank	Checking	500.00		View register ▾
11000	11000 Accounts Receivable	Accounts receivable (	Accounts Receivable (	79,774.18		View register ▾
12000	12000 Undeposited Fund	Other Current Assets	Undeposited Funds	2,440.00		View register ▾
12100	12100 Inventory Asset	Other Current Assets	Other Current Assets	30,677.02		View register ▾

Batch Edit button

FIGURE 13-9: From the Chart of Accounts page, you can add and edit accounts.

TIP

You also can open the Chart of Accounts from the Accountant Tools button. All roads lead to Rome.

If you chose to enable the option to use account numbers while you were reviewing company settings (refer to Figure 13-8), the Chart of Accounts page displays a column for account numbers at the left edge of the page and the Batch Edit button in the upper right corner — it looks like a pencil. You can use the Batch Edit button to add account numbers, as described later in this chapter in the section "Adding account numbers."

Importing a Chart of Accounts

When you create a new company, QBO automatically sets up the Chart of Accounts it thinks you'll need. But you don't need to use it. Instead, you can replace it by importing a Chart of Accounts that you've set up in Excel or as a CSV file that can include sub-accounts along with their parent accounts, if your client's company needs sub-accounts.

REMEMBER

At the time I wrote this, there was an issue importing sub-accounts if the structure of the parent and sub-account was separated by a period. You could import the sub-accounts as parent accounts, but then you needed to edit them to make them sub-accounts.

The file you import needs to follow a particular format, and you can download a sample file to get the hang of the layout before you set up your file. On the Chart of Accounts page, click the arrow beside the New button and then click Import (refer to Figure 13-9). QBO displays the Import Accounts page shown in Figure 13-10. Click the Download a Sample File link and open the file in Excel to see the format your file should follow.

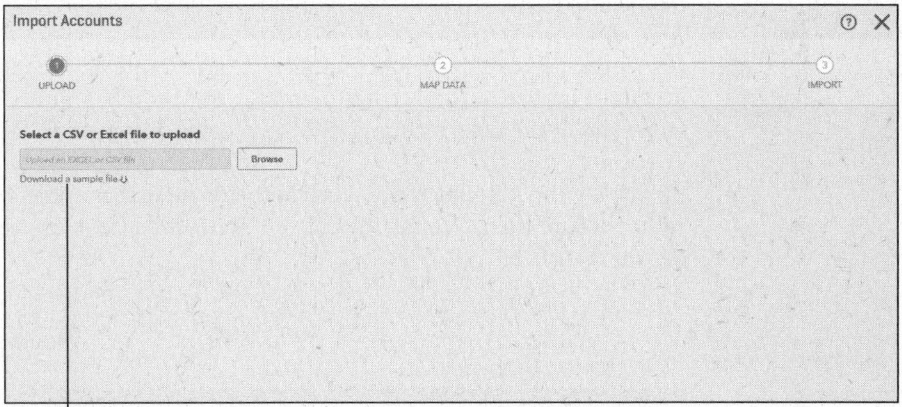

Import Accounts		
● UPLOAD	② MAP DATA	③ IMPORT

Select a CSV or Excel file to upload

Upload an EXCEL or CSV file	Browse

Download a sample file ⬇

FIGURE 13-10:
The Import Accounts page.

Click here.

Once you set up your Chart of Accounts file, you return to the Import Accounts page; click the Browse button to select your file and click Next in the lower right corner of the Import Accounts page. On the page that appears, shown in Figure 13-11, you map the headings in your file to the fields in QBO by selecting your field names from the list boxes in the Your Field column of the table; then, click Next.

QBO displays the accounts it expects to import; if all looks well, click Import and QBO imports your Chart of Accounts.

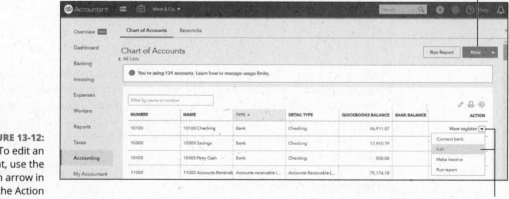

FIGURE 13-11:
Map the fields in
your file to the
fields in QBO.

Editing or adding accounts

You might need to edit an account to change an account's Category Type or its name, and you use the Account window to make the change.

TIP

If you decide to add account numbers to the Chart of Accounts, you can add an account number in the Account window, but there's a much easier way, which I show you in the next section, "Adding account numbers."

To display the Account window, click the down arrow in the Action column at the right side of the account and, from the menu that appears, click Edit (see Figure 13-12).

Click to create a new account.

FIGURE 13-12:
To edit an
account, use the
down arrow in
the Action
column.

Click to edit an account.

Or, if you need to create a new account, click the New button above the list. The window you see when creating a new account looks just like the one you see when you edit an existing account.

TIP

You can click View Register beside any Asset, Liability, or Equity account to display the account's register. Retained Earnings is the exception; it functions like Income and Expense accounts. Beside any Income or Expense account, you can click Run Report to display a QuickReport for the account.

Adding account numbers

I promised I'd show you an easy way to add account numbers to a QBO company Chart of Accounts. First, make sure you enable the setting on the Advanced tab of the Settings dialog box (in the Chart of Accounts section) shown previously in Figure 13-8.

Then, on the Chart of Accounts page, click the Batch Edit button (the one that looks like a pencil on the right side of the table above the table headings) to display the page shown in Figure 13-13.

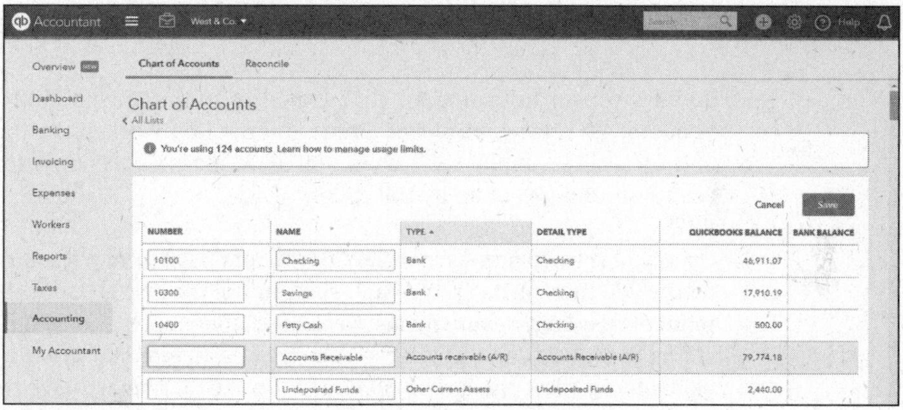

FIGURE 13-13:
Use this page to set up account numbers for the Chart of Accounts.

Type account numbers in the Number column. Save buttons appear at the top- and bottom-right corners of the page (you can't see the bottom of the page in Figure 13-13); click either button after you finish entering the account numbers.

TIP

Because a QBOA session times out by default after 60 minutes of non-use, you might want to save periodically as you enter account numbers. Also, after you enter account numbers, you can sort the Chart of Accounts in account-number order by clicking Number in the column headings on the Chart of Accounts page.

Reviewing list information

You also can review list information. Using the links in the Navigation bar, you can view overview information about customers, vendors, and employees. To view customers, as shown in Figure 13-14, you click Sales in the Navigation bar (it might say Invoicing, depending on the choices made when creating the company) and then click Customers.

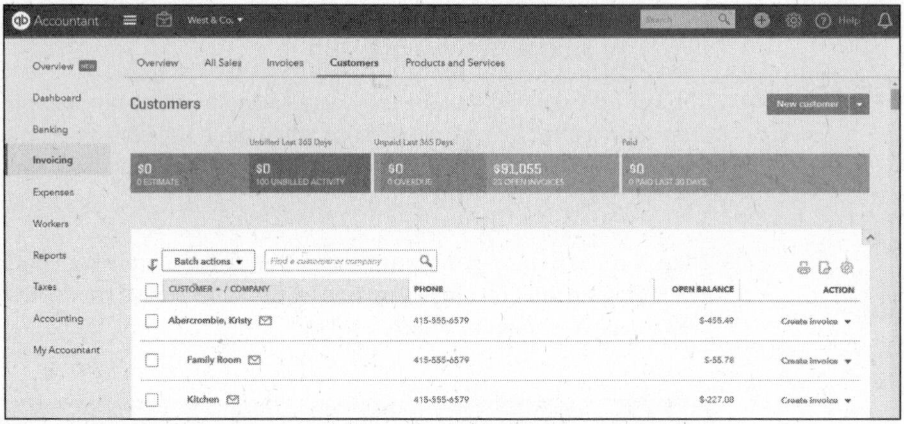

FIGURE 13-14:
The Customers
page.

To view vendor information, click Expenses in the Navigation bar and then click Vendors. To review employee information, click Workers in the Navigation bar and then click Employees. When you click Workers ⇨ Contractors, QBO displays the 1099 vendors set up by the client.

On any of these pages except the Contractors page (and payroll needs to be set up before you can use its status bar), you can use the status bar at the top of the page to identify activity over the last year and, if you click one of the elements on the status bar, QBO filters the list to view that particular subset of the list. For example, you can filter the list of customers on the Customers page to view only those customers with overdue invoices or only those customers with unbilled activity. And you can use the Batch Actions button (just above the table) to perform, well, batch actions, such as emailing a batch of customers. If your list is long, use the text box beside the Batch Actions button to search for a particular list entry. You also can sort the list by name or by open balance; just click the appropriate heading below the Batch Actions button. Note that you can import names into a people list; for more information, see Chapter 4.

To review other lists, click the Gear button in the QBOA toolbar. In the Lists section of the Gear menu that appears, you can opt to view any of three common lists (the Products and Services list, the Recurring Transactions list, or the

Attachments list). Or, you can click All Lists at the top of the Lists section to display the Lists page shown in Figure 13-15, which you can use to navigate to any list other than a people-oriented list.

For more extensive details on working with lists, see Chapter 4.

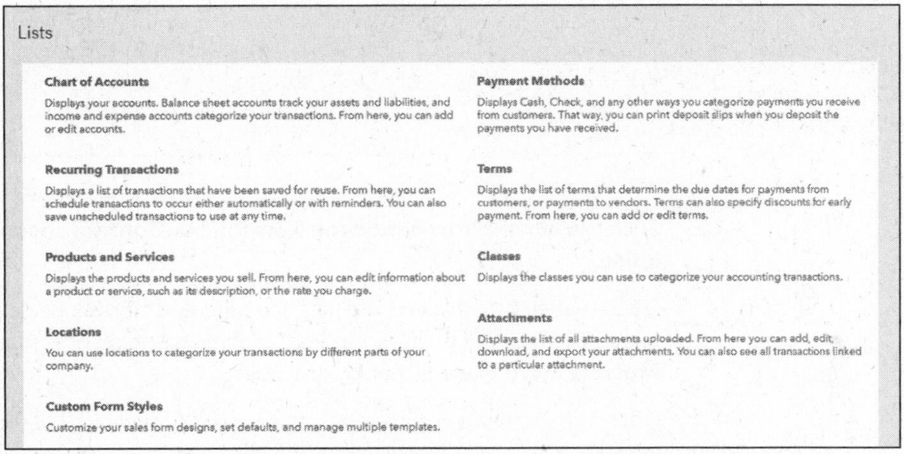

Lists

Chart of Accounts
Displays your accounts. Balance sheet accounts track your assets and liabilities, and income and expense accounts categorize your transactions. From here, you can add or edit accounts.

Payment Methods
Displays Cash, Check, and any other ways you categorize payments you receive from customers. That way, you can print deposit slips when you deposit the payments you have received.

Recurring Transactions
Displays a list of transactions that have been saved for reuse. From here, you can schedule transactions to occur either automatically or with reminders. You can also save unscheduled transactions to use at any time.

Terms
Displays the list of terms that determine the due dates for payments from customers, or payments to vendors. Terms can also specify discounts for early payment. From here, you can add or edit terms.

Products and Services
Displays the products and services you sell. From here, you can edit information about a product or service, such as its description, or the rate you charge.

Classes
Displays the classes you can use to categorize your accounting transactions.

Locations
You can use locations to categorize your transactions by different parts of your company.

Attachments
Displays the list of all attachments uploaded. From here you can add, edit, download, and export your attachments. You can also see all transactions linked to a particular attachment.

Custom Form Styles
Customize your sales form designs, set defaults, and manage multiple templates.

FIGURE 13-15: Use this page to open any list other than the Customers, Vendors, or Employees list.

Exporting and importing bank feed rules

When your client takes advantage of bank feeds and downloads transactions from the bank to his QBO company, you can help ensure that the transactions post properly. In many cases, the rules used by one client can apply to another, so, rather than re-creating rules, export them from one client and import them to another.

When you export rules, QBO exports all the rules in the client's company. You can then selectively import rules using the Import Rules wizard.

To export rules from a client company, open that company and follow these steps:

1. **Choose Banking ⇨ Rules from the Navigation bar.**

QBO displays the Rules page (see Figure 13-16).

2. **Click the down arrow beside the New Rule button.**

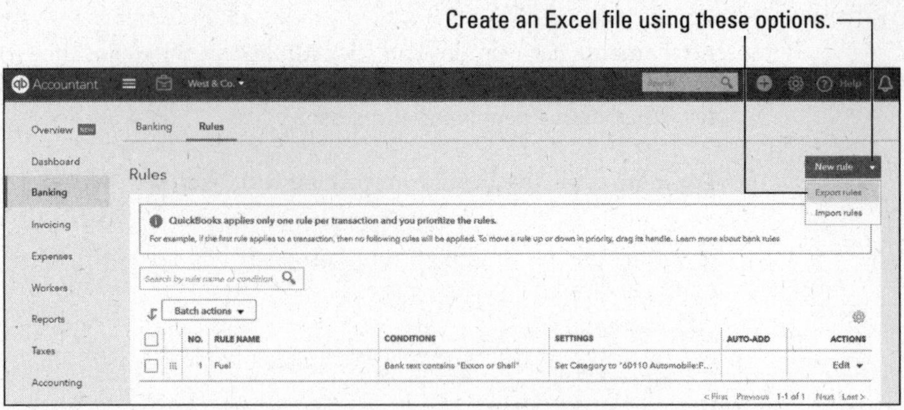

Create an Excel file using these options. ──────

FIGURE 13-16:
Use this page to export rules from one client and import them into another.

3. **Click the down arrow beside the New Rule button and choose Export Rules.**

   QBO creates an Excel file containing the rules and stores it in your Downloads folder. The name of the file includes the name of the client whose rules you exported and the words "Bank_Feed_Rules."

   QBO displays the directions for what you do next — which I outline in the following steps. Click Close in the QBO message.

4. **Switch to the company to which you want to import these rules.**

5. **Repeat the preceding Steps 1 to 3; in Step 3, choose Import Rules.**

   QBO starts a wizard that helps you import the rules.

6. **On the first Import Rules wizard screen, select the file you created in Step 3 and click Next.**

7. **On the second wizard screen, select the rules you want to import and click Next.**

8. **On the third wizard screen, you have the option to select categories for the rules that match the Chart of Accounts of the client to which you are importing the rules; make any changes and, when you finish, click Import.**

   QBO tells you how many rules imported successfully.

9. **Click Finish.**

   QBO redisplays the Rules page for the client you opened in Step 4, where you can verify that the rules you wanted to import appear.

For more detail on working with rules, see Chapter 8.

Chapter **14**

Working in a Client's Company

You work in a client's QBO company in much the same way your client does; see Chapters 4 to 10 for detailed information. In this chapter, I focus on ways you can navigate easily, search for and review transactions, and communicate with clients.

Making Navigation Easy

Much of mouse navigation is obvious; click here and click there. But, you can use a few not-so-obvious tricks to navigate easily, including some keyboard shortcuts. Some common navigation techniques are specific to Chrome; see Chapters 17 and 18 for more information.

Using keyboard shortcuts

Hidden away in QBO companies are keyboard shortcuts that you might want to use. I show them here in Figure 14-1, and you also can find them on this book's cheat sheet.

To get this cheat sheet, simply go to www.dummies.com and search for "QuickBooks Online For Dummies Cheat Sheet" in the Search box.

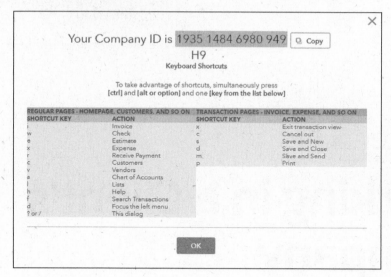

Your Company ID is 1935 1484 6980 949   Copy
H9

Keyboard Shortcuts

To take advantage of shortcuts, simultaneously press
[ctrl] and [alt or option] and one [key from the list below]

REGULAR PAGES - HOMEPAGE, CUSTOMERS, AND SO ON		TRANSACTION PAGES - INVOICE, EXPENSE, AND SO ON	
SHORTCUT KEY	ACTION	SHORTCUT KEY	ACTION
i	Invoice	x	Exit transaction view
w	Check	c	Cancel out
e	Estimate	s	Save and New
x	Expense	d	Save and Close
r	Receive Payment	m	Save and Send
c	Customers	p	Print
v	Vendors		
a	Chart of Accounts		
l	Lists		
h	Help		
f	Search Transactions		
d	Focus the left menu		
? or /	This dialog		

OK

To view these shortcuts (and the current client QBO Company ID), press and hold Ctrl+Alt and then press the forward slash (/) key. Mac users, substitute Option for Alt here and in the next paragraph. If you press Ctrl+Alt+/ without opening a client QBO company, the Company ID you see is your own.

To use any of these shortcuts, press and hold Ctrl+Alt and then press the appropriate key to perform its associated action. For example, to open the Invoice window, press Ctrl+Alt+I.

Opening multiple windows

Many times, accountants want to work with multiple windows, and you can do that in QBO. Within the same QBO company, you can duplicate a browser tab using the New Window command on the Accountant Tools menu on the QBOA toolbar (see Figure 14-2). You can read more about the other commands on the Accountant Tools menu in Chapter 15.

TIP

If you're using Chrome, you also can duplicate a browser tab by right-clicking the tab and choosing Duplicate or, if you're a keyboard person, press Alt+D followed by Alt+Enter (that would be the same as holding down the Alt key and pressing D followed by pressing Enter). In Firefox, you can duplicate a browser tab by clicking in the address bar and pressing Alt+Enter.

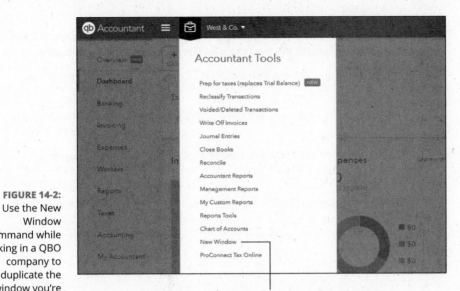

FIGURE 14-2:
Use the New
Window
command while
working in a QBO
company to
duplicate the
window you're
viewing.

Click this option to duplicate the current browser tab.

When you click the New Window command, QBO opens a new browser tab and displays the same information that appears in the original browser tab. But, from that point, you can display different information for the same company in each browser tab. And, if you're working in Chrome on multiple monitors, you can split the tabs onto different monitors. Drag the tab you want to place on a different monitor in a downward direction, and it splits away from the browser. You can immediately drag it to another monitor, or you can release the mouse button, in which case a second instance of Chrome appears. You can then drag either instance to a different monitor.

The same technique works in Firefox; drag a Firefox tab downward and release the mouse button. The tab splits away and appears in a second instance of Firefox. You can then drag either instance to a different monitor.

TIP

If you're a fan of "split screen," you can use a Windows shortcut to display two tabs side by side. Follow these steps in either Chrome or Firefox:

There's no short, easy way to display two windows one on top of the other. You have to manually resize the windows and place them where you want them.

TIP

1. **Duplicate a browser tab using any technique already described.**

2. **Drag the current tab down.**

   The browser displays the tab you dragged in its own browser window.

3. **Press and hold the Windows key (the one that appears between the left Ctrl and the left Alt keys on the keyboard) and press an arrow key:**

- Press the left arrow key to pin the active window to the left side of the monitor.

- Press the right arrow key to pin the active window to the right side of the monitor.

4. **Click the other available window to make it the active window and repeat Step 3.**

In Figure 14-3, I displayed the Balance Sheet (on the left) and then created a second browser window where I drilled down to display the transactions in the checking account. Then, I pinned the two windows side by side onscreen.

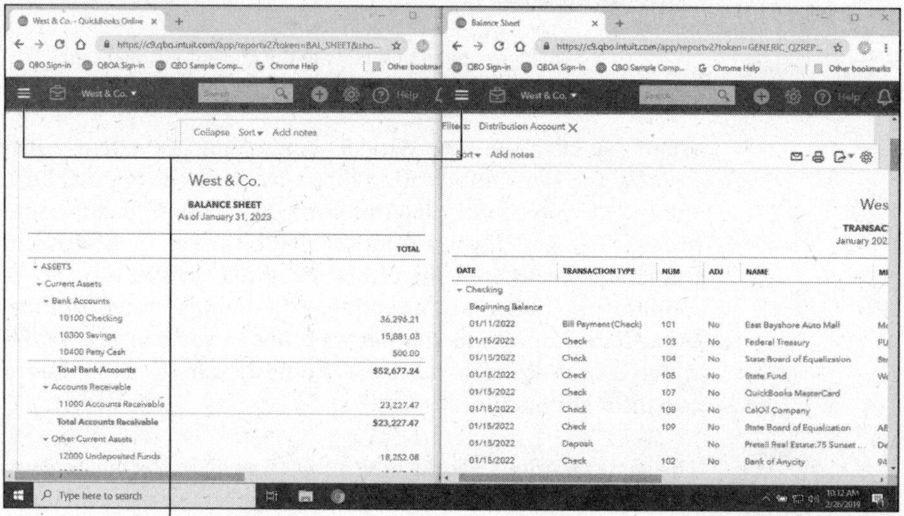

FIGURE 14-3: Two windows pinned side by side.

Click to hide the Navigation bar.

TIP

You can click the menu button in either or both windows to hide the Navigation bar (giving more screen real estate to the data as I did in Figure 14-3).

When you finish working in two windows, simply close one and maximize the other.

Working in two companies simultaneously

Suppose that you're done working with one client and want to open a different client. As described in Chapter 12, you can click the Go to Client's QuickBooks button on the QBOA toolbar and select a new client. Or, you can click the Accountant button in the upper left corner of the QBOA interface to redisplay the Clients page and then click the QuickBooks icon for the client QBO company you now want to open. Either way, QBOA displays the information for the newly selected client.

That brings up the question, "How do I work in two different companies simultaneously?" Well, you can open a different browser, sign in to QBOA, and open a second client QBO company. For example, if you're working in Chrome, you could open Firefox using the same QBOA login information. You can then open two different companies, as I did in Figure 14-4.

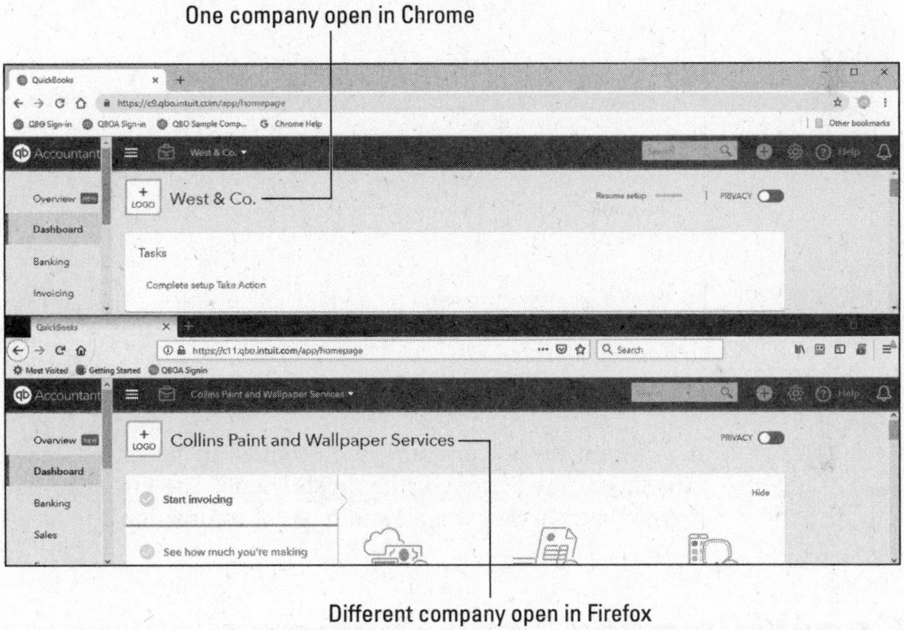

One company open in Chrome

FIGURE 14-4:
To work in two companies at the same time, you can use two browsers.

Different company open in Firefox

If you're working in Chrome, you also can take advantage of Chrome users and open Chrome as a different user. You'd have, effectively, two instances of Chrome running simultaneously. See Chapter 17 for more information on Chrome users.

Examining Available Transaction Types

In Chapters 5 to 9, I cover transactions in a fair amount of detail, so I'm not going to repeat that information here. But you can see the available transactions by opening a client QBO company and then clicking the Create menu (the plus sign). Figure 14-5 shows the Create menu open; remember that the Create menu button appears as a plus sign before you click it and an X after you click it.

Available transactions are organized on the menu by the type of people to which they pertain. And the Create menu contains an "Other" category for transactions that don't pertain to particular types of people — like bank deposits.

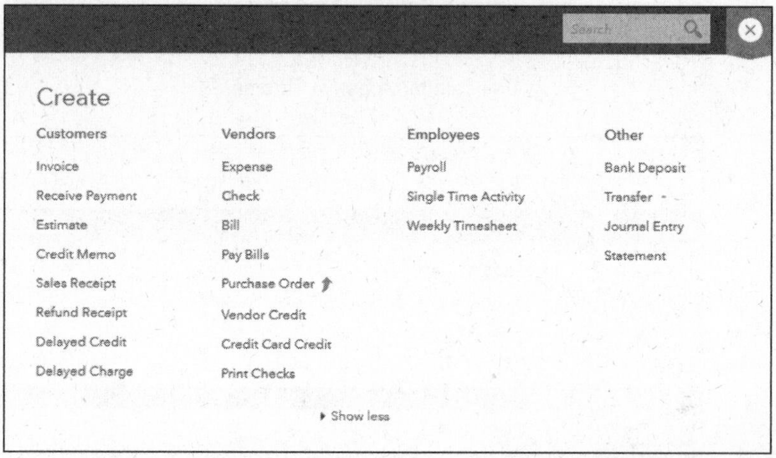

Create

Customers	Vendors	Employees	Other
Invoice	Expense	Payroll	Bank Deposit
Receive Payment	Check	Single Time Activity	Transfer
Estimate	Bill	Weekly Timesheet	Journal Entry
Credit Memo	Pay Bills		Statement
Sales Receipt	Purchase Order		
Refund Receipt	Vendor Credit		
Delayed Credit	Credit Card Credit		
Delayed Charge	Print Checks		

▶ Show less

FIGURE 14-5:
The transactions you can create while working in a QBO company.

If you want to view only the more commonly used transactions, click the Show Less link at the bottom of the Create menu. The link changes to the Show More link so that you can redisplay all types of transactions.

Searching for Transactions

More often than not, you'll be searching for transactions in a client QBO company rather than creating them. You can search for transactions using the Search box on the QBOA toolbar at the top of the client QBO company window (see Figure 14-6). When you click in the Search box, QBO displays a list of recent transactions and reports.

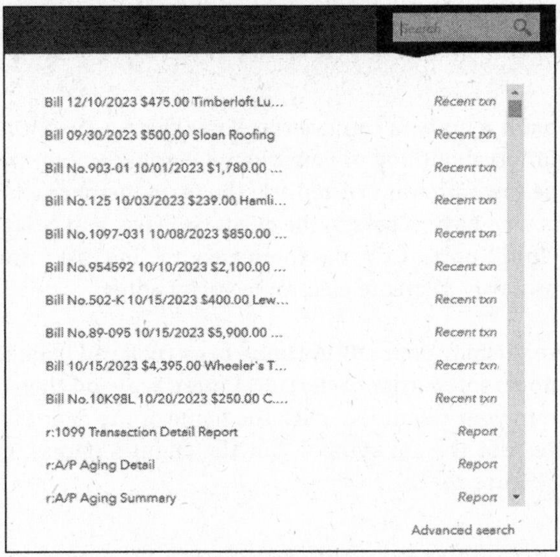
Search
Bill 12/10/2023 $475.00 Timberloft Lu...
Recent txn
Bill 09/30/2023 $500.00 Sloan Roofing
Recent txn
Bill No.903-01 10/01/2023 $1,780.00 ...
Recent txn
Bill No.125 10/03/2023 $239.00 Hamli...
Recent txn
Bill No.1097-031 10/08/2023 $850.00 ...
Recent txn
Bill No.954592 10/10/2023 $2,100.00 ...
Recent txn
Bill No.502-K 10/15/2023 $400.00 Lew...
Recent txn
Bill No.89-095 10/15/2023 $5,900.00 ...
Recent txn
Bill 10/15/2023 $4,395.00 Wheeler's T...
Recent txn
Bill No.10K98L 10/20/2023 $250.00 C....
Recent txn
r:1099 Transaction Detail Report
Report
r:A/P Aging Detail
Report
r:A/P Aging Summary
Report
Advanced search

FIGURE 14-6: Type any phrase you want to use as a search filter or click Advanced Search at the bottom of the Search list.

If you see the transaction or report you want, you can click it to open it in the appropriate window. If you *don't* see the transaction or report you want, you have a couple of options.

First, you can type in the Search box, and QBO responds with sample results. If you still don't see the result you want, try your second option: Click Advanced Search in the lower right corner of the menu, and QBO displays the Search page (see Figure 14-7).

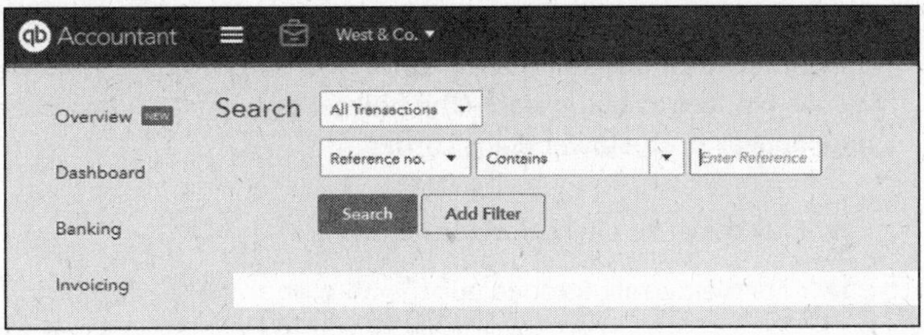
Accountant
West & Co.
Overview
NEW
Search
All Transactions
Dashboard
Reference no.
Contains
Enter Reference
Banking
Search
Add Filter
Invoicing

FIGURE 14-7: Set criteria for a more specifically defined search.

You can limit the search to a particular transaction type, choose to search for any of several types of data, and specify whether the search should contain, not contain, be equal to, or not be equal to the search criteria.

TIP

From any transaction window, you can view recent transactions of that type by clicking the button that appears in the transaction's title bar, immediately to the left of the name of the transaction type. The button image looks a bit like a clock.

Making Client Notes

You and your team members can use the Notes feature in QBOA to document any kind of information about any of your clients. For each note, QBOA automatically assigns the time the note was created and the team member who created the note. Team members who have access to the client can view and edit that client's notes. And, you can "pin" notes to make them easy to find. You can think of QBOA's Notes feature as a way to create electronic sticky notes.

To create a note, display your QBOA Home page (you can click the QB Accountant symbol in the upper left corner of the QBOA interface) and then click Clients in the Navigation bar. In your Client list, click the name of the client for whom you want to create a note (not the QB symbol, but the client's name). QBOA displays the page shown in Figure 14-8.

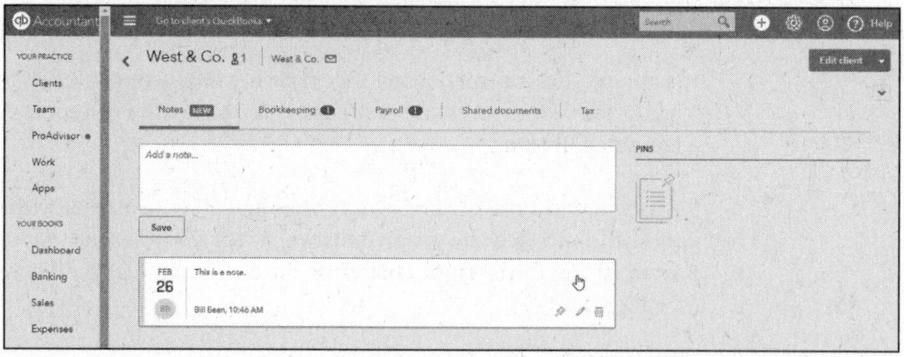

FIGURE 14-8: The page where you create a client note.

Type your note and click Save. Once you save a note, you can pin it; move the mouse pointer over the note (the pointer appears as a hand) and options for the note appear in the lower right corner:

>> Click the push-pin button to pin the note

>> Click the pencil button to edit the note, and

>> Click the trash can button to delete the note.

Communicating with a Client

Communication is essential in all walks of life, including between a client and an accountant. You can use tools in QBO and QBOA to communicate with your clients who have QBO subscriptions.

TIP

If you prefer, you can skip using QBOA and QBO to communicate and just use email.

For example, you can request that your client send you a bank statement. You use Client Requests to communicate; you send a message from QBOA and it appears on the My Accountant page of the client's QBO company. Follow these steps:

1. **From QBOA, click Work in the Navigation pane.**

   You can read more about the purpose and functioning of the Work page in Chapter 15.

2. **Click Create Client Request.**

   QBOA displays the Client Request panel on the right side of the screen (see Figure 14-9).

3. **Type a name for the request.**

   Think of this as the subject line of an email message.

4. **Select a client.**

   Only clients with QBO subscriptions appear in the list.

5. Supply the due date for the request.

6. Optionally, complete the rest of the fields on the request form, including adding any documents you want to send to your client.

7. You can optionally select the Notify Client check box to send a QBOA-generated email to the client, notifying him of the request.

8. Click Publish to Client's QuickBooks.

Create client request

Request name *

Bank Statement

Client *   Due date *

West & Co.   ▼   03/01/2019

Status

To do   ▼

Details

Maureen, I need all your bank statements for 2018. Thanks, Bill.

▼ Documents

Adding a doc here also shares it with your client in QuickBooks.

+ Add document

✓ Notify client   Publish to client's QuickBooks

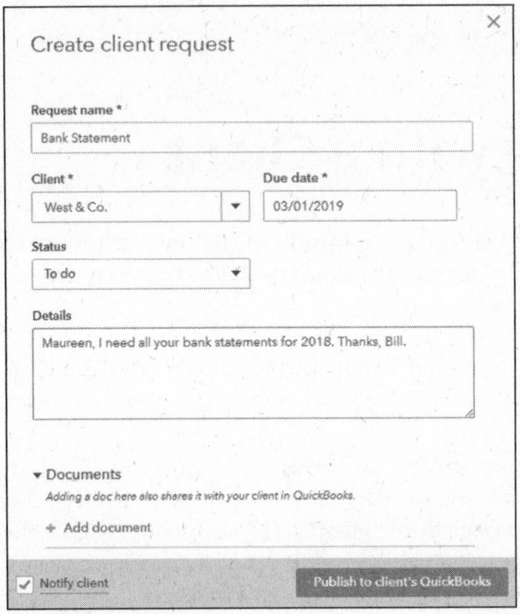

FIGURE 14-9:
Use this panel to communicate with a QBO client in a general way.

If you selected Notify Client in Step 7, QBOA displays a preview of the message you will be sending to your client (see Figure 14-10). After you review it, click Publish and Send Email.

When your client opens his QBO company, he can click My Accountant in the Navigation pane to see the message and respond to it (see Figure 14-11).

To respond to the message using QBO, the client clicks the message on the My Accountant page to display a panel like the one shown in Figure 14-12, where the client can write a message and attach any needed documents.

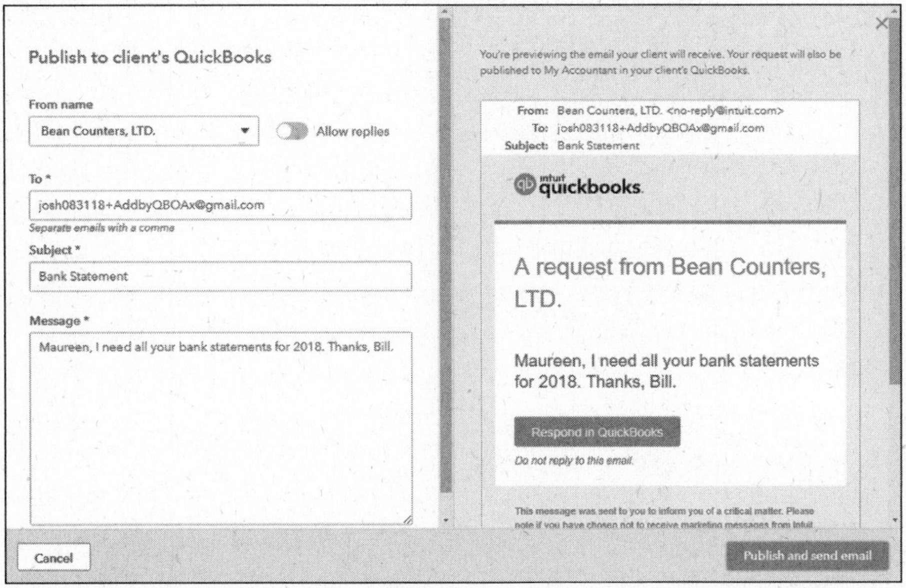

FIGURE 14-10:
A preview of a
Client Request
message.

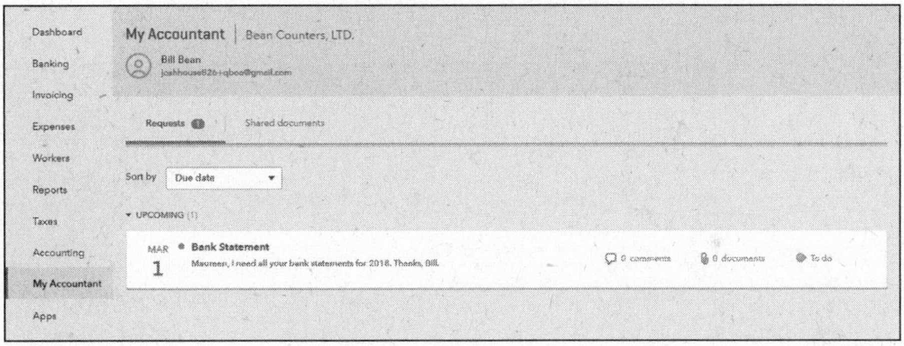

FIGURE 14-11:
A Client Request
in a client's QBO
company.

Documents can be no larger than 30MB.

Once you receive a document from a client, you can retrieve it in QBOA. Click Clients from the Navigation pane and, in the Client list, click the name of the client. QBOA opens the client's Details page, where you click the Shared Documents tab shown in Figure 14-13.

From there, you can download the document or click the link in the Request column to view/update the original request. Any changes you make appear on the Work tab.

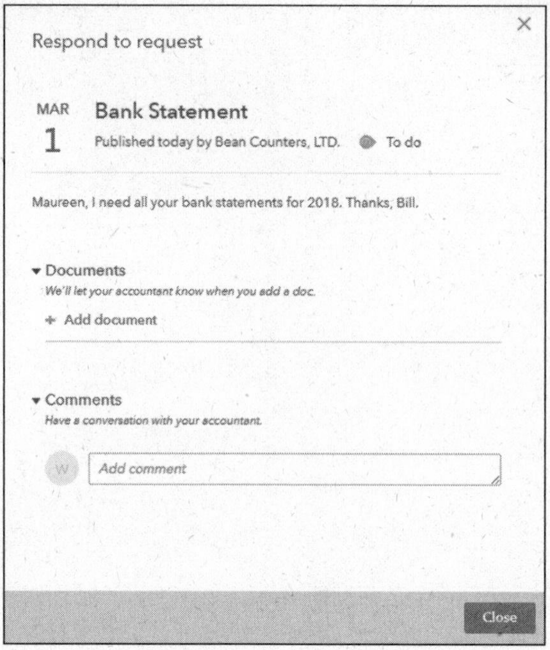

FIGURE 14-12:
The panel your client uses to respond to a Client Request you generated.

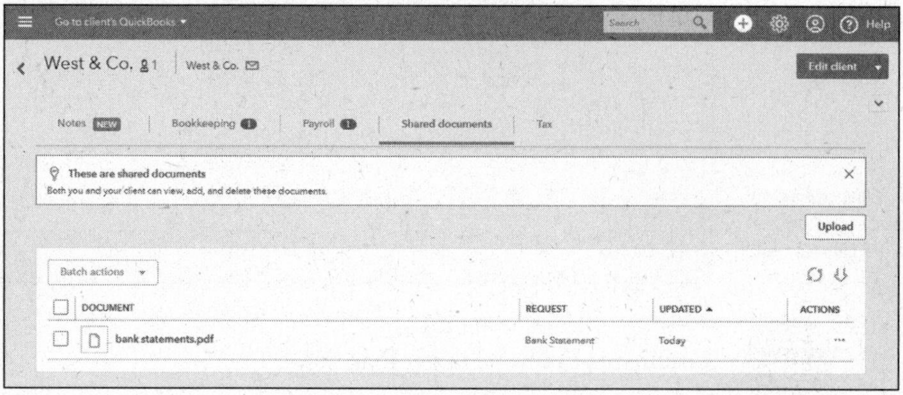

FIGURE 14-13:
The Shared Documents page in a client QBO company after an accountant receives a client's documents.

Chapter **15**

Using Accountant Tools

Accountant tools are available to anybody who opens a client QBO company from QBOA.

You can become a user in a QBO company in one of two ways:

» As described in Chapter 12, your client can invite you to be the accountant user on his account. But each QBO company can have only two accountant users.

» As described in Chapter 11, the master administrator of the QBOA account can set up users. Any user established by the master administrator can log in to QBOA, open any client QBO company for which the user has privileges, and use the tools found on the Accountant Tools menu that I describe in this chapter.

In addition to the tools found on the Accountant Tools menu, this chapter covers reporting and paying sales tax — an activity that accountants often perform for their clients, so I'll start off with that information — and using QBOA's Work Flow feature.

Reporting and Paying Sales Taxes

You or your client can manage and pay sales tax. Open any client QBO company and, in the Navigation bar on the left, click Taxes and then Sales Tax to display the Sales Tax Center. On the Sales Tax Center page you'll see all sales tax returns that are due, including any that are overdue. To file and pay a particular return, click the View Return button on the right side of the page beside the return you want to file. QBO displays a page similar to the one shown in Figure 15-1.

The first time QBO displays the Sales Tax Center, you are prompted to set up sales taxes; a wizard walks you through the process.

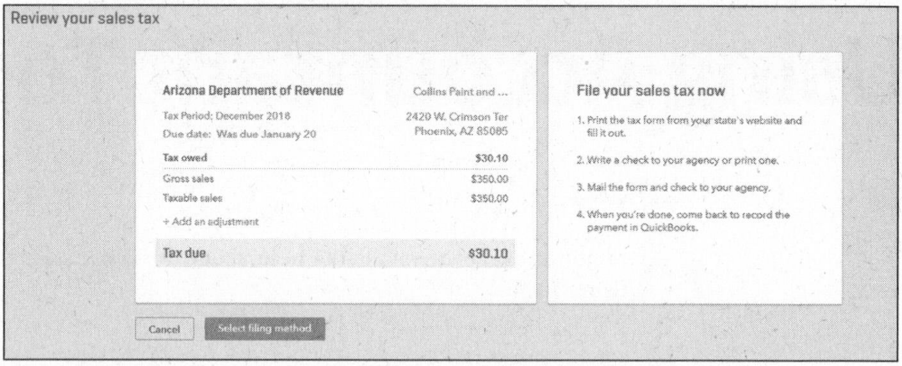

Review your sales tax

Arizona Department of Revenue		Collins Paint and ...
Tax Period: December 2016		2420 W. Crimson Ter
Due date: Was due January 20		Phoenix, AZ 85085
Tax owed	**$30.10**	
Gross sales	$350.00	
Taxable sales	$350.00	
+ Add an adjustment		
Tax due	**$30.10**	

File your sales tax now

1. Print the tax form from your state's website and fill it out.
2. Write a check to your agency or print one.
3. Mail the form and check to your agency.
4. When you're done, come back to record the payment in QuickBooks.

Cancel   Select filing method

FIGURE 15-1:
Reviewing a sales tax return.

If you need to add a sales tax adjustment, click the Add an Adjustment link and, in the panel that appears on the right side of the screen, provide a reason for the adjustment, select an account and an amount for the adjustment, and click the Add button in the lower right corner of the Add an Adjustment panel.

When QBO redisplays the Review Your Sales Taxes page, click the Select Filing Method button to continue the payment and filing process; QBO displays the Select a Filing Method page, where you can choose E-File if it's available. If not, click the File Manually button. In my example E-File was not available, so choosing File Manually produced the screen shown in Figure 15-2.

QBO calculates and displays the amount due to your sales tax agency, and you can confirm the amount or change it. Be aware that, although you can change the amount due that QBO supplies, you risk underpaying your sales tax liability. To see the details of the amount due, click the Report link in the first step, "Download Your Full Report," to view the Sales Tax Liability report, which breaks down the tax amount due.

File manually

Total tax payment	$30.10
Tax due	**$30.10**

1. Download your full report.
2. Fill out the tax form on your tax agency's website.
3. Send the form and payment to your agency.
4. Don't forget to record the payment!

Record payment

Tax amount	Payment date	Bank account
30.10	01/31/2019	10100 Checking ▼

Cancel   Record payment

To complete the payment and sales tax filing, supply a Payment Date and a bank account from which to pay the liability, and click the Record Payment button.

If you need to set up sales taxes in your client's QBO company, see Chapter 4 for details on the process.

TIP

Managing Your Practice

Before diving into using the QBOA tools available while you work in a client's QBO company, take a look at the Work page in the Navigation pane, which functions as a practice management tool. Having such a tool in QBOA enables you to centralize practice management, because all team members in your firm have access to the Work page in QBOA.

It's important to understand that your clients don't see the Work page — it is available only in QBOA, so only you and your team members see the Work page. Further, the information each team member sees on the Work page is specific only to his clients — the ones to whom your team member has access.

REMEMBER

The Work page enables you to track what needs to happen for both your clients and your own firm. And, although the terminology used on the Work page refers to projects, bear in mind that these projects are entirely different from the projects your clients can create in QBO.

Understanding the Grid view

When you click Work in the Navigation bar, QBOA displays the default Grid view of the page (see Figure 15-3). The Grid view displays task cards organized into date ranges (Due Today, This Week, Next Week, and in the Next 30 days).

The client name

The project associated with this task

The task name

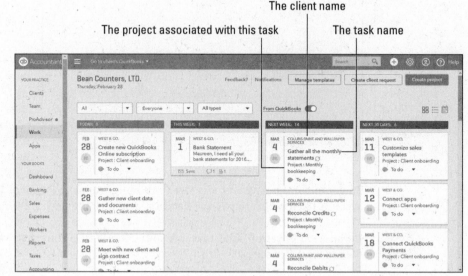

FIGURE 15-3:
The Grid view of the Work page in QBOA.

Each task card of a given project identifies the client for whom the work needs to be done (or, your own firm, if the project isn't for a client) as well as the project name. Uniquely on each task card, you'll find the task name (refer to Figure 15-3).

You can control some of what you see on the Grid view of the Work page. For example, you can filter the page to display information for all clients, your firm, particular clients, or specific team members. The Work feature also uses data in client QBO companies to automatically display deadlines you need to meet and things you need to do, such as payroll deadlines and reconciling connected banking transactions. If you don't want to see this automatically created information, you can click the From QuickBooks slider.

REMEMBER

At the present time, the Work feature automatically suggests actions to take associated only with QBO; the Work feature doesn't connect to other products like ProConnect Tax Online.

Because the Grid view organizes tasks by due date, you won't see any type of visual connection between tasks; that is, no lines appear, connecting tasks to each other, because the Grid view isn't a flow chart.

Grid view isn't the only view available on the Work page; you can read about List view and Calendar view later in this chapter, after I discuss creating projects and tasks.

Creating projects and tasks

As described in Chapter 14, you can use the Work page to create client requests. With respect to practice management, you use the Work page to create *projects*, which represent things that need to be done. You break each project down into *tasks*, which are subsets of the project that provide more detail about what needs to be done to complete the project. You create tasks as part of a project, but you can assign different team members to different tasks on the same project. Projects are typically general things you need to accomplish by a specified deadline date, and tasks describe the specific things you need to do to complete the project.

As you create a project, you assign a deadline date to the project, and you assign due dates to each task in the project. You identify the client with whom the project is associated and the team member who has responsibility for the project. Or, you can specify that the project is an internal one that affects your firm but not any of your clients.

TIP

QBOA contains project templates that help you quickly create commonly needed projects, such as Monthly Bookkeeping or Client Onboarding. When you use one of these templates, QBOA creates not only the project but all the tasks associated with the project. You can then edit the project as needed.

Creating a project

To try to keep this information as easy to follow as possible, I'm going to cover creating projects separately from creating tasks — even though you can, and probably will, create tasks when you create projects. But, I'll take this in bite-size chunks. To create a project, follow these steps:

1. **Click Work in the Navigation pane.**

   QBOA displays the Work page for your firm.

2. **Click Create Project in the upper right corner of the page (refer to Figure 15-3).**

   QBOA opens a panel on the right side of the page that you use to create a project (see Figure 15-4).

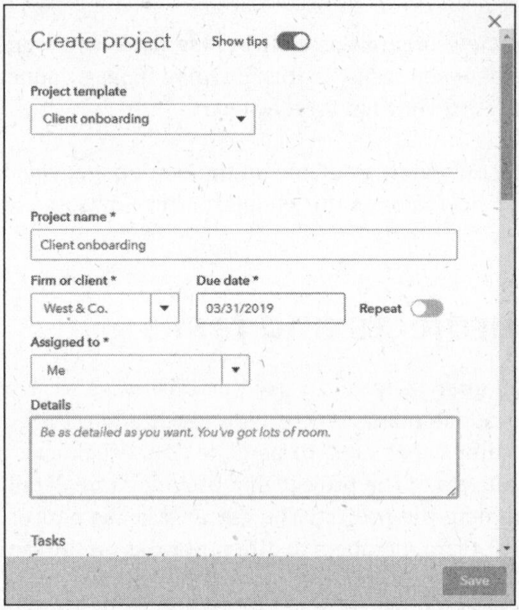

FIGURE 15-4:
Creating a project using a template.

3. **If your project falls into one of the predefined template categories of Bi-weekly Payroll, Client Onboard, Monthly Bookkeeping, or Yearly taxes, select the template from the Project Template list box.**

    QBOA adds the tasks associated with the project template to the project, assigning each task a due date of "tomorrow." You can edit and reorganize the tasks; see the next section, "Working with tasks."

4. **Fill in a name for the project.**

    If you selected a project template, QBOA fills in the project name using the project template name.

5. **From the Firm or Client list box, select the QBO client with whom the project is associated.**

    If the project applies only to your firm and no client, select My Firm.

6. **Set a project due date.**

    The due date you set for the project is a constraint; if you add tasks to the project, you won't be able to set due dates for the tasks that occur after the end of the project.

7. **Using the Assigned To list box, assign the project to one of your team members.**

    You can add details for the project if you want.

TIP

Some projects, like reconciling a bank statement, need to repeat on a regular basis; for those projects, click the Repeat slider to set up the timeframe QBOA should use to repeat the project.

Working with tasks

Now that you've created a project, you can work with the project's tasks. You can

>> Add and delete tasks,

>> Change the due dates QBOA assigns to the tasks, and

>> Reorganize the order of tasks in a project.

1. **Add a task to a project by clicking the Add a Task button at the bottom of the list of tasks.**

   QBOA displays a form for task information (see Figure 15-5).

2. **Supply a task name, due date, the team member to whom you want to assign the task, and any pertinent details about the task, such as the QBO commands used to accomplish the task.**

   There is no limit to the number of tasks you can create.

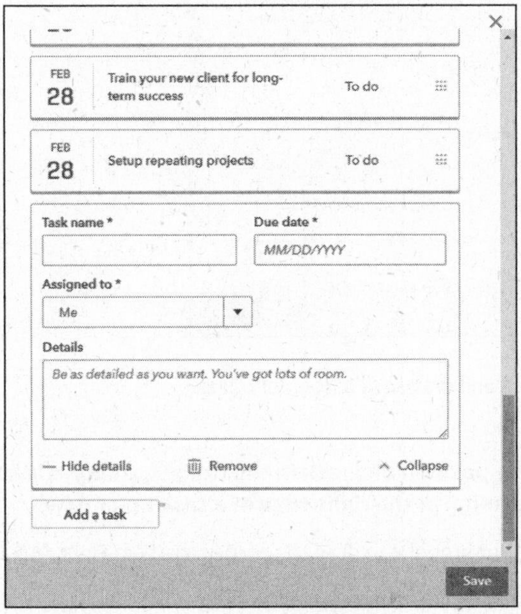

<table>
<tr><td>FEB
28</td><td>Train your new client for long-term success</td><td>To do</td><td>⠿</td></tr>
</table>

<table>
<tr><td>FEB
28</td><td>Setup repeating projects</td><td>To do</td><td>⠿</td></tr>
</table>

Task name *

Due date *
MM/DD/YYYY

Assigned to *
Me ▼

Details
Be as detailed as you want. You've got lots of room.

— Hide details   🗑 Remove   ∧ Collapse

Add a task

Save

FIGURE 15-5:
Supply a task name and due date, and assign it to a team member of the firm.

3. **To work with a different task, collapse the one you're currently working on by clicking Collapse in the lower right corner of the task card.**

   You don't save individual tasks; instead, you save the project, which saves the task information.

4. **To delete a task or change its information, click the task.**

   QBOA displays the details of the task (see Figure 15-6).

   - To change the task, simply supply the new information.
   - To delete the task, click the Remove link.

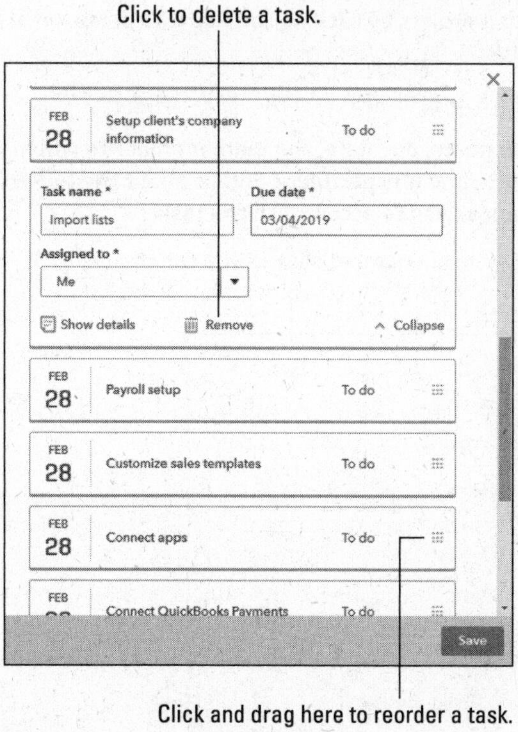

Click to delete a task.

FIGURE 15-6:
Click a task to edit
or delete it, or
drag it to
reorder it.

Click and drag here to reorder a task.

5. **To change the position of a task in the project, collapse it and then drag the square symbol at the right edge of a task up or down.**

   You can see the symbol you drag to reorder a task in Figure 15-6.

6. **Click Save to save the project and its tasks.**

   QBOA redisplays the Work page, and your new projects and tasks appear on it.

Updating task status

As you make progress on a task, you can update its status directly from the Grid view of the Work page. Click the down arrow on a task card to change its status (see Figure 15-7).

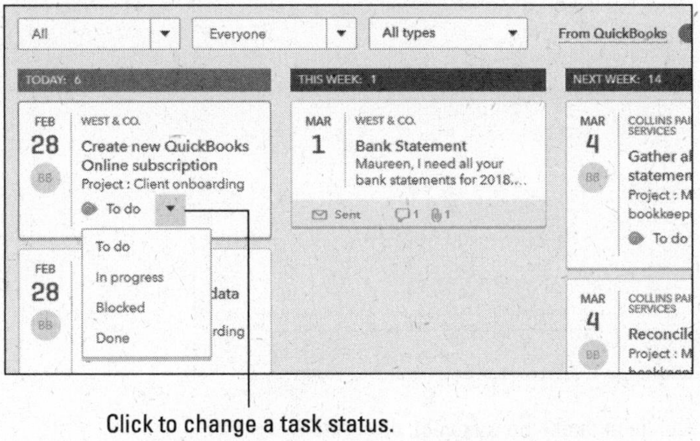

FIGURE 15-7:
Use the down arrow on a task or project card to display the list of available statuses.

Click to change a task status.

Tasks can have a status of To Do, In Progress, Blocked, or Done. You use the Blocked status when something is stopping you from completing a task.

Editing and deleting project information

You can edit any project or task except those created automatically from a QBO company — you can only hide or display those automatically created tasks using the From QuickBooks slider.

Regardless of the view you're displaying on the Work page, to edit any project or task you created, click any task in the project. QBOA then opens the Edit Project panel on the right side of the screen and displays the information of the task you clicked.

You can change the project information by editing the top portion of the Edit Project panel. You can delete any project from the Edit Project panel by clicking the trash can icon in the lower left corner of the panel (see Figure 15-8).

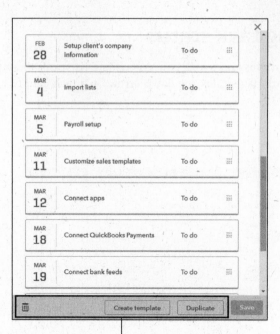

FIGURE 15-8:
Delete or
duplicate a
project or create
a template
from it.

Delete or duplicate a project, or create a
template of it using these tools.

Many of the projects you create are similar to each other, so save yourself some work and duplicate an existing project to create a new one. You also can use an existing project to create a template for subsequent similar projects. From the Edit Project panel, duplicate the project by clicking the Duplicate button. To create a template from the project, click Create Template.

Although you can edit project and task information, you cannot change a project into a task or a task into a project.

To close the Edit Project panel, click the X in the upper right corner of the panel.

Working in the List view

The Grid view of the Work page — the default view shown earlier in Figures 15-3 and 15-7 — is limited in what it can display because the cards take up quite bit of screen real estate. You can view your projects and tasks in List view, as shown in Figure 15-9, by clicking the List View button in the upper right corner of the Work page (just below the Create Project button).

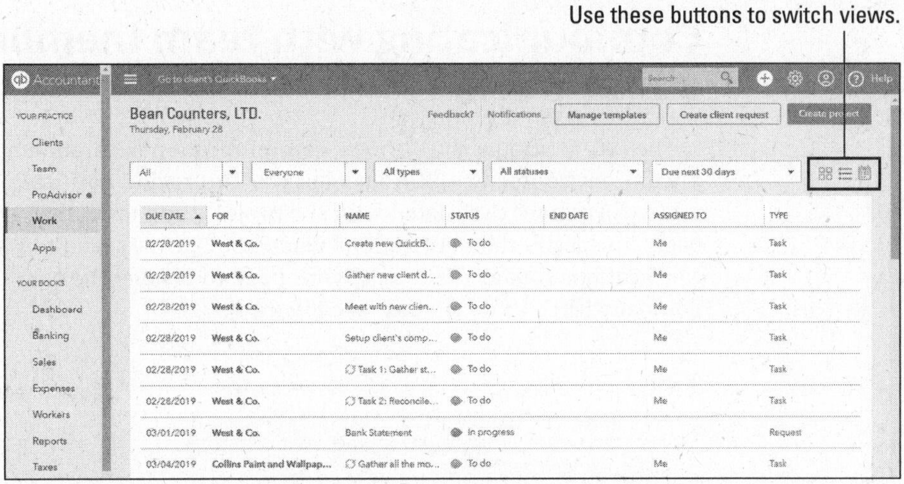

Use these buttons to switch views.

FIGURE 15-9:
The Work page in
List view.

From this view, you have additional filters available to you. In addition to filtering for a client, a team member, and a type of work (project, task, or client request), you also can filter by status and set a date range of interest to you. And, you can still edit any project or task; simply click anywhere on the project's or task's line to display the Edit Project panel shown earlier in Figure 15-8.

Working in the Calendar view

The Calendar view, shown in Figure 15-10, displays the tasks due for any selected date. On the calendar, you'll see the number of tasks due on each date. When you click a date, QBOA uses the right side of the Calendar view to show the tasks due on that date.

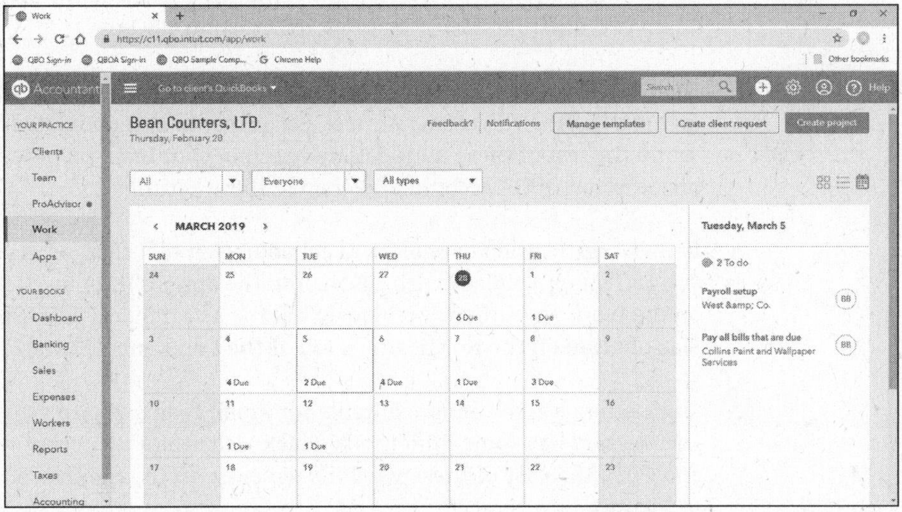

FIGURE 15-10:
Calendar view
presents project
tasks by due date.

Communicating with team members about work

At the risk of stating the obvious, communication is paramount when working in a team environment. QBOA enables you to provide notifications by email for a variety of actions associated with the projects and tasks that appear on the Work page. To specify the notifications you want QBOA to send to your team, click the Notifications link at the top of Work page to display the Notifications tab of the Company Settings dialog box (see Figure 15-11).

Click to edit Work notifications.

Company	**Work notifications**		
Notifications			
	Email	Stay up-to-date on your work. When you get a new work assignment, or when someone makes a change to your projects or tasks, we send a notification to your inbox at:	
Sales		joshhouse826+qboa@gmail.com	
Expenses		New assignments	On
Payments		Due dates	On
		Details	Off
Advanced		Status	Off
		Name	Off
		Assignees	Off
		Deletions	Off
	Slack	Get new work assignments, status updates, and due date reminders, right in Slack. Use any channel, or set up private channels. New to Slack? Learn More	Connect Work to Slack

FIGURE 15-11: Set up email notifications for team members regarding work.

Click to connect QBOA to Slack.

Click the pencil in the upper right corner of the Email section to turn on and off email notifications for various actions that take place on the Work page. Click Save when you finish, followed by Done to return to QBOA.

TIP

Each team member controls the notifications he receives. By default, each team member gets notifications of new assignments and due dates by default, but, to set up the rest of these notifications, each of your team members needs to log into his personal QBOA account and change these settings.

If your organization uses Slack, a collaboration tool that helps your team connect, you can integrate Slack with QBOA. Add the app to QBOA by clicking Connect Now on the Work page. If you previously hid the ad for Slack, click the Connect Work to Slack button on the Notifications tab of the Company Settings dialog box.

Slack offers a free version suitable for small teams wanting to try out Slack; the free version has some limitations. Slack also offers two "pay" versions: Standard and Plus; the cost of these versions depends on the number of active Slack users per month.

Facilitating Accountant Activities

Accountants often need to reclassify transactions, examine voided and deleted transactions, write off invoices, and perform other activities. QBOA contains tools to make performing these activities easy.

To view and use the tools QBOA makes available to accountants, open any client QBO company. Then, on the QBOA toolbar, click the Accountant Tools button (the one that looks like a suitcase). QBOA displays the Accountant Tools menu, shown in Figure 15-12.

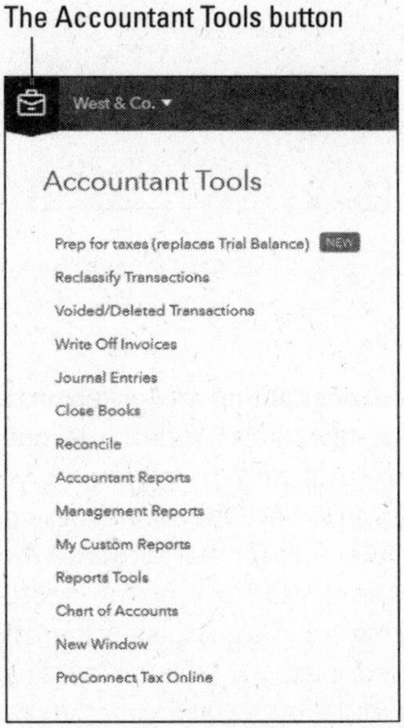

The Accountant Tools button

Accountant Tools

Prep for taxes (replaces Trial Balance) [NEW]
Reclassify Transactions
Voided/Deleted Transactions
Write Off Invoices
Journal Entries
Close Books
Reconcile
Accountant Reports
Management Reports
My Custom Reports
Reports Tools
Chart of Accounts
New Window
ProConnect Tax Online

FIGURE 15-12:
The Accountant Tools menu contains commands specifically designed to aid the accountant.

Understanding the Prep for Taxes page

You use the Prep for Taxes tool to adjust and review accounts before preparing the client's taxes. The Prep for Taxes page replaces the Trial Balance page. Personally, I feel the title "Prep for Taxes" title is a bit misleading; the page is well-designed to help you find accounts that need year-end adjustments and easily make them by providing a link to the Journal Entry transaction. I feel the name really isn't clear, and, if asked, I would have suggested the page be named "Make Year-End Adjustments," for the sake of clarity. But, no matter.

The page you see initially presents a working trial balance like the one shown in Figures 15-13.

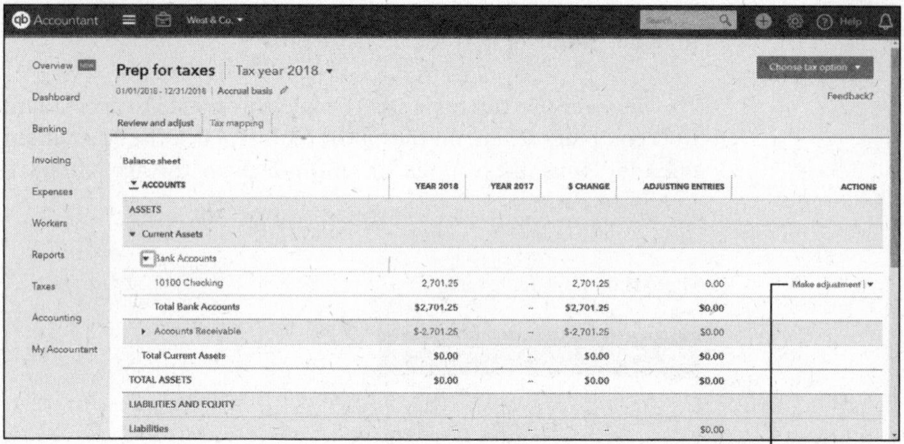

FIGURE 15-13:
The Review and
Adjust tab of the
Prep for Taxes
page.

Click here to make an adjusting journal entry.

>> **The values in the Unadjusted Balance column are locked on the page to protect the integrity of the data.** If you click the carats beside the various headings (that is, Current Assets, Bank Accounts, and so on; refer to Figure 15-13), you'll find that you can click the Make Adjustment link in the Actions column beside an appropriate account to create adjusting journal entries for that account. When you click the link, QBOA opens a journal entry window, where you can record the adjusting entry — and QBOA automatically selects the Is Adjusting Journal Entry? check box. Once you save the entry, QBOA redisplays the Prep for Taxes page and indicates that you made a change (see Figure 15-14). If you accept the change, QBOA updates the Prep for Taxes page to incorporate your adjustment; in addition, QBOA changes the Adjusted Balance column to reflect your adjustment.

>> **You can click any dollar value that appears as a link to view a report of all transactions that make up that balance.** From the report, you can drill down to a particular transaction and, if necessary, change it. After you save the transaction and redisplay the report, you can click the Back to Prep for Taxes link at the top of the report page to redisplay the Prep for Taxes page. Once again, QBOA indicates that you made a change, and, after you accept the change, updates the Prep for Taxes page to incorporate the change.

> » **You can use the down arrow in the Actions column to add notes and attach documents to a particular line.** This helps you remember why you made a particular adjustment.

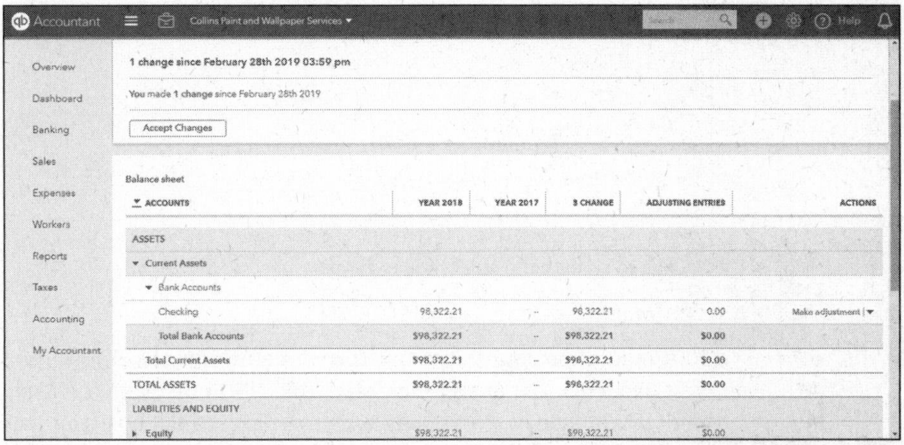

FIGURE 15-14:
The Prep for Taxes page after you make an adjusting entry and before you accept the entry.

If you use ProConnect Tax Online, Intuit's cloud-based tax preparation software, to prepare a client's tax return, then you'll want to make sure that your client's accounts are mapped properly to lines on tax forms. The Prep for Taxes feature automatically maps most account balances to lines on tax forms you'll file for corporations using IRS Form 1120 (for corporations) or 1120s, partnerships that use IRS Form 1065, nonprofits that use IRS Form 990, and sole proprietorships using IRS Form 1040. For other business organization types, you can manually assign accounts to tax form lines. You also can manually assign lines on tax forms for accounts the tool doesn't recognize, and you can change tax line assignments as needed. Note that the View Tax Return button appears unavailable if you have not yet selected a tax form for the QBO client company.

Click the Tax Mapping tab on the Prep for Taxes page to see the page you use to map last year's client QBO company information directly into tax forms (see Figure 15-15).

TIP

If you haven't yet selected a tax form for the QBO company, the first time you select the Tax Mapping tab, you'll be prompted to select one. Or, you can click the Edit button (the pencil) beside the selected form at the bottom left side of the Prep for Taxes page and select a tax form; refer to Figure 15-15.

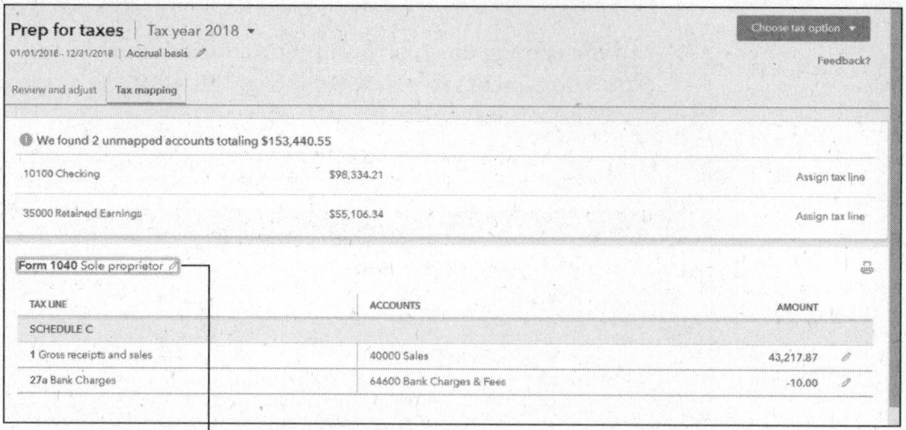

Prep for taxes | Tax year 2018 ▾

Choose tax option ▾

01/01/2018 - 12/31/2018 | Accrual basis 🖉

Feedback?

Review and adjust   **Tax mapping**

ⓘ We found 2 unmapped accounts totaling $153,440.55

| 10100 Checking | $98,334.21 | Assign tax line |
| 35000 Retained Earnings | $55,106.34 | Assign tax line |

Form 1040 Sole proprietor 🖉

TAX LINE	ACCOUNTS	AMOUNT
SCHEDULE C		
1 Gross receipts and sales	40000 Sales	43,217.87 🖉
27a Bank Charges	64600 Bank Charges & Fees	-10.00 🖉

Click to change the selected tax form.

FIGURE 15-15:
The Tax Mapping tab of the Trial Balance page.

To assign an account to a tax form line or edit the line to which an account is assigned, click the Assign Tax Line link. QBOA displays the Assign Tax Line panel on the right side of the screen, which contains a list box from which you select the appropriate tax form line, and then click Save.

When you finish reviewing the Prep for Taxes page and making adjustments to entries, you can click the Choose Tax Option button in the upper right corner of the page and then click Create New Return or Update Existing Return (as appropriate) to transfer the information to ProConnect Tax Online and generate a tax return. You don't pay anything to use the Prep for Taxes feature; you pay only when you print or E-file a return from ProConnect Tax Online.

REMEMBER

If you don't use ProConnect Tax Online or you are not the tax preparer, you have the option to export the adjustments to a comma-separated values (CSV) file (readable by Excel) so that you can import them into a separate application. Choose the Export CSV File option on the Choose Tax Return button.

Reclassifying transactions

When you choose Reclassify Transactions from the Accountant Tools menu, the Reclassify Transactions page appears (see Figure 15-16). You can use this page to reclassify transactions without worrying about the company's closing date.

You use the information in the Accounts section on the left side of the page and the Transactions section on the right side of the page to filter for the date range and type of accounts (Profit and Loss or Balance Sheet) you want to consider. You then select an account on the left side of the page, and QBOA displays transactions that meet the criteria on the right side of the page. You can reclassify, individually or as a group, transactions that display a green circle.

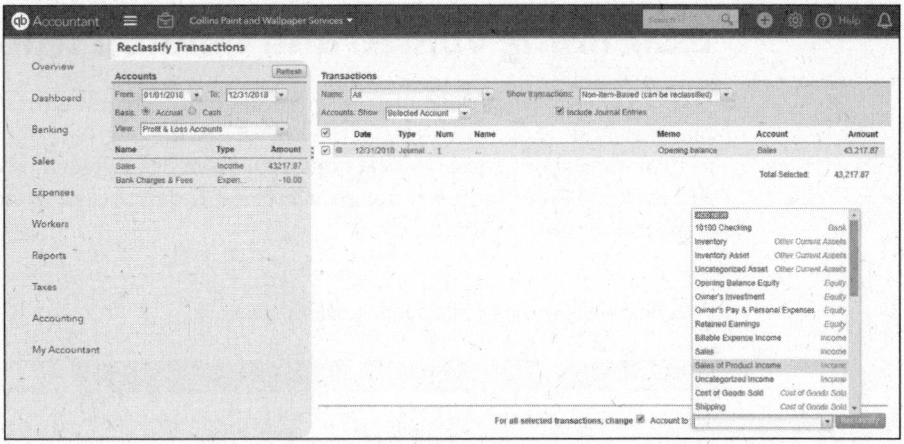

FIGURE 15-16:
Use this page to reclassify transactions.

Follow these steps to reclassify transactions:

1. **On the left side of the page, set the date range you want to consider, along with the accounting basis.**

2. **From the View list box, select the type of accounts you want to consider — Profit & Loss accounts or Balance Sheet accounts.**

3. **Click an account in the list below the View list box to examine that account's transactions.**

   The transactions in the account appear on the right side of the page.

4. **Above the list of transactions on the right side of the page, set filters to display the types of transactions that you might consider reclassifying.**

   You can make changes to transactions that display green circles. You can also click a transaction to open it in its transaction window and then make changes to it.

5. **To change several transactions simultaneously, select them by clicking the check box beside them.**

6. **Below the list of transactions, select the For Select Transactions, Change check box.**

7. **From the Account To list, specify a different account.**

   If Class Tracking is turned on, you'll also see a field to change the assigned class, the same way you can change an account.

8. **Click the Reclassify button.**

Examining voided and deleted transactions

You can click Voided/Deleted Transactions on the Accountant Tools menu to display the Audit Log. The default view of the Audit Log (see Figure 15-17) shows information about those transactions that have been voided or deleted. But, you can click the Filter button to set a variety of different filters to view other types of transactions and events.

Click display more than voided or deleted transactions.

Writing off invoices

Choosing Write Off Invoices from the Accountant Tools menu displays the Write Off Invoices page, which enables you to view invoices you might want to write off, and then write them off to an account of your choice. At the top of the page, you set filters to display the invoices you want to review. Select the age of the invoices to view those

>> Greater than 180 days

>> Greater than 120 days

>> In the current accounting period

>> In a custom date range you set

You also can set a balance limit.

As shown in Figure 15-18, QBOA displays the date, age, invoice number, customer name, original invoice amount, and the amount still due on the invoice. To write off any invoices, click the check box beside them. Then, at the bottom of the page, select the account you want to use to write off the invoices and click the Preview and Write Off button.

WARNING

The Write Off feature does not make adjusting entries in the current period; instead, it makes adjustments in the period in which the transaction was originally created — and can negatively affect closed periods. To write off an item in a closed period, see this article online: `https://community.intuit.com/ articles/1145951-write-off-bad-debt`.

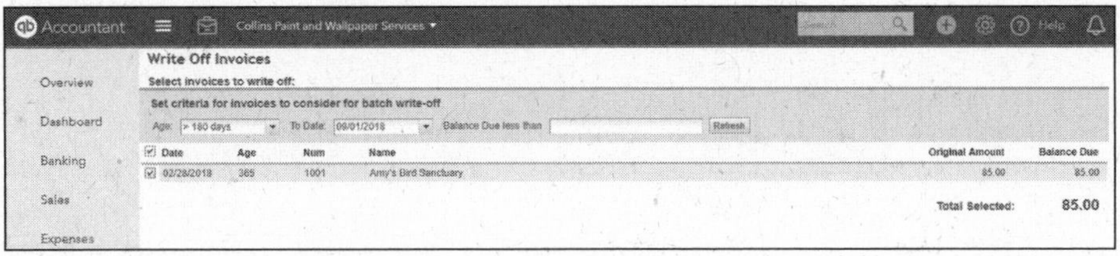

FIGURE 15-18:
Writing off
invoices.

QBOA displays the Confirm Write Off dialog box shown in Figure 15-19. If the information in the dialog box is correct, click Write Off. Otherwise, click Cancel.

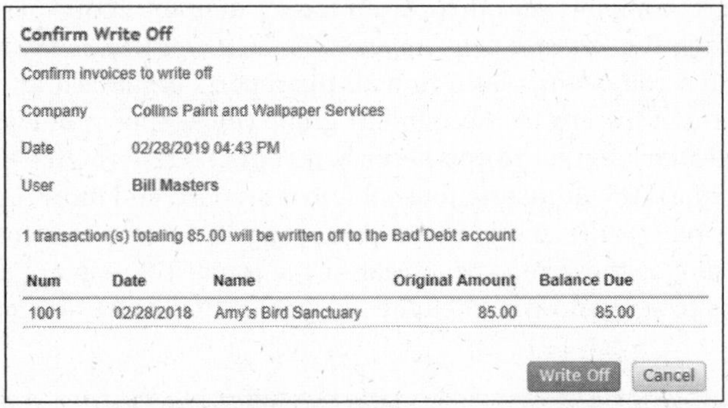

FIGURE 15-19:
Confirm that you
want to write off
the selected
invoices.

Closing the books

You use the Close Books command on the Accountant Tools menu to display the Advanced page of the QBO company's Account and Settings dialog box, shown in Figure 15-20. You can click anywhere in the Accounting section to edit the fields in that section, which include the closing date for the books.

You can set a closing date and then allow changes prior to the closing date after QBO issues a warning, or you can require a password to enter changes prior to the closing date. Click Done to save your changes.

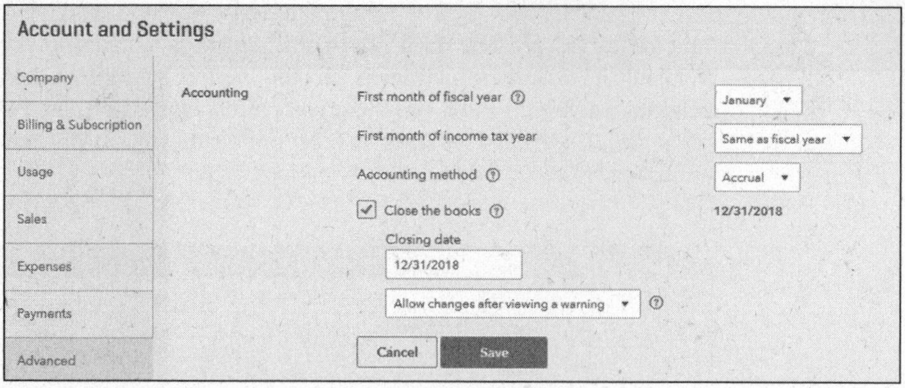

FIGURE 15-20:
Setting a
closing date.

Reviewing reports

Reports in QBOA work the same way as reports in QBO; see Chapter 10 for details.

But, QBOA contains some reports of particular interest to accountants. If you open a client QBO company and then, from the Accountant Tools menu, click Accountant Reports, the Reports page appears. Reports marked as favorites appear first and, if you scroll down, you'll find all the reports organized into various groups. The Reports in the For My Accountant group (most appear in Figure 15-21) might be of particular interest to you because it contains reports like the Adjusted Trial Balance report, the Adjusting Journal Entries report, and more. I couldn't show all of them; when you're checking out these reports, be sure to scroll down the page. To make any of these reports appear at the top of the Reports page (so that you don't need to scroll down), click the star beside the report to mark it as a favorite.

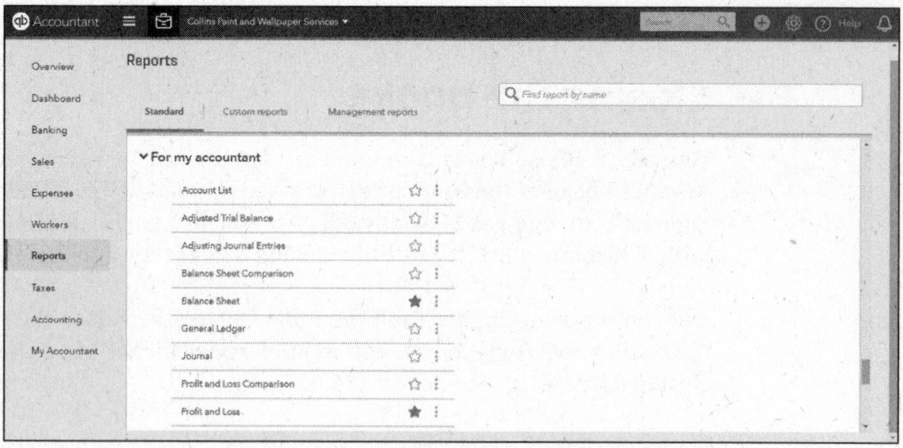

FIGURE 15-21:
Accountant-
oriented reports
available in
QBOA.

If you choose Management Reports from the Accountant Tools menu (or if you click the Management Reports tab that appears on the Reports page shown in Figure 15-21), QBOA lists two customized management-style reports: Basic Company Financials and Expanded Company Financials. Both reports display a collection of reports, complete with an elegant cover page and a table of contents. Click the View link in the Action column for either report to view them onscreen, or download them to your computer as PDF files.

The Expanded Company Financials report contains the P&L, Balance Sheet, Statement of Cash Flows, and the A/R Aging Detail and A/P Aging Detail reports. The Basic Company Financials report contains all reports except the Aging Detail reports. If you click the down arrow in the Actions column and then click Edit, you can edit either report package to add or delete reports and modify the appearance of pages in the report, including determining whether pages such as the table of contents appear in the report. Using the same down arrow in the Action column, you can send these reports via email, export the information to PDF files or DOCX files, and make copies of them so that you can make your own set of management reports.

TIP

Copying one of these reports before you change it is a great idea; that way, you keep the original report intact but create your own version of it as well.

If you choose My Custom Reports from the Accountant Tools menu or the Custom Reports tab on the Reports page, reports you have customized and saved appear. And you can click Reports Tools on the Accountant Tools menu to set default report dates and the accounting basis. You also can see account reconciliation status for cash and credit card accounts and view and set company closing date information.

WARNING

Be aware that any changes you make using Report Tools resets all default report dates and the accounting basis, even if you run the report from the Reports screen. So, if your report comes up using an unexpected set of dates or accounting basis, check the values set under Report Tools.

Also on the Accountant Tools menu, you'll find the Reports Tools command. When you choose this command, QBOA displays the Report and Tool Defaults page, which enables you to set default dates you want to use for reports and tools in the client QBO company. These default dates don't apply to payroll reports, because Payroll is a separate product, nor do they apply to Quick Reports, which you run from the Chart of Accounts page; the Quick Reports period automatically defaults to Since 90 Days Ago.

TIP

The Report and Tool Defaults page also shows whether the books are closed and provides a button to close the books, and the page shows you the reconciliation status of bank and credit card accounts.

A brief look at other accountant tools

The Accountant Tools menu contains a few other tools that make an accountant's life easier, such as the Reconcile page; from this page, you can opt to reconcile an account you select, or you can review existing reconciliation reports. For more detail on reconciling accounts, see Chapter 8.

Also from the Accountant Tools menu, you can choose Journal Entries to display the Journal Entry window, or Chart of Accounts to display the Chart of Accounts window; I describe working in the Chart of Accounts window in Chapter 13. You also can use the New Window command described in Chapter 14 to quickly open a new window in QBOA.

Last, from the Accountant Tools menu, you can choose ProConnect Tax Online, which opens a new browser window and takes you to the Tax Hub of ProConnect Tax Online, where you can see the status of your clients' tax returns. ProConnect Tax Online connects to your QBOA account but is actually a separate product with its own menus in the Navigation bar.

4

The Part of Tens

Chapter **16**

Almost Ten Things about the Chrome Browser Interface

C hrome — officially Google Chrome — is the free web browser created by Google, Inc., an American-based multinational corporation that focuses on Internet-related products and services, such as Gmail for email, Google maps, and Google Docs, just to name a few. Most of Google's profits come from online advertising technologies.

You can use QuickBooks Online (QBO) and QuickBooks Online Accountant (QBOA) in the Chrome, Firefox, Safari, and Internet Explorer browsers. You also can use Microsoft Edge, but not to export to the QuickBooks Desktop product. In my experience, I found that QBO and QBOA work best in Chrome. If you're not familiar with Chrome or haven't worked much in it, this chapter and Chapter 17 are designed to help you become adept at using Chrome with QBO and QBOA.

This chapter focuses on helping you become familiar with the Chrome interface and make use of it. Figure 16-1 shows you how Chrome looks shortly after you install and open it; don't forget to refer back to this figure as you read the chapter.

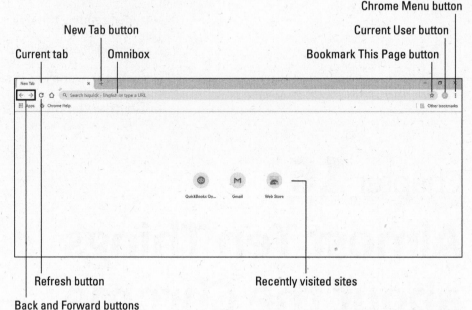

Chrome Menu button

Current User button

New Tab button

Bookmark This Page button

Current tab   Omnibox

FIGURE 16-1:
Reviewing the
Chrome interface.

Refresh button

Recently visited sites

Back and Forward buttons

TIP

If you don't already have Chrome installed on your computer, you can visit www. google.com/chrome. From this web page, you can download and install Chrome.

Understanding Users

The Current User button near the top right corner of the screen represents a Chrome user. The icon may appear generically, as you see it in Figure 16-1, or it may display your name or email address. In Chrome, you can set up multiple users, each of whom can have different Chrome settings. In this way, each person using Chrome on a single computer can customize the program, saving his or her own bookmarks, passwords, and more. See Chapter 17 to learn how to create a Chrome user.

Windows and Tabs

You can open Chrome more than once to view multiple web pages — a process called *opening a new window*.

To open a new window, first open Chrome. Then, press Ctrl+N, and a second instance of the Chrome browser appears. In Figure 16-2, I've resized Chrome's second window so that you can see both instances of Chrome. Also notice that two buttons for Chrome appear in the Windows taskbar.

Two instances of Chrome

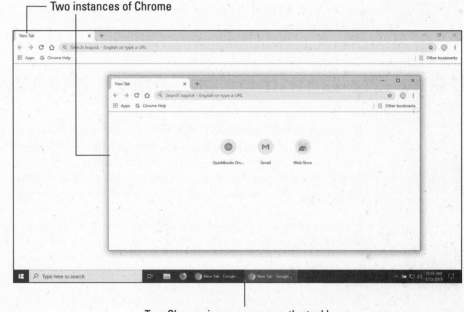

FIGURE 16-2:
When you open a new Chrome window, two instances of Chrome run simultaneously.

Two Chrome icons appear on the taskbar.

But, in most cases, you don't need to open multiple instances of Chrome; you can use Chrome's tabs to display multiple web pages while you work.

Tabs appear at the top of the Chrome window and initially display the same short-cuts you see when you open a new window. You can add a tab by clicking the New Tab button, which appears just beside the last open tab (refer to Figure 16-1). And, you can close any tab by clicking the X that appears in the tab. You also can repo-sition tabs in the Chrome window by dragging a tab's title.

In either a new window or a new tab, you navigate to a new website using the Omnibox (read on).

Using the Omnibox to Visit a Web Page

You've probably heard of the *address bar* in other browsers; Chrome refers to the text box at the top of the browser as the *Omnibox* because it's a multi-purpose box.

To visit a web page, type the address of the web page into the Omnibox and either press Enter or click the Refresh button. After you've visited a few websites, you can click the Back and Forward buttons to revisit pages you have recently visited in the order you visited them.

TIP

If you right-click or click and hold either the Back button or the Forward button, you can view a historical list of the websites you have visited. You can left-click one to return to it.

Using the Omnibox to Search the Web

Chrome uses the Omnibox to combine the functions of navigating to websites and searching the Internet; as you might expect, Chrome uses Google's search engine by default. You can type a search term into the Omnibox, and as you type, suggestions driven by Google's search technology appear. You can then click a suggestion to navigate to the associated Google search page or web page.

An icon appears to the left of each suggestion in the Omnibox; the icon indicates the type of suggestion:

>> A magnifying glass identifies the term for which you are searching.

>> Various other icons identify a suggestion as a potential page you might want to visit.

What's the Star?

You can easily save the web address of a site you visit frequently so that you don't have to type the address each time you want to visit the site. In Chrome, saving a web address is called *bookmarking*, and you click the star icon to create a bookmark for the web page you are currently viewing. You can read more about working with bookmarks, including managing bookmarks, in Chapter 17.

Examining the Chrome Menu

You can click the Chrome Menu button in the upper right corner of the Chrome window (see Figure 16-3) to view a series of commands that help you work in Chrome.

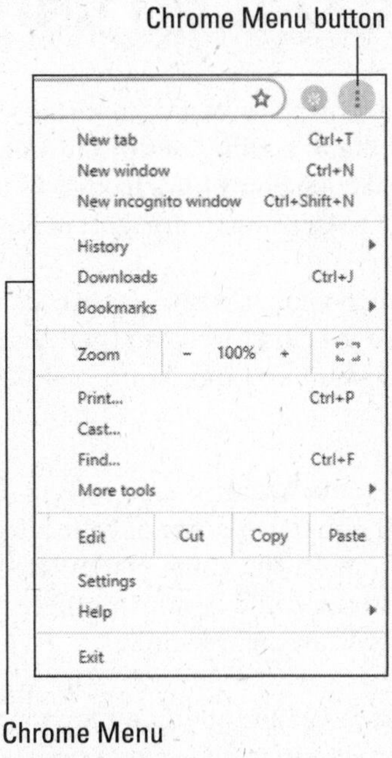

Chrome Menu button

New tab		Ctrl+T
New window		Ctrl+N
New incognito window		Ctrl+Shift+N
History		▶
Downloads		Ctrl+J
Bookmarks		▶
Zoom	– 100% +	⤢
Print...		Ctrl+P
Cast...		
Find...		Ctrl+F
More tools		▶
Edit	Cut Copy	Paste
Settings		
Help		▶
Exit		

FIGURE 16-3:
The Google
Chrome Menu.

Chrome Menu

Using options on the Chrome Menu, you can

» Work with bookmarks (described in Chapter 17).

» Reopen recently closed tabs.

» Copy and paste text.

» Save a web page.

» Clear browsing data.

» Find text on a web page.

» Print a web page.

» View files you have downloaded.

» Make changes to Chrome's settings.

The options available to you on the Chrome Menu aren't limited to the ones I've listed — there are too many for me to list them all. But, for example, if you want to see how your web browsing affects your computer's use of memory, you can choose Chrome Menu ⇨ More Tools ⇨ Task Manager.

About Signing In to (and Out of) Chrome

I'm going to repeat myself in this section because it's important for you to understand the ramifications of signing in and signing out of Chrome. Let me start by saying — emphasizing, in fact — that you don't have to sign in to use Chrome. In particular, you don't need to sign in to Chrome to use QBO or QBOA.

That said, why sign in? If you sign in, bookmarks and passwords you save, browsing history, and settings are saved to the cloud. You can then sign in to Chrome on a different computer and use all your settings from that computer or any computer.

The act of signing in can result in some negative side effects. Even though you sign out of Chrome, Chrome can still remember some of your information, making it visible to anyone who uses Chrome on the same computer. And, on a public computer, leaving traces of your activity could result in others gaining access to your personal information, email, and saved passwords.

WARNING

I strongly urge you to avoid signing in to Chrome if you are using a public computer. Remember, you don't need to sign in to Chrome to use QBO or QBOA. And, I'll be repeating this warning again in this section (editors, take note that I know I'm going to repeat myself) because it's important to the security of your financial data.

If you want to sign in to Chrome, you need a Google account. If you have a Gmail email address, you already have an account, and you can skip the section "Creating a Google account."

Creating a Google account

If you don't have a Google account, you can easily create one; creating a Google account automatically creates a Gmail email address. Once you have a Google account, you can use Google services such as Gmail, Google Docs, and Google Calendar. Follow these steps to create a Google account:

REMEMBER

If you already have a Gmail email address, you already have a Google account. Skip these steps and continue in the next section, "Signing In to Chrome." The following steps help you create a Google account and simultaneously sign in to it.

1. **Navigate to** `http://www.google.com/chrome`.

2. **Click the Sign In button in the top right corner of the page.**

3. **On the page that appears, click the More Options link and then click Create Account.**

    The More Options link appears below the box where you would ordinarily provide your email address.

4. **Provide the requested information.**

    The requested information includes your name, a username, which is a proposed Gmail email address and associated password, birth date, gender, mobile phone number, current email address, and the country in which you live. Note that your mobile phone number is actually optional.

5. **Click the Next Step button.**

6. **Scroll down and check the I agree to the Google Terms of Service and Privacy Policy box.**

    You can click the links for Terms of Service and Privacy Policy to review the statements.

7. **Click Next Step.**

    At this point, you might be prompted to verify your account using either a text message or a voice call; select a method and, when you receive the verification information, provide it onscreen. You'll see the Welcome! screen and your new Gmail address.

8. **Click Continue.**

    Google displays the page found at `www.google.com`. And, you'll be signed in to your Google account. Some new buttons you can use to navigate while signed in to your account appear in the upper right corner of the page (see Figure 16-4).

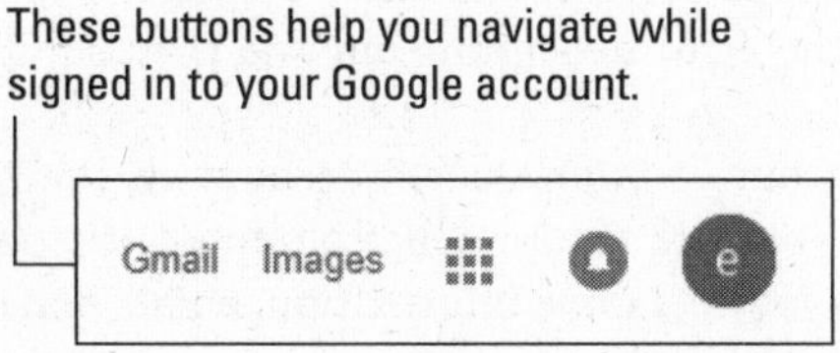

FIGURE 16-4: The buttons in the upper right corner are associated with your Google account.

These buttons help you navigate while signed in to your Google account.

Gmail   Images

Signing In to Chrome

If you sign in to the Chrome browser, bookmarks and passwords you save, browsing history, and settings are available to you from any computer. But you don't want to create a new account each time you want to sign in to Chrome, so, there must be another way to sign in, right? Right.

WARNING

Avoid signing in to Chrome if you are using a public computer, because signing out might not remove all your information, leaving it visible to anyone who uses Chrome on the computer.

To sign in to Chrome, follow these steps:

1. **Type www.google.com in the Omnibox and press Enter.**

2. **Click Sign in to Chrome in the upper right corner of the page that appears.**

   The sign-in form appears, requesting your Google Account email.

3. **Type your email address and click Next.**

4. **Type your password and click Next.**

   An icon replaces the Sign In button in the upper right corner, letting you know you are signed in to Chrome. The page looks just like the one shown previously in Figure 16-4.

REMEMBER

You can synchronize Chrome settings across your devices—a useful feature to make using Chrome easier to use on multiple devices. To turn on synchronization, click the User button at the top right portion of the Chrome window, choose Turn On Sync from the menu that appears, and follow the onscreen prompts.

Signing Out of Chrome

You should sign out of your Google account when you finish using Chrome, or when you no longer want changes you make on your computer saved to your Google account and synced to Google Chrome on your other devices. Signing out also can help if you think an error with Chrome's synchronization has occurred, and you want to try to fix the error by signing out and then signing in again.

By default, when you sign out of your Google account in the browser window, you leave behind traces of yourself. On a public computer, it's possible that other people might gain access to your personal information, email, and saved passwords.

So, if you're using a public computer and you want to eliminate all traces of your visit, sign out of Chrome and then delete saved information on the computer. Use this two-part process.

On your own private computer, deleting all traces of the user who signed in might be a bit more drastic than you want. You can opt to clear history separately and less drastically; see Chapter 17 for details on clearing history. But, if you're working on a public computer, you should delete all traces of your visit.

First, sign out of Chrome by clicking the button in the upper right corner that represents your Google account (see Figure 16-5) and then clicking the Sign Out button. Google signs you out of your Google account and Chrome.

Click to see Google account sign-in information and to sign out.

FIGURE 16-5:
Click the icon that represents your Google account and then click Sign Out.

Gmail Images

edward jones
ejxxxx263@gmail.com
Privacy

Change Google Account

Add account   Sign out

Then, follow these steps to eliminate all traces that you signed in:

1. **Click the Chrome Menu button to open the Chrome Menu (refer to Figure 16-3 for the location of the Chrome Menu button).**

2. **Click Settings.**

   The Chrome Settings page appears (see Figure 16-6).

3. **Click the Settings menu (three parallel horizontal bars at the upper left portion of the Chrome Settings page that don't appear in Figure 16-6).**

4. **Click the small downward pointing arrow beside Advanced and then click Privacy and Security.**

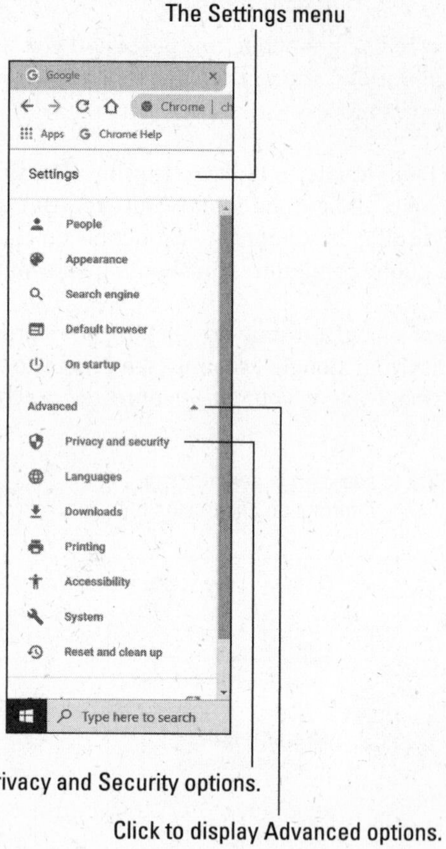

The Settings menu

FIGURE 16-6: Click to display Privacy and Security options.
The Chrome
Settings menu. Click to display Advanced options.

FIGURE 16-6:
The Chrome
Settings menu.

5. **Toward the bottom of the Privacy and Security section, click Clear Browsing History.**

The Clear Browsing Data dialog box appears (see Figure 16-7).

6. **Click the Advanced tab to view and select the items you want to delete.**

Remember, if you're working on a public computer, you want to delete everything.

7. **Click Clear Data.**

Chrome clears the elements you selected and redisplays the Settings page; you can now close the browser.

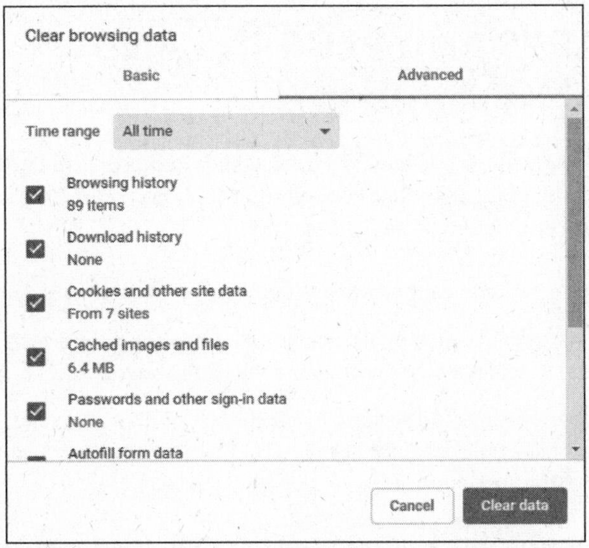

FIGURE 16-7:
Use this dialog
box to clear your
browsing data
from the local
computer.

Using the Chrome Web Store

You can enhance the capabilities of Chrome using web apps, plug-ins, and extensions such as calculators, ad blockers, or password managers. These browser-capable enhancers work like software you install on your computer, phone, or tablet, but they typically function within Chrome.

You can obtain web apps, plug-ins, and extensions from the Chrome Web Store found at `https://chrome.google.com/webstore`. The Chrome Web Store provides tools you can use to search for web apps, plug-ins, and extensions.

Web apps you install should appear on the New Tab page, from which you can launch them. You also can remove a web app by right-clicking it on the New Tab page and then clicking Remove from Chrome.

Extensions run by default when you open Chrome. You can view a list of installed extensions from the Settings page. Choose Chrome Menu⇨More Tools⇨Extensions to display the installed extensions. In Figure 16-8, you can see that I use an extension called RoboForm Password Manager, which helps me avoid reusing the same password at multiple websites.

WEB APPS AND PLUG-INS AND EXTENSIONS, OH MY!

So what exactly is a web app and how does it differ from a plug-in or extension? Honestly, for the purposes of this book, you probably don't care. But, for better or for worse, here are some simple definitions:

- Web apps run inside your browser with their own dedicated user interface.

- Extensions, unlike web apps, do not typically have a user interface. Instead, they extend the functionality of Chrome and the websites you view using Chrome.

- Plug-ins are similar to extensions in that they extend functionality by helping Chrome process special types of web content, but a plug-in affects only the specific web page that contains it.

So, as you can see, each has a technical definition that distinguishes it from the others, but, for most of us, the bottom line is this: All of them enhance the capabilities of a browser by providing some functionality that the browser does not, inherently, provide.

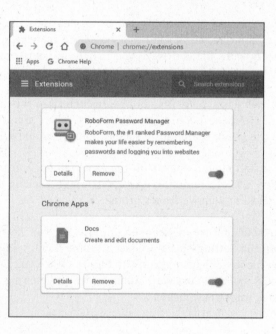

FIGURE 16-8: You can view and enable or disable extensions from the Settings page.

You might want to disable an extension if you suspect it is causing a conflict as you work; uncheck the Enabled check box beside the extension. If the extension proves to be the source of your problem, you can delete it by clicking the trash can icon beside it.

TIP

If you click the Get More Extensions link at the bottom of the Extensions page, Chrome opens a new tab and takes you to the Chrome Web Store, where it displays, by default, available extensions.

Plug-ins enable certain types of web content that browsers can't process. When Chrome encounters a plug-in on a web page, Chrome allows the plug-in to perform its function. Learn more about managing plug-ins in Chapter 17.

Selecting a Theme

You can use *themes* to change the appearance of Chrome. Themes can change the color of the Chrome window, or they can add background pictures to the entire browser. The idea here is to provide some interest to the browser page background.

You can find available themes in the Chrome Web Store; choose Chrome Menu ⇨ Settings. Click the Settings menu (the three parallel horizontal lines in the upper left corner of the page that appears) and then click Appearance. In the Appearance section, under Themes, click Open Chrome Web Store. The Chrome Web Store opens to a page where you can preview themes.

If you install a theme and then later change your mind about using it, choose Chrome Menu ⇨ Settings. Then, click the Settings menu and click Appearance. In the Appearance section, under Themes, click Reset to Default.

Chapter **17**

Ten or so Ways to Use Chrome Effectively

Chapter 16 helps you understand and work with the Chrome interface. This chapter introduces some browser tips and tricks that can make using Chrome easier and more effective both in general and specifically with QBO and QBOA.

Setting a Home Page

Many browsers sport a button that you can click to return to your *Home page* — the page that appears when you open the browser. When you open Chrome, by default, the New Tab page appears. Although Chrome doesn't show the Home page button by default, you can display it and also set a page that will appear when you click the Home page button. Note that Chrome doesn't display the page you set as the Home page when you open the browser; instead, the Home page appears when you click the Home page button.

Before you begin the following steps, make sure you know the web address of the page you want to set as your Home page:

1. **Choose Chrome Menu ➪ Settings.**

The Settings tab appears.

2. **In the Appearance section, click the Show Home button check box.**

The Home button appears between the Refresh button and the Omnibox (see Figure 17-1). At this point, Chrome defaults to opening the New Tab page whenever you click the Home button.

Home button   Show Home Button check box

FIGURE 17-1:
Adding the Home button and setting a Home page.

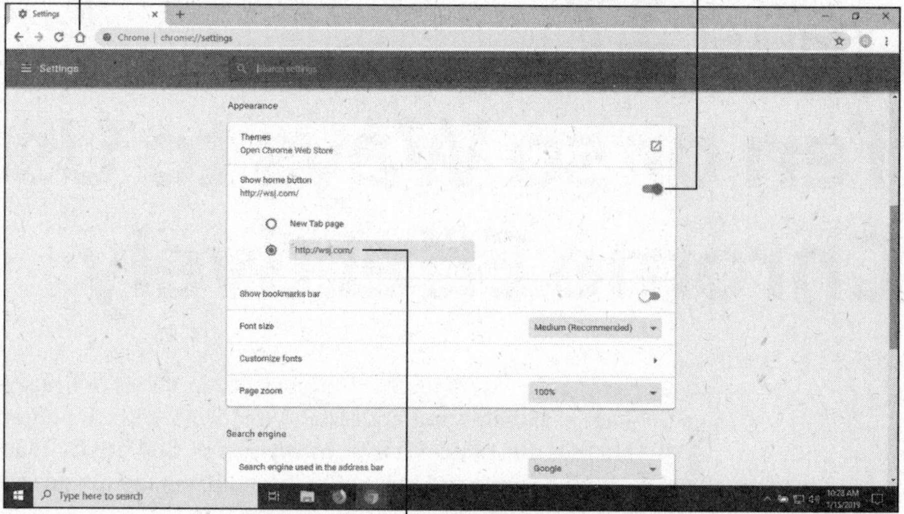

Click to set a Home page address.

3. **Click Enter Custom Web Address and type a web address.**

Close the Settings tab (there's no "save" button or option; Chrome automatically saves your changes).

When you click the Home button, Chrome displays the page you set as your Home page.

If you open certain sites every time you start Chrome, you can pin each page as a tab. See the section "Duplicating and Pinning Tabs."

Chrome and Security

Chrome includes several tools that help to keep you safe online. As you are no doubt aware, bad things can happen as you browse the Internet. You can run into *phishing* schemes, where someone tries to trick you into sharing personal or sensitive information, usually through a fake website, some of which look extremely genuine. You also can run into websites that have been hacked and contain *malware* that tries to install itself on your computer, often without your knowledge; malware usually tries to harm you and your computer in some way, from simply messing up your computer's behavior to trying to steal information.

Chrome includes technology, enabled by default, that helps protect you from phishing schemes and malware, displaying a warning whenever you visit a potentially dangerous page.

Chrome also uses a technique called *sandboxing* to open websites. Sandboxing isolates computer processes from anything else happening on the machine. If a sandboxed process crashes or becomes infected with malware, the rest of your computer remains unaffected. Each tab in Chrome opens as a separate process, completely independent of other tabs. If a website contains malware, the sandboxing technique isolates the malware to that browser tab; the malware can't jump to another Chrome tab or to your computer. You eliminate the malware threat when you close the infected website's browser tab.

Using *plug-ins,* hackers can gain access to your computer. Plug-ins are small add-on programs for browsers. Because they are add-on programs, plug-ins can become out-of-date and hackers can use them to try to introduce malware onto your computer. Adobe Flash Player is one of the most popular browser plug-ins; it is used most often to view video content. Out-of-date versions of Adobe Flash Player are also notorious for introducing malware into computers. Chrome reduces the threat that Adobe Flash Player poses by directly integrating it into Chrome. Because of this integration, updates for Adobe Flash Player are included in Chrome updates.

Chrome also regularly checks for the latest security update without any action on your part. By integrating Adobe Flash Player and regularly checking for security updates, Chrome greatly reduces the danger of malware infection.

To view the default security measures, you can follow the next steps:

1. **Choose Chrome Menu ⇨ Settings.**

   Don't change security settings unless you really know what you're doing.

2. **Scroll to the bottom of the page and click Advanced.**

   - In the Privacy and Security section, the Safe Browsing option warns you if Chrome detects that the site you're trying to visit might contain phishing or other malware.

   - The Manage Certificates option enables you to manage various HTTPS/SSL certificates and settings.

Chrome and Privacy

Chrome enables you to control the information you share online. For example, you can change your privacy settings, delete your browsing history, and browse in Incognito mode. To adjust privacy settings, follow these steps:

1. **Choose Chrome Menu ⇨ Settings.**

2. **Scroll to the bottom of the Settings page and click Advanced.**

3. **In the Privacy and Security section, click Content Settings.**

   Chrome displays a variety of changes you can make. Below, I'm going to list the settings you might be most likely to change. If I don't cover a setting you want to change, you can search for help on that setting at https://support. google.com/chrome/.

Handling cookies

You can control how Chrome handles cookies. In most cases, websites you visit place *cookies* on your computer for the purpose of recognizing your specific browser/computer combination if you return to the site. Chrome allows cookies by default, because they are typically harmless, but cookies can allow sites to track your navigation during your visit to those sites.

TIP

Third-party cookies are cookies placed on your computer by one website for some other website. To increase privacy, most people block third-party cookies. That way, only the website you visit — and not any of its affiliates — knows about you and your browsing habits.

Chrome and JavaScript

You can control whether Chrome runs JavaScript, which web developers often use to make their sites more interactive. If you disable JavaScript, you might find that some sites don't work properly.

Flash

Plug-ins such as Adobe Flash Player appear on specific websites and are used by website developers to process web content that browsers can't inherently handle. Chrome sets the Flash option for each session of Chrome and retains the setting until you quit Chrome. Chrome's recommended setting for Flash is to ask you first before allowing Flash to run.

Working in Incognito mode

If you work in *Incognito mode,* you can browse the web without recording a history of the websites you have visited and without storing cookies. Using Incognito mode doesn't make Chrome more secure; it simply enhances your privacy by preventing Chrome from keeping a record of the sites you have visited during that particular browsing session. Even in Incognito mode, you shouldn't visit websites that you wouldn't feel safe viewing in a regular Chrome window.

To use Incognito mode, choose Chrome Menu⇨New Incognito Window. A new instance of Chrome opens; notice that two buttons for Chrome appear on the Windows taskbar. The new Chrome instance displays an Incognito window like the one shown in Figure 17-2, and the Incognito icon appears in the upper right corner of the browser window, immediately to the left of the Chrome menu. You use an Incognito window the same way that you use the regular Chrome window; while you work, Chrome doesn't record a history of the sites you visit nor does Chrome allow sites to store cookies on your computer.

Incognito icon

FIGURE 17-2: An Incognito window.

To stop browsing incognito, you must close the instance of Chrome that's running incognito.

Deleting browsing history

Like all browsers, if you work in a regular Chrome window (rather than an Incognito window), Chrome keeps track of the websites you have visited during each browsing session. Browsers save your browsing history, among other reasons, to decrease the time you wait to see a web page that you have previously visited. And browser history can help you return to a website you visited previously even though you can't remember the website's address.

To view your browsing history, choose Chrome Menu ➪ History ➪ History. A page similar to the one shown in Figure 17-3 appears; your browsing history is organized by date and time, with the most recent sites you visited appearing first. You can click any entry to redisplay that web page.

You also can delete all or only part of your browsing history, typically to maintain your privacy. To clear selected sites, click the check box beside each site; the number of sites you select appears in a bar across the top of the Chrome History page. To delete the selected sites, click Delete at the right end of the bar.

To clear all (or selected portions) of your browsing history, click the Clear Browsing Data link on the left side of the Chrome History page. The dialog box shown in Figure 17-4 appears; you can choose the type of data you want to delete and the timeframe over which to delete that data.

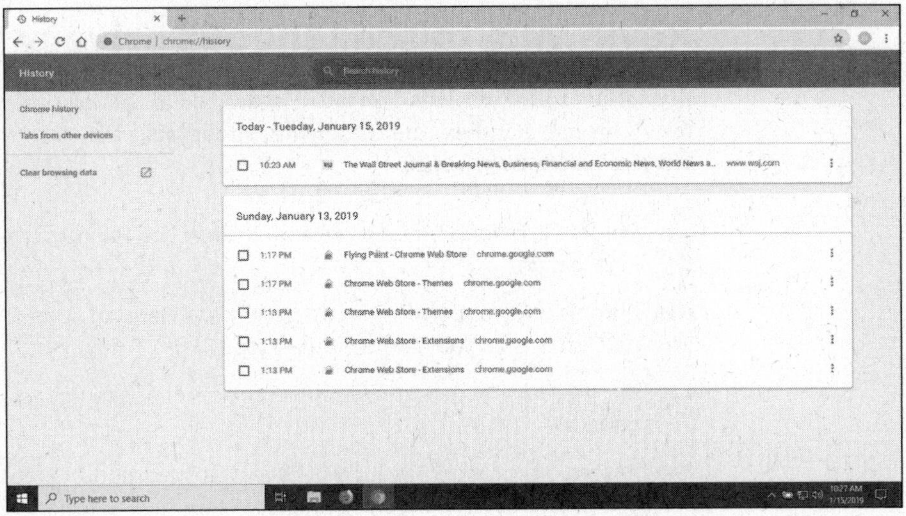

FIGURE 17-3:
Use your
browsing history
to revisit a web
page you visited
previously.

![Chrome History window showing browsing history entries for Today - Tuesday, January 15, 2019 and Sunday, January 13, 2019]

FIGURE 17-3:
Use your
browsing history
to revisit a web
page you visited
previously.

![Clear browsing data dialog box with Basic and Advanced tabs, Time range dropdown showing Last hour, Last 24 hours, Last 7 days, Last 4 weeks, All time, and checkboxes for browsing data types]

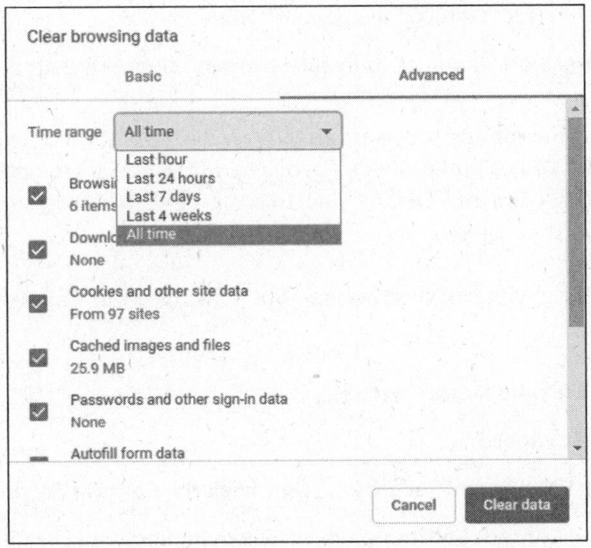

FIGURE 17-4:
Use this dialog
box to delete
browsing history.

REMEMBER

If you delete all of your cookies, you might need to re-identify yourself at websites where you were previously "known," such as your bank's website. The process involves getting a code from the website and entering it, typically along with your password at that site, so that you can verify that you are, indeed, the user the website thinks you are.

Reviewing miscellaneous privacy settings

In addition to the settings previously described in this section, you can control the way Chrome handles the following situations; the following list describes Chrome's default behavior:

» Chrome asks for permission whenever a website wants to use your location information.

» Chrome asks for permission whenever a site wants to automatically show notifications on your computer desktop.

» Chrome asks for permission whenever sites or apps want access to USB devices.

» Chrome asks for permission whenever websites request access to your computer's camera and microphone.

» Chrome asks for permission if a website wants to bypass Chrome's sandbox technology and directly access your computer.

» Chrome blocks pop-ups from appearing and cluttering your screen.

TIP

To use Chrome (or any browser) effectively with QBO and QBOA, you cannot block *all* pop-ups. You can take advantage of a tool Intuit offers to optimize your browser for use with QBO and QBOA. Visit https://fixit.intuit.com and follow the prompts on the page.

Using Chrome, you can turn on pop-ups selectively for any website. Follow these steps:

1. **Click Chrome Menu ⇨ Settings.**

2. **Click Advanced.**

3. **In the Privacy and Security section, click the Content Settings button.**

4. **On the Content Settings page, scroll down, find, and click Pop-ups and Redirects.**

   The page where you manage pop-up exceptions appears (see Figure 17-5).

5. **Click Add to display the Add a Site dialog box.**

6. **Type the address of the site you want to add.**

7. **Click Add.**

8. **Repeat Steps 5 to 7 for each website on which you want to permit pop-ups.**

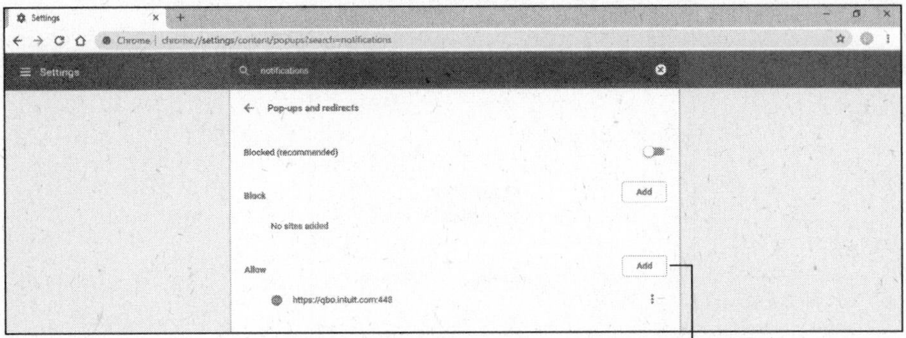

FIGURE 17-5:
Use this page to
identify websites
whose pop-ups
you want to allow
or deny.

Click here to add websites for which you want to allow pop-ups.

Using Google tools to manage privacy

Although Google can collect a lot of information about you, you can control just how much information it collects using its privacy management tools. Sign in to your account at `https://myaccount.google.com/intro`; from this website, you can, for example, use the Ads Settings to adjust the ads Chrome shows you.

Using Bookmarks in Chrome

Bookmarks enable you to save a web page address so that you can easily return to it. In this section, you learn to

» Create a bookmark.

» Use a bookmark to display its associated web page.

» Display the Bookmarks bar in Chrome to make bookmarks more accessible.

» Organize bookmarks by renaming them, placing them into folders, changing the order in which they appear when you view bookmarks, and deleting bookmarks you no longer need.

Creating a bookmark

Creating a bookmark is easy. First, navigate to the web page you want to bookmark. For example, you might want to bookmark the QBO or QBOA sign-in page. Then click the Bookmark This Page button (the one that looks like a star) at the right edge of the Omnibox, press Ctrl+D, or choose Chrome Menu➪Bookmarks➪Bookmark This Page. The Bookmark Added dialog box appears (see Figure 17-6).

FIGURE 17-6:
This dialog box
appears when
you create a
bookmark.

You can change the bookmark's name (I shortened mine) and the folder in which Chrome stores it. By default, Chrome offers two folders:

>> The Bookmarks bar folder and

>> The Other Bookmarks folder.

Choose one of these folders, click Done, and Chrome saves your bookmark. All bookmarks you create appear at the bottom of the Bookmarks menu; choose Chrome Menu⇨Bookmarks to see them. If you place the bookmarks you use most often on the Bookmarks bar, they can be easily visible and available for use, as you'll see in the next section.

So, logically, because you're an organized human being, you want to know if you can create your own folders and organize your bookmarks using your organizational style. Yes, you can, using the Bookmark Manager, and you can read more about the Bookmark Manager later in this chapter in the section "Managing bookmarks."

REMEMBER

Bookmarks can "break" and display "page not found" messages (error code 404). If this happens, manually navigate to the page and save the bookmark again, overwriting the original bookmark.

Displaying the Bookmarks bar

By default, Chrome saves your bookmarks to the Bookmarks bar, which appears just below the Omnibox every time you open the New Tab page (see Figure 17-7).

FIGURE 17-7:
Take
advantage of the
Bookmarks bar.

Bookmarks bar

The Bookmarks bar makes using bookmarks faster and easier because bookmarks are always visible. You can simply click the appropriate bookmark on the Bookmarks bar to display its associated web page.

To take full advantage of the Bookmarks bar, you should display it on all Chrome tabs (rather than just the New Tab tab). Press Ctrl+Shift+B or choose Chrome Menu ⇨ Bookmarks ⇨ Show Bookmarks bar (see Figure 17-8).

FIGURE 17-8:
Opt to display the
Bookmarks bar
on all tabs in
Chrome.

Click to show the Bookmarks bar on all tabs.

Chrome displays as many bookmarks as possible on the Bookmarks bar, based on the names you give to your bookmarks: the shorter the name, the more bookmarks Chrome can display. But, you can easily get to the bookmarks you can't see by clicking the small button containing two right-pointing arrows at the right edge of the Bookmarks bar.

Importing bookmarks

If you've been working in a different browser and want to copy your bookmarks from that browser to Chrome, no problem. Choose Chrome Menu ⇨ Bookmarks ⇨ Import Bookmarks and Settings. The Import Bookmarks and Settings dialog box appears (see Figure 17-9).

Select the browser from which to import bookmarks and settings and select or deselect the check boxes beside the items you want to import; different browsers offer different importing options. Then, click Import, and Chrome imports the information. The imported bookmarks appear in a folder on the Bookmarks bar, and you can use the Bookmark Manager, described in the next section, to reorganize these bookmarks.

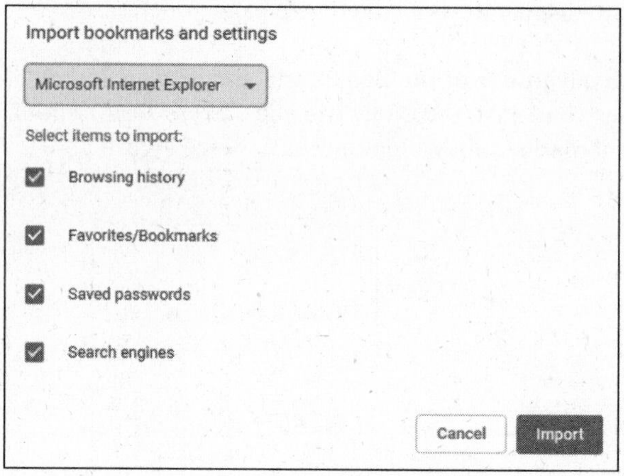

Import bookmarks and settings

Microsoft Internet Explorer ▾

Select items to import:

☑ Browsing history

☑ Favorites/Bookmarks

☑ Saved passwords

☑ Search engines

Cancel   Import

FIGURE 17-9:
Use this dialog box to identify what you want to import.

Managing bookmarks

If you're like me, you'll learn to love bookmarks — perhaps to your detriment. As you accumulate bookmarks, finding them to be able to use them becomes a project. You have a few avenues available to you:

» You can organize your bookmarks by repositioning them on the Bookmarks bar and on the list of bookmarks on the Bookmarks menu (choose Chrome Menu ⇨ Bookmarks).

» You can create folders for your bookmarks and place bookmarks in the appropriate folder.

» You can search for a bookmark.

To reposition bookmarks, you can drag them on the Bookmarks bar or on the list of bookmarks that appears at the bottom of the Bookmarks menu. A black line (vertical if you're dragging on the Bookmarks bar or horizontal if you're dragging on the list of bookmarks) helps you locate the new position for the bookmark; simply release the mouse button when the bookmark appears where you want it to appear.

You also can use the Bookmark Manager to reorder bookmarks; in addition, using the Bookmark Manager Organize menu, you can create folders and organize bookmarks into those folders, delete bookmarks and folders you no longer need, rename bookmarks, and search for bookmarks.

To open the Bookmark Manager, choose Chrome Menu ⇨ Bookmarks ⇨ Bookmark Manager. A page like the one shown in Figure 17-10 appears.

Bookmarks search box   Bookmark Manager Organize menu

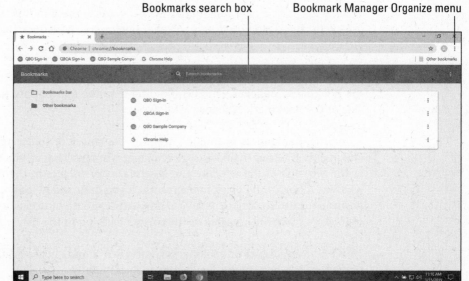

FIGURE 17-10:
The Bookmark
Manager.

TIP

The Bookmark Manager window works the same way that Windows Explorer and File Explorer work; if you're familiar with Windows Explorer or File Explorer, you already know many of the techniques you use to organize bookmarks.

The left pane displays existing folders, and the right pane shows the bookmarks in the folder you select in the left pane. You use the Organize button at the right edge of the Bookmark Manager window to make organizational changes.

TIP

To delete any bookmark or folder except the Bookmarks bar folder and the Other Bookmarks folder, click the bookmark or folder and then press the Delete key on your keyboard. Nope, you can't delete the Bookmarks bar folder or the Other Bookmarks folder.

You can use folders to organize bookmarks; I like to organize my bookmarks by subject. Although you can add new folders to the Other Bookmarks folder at the bottom of the list on the left, I suggest that you confine your organization to the

Bookmarks bar folder. You can compare keeping all your bookmarks on the Bookmarks bar to owning only one file cabinet. The cabinet has multiple drawers (folders, in this analogy), but you need to search only one cabinet to find what you need. Finding a particular bookmark will be easier if you use only the Bookmarks bar folder.

To create a new folder on the Bookmarks bar, open the Bookmark Manager Organize menu and choose Add Folder. Type a name for the new folder, and press Enter.

When you create a new bookmark that you want to place in this folder, select this folder in the Folder list box of the Bookmark Added dialog box (refer to Figure 17-6).

To add an existing bookmark to a folder, click the bookmark on the right side of the Bookmark Manager window and drag it to the appropriate folder on the left side of the Bookmark Manager window.

To reorder bookmarks or folders, drag the bookmark or folder up or down in the list on either side of the Bookmark Manager window. That is, you can drag folders in the left side of the window and bookmarks or folders in the right side of the window. A horizontal black line appears as you drag and helps you locate the new position for the bookmark or folder; release the mouse button when the bookmark or folder's black line appears at the correct location in the list.

To rename any folder or bookmark, right-click it and choose Edit from the menu that appears. Then, type a new name and press Enter.

Suppose that, after this wonderful organizing you've done, you can't remember where you put a particular bookmark. No problem. Use the Bookmarks Search box (refer to Figure 17-10). Type an address or search term into the Search box and press Enter. Chrome displays any bookmarks that match the address or search term. To cancel the search and redisplay all your bookmarks, click the X that appears in the Search box.

When you finish working in the Bookmark Manager window, click the X that appears in the tab's name.

Duplicating and Pinning Tabs

Chapter 16 describes how to open multiple tabs as you browse in Chrome and how to reposition tabs within the Chrome window.

At times, you might find it useful to duplicate a QuickBooks company tab you've already opened so that you have that tab open twice — or, so that you can open two different tabs for the same company simultaneously. To duplicate any tab, right-click the tab and choose Duplicate from the shortcut menu that appears (see Figure 17-11). Chrome automatically opens another tab using the web address of the duplicated tab. You can then work on the tabs independently of each other, switching to different tabs in the same company.

Click to duplicate a browser tab.

QuickBooks			
← → C ⌂ 🔒	New tab	Ctrl+T	
QBO Sign-in QBOA	Reload	Ctrl+R	
	Duplicate		
quickbooks	Pin tab		
	Mute site		
Dashboard	Close tab	Ctrl+W	
	Close other tabs		
Banking	Close tabs to the right		
Sales	Reopen closed tab	Ctrl+Shift+T	
	Bookmark all tabs...	Ctrl+Shift+D	
Expenses	See how much you're mak		

FIGURE 17-11:
Duplicate a browser tab in Chrome.

You might also find it useful to *pin* a particular Chrome tab; pinned tabs open automatically whenever you start Chrome. To pin a tab, right-click the tab and choose Pin Tab from the shortcut menu that appears (refer to Figure 17-11).

TIP

If you decide you no longer want a pinned tab to appear each time you open Chrome, right-click the pinned tab and click Unpin Tab from the menu that appears. As you might expect, the Unpin Tab command appears only if you previously pinned the tab.

Using Chrome on Multiple Monitors

Here's another tab-related trick: If you have more than one monitor, you can pull one tab out of the Chrome window and drag it to your other monitor so that you can work in QBO/QBOA on multiple screens. Again, because tabs in Chrome function independently, the work you do in each window is independent of the other.

To pull a tab, click and drag the tab; a preview of the new window appears. Release the mouse button and the tab appears in a new window onscreen. If you didn't drag the tab to a different monitor, no problem. Just drag the new window by its title bar to your second monitor. (Yes, if you have three monitors, you can repeat this process.)

Working with Chrome Users

In Chapter 16, I explain that you can set up and use multiple users, each of whom can have different Chrome settings. At that time, I promised that I'd show you how to set up multiple Chrome users — and, here we are.

Adding a Chrome user

If you want to log in to two different QBO companies from a single QBO account, you can use different Chrome users. To create a user, choose Chrome Menu⇨ Settings to display the Settings tab. In the People section, click Manage Other People to display the dialog box shown in Figure 17-12.

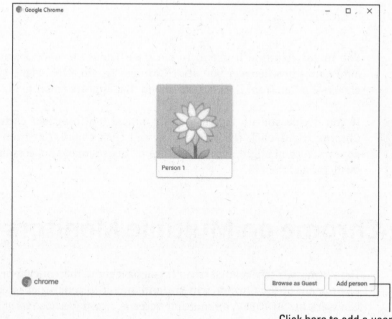

FIGURE 17-12: Use this dialog box to start the process of adding a user.

Click here to add a user.

Click Add Person in the lower right corner to display the dialog box shown in Figure 17-13. Enter a name for the user and select an icon for the new user; the icon appears in the Current User button in the upper right corner of the Chrome window, and the username appears when you click the Current User button. Optionally, you can create a desktop shortcut for the user so that the user can quickly and easily open his or her own version of Chrome. Then click Add.

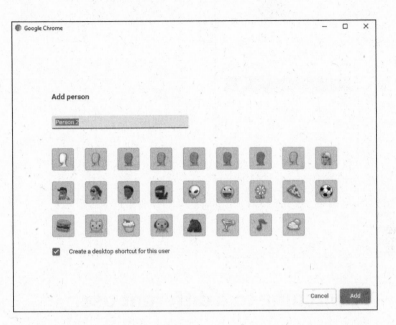

FIGURE 17-13: Establish settings for the new user.

Another instance of Chrome opens, and you'll see two buttons on the Windows taskbar. You can identify the current user by looking at the Current User button in the upper right corner of the browser, and you can easily switch from one user to another.

Opening a different user

Say that you have opened only one instance of Chrome, so only one button appears on the Windows taskbar. To open a different user, click the Current User button, and Chrome displays a window listing the currently defined users (see Figure 17-14); click one or click Manage People to go through the process of creating a new user.

Assuming you select an existing user, Chrome opens a new browser window for that user. If you don't maximize Chrome, you can easily see the open windows.

Click here to switch users.

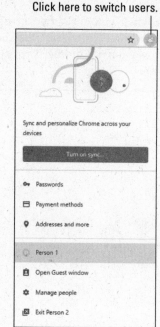

Switching to a different user

To switch users — that is, to stop using one user and start using another — click the Current User button and choose the last command on the menu to exit from the currently opened user. Chrome then displays a window similar to the one shown in Figure 17-15. Click a user to open a Chrome window for that user.

Removing a user you no longer need

When you move the mouse pointer over any user's picture in the dialog box shown in Figure 17-15, a menu of three small dots appears in the upper right corner of the user's picture. To remove a user, follow these steps:

1. **Click the Current User button.**

2. **Click Manage People.**

   A window like the one shown in Figure 17-15 appears.

3. **Slide the mouse pointer over the icon of the user you want to remove.**

   A menu icon (three vertical dots) appears.

4. **Click the menu icon.**

5. **Click Remove This Person.**

   Chrome asks you to confirm.

6. **Click the Remove This Person button.**

   Chrome removes the user.

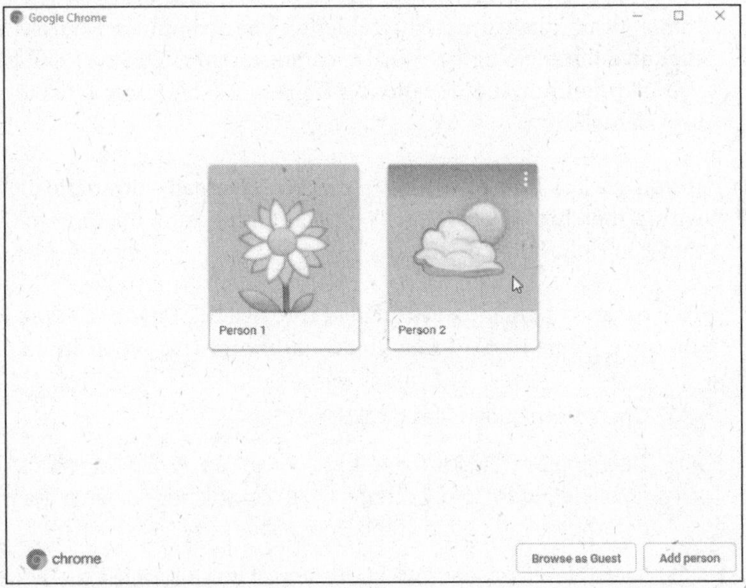

FIGURE 17-15:
Use this window
to select a
Chrome user.

Zooming In and Out

There are times when tired eyes need help; fortunately, you can zoom in and out of Chrome's windows easily. Press Ctrl++ (plus sign) to make the information in the window larger (known as *zooming in*) and Ctrl+- (minus sign) to reduce the size of the information in the window (you guessed it: *zooming out*).

WARNING Be aware that, whereas zooming is great for enlarging text, zooming can also alter how web pages appear, even to the point of hiding content that would otherwise be visible. So, if something seems to be missing, try resetting the zoom factor to 100%.

Downloading Files

Chrome can display many different types of documents, media, and other files, such as PDF and MP3 files. But, you might need to save a file to your computer.

Instead of clicking the file's link — which is always tempting — right-click the link and, from the menu that appears, click Save Link As. Then, in the dialog box that appears, navigate to the folder on your computer where you want to save the file, give the file a name you'll recognize, and click Save. The file downloads, and you can monitor the download progress in the lower left corner of the Chrome browser window.

REMEMBER

If you click a link to a file, it might download automatically or it might open within the Chrome browser. To prevent a file from opening in Chrome, make sure that you right-click the link.

To view and open any downloaded file, use the Downloads tab (see Figure 17-16). Choose Chrome Menu ⇨ Downloads. From this tab, you can

» Open downloaded files by clicking them.

» Open the Downloads folder by clicking the Show in Folder link below any downloaded file, or by clicking Open Downloads Folder in the menu (three dots) at the right edge of the Downloads page.

» Search for downloads using the Search box just below the Bookmarks bar.

» Clear the Downloads list using the menu (three dots) at the right edge of the Downloads title bar to click the Clear All link.

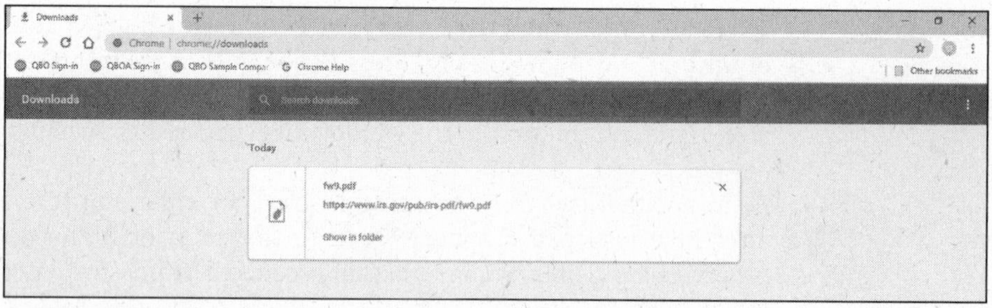

FIGURE 17-16:
Files you've
downloaded
using Chrome.

You can use the Chrome browser on mobile devices as well as on desktop computers (of course you can!). Chrome works on both iOS and Android, and the Chrome app is typically preinstalled on Android devices because Android and Chrome are both Google products. Chrome on a mobile device functions pretty much the same way that Chrome on a desktop computer does.

Appendix **A**

QBO, QuickBooks Desktop, and Data Conversion

A lthough you can import most data from a QuickBooks Desktop company into QBO, not everything converts. In some cases, some things convert completely or have counterparts in QBO. And, some things convert partially or have simply been replaced by QBO features. But in some cases, things don't convert and there's no QBO substitute feature.

This appendix explores the data conversion that occurs when you import data from a QuickBooks Desktop company to give you a sense of what you can expect.

REMEMBER

Everything you read in this chapter assumes that you are converting a company from QuickBooks Desktop 2016 or later. If you are trying to convert a company from an older version of QuickBooks Desktop, you are likely to run into problems, so, first, back up your data and store the backup in a safe place. Then, download a free 30-day trial version of the latest edition of QuickBooks Desktop — 2019 when I wrote this — for your country (U.S., Canada, or UK) and install it alongside your existing version of QuickBooks Desktop. You cannot register or activate the free trial; if you do, the process will fail and you'll be locked out of QuickBooks Desktop. You'll want to keep your existing version (instead of over-writing it with the trial) so that you can refer back to your data if needed. When I wrote this, trial versions were available at this web address: `https://community.intuit.com/articles/1207255-quickbooks-desktop-trial-links`. You use the trial version to update your company data before you attempt importing it to QBO. See Chapter 12 for details. If you're a QuickBooks Premier Desktop edition user, download the QuickBooks Pro Desktop trial; it will work with your data.

What Doesn't Import

Because most of your QuickBooks Desktop data will import, I'll start by identifying what won't import. Table A-1 provides that information.

There. Now, that wasn't painful, was it?

TABLE A-1   **QuickBooks Desktop Data that Won't Import**

What Doesn't Import	Recommendation
QuickBooks Desktop usernames and passwords	QBO requires each user who has access to a company to log in using a password. Existing QuickBooks Desktop users do not automatically have access to QBO. Instead the company master administrator will need to re-invite users from QBO to gain access.
	Be aware that, in QBO, you can limit the user's ability to see and use different parts of QBO, but you can't control access at the level of transactions as you can in QuickBooks Desktop.
Shortcut list and icon bar settings	QBO has its own keyboard shortcuts. While working in QBO, press Ctrl+Alt+? to see the shortcut menu.
Price levels	QBO currently doesn't support price levels or any automatic way to adjust prices. If you have price levels defined in your QuickBooks Desktop data file, the conversion process won't convert them to QBO.
Reminders	Reminders don't convert to QBO. Use an external calendar (probably your best bet) or try using recurring transactions set to remind you instead of scheduling themselves.

What Doesn't Import	Recommendation
Vehicle list	You'll need to set up vehicles as fixed assets and, if you don't buy vehicles outright, you'll need to set up corresponding loans for each vehicle.
Reconciliation reports	Save your reconciliation reports in QuickBooks Desktop to access them later. In QBO, just continue reconciling where you left off. And, although reconciliation reports don't convert, all reconciled transactions in registers convert as reconciled transactions in QBO.
Subtotal items	You can add subtotals to transaction documents using the method described in Chapter 6.
Recurring credit card charges	Cancel each existing Automatic Credit Card recurring charge from your Merchant Center, and re-create it in QBO as a recurring sales receipt. Note: All other recurring transactions will import.
Memorized reports	Find a similar report in QBO and customize it to your preference.
Audit trail	Your desktop audit trail won't import, but all new changes you make in QBO going forward will be captured in the QBO audit log.
Inventory from QuickBooks for Mac	QuickBooks for Mac isn't capable of exporting inventory to QBO. Instead, you can save your QuickBooks for Mac company as a QuickBooks for Windows file and export it from a Windows machine running QuickBooks Desktop.

Features Not Fully Available in QBO

Currently, Intuit doesn't recommend QBO to QuickBooks Desktop users who need the following features:

>> To Do notes

>> Complete Job Costing

>> Sales Orders

>> Fixed Asset Tracking

>> Estimate to Actual Reporting

If you need one of these features and you choose to use QBO, you might be able to find an app that can integrate these features with QBO. Check out the QBO App Center at Apps.Intuit.com to see a full list.

REMEMBER

Mileage tracking is available only in QBSE; for other versions of QBO, you might be able to find an add-on app that works for you.

Looking at List Limitations

Most information stored in QuickBooks Desktop lists converts during the import process, but, as you'd expect, there are some limitations. In the following sections, I've excluded the Item list; I cover inventory and items in the section "Examining Inventory and the Items List" later in this Appendix. Generally speaking, inventory converts, but you might run into some trouble.

Chart of Accounts

In your Chart of Accounts, the bank account number and notes, if you've entered any, don't convert. To learn more about editing the Chart of Accounts, see Chapter 3.

QBO has an additional level of account typing, called the *detail type,* that you won't find in QuickBooks Desktop. For example, expense accounts in QBO can have a number of detail types, such as Auto, Equipment Rental, Legal & Professional Fees, and so on.

When the detail type for an account is obvious — for the Undeposited Funds account, for example — the import process assigns the appropriate detail type. But, when the detail type isn't obvious — and it's not obvious in most cases — the import process assigns a generic detail type within the type, such as Other Miscellaneous Expense, that you can edit later.

To update detail types after importing, run the Account List report (Reports ⇨ All Reports ⇨ Accountant Reports ⇨ Account List) to review the detail types that the import process assigned. If you click on a line in the report, the Edit Account window appears, and you can update the detail type.

Customers and jobs

The import process converts all of your customers from QuickBooks Desktop to QBO. And, all of your jobs in QuickBooks Desktop convert to *sub-customers* in QBO. Unfortunately, the import process doesn't convert all customer detail and job information.

The import process converts the following customer and job information:

Customer	Email
Company Name	Terms
Mr./Ms./?	Bill to Address (except Note)
First Name	Ship To Address (except Note)
M.I.	
Last Name	Tax code/item
Phone	Preferred Payment Method
FAX	Note (up to 4000 characters)
Alt Ph.	

REMEMBER

The Ship To Address converts, but not perfectly. The import process places the entire address in the main address field, leaving City, State, Zip Code, and Country blank.

But, the following customer and job information doesn't convert:

Inactive status	Credit Limit
Contact	Job Status
Alt. Contact	Start Date
Customer Type	Projected End
Rep	End Date
Price Level	Job Description
Custom Fields	Job Type
Account	Credit Card Information

Note that Inactive status remains as long as there are no unbilled charges imported.

Group Items

Group items convert to *bundles* in QBO. You can use QBO bundles on sales-related documents only. If you have group items on a purchasing-related document in QuickBooks Desktop, the import process presents each item in the group on a separate detail line, effectively "ungrouping" the group item.

Inactive list elements

In your QuickBooks Desktop data file, if you have any inactive accounts, customers, or vendors that have open balances, the import process converts those accounts, customers, or vendors as regular, active elements. If the inactive element has no balance, the import process converts the element as an inactive element; QBO treats inactive elements as deleted elements.

Other names

QBO currently doesn't have an Other Names list, so the import process imports all elements on the Other Names list as vendors in QBO.

Recurring transactions

The import process converts memorized transactions, but you will be able to see your memorized transactions only in QBO Plus, which supports recurring templates. If you import to any other version of QBO, you won't be able to see your memorized transactions — but they'll be waiting for you if you upgrade your QBO subscription to QBO Plus.

QBO Simple Start users should delete all recurring transactions and templates from QuickBooks Desktop before importing into QBO Simple Start to avoid errors after importing.

Sales tax items

After you import a QuickBooks Desktop data file, QBO will contain at least two sales tax payable accounts on the Chart of Accounts: one for each old Sales Tax Payable account from QuickBooks Desktop, and one for each Sales Tax Agency Payable account in the new QBO, which QBO sets up automatically for each jurisdiction during the import process. Moving forward, QBO only uses the new Sales Tax Agency Payable account, and all sales tax will be managed from the Sales Tax Center.

The import process doesn't convert sales tax group items as group items; instead, they appear as individual lines on transactions. But you can set up combined sales tax items in QBO. QBO doesn't support the three-character tax codes associated with sales tax items in QuickBooks Desktop.

Sales tax payments post as regular checks, and sales tax adjustments post as journal entries.

Ship Via list

The import process converts the information stored in the QuickBooks Desktop Ship Via list, but doesn't maintain it as a list in QBO. When you record Ship Via information on transactions in QBO, you'll enter the shipping method in a text box, instead of selecting it from a list.

Subtotals

Subtotal items appear on invoices in QBO, but they don't calculate. Instead, they appear in the Description field for that line on the invoice

Types for customers, jobs, and vendors

QBO currently doesn't have a way to categorize customers, vendors, or jobs with types the way you can with QuickBooks Desktop. If you have types in your QuickBooks Desktop data file, the import process doesn't convert them to QBO. And, when the import process converts customers, vendors, and jobs, it ignores the type.

Vendors

As with customers and jobs, the import process converts all of your vendors, but not all of their detail.

The import process converts the following vendor-related information:

Vendor	Email
Company Name	Terms
Mr./Ms.	Print on Check as
First Name	Address
M.I.	Account
Last Name	Tax ID
Phone	1099 (US only)
FAX	

But, the import process does *not* convert the following vendor-related information:

Contact	Credit Limit
Alt. Contact	Custom Fields
Note	Alt. Contact
Inactive	Alt Ph.
Vendor Type	

Exploring Payroll Conversion

Most QuickBooks Desktop payroll information converts to QBO Payroll (QBOP), with some exceptions. For example, the import process converts invalid employee addresses, but you will need to fix them after the fact.

The import process won't convert

>> Pay types that QBOP doesn't support,

>> Invalid social security numbers (SSNs) and employer identification numbers (EINs), and

>> Addresses for states outside those Intuit supports, such as Payroll Setup wizard, AS, and VI.

REMEMBER

Paychecks and liability payments convert as regular checks rather than as payroll transactions in QBOP. But, during QBO Payroll setup, you can enter year-to-date amounts to reflect paychecks and liability payments made prior to conversion.

Liability refunds, adjustment transactions, and opening balance transactions that affect accounts convert to journal entries.

Employee pay schedules and payroll items convert, but you might have to manually map some of them to QBOP pay types so that QBOP can calculate them if they are supported. The first time you display the Employees page in QBO, you'll see the Complete Payroll Setup button. As you complete payroll setup, you will be prompted to map any payroll elements the import process found in your QuickBooks Desktop company that it couldn't match to QBOP. See the "Map Your Custom Pay Types" section in "What to do after converting from QuickBooks Desktop for Windows or Mac to QuickBooks Online" for more information.

REMEMBER

The import process doesn't convert pay types that QBOP doesn't support. If you don't see any choices to map a pay type, you can choose the Skip For Now option, but be aware that you can't go back and map your pay types later. If you choose Skip For Now, you will need to manually create pay types for your employees to complete payroll setup.

After importing payroll information, you'll need to fill out an interview to complete payroll setup, establishing information such as company contributions, before you'll be able to create paychecks. You might also need to enter year-to-date payroll information for each employee; in most cases, the import process converts this information, and you only need to verify the totals. But, if the information is missing, you need to enter it, and the interview guides you through entering these year-to-date totals in order to get going again.

Completing payroll setup

To complete your payroll setup, follow these steps:

1. **Select Workers from the left menu and then click Employees.**

2. **Click the Get Started button.**

3. **On the My Payroll screen that appears (see Figure A-1), in the Paid in [Year] column, be sure each employee who received a paycheck this year is switched to Yes.**

    Employees who have not been paid in the current year are automatically listed as No.

    The Paid in [Year] column appears only before you complete payroll setup.

4. **Click Complete Payroll Setup to enter and/or verify your year-to-date payroll totals and employee information.**

    Use the Payroll Summary report in QuickBooks Desktop to help you; enter the year-to-date numbers in QBO as positive numbers, even though they appear negative on the report.

    You don't have to complete payroll setup in a single sitting; you can come back and the Payroll Setup wizard picks up where you left off. You *do* need to complete payroll setup before you can pay employees.

REMEMBER

If you reported Group Term Life Insurance or S-Corp Owners Health Insurance, the import process recalculates net pay using QBOP calculations. Be sure to keep this in mind when comparing your QBO Payroll Summary reports to your Quick-Books Desktop Summary reports.

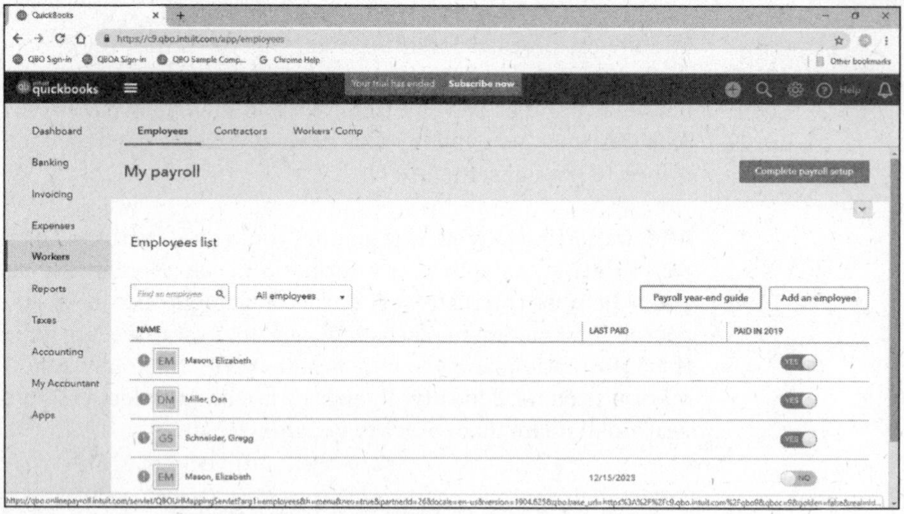

FIGURE A-1:
The Employees
page after
importing data
but before
completing
setup.

Special payroll notes

Here are a few final notes to remember when importing payroll data:

» If you were using E-services to pay or file your taxes electronically, you
will need to re-enroll for this service in QBO. Simply log in and follow the
steps on the Payroll Preferences page (Gear ➪ Payroll Settings) to enroll
for Electronic Services.

QuickBooks MAC USERS AND IOP

If you are using Intuit Online Payroll (IOP) to bring transactions into QB Mac, you can
continue to use it if you want. Be aware, though, that typically QBO accounts start with
having QBO Payroll (QBOP) attached. So, to continue to use your standalone payroll,
you'll have to cancel QBOP.

After cancelling QBOP, you change the export preferences in IOP and begin sending the
transactions straight to QBO. For more information, see "Setup Export of IOP Data
to QuickBooks Online (QBO)."

If you prefer to start using QBOP, complete the steps in the section "Completing payroll
setup."

> **>>** If you were using or want to use direct deposit for your employees, you need to add your employer and employee's individual bank account information. This can be done from the Payroll Preferences page (Gear ⇨ Payroll Settings), or from the Employee setup page (in the Navigation bar, click Employees and then edit the appropriate employee's pay details on the Employee Details page).

Examining Inventory and the Items List

QBO Plus tracks inventory using the First-in–First-out (FIFO) method in accrual only. When you select the option to import inventory, the import process asks you to choose a date, which it uses to recalculate your inventory based on FIFO calculations. The import process brings over your current item quantities, item accounts, and details, excluding unit of measure (UM), because QBO contains no corresponding feature. When the import process completes, you do not need to do any work to your inventory.

But, you might run into some difficulties getting inventory imported into QBO. If you don't see any of your inventory in QBO within 24 hours of importing it, you will probably receive an email error message with the subject line, "There was a problem copying your company file to QuickBooks Online." The email will contain an attachment that describes the problems the import process encountered, and typically those problems revolve around the recalculation of inventory using the FIFO method on an accrual basis. In this case, review the Inventory/Stock section of "What data doesn't convert from QuickBooks Desktop to QuickBooks Online?" an online article updated regularly by Intuit folks, to resolve the issues. The article walks you through the process of resolving the issues encountered in the import process.

Examining Other Special Cases

The rest of this appendix presents notes on the way the import process treats most common areas in QuickBooks Desktop.

Bills

The import process converts item receipts into bills. The Bill Received check box doesn't convert.

Bill payments

A discount applied to a bill in QuickBooks Desktop converts to a Vendor Credit in QBO. The import process replaces the address on each bill payment check with the Vendor address in the Vendor list.

Budgets

The import process converts only Profit & Loss budget types to QBO, because those are the only budget types that QBO currently supports.

Closing date

The import process converts your QuickBooks Desktop closing date, but not the Closing Date password. After importing, the Exceptions to Closing Date report in QBO won't show the exceptions that you had accumulated in QuickBooks Desktop. Instead, QBO will track new exceptions that occur in QBO, beginning on the date that you convert your company file.

Credit card charges

The import process converts all credit card charges in your QuickBooks Desktop data file to QBO. QBO has no specific "Credit Card Charge" transaction, so the import process converts credit card transactions to expenses.

The import process converts credit card credits to the corresponding QBO Credit Card Credit transaction, and bill payments made by credit card to QBO bill payments.

Custom fields

QBO currently doesn't support custom fields on customers, vendors, employees, or items. Instead, these fields appear only on transactions, and you are limited to displaying a limit of three custom fields on transactions. Therefore, custom fields from QuickBooks Desktop won't be converted.

Information in the Sales Rep field in QuickBooks Desktop converts to a customer field on sales forms in QBO.

Discounts

Although you can define terms to specify the discount to be given in the event of early payment for invoices, QBO doesn't automatically calculate discounts when you receive a payment. When converting QuickBooks Desktop data, the import process converts discounts already given to customers for early payment of invoices to credit memos applied to the customer's outstanding balance.

On the vendor side of things, the import process works similarly, converting discounts you take when you pay a vendor's bill to vendor credits applied to the vendor's outstanding balance.

Documents

Any documents listed under the Company menu do not transfer over, and attachments on transactions don't convert.

Finance charges

The import process converts finance charge invoices existing in QuickBooks Desktop to invoices in QBO with no data loss.

REMEMBER

QBO currently doesn't have an automatic way to assess finance charges for late customer payments. You can run a report to see which customers are overdue and manually add finance charges that will appear on the customers' next invoices.

Notice that if you use finance charges in QuickBooks Desktop, after importing, QBO has an element on the Products and Services page called Finance Charge. This element has the same rate and account used by your QuickBooks Desktop finance charge setup.

To assess the finance charge after importing, create an invoice using the finance charge element. Based on the overdue report, manually enter the amount due for the late penalty charges as a line item on the invoice.

Invoices

Because there are some features in QuickBooks Desktop that aren't available in QBO, the import process translates the following invoice data during conversion:

» PO No. translates to Custom Field 1.

» Sales Rep initials translate to Custom Field.

>> Subtotals appear in the Description field for that line on the QBO invoice, but they don't calculate. See Chapter 6 to learn how to customize QBO forms to include subtotals.

REMEMBER

Progress invoices — invoices based on estimates — and their extra fields are not converted. In QBO, you won't find Est Qty, Est Rate, Est Amt, Prior Qty, Prior Avg Qty, Prior Avg Rate, Rate, Prior Amt, Prior %, Curr %, and Total %.

The following elements on invoices don't convert:

>> In the Customer Fields section, the Other field and the Customer custom fields

>> In the Item Detail section, Other 1, Other 2, and Item custom fields

>> In the Options and Others section, sales form templates, logos, long text disclaimers, and tax names

TIP

Even though the import process doesn't convert your logo, you can add your logo to sales forms in QBO.

Journal entries

Journal entries import entirely, with the single exception of a journal entry's billable status; you can't make a journal entry billable in QBO.

In rare cases, if QBO cannot re-create the original transaction, the import process converts transactions such as checks or invoices in a QuickBooks Desktop data file into general journal transactions. For example, if the import process comes across a check that uses an income account rather than a bank account as its source account, the transaction converts to a general journal entry.

Customized sales form templates

The import process doesn't convert custom sales templates, but you can create a completely new custom template in QBO. See Chapter 3 for details.

Merchant account service

To transfer your existing QuickBooks Merchant Service account to QBO, you need to unlink and relink your merchant account. To learn how, see the online article "Link your merchant account."

Multicurrency

The import process converts multicurrency transactions into QBO. But, be aware that you can create multicurrency transactions in QuickBooks Desktop in ways that QBO doesn't support. For example, you can create transactions in QuickBooks Desktop that use three different currency types, but QBO supports only two currency types on any single transaction. Any QuickBooks Desktop transaction that contains more than two currency types won't import into QBO.

You may also see penny rounding differences in QBO on transactions that are calculating multicurrency.

WARNING

QuickBooks Desktop supports some currency types that QBO doesn't support, and these QuickBooks Desktop transactions might cause difficulty when you import your data into QBO. Read the Multicurrency section of the online article "What data doesn't convert from QuickBooks Desktop to QuickBooks Online?" for details on resolving these and other multicurrency issues.

Online bill payment

The import process converts checks marked "To be Sent," but does not convert their online bill payment status.

Intuit has partnered with Bill.com to provide Online Bill Payment in QBO. To use Online Bill Payment in QBO, you must sign up for the service — and it has different features than you find using the regular Bill.com app. Further, if you currently have a Bill.com account, you cannot use it with QBO. For details, you can review the online article "What is Online Bill Pay?"

Pending sales

Because QBO currently doesn't have a way to mark a sale as pending, the import process doesn't convert any pending transactions from your QuickBooks Desktop data file. QBO Essentials and Plus have the Delayed Charge form, which is a non-posting sales transaction.

Print mailing labels

QBO currently doesn't print mailing labels. As an alternative, you can create a report of customer, vendor, or employee addresses, copy the report to Excel, and use the data to print mailing labels from Excel.

Purchase orders

The import process will not link closed purchase orders to their corresponding bill.

Receive items

The import process converts all the ways you can receive items in QuickBooks Desktop — Receive Item & Enter Bill, Receive Item, and Enter Bill for Received Items — to bills in QBO.

Reimbursable expenses

QBO has billable expenses, which are similar to reimbursable expenses in Quick-Books Desktop. QBO billable expenses differ from QuickBooks Desktop reimbursable expenses in that, in QBO, you specify the markup percentage when creating the purchase rather than when creating an invoice.

The import process converts reimbursable expenses and time that have not yet been billed in QuickBooks Desktop to billable expenses in QBO.

Reports

QBO doesn't have all the reports that QuickBooks Desktop does, and some of the similar reports differ slightly.

Although your Accrual Basis reports will match in both products, your Cash Basis reports may not match because cash basis calculations are somewhat subjective. Be aware that there are several differences in how the two products calculate what is considered paid.

Consider the use of negative lines on invoices. Suppose you have a service income line of $1000 and a discount of $ -100 and no payments:

>> In QuickBooks Desktop, the cash basis P&L report shows no portion of an unpaid invoice.

>> In QBO, your cash basis P&L report will show $100 of income and $ -100 of discount.

As payments are received for this invoice:

>> In QuickBooks Desktop, the cash basis P&L report prorates the amount of the discount that appears.

>> In QBO, the cash basis P&L report continues to show the entire amount.

Report customization

Although QBO doesn't have all the report customization options that QuickBooks Desktop has, QBO does offer extensive filtering and supports exporting a report to Excel for further filtering if necessary. And, you can save your QBO report customizations — the equivalent of memorizing a QuickBooks Desktop report — and schedule the report to be automatically sent from QBO.

Sales rep

As mentioned earlier in this appendix, the import process converts any sales rep names or initials you recorded in transactions in your QuickBooks Desktop file to the corresponding transaction in QBO, with one difference: The sales rep information appears as a custom field in QBO.

You can continue to supply sales rep information on sales transactions in QBO and filter reports by Sales Rep. However, when assigning sales reps to sales transactions, you'll need to enter the name because QBO maintains no Sales Rep list.

Tax support

QBO currently doesn't export information to TurboTax or other tax preparation programs, and QBO doesn't support tax line mapping in the Chart of Accounts. However, QBO has an additional level of account types, called *detail types,* that might help you make tax line assignments to accounts when tax support is available.

That being said, accountants can use QuickBooks Online Accountant (QBOA) to access a QBO file; QBOA contains the Book to Tax feature, which integrates with Intuit Tax Online.

Terms

QBO has a terms feature that is very similar to the terms feature in QuickBooks Desktop. The terms automatically calculate the due date from the transaction date.

However, QBO doesn't have an associated feature to assess finance charges associated with the terms you assign. And, as mentioned earlier, you can use terms for discounts for early payments, but QBO doesn't automatically calculate the discount amount. So, if a customer pays early enough to qualify for a discount, you'll need to edit the invoice to manually add the discount.

The import process imports terms without change with the following additional exceptions:

» In QuickBooks Desktop, a job can't have its own terms; it inherits its terms from its parent customer.

» In QBO, the equivalent to a job (a sub-customer) can have terms, so you can edit the terms later to make them different from those of the parent customer.

Write letters

QBO currently doesn't have an automated way to use your data to generate customized letters.

Index

B

C

displaying
  Account window, 324
  Bookmarks bar, 388–389
  rows, 182
documents, import procedure and, 411
Done button, 49
double-entry bookkeeping, 179
downloaded activity, managing, 204–216
downloading files, 398
Downloads tab (Chrome), 398
Draw account, 66
due dates, for payroll taxes, 244
duplicating
  browser tabs, 330
  tabs, 259, 392–393

E

Edit button, 84
Edit Project panel, 349–350
Edit User dialog box, 280
editing
  accounts, 64, 324–325
  inventory quantity adjustments, 106–107
  project information, 349–350
  transactions, 182–186
Electronic Federal Tax Payment System (EFTPS), 245
Emails tab, 49
employees
  process of payroll for, 226
  use of timesheets by, 238
employers, seasoned, 227
Enable Editing button, 87
enabling Projects feature in customer lists, 139
entering
  bills, 126–127
  purchase orders, 119–126
  sales receipts, 166–167
  single time activities, 173–174
  transactions, 182–186
Essentials version, 22, 24, 26

establishing
  categories, 92–93
  company settings, 45–56
  rules to accept transactions, 210–216
estimates
  about, 157
  converting to invoices, 161–163
  copying existing, 163–164
  copying to purchase orders, 160–161
  preparing, 158–160
Excel (Microsoft)
  app for, 75
  data file layout in, 77
  exporting lists to, 87–88
  exporting reports to using Chrome, 263
  importing transactions via, 202–203
Excel Mobile app, 75
excluding transactions, 206–207
Expanded Company Financials report, 361
expenses
  creating, 117–119
  preferences for, 52–53
  reviewing, 253–254
Expenses Performance management report, 257
Expenses tab (Account and Settings dialog box), 52–53
exporting
  bank feed rules, 327–328
  lists to Excel, 87–88
  reports to Excel using Chrome, 263
extension, 376–377
EZShield's Detect & Defend, 13

F

facilitating accountant activities, 353–362
Federal Form 941, 246–247
files, downloading, 398
Filter funnel button, 187
filtering transactions, 187–189
finance charges, import procedure and, 411
financial institutions, connecting accounts to, 192–203

L

Lead Accountant role, 280
List view (Work page), 350–351
lists
about, 73
adding new people to, 79–83
batches, 88–89
changing settings for, 89–91
exporting to Excel, 87–88
importing people into, 73–77
limitations of, 402–406
other, 109
Products and Services, 91–108
reviewing information, 326–327
searching for people, 83–89
sorting, 87

M

Macs, QuickBooks on, 408
Management Reports tab, 256, 361
managing
appearance of bank accounts, 191–192
appearance of client list, 281–282
bookmarks, 390–392
cookies, 382–383
downloaded activity, 204–216
invoice status, 155–156
overpayments, 154
payroll taxes, 244–247
projects, 137–144
your practice, 343–352
master administrator, 277
memo field, 214
Menu button, 274
merchant account service, import procedure and, 412
Messages section, 47
Microsoft Excel
app for, 75
data file layout in, 77
exporting lists to, 87–88

exporting reports to using Chrome, 263
importing transactions via, 202–203
mobile apps, 12, 145
monitors, using Chrome on multiple, 393–394
More button, 92
Multicurrency feature
about, 56–57
Chart of Accounts and, 63, 65
how it changes QBO, 58
import procedure and, 413
turning on, 58–59
My Accountant page (QBO), 337

N

names, list limitations and, 404
navigating client company, 329–333
Navigation bar, 42, 273
New Style button, 145
New Transaction button, 84, 112
New Window command, 317
Nitro Reader, 167
Non-billable Time report, 143
non-inventory items, adding, 94–97
non-posting transactions, 157

O

Omnibox, 367–368
online bill payment, import procedure and, 413
Online Delivery section, 48
Open dialog box, 115
opening
Bookmark Manager, 391
Chart of Accounts, 322
client company, 315–316
multiple windows, 330–332
users in Chrome, 395–396
windows, 367
Opening Balance Equity (Equity) account, 68
optimizing browsers, 386
order of rules, 210
organizing bookmarks, 391–392

About the Author

Elaine Marmel is President of Marmel Enterprises, LLC., an organization that specializes in technical writing and software training. Elaine has an MBA from Cornell University and has worked on projects to build financial management systems for New York City and Washington, D.C., training more than 600 employees to use these systems. This prior experience provided the foundation for Marmel Enterprises, LLC., to help small businesses implement computerized accounting systems.

Elaine spends most of her time writing: She has authored and co-authored more than 90 books about software products, including Windows, QuickBooks Desktop, QuickBooks Online, Quicken for Windows, Quicken for DOS, Microsoft Project, Microsoft Excel, Microsoft Word for Windows, Word for the Mac, 1-2-3 for Windows, and Lotus Notes. From 1994 to 2006, she was also the contributing editor for the monthly publications *Inside Peachtree for Windows, Inside QuickBooks,* and *Inside Timeslips* magazines.

Elaine left her native Chicago for the warmer climes of Arizona (by way of Cincinnati, OH; Jerusalem, Israel; Ithaca, NY; Washington, D.C.; and Tampa, FL) where she basks in the sun with her PC and her dog, Jack, and cross-stitches.

Author's Acknowledgments

A book is not the work of just the author. Instead, it is really a team effort. I have a marvelous team, and I'd like to acknowledge and thank all the folks who made this book possible. Thanks to Katie Mohr for the opportunity to write this book. Thank you, Dan Delong, for stepping up and taking on the role of technical editor. You eased my way as I worked with QBO and QBOA, and you kept me honest, but you didn't stop there; your insights make the book a better book — and that's probably the highest compliment I can pay. Last, but certainly not least, thank you seems inadequate, Scott and Maureen Tullis, for the outstanding job you did to guarantee that my manuscript was accurate and understandable and to manage everything involved in producing this book; you did a great job (as always) and really made my life easy.

Publisher's Acknowledgments

Executive Editor: Katie Mohr
Development Editor/Copy Editor: Scott Tullis
Technical Editor: Dan DeLong

Production Editor: Mohammed Zafar Ali
Project Manager: Maureen Tullis
Cover Image: © andresr/Getty Images

Leverage the power

Dummies is the global leader in the reference category and one of the most trusted and highly regarded brands in the world. No longer just focused on books, customers now have access to the dummies content they need in the format they want. Together we'll craft a solution that engages your customers, stands out from the competition, and helps you meet your goals.

Advertising & Sponsorships

Connect with an engaged audience on a powerful multimedia site, and position your message alongside expert how-to content. Dummies.com is a one-stop shop for free, online information and know-how curated by a team of experts.

- Targeted ads
- Video
- Email Marketing
- Microsites
- Sweepstakes sponsorship

20 MILLION PAGE VIEWS EVERY SINGLE MONTH

15 MILLION UNIQUE VISITORS PER MONTH

43% OF ALL VISITORS ACCESS THE SITE VIA THEIR MOBILE DEVICES

700,000 NEWSLETTER SUBSCRIPTIONS TO THE INBOXES OF *300,000* UNIQUE INDIVIDUALS EVERY WEEK

# of dummies

Custom Publishing

Reach a global audience in any language by creating a solution that will differentiate you from competitors, amplify your message, and encourage customers to make a buying decision.

- Apps
- Books
- eBooks
- Video
- Audio
- Webinars

Brand Licensing & Content

Leverage the strength of the world's most popular reference brand to reach new audiences and channels of distribution.

For more information, visit dummies.com/biz

PERSONAL ENRICHMENT

Staying Sharp
9781119187790
USA $26.00
CAN $31.99
UK £19.99

Facebook
9781119179030
USA $21.99
CAN $25.99
UK £16.99

Guitar
9781119293354
USA $24.99
CAN $29.99
UK £17.99

Investing
9781119293347
USA $22.99
CAN $27.99
UK £16.99

Beekeeping
9781119310068
USA $22.99
CAN $27.99
UK £16.99

Digital Photography
9781119235606
USA $24.99
CAN $29.99
UK £17.99

Meditation
9781119251163
USA $24.99
CAN $29.99
UK £17.99

Pregnancy
9781119235491
USA $26.99
CAN $31.99
UK £19.99

Samsung Galaxy S7
9781119279952
USA $24.99
CAN $29.99
UK £17.99

iPhone
9781119283133
USA $24.99
CAN $29.99
UK £17.99

Crocheting
9781119287117
USA $24.99
CAN $29.99
UK £16.99

Nutrition
9781119130246
USA $22.99
CAN $27.99
UK £16.99

PROFESSIONAL DEVELOPMENT

Windows 10
9781119311041
USA $24.99
CAN $29.99
UK £17.99

AutoCAD
9781119255796
USA $39.99
CAN $47.99
UK £27.99

Excel 2016
9781119293439
USA $26.99
CAN $31.99
UK £19.99

QuickBooks 2017
9781119281467
USA $26.99
CAN $31.99
UK £19.99

macOS Sierra
9781119280651
USA $29.99
CAN $35.99
UK £21.99

LinkedIn
9781119251132
USA $24.99
CAN $29.99
UK £17.99

Windows 10
9781119310563
USA $34.00
CAN $41.99
UK £24.99

SharePoint 2016
9781119181705
USA $29.99
CAN $35.99
UK £21.99

Fundamental Analysis
9781119263593
USA $26.99
CAN $31.99
UK £19.99

Networking
9781119257769
USA $29.99
CAN $35.99
UK £21.99

Office 2016
9781119293477
USA $26.99
CAN $31.99
UK £19.99

Office 365
9781119265313
USA $24.99
CAN $29.99
UK £17.99

Salesforce.com
9781119239314
USA $29.99
CAN $35.99
UK £21.99

Coding
9781119293323
USA $29.99
CAN $35.99
UK £21.99

dummies.com

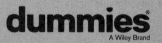

dummies
A Wiley Brand